AUSTRALIA

to

ZIMBABWE

A RHYMING ROMP AROUND THE WORLD TO 24 COUNTRIES

TRAVEL GUIDE: RUTH FITTS ✈

LOVE THE WORLD BOOKS ✈

WHY THESE 24 COUNTRIES? →

There tend to be two types of geography books: books about one country, or about every country. When atlases cover every country on earth, they don't have space to really explore any one. When books explore just one country, readers miss the chance to compare cultures and to discover places they never knew they were interested in. This book explores 24 countries (one from each letter of the alphabet except W and X).

The countries were chosen to give a good overview of many of the different regions and cultures of the world. From some of the biggest countries to some of the smallest, from former empires to former colonies, each country has its own national story to tell and national treasures to share. Beyond visiting these 24 nations, this book aims to give readers the globetrotting skills and desire to keep traveling until they discover them all!

Author and Designer: Ruth Fitts
Editor: Elizabeth Larson Richardson

Published by
Love the World Books
4424 Volta Place NW
Washington, DC 20007

Visit: www.australiatozimbabwe.com

Printed in China
10 9 8 7 6 5 4 3 2 1
First Edition

Library of Congress Control Number: 2015905096

ISBN: 978-0-9962495-7-7

TRAVEL ITINERARY

INTRODUCTION
Finding Your Map • Orientation • Navigating the Activity Pages 1

Australia 6

Brazil 18

China 28

Denmark 42

Ethiopia 52

France 67

Ghana 79

Haiti 93

India 106

Japan 124

Kazakhstan 138

Lebanon 152

Mexico 166

Nigeria 182

Oman 196

Peru 208

Qatar 224

Russia 236

Spain 248

Turkey 261

United Kingdom . . . 274

Vietnam 284

World Map 296

X marks our travels . 297

Yemen 298

Zimbabwe 311

CONCLUSION
Country Comparisons • Lists of Maps & Activities 323

This book is dedicated
to my hometown of Selma, Alabama,
which first taught me the crucial importance
of cross-cultural understanding…and that a place
is not its publicity.
And to the many strangers around the world who have welcomed
me and rescued me from disasters large and small, making me feel that
the world is my home and all its people my family.

"Oh mankind! We have created you male and female, and
made you into nations and tribes, that you
may come to know one another."
Qu'ran, Al-Hujurat 49:13

"And who is my neighbor?"
Luke 10:29

FINDING YOUR MAP

(An Introduction)

Way back in your head

in a near hidden place

(In between your two ears

and behind your *dear face*)

There's a long winding hallway

of stuffed storage rooms

like FACTS TO FORGET

and **10,000 TUNES.**

Near **History Before Me**

(Events Long Ago),

There's a door labeled **WHERE?**

(All the places to Go).

In this room is where **DESERTS**

and ***oceans*** are filed

Next to MONUMENTS, **MOUNTAINS**

and animals WILD!

Here where ***capitals*, *CLIMATES***

and peoples are squirreled,

You will find on the wall

YOUR OWN MAP OF THE WORLD.

Where?
(All the Places
to Go)

Take a look at your map →

tell me **what do you see?**

Is it teeming with people

↓

or just land and sea?

↓

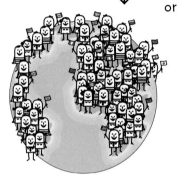

Is it filled with detail,

endless **COLORFUL SPRAWL?**

OR do vast empty spaces

show not much at all?

Is your map made with pictures?

Or **black wavy lines?** →

Are your labels quite clear,

or perhaps less defined?

Do they warn: **Here be Dragons!**

or **PARTS QUITE UNKNOWN!**

Or, inspired by the news, are there

PROBLEM-FILLED ZONES?

Are there signs,

this is where my nice neighbor is from →

• MUSIC HERE MAKES ME DANCE •

↓

Or **THE FOOD HERE IS YUM!**

*For fun, try drawing your own world map and adding labels and illustrations!

Whatever that map

that you see on your wall,

Every day is your chance

to expand and redraw.

For the words above read:

EVERY PLACE I COULD ROAM
THIS IS MY WORLD,

MY VERY OWN HOME.

So take down that map,

lay it flat on the floor.

Let's **step into your world**

and head out to explore!

Let's set out to TRAVEL

and **SEE** what we **SEE**

Visiting countries
From **A** through to **Z**!

ORIENTATION

Before we start our alphabetical voyage around the world
to 24 countries, here's a guide to how we'll travel!

Each country visit has 3 STOPS:

➡ **MEET** the country with
a **RHYMING** *Whirlwind* **INTRODUCTION**

➡ **SEE** the country by
SIGHT-SEEING with **PHOTOS** & captions

➡ **EXPERIENCE** the country's culture with
ACTIVITIES to make, explore and have fun!

There's no right way to travel. Take a globetrotting trip around the world

through introductions to all 24 countries, or visit one country at a time.

Just go sightseeing, or stop for lots of cultural activities.

Follow your interests to keep exploring and having fun all over the world!

NAVIGATING THE ACTIVITY PAGES:

Love MUSIC? Look for this icon to find fabulous music ➜ recommendations for every country. Transport yourself on a sound wave, sing their national songs and dance along to popular music videos. Links to all songs can be found on www.australiatozimbabwe.com

Love to EAT? Look for this icon to find yummy recipes ➜ for every country. Get your chef's hat and have fun making and tasting culinary delights from all 24 countries. All recipes are based on ingredients you already have on your shelf or can get at most grocery stores. Get an adult assistant to be safe.

Want to SEE the World? Look out for this Icon ➜ to find recommendations for movies and fun videos about life in each country. There are plenty of short gems under 5 minutes, as well as longer films and fascinating documentaries. Movies are available to stream online and all other videos can be found on YouTube. Check out www.australiatozimbabwe.com for help finding these must-sees.

Love to MAKE & CREATE? Look for this icon ➜ to find construction, craft and art activities.

Love GAMES? Look for this icon to find fun games ➜ from around the world.

Love READING or just a good STORY? Look out for this icon to find fantastic folktales, captivating ➜ stories, travel guides and fun nonfiction for every country.

Love to INVESTIGATE and RESEARCH? Look for ME to find interesting topics you might like to ➜ explore more!

Visit www.australiatozimbabwe.com for links to online activities. See page 329 for a list of activities.

A is for Australia

INDIAN OCEAN

DARWIN

Coral Sea

GREAT BARRIER REEF

PACIFIC OCEAN

GREAT DIVIDING RANGE

ALICE SPRINGS

Uluru

BRISBANE

PERTH

ADELAIDE

SYDNEY

CANBERRA

MELBOURNE

INDIAN OCEAN

TASMANIA

Aboriginal Dancer Performing

Our **A** is **Australia**

or **"OZ"** as it's known.

Aboriginal nations

first called this land home.

They've lived here at least

45,000 years

In a land filled with sights

you can only find here:

Dingo

Kangaroo

Teddy bears called KOALAS
and red *kangaroos*,
whirling **boomerangs**, DINGOES
and **didgeridoos!**

It is here you can see
playful *platypus* swim,
a KOOKABURRA laugh
and a **crocodile** grin!

Kookaburra

Aboriginal Man
Playing a Didgeridoo

Though you better BEWARE
of the salties' **SHARP TEETH**,
you can swim with the fish
on the **GREAT BARRIER REEF.**

"A Salty"
Saltwater Crocodile

The Aussies are friendly
and so they will greet you,
"G'day mate! How ARE ya?"
if ever they meet you.

Great Barrier Reef

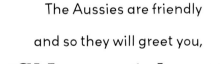

They're so easygoing
and rarely uptight,
their motto's **"NO WORRIES!"**
or "Mate, she'll be right."

Convict Chains

Captain Cook

In 1770,

Australia was claimed

By **Captain James Cook**

for the British domain.

It became a new colony

named "New South Wales"

Where British sent **CONVICTS**

instead of to jails.

Gold

And then came the **GOLD RUSH**

that doubled their number.

Men came here for riches,

then settled Down Under.

Sheep

Australians today

are outnumbered by **SHEEP**.

Try to count all their flocks

and you'll fall right to sleep!

Sydney Opera House

Outback

The capital's Canberra, [CAN-ber-rah]

the opera's in Sydney,

The **OUTBACK** is inland,

away from the cities.

From Melbourne to Brisbane,

from Darwin to Perth

Aussies live on the coast

where they **swim** and they **SURF**.

Vegemite Toast

They love food from the **BARBIE**

and **VEGEMITE** toast,

A "brekkie" non-Aussies

will likely think GROSS.

Beach Christmas

They have **CHRISTMAS** in summer

and wintry Julys.

They have **WOMBATS** and **EMUS**

and trillions of **flies!**

Wombat

This continent's filled

with unique sights and wonders,

our A is **AUSTRALIA**,

the ace land Down Under!

Emu

G'day mate!

← The **Australian Flag** has three features:
1. The **Southern Cross** on the right half is a constellation visible only in the Southern Hemisphere.
2. The **Commonwealth Star** (*left*) is the seven-pointed star for Australia's original states plus its territories.
3. The **Union Jack** (*top left*) is the flag of the United Kingdom. Australia was a British colony that became independent in 1901. Though Australia now has its own government, they still accept the British king or queen as their monarch.

The name **AUSTRALIA** comes from the Latin word *australis*, which means "southern." Australia and Antarctica are the only continents located solely in the Southern Hemisphere. "Oz" is a popular nickname for Australia.

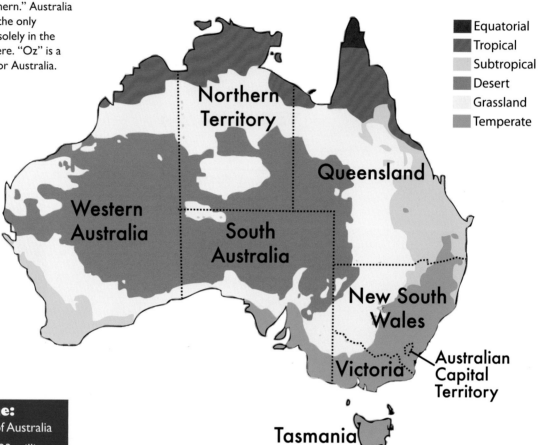

Equatorial
Tropical
Subtropical
Desert
Grassland
Temperate

Northern Territory

Queensland

Western Australia

South Australia

New South Wales

Victoria

Australian Capital Territory

Tasmania

Official Name: Commonwealth of Australia

Population: 23 million

Capital: Canberra

Largest Cities: Sydney, Melbourne, Brisbane

Comparative Size: Slightly smaller than the contiguous United States, the 6th-largest country, the smallest continent

Language: English (*18% of Australians speak another language at home.*)

Religion: Christian 67%, Buddhist 2.7%, Muslim 2.4%, Hindu 1.4%, unaffiliated 22%

Currency: Australian dollar

Key Industry: Mining

Where in the world is Australia?

GEOGRAPHICAL NOTES

◉ Australia is the **second driest continent** after Antarctica. Much of the interior of the country, the OUTBACK, is desert, and very few people live there.

◉ Australia has **six states** (Western Australia, South Australia, Queensland, New South Wales, Victoria, Tasmania) and **two territories** (the Northern Territory and the Australian Capital Territory).

Aboriginal Dancer

← **Aboriginal** peoples have lived in Australia for over 45,000 years and now make up about 2.5% of the population. There are many different Aboriginal nations and cultures and over 200 different languages.

Kangaroo

Koala

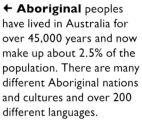
David Wirrpanda is a famous former → *Australia Rules Football player of Aboriginal descent. See more about Australia Rules Football or "Footy" on pages 13 & 16.*

↑ **Kangaroos** and **koalas** are ↑ both *marsupials,* which means they carry their babies in a pouch on their body. Australia is home to many marsupials and animals not found anywhere else in the world.

Playing a Didgeridoo

← A **didgeridoo** is an Aboriginal musical instrument also known as a "drone pipe." It was created over 1,500 years ago and its droning buzz is one of the best known sounds of Australia. →

Didgeridoo

Dingo

The duck-billed, beaver-tailed **platypus** may be one of the oddest Australian animals. It is a *monotreme,* a mammal that lays eggs, and the males have a spur on their back feet that is venomous. ↓

Platypus

↑ **Dingoes** are wild dogs that roam the Australian outback hunting for food. They eat rabbits, possums, wombats, sheep and even kangaroos.

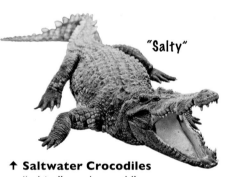
"Salty"

Kookaburra

← The **kookaburra** is a large kingfisher bird that is famous for its laughter-like call.

↓ **Boomerangs** are Aboriginal throwing sticks that have been used for both hunting and games for over 10,000 years. Not all boomerangs are designed to be "returning," those used for hunting must fly straight.

↑ **Saltwater Crocodiles** or "salties" are the world's largest living reptile and can grow to more than 18 feet in length. Found only in Northern Australia and Southeast Asia, they are fierce, intelligent predators and can attack humans.

Clownfish & Surgeonfish

Boomerang

Great Barrier Reef

← ↑ The **Great Barrier Reef** is the world's largest coral reef. Coral reefs are the "rainforest of the ocean" containing 25% of all marine species, including tropical fish, like clownfish. Off the coast of Queensland, the Great Barrier Reef is one of Australia's top tourist destinations.

← **"No worries"** has been described as Australia's national motto. Similar to the American "no problem," it can mean "don't worry about that," "you're welcome," or "sure thing." It expresses feelings of friendliness, ease and optimism.

Captain James → **Cook** claimed Australia for the British Empire in 1770. A **penal colony** for convicts was founded in what is now Sydney on January 26, 1788. January 26 is now celebrated as **Australia Day**.

Leg Shackles for Convicts

← Until the United States declared its independence in 1776, the British used their American colonies as **penal colonies,** sending British citizens convicted of small crimes to be sold there as indentured servants. Five years after America won its independence (1783) and stopped accepting convicts, Australia's penal colony was founded to relieve Britain's overcrowded jails. These convicts became unpaid laborers working to build the new colony.

↑ An Australian five-dollar bill or "fiver" with the face of their queen, Elizabeth II.

Sheep

↑ There are about 120 million **sheep** in Australia, about five times the number of people. Australia is the leading producer of wool worldwide.

Gold

↑ **Gold** rushes in the 1850s more than doubled Australia's population. Mining gold and other minerals continues to be one of Australia's most important industries.

Outback

↑ The **Outback** is any remote, dry part of Australia. The Outback tends to be in the interior of the country where there are several deserts. It is also known as the "bush" or the "never-never."

Uluru or Ayer's Rock is the world's second largest rock. A sacred site for the local Aboriginal people, the *Anangu*, Uluru is one large sandstone that is over five miles around and 100 feet high. Uluru is Australia's most famous natural landmark. ↓

Sydney Opera House

↑ Designed to look like a ship in full sail, **Sydney Opera House** is one of the most recognized symbols of Australia. Completed in 1973, it is considered an architectural feat of the 20th century.

↑ Did you know that 12% of Australians have **Asian ancestry**? Australia is a nation of immigrants and 45% of Australians today are either immigrants or the children of immigrants. Many new immigrants to Australia are from Asian countries including India, China, the Philippines, Vietnam and Malaysia.

Uluru

Barron Falls

Great Dividing Range

↑ Although a large part of Australia is both dry and flat, there are tropical rainforests in the far north and the **Great Dividing Range** runs down the eastern side of the country. The mountains actually contribute to the dryness of the interior. They stop moist air coming in from the ocean and keep most of the rain on the coast, where the majority of Australians live.

Swimmers

← **Swimming** and **surfing** → are very popular sports in Australia, and Australians are some of the top competitive surfers and swimmers in the world.

Surfing

Australians → love to cook out with friends and have a "**barbie**." Sausages, also called "snags," are very popular to grill up, as well as steaks and shrimp.

Snags on the "Barbie"

Australia Rules → Football or "footy" is played on an oval field with four goal posts at each end. Two teams of eight players each compete to make goals. They can advance the ball using any part of their body, though they cannot throw the ball or hold it. Cricket, swimming and footy are the most popular sports in Australia.

Footy

← **Vegemite** is a salty spread made of brewer's yeast that is rich in vitamin B. Vegemite sandwiches are as popular in Australia as peanut butter and jelly are in the United States. ↓

Flies

Wombat

Vegemite Toast

In the summer, there are ↑ so many **flies** in parts of Australia that waving them away from one's face is jokingly known as the "Australian national salute." Early British settlers developed the ← cork hat to keep flies away from their faces. The swinging movement of the corks naturally shoos flies. Cork hats are rarely used today, but they remain a symbol of Australia.

↑ The **wombat** is a marsupial native to southeast Australia and Tasmania. Wombats burrow underground and have a backward-facing pouch so dirt won't get in when they are digging.

Cork Hat

Emu

← **Emus** are the second largest birds in the world (after ostriches). Emus cannot fly but they can run at speeds of up to 30 mph (50 km/h).

Gold Coast

↑ Gold Coast, Queensland, typifies the Australian ideal of a **city on the beach**. Most Australians live in cities along the coastline, and very few live "outback" in the interior.

Christmas

↑ As Australia is in the Southern Hemisphere, their summer is December to February. This makes the weather quite warm at **Christmas**, when many families choose to celebrate at the beach.

SPEAK AUSSIE!
or "Strine"

Mate: friend
Barbie: barbecue
Brekkie: breakfast
S'arvo: this afternoon
Mate, can you come to the barbie s'arvo?
No worries: No problem, you're welcome, that's okay.
She'll be right: Don't worry, everything will be alright.
She's apples: All is well.
Ace: splendid, excellent

Listen to the SOUNDS of AUSTRALIA

Listen to a:

Didgeridoo The droning buzz of the didgeridoo is a sound distinctive to Australia. Didgeridoo players can hold notes for longer than 40 minutes through a technique called "circular breathing" (breathing in through the nose while blowing out through the mouth.) Online, you can also learn how to make and play your own didgeridoo with just PVC pipe and beeswax. **YOUTUBE SEARCH:** didgeridoo, "How to make a didgeridoo"

Learn how to sing:

Waltzing Matilda "Waltzing Matilda" is a traditional bush ballad that is so beloved in Australia that some consider it their unofficial national anthem. Filled with slang from Australia's Outback, it takes some time for non-Aussies to translate the story, but the catchy chorus and melody will keep you singing, even if you can't remember the meaning of all of the "Strine." Waltzing Matilda was written in 1895 by Banjo Peterson. **YOUTUBE SEARCH:** Waltzing Matilda lyrics

Other Song Recommendations:
"G'day, G'day" by Slim Dusty
"Kookaburra Sits in an Old Gum Tree," a traditional song

SPEAK STRINE!

Strine is a shortening of the word "Australian" and means Australian English. Many of their colorful expressions use both abbreviation and rhyming slang. **Rhyming slang** refers to something by another common word that rhymes with it. For instance, "Let's take a *Captain Cook*" means "Let's take a *look*." Here are a few other examples of Strine:

Noah: Shark. Sharks used to be called "Noah's Arks" but have since been shortened to just "noahs"

Esky: Cooler. Food and drink coolers used to be called "Eskimos" after a brand name until it was shortened. "Esky lidder" is slang for a boogie board.

Steak and Kidney: Sydney, Australia's largest city.

Pat Malone: Alone. He's sitting on his Pat Malone.

Bag of Fruit: Men's suit. *He's got on his new bag of fruit.*

China Plate: Mate, sometimes shortened just to *China.*

Frog and Toad: Road. *China, let's hit the frog 'n toad.*

He's got tickets on himself. He's opinionated and conceited. *Don't listen to him mate, he's got tickets on himself.*

VISIT this fabulous website created by the National Museum of Australia for comic lessons in Strine: **www.nma.gov.au/kidz/aussie_english_for_the_beginner**

BAKE AUSTRALIAN
ANZAC BISCUITS

ANZAC biscuits were developed during World War I (1914–1918) as a treat to send troops stationed abroad. **ANZAC** stands for Australian and New Zealand Army Corps. As there was an egg shortage during the war, the recipe uses no eggs, and the biscuits (that Americans would call cookies) kept well for long naval transportation. ANZAC biscuits are still very popular in Australia, particularly around ANZAC Day, a national holiday on April 25 that is similar to Memorial Day or Veteran's Day in the United States.

1 cup flour
1 cup dry oatmeal
1 cup dried shredded coconut
1 cup brown sugar
1/2 cup butter
2 heaping* tablespoons golden syrup**
1 teaspoon baking soda
2 heaping* tablespoons water

1. Combine flour, oatmeal, coconut and sugar in a bowl.
2. Melt the butter and syrup over low heat in a sauce pan.
3. Mix the baking soda with water and add to butter and syrup.
4. Mix wet and dry ingredients.
5. Drop spoonfuls of the dough onto a greased cookie sheet. Allow room for cookies to spread during baking.
6. Bake at 350°F for 15–20 minutes.

*Australian tablespoons are slightly larger than American.
**If you can't find golden syrup, use either honey or corn syrup.

MAKE YOUR OWN BOOMERANG!

Needed:

1 piece white paper

Cardboard from cereal box or similar

Scissors

Pencil/Pen

Clear tape (optional)

1. Trace boomerang pattern outline below on white paper (or photocopy).

2. Cut out and place on top of cardboard.

3. Tape paper pattern to cardboard, or outline shape on cardboard.

4. Cut out the shape from cardboard.

5. Bend each blade lightly along a line running down the middle (see pattern) so that the edges face down and the middle tents up slightly. ^

6. Place the boomerang down on the table so that all the blade edges are touching the table.

7. Put a finger on the center of the boomerang, holding it down. Then gently pull up on the end of each blade so that the blade ends are raised slightly above the boomerang's center.

8. Your boomerang is ready to throw!

How to Throw Your Boomerang

1. OVERHAND: Hold your boomerang vertically, pinching a blade between your thumb and your first finger. Bend your elbow in front of you so the boomerang is roughly at ear height. The center should be curved away from you, with the points of the tented blades facing toward you.

2. SLIGHTLY TILTED: Tilt your boomerang slightly / away from your body.

3. SPINNING: Extend your arm and flick your wrist forward when you throw it. The wrist motion is somewhat similar to knocking on a door and makes the boomerang spin. The boomerang must be spinning in order to return. Make sure you are not throwing the boomerang toward the ground, it should be thrown slightly upward.

4. PRACTICE: For most people, it takes a little experimentation and practice before they can get their boomerang to return directly to them every time.

bend

bend

bend

← *Once you've made your boomerang and learned how to use it, you can decorate it with markers!*

RESEARCH:

How to Avoid Being Eaten by a Saltwater Crocodile!

Saltwater crocodiles are incredibly good hunters and their attacks on humans, though relatively rare, are a fact of life in Northern Australia. On average, a person is killed by a saltwater crocodile once every two years in Australia. Look online to find all the things you can do to avoid becoming a salty's meal.

Differences between Australia and New Zealand

Though both countries are located "Down Under," Aussies and Kiwis (New Zealanders) have very distinct histories, climates, wildlife and cultures. Create a chart comparing their similarities and differences. Label one column "Australia" and another "New Zealand." Then list categories like: original inhabitants, flag, colonized by, population, nickname, climate, favorite foods, size, language and national symbols.

READ:

Possum Magic by Mem Fox. A culinary and geographical journey around Australia in search of magic. Ages 4 & up.

The Biggest Toad in Australia by Susan Roth. A story from the Aboriginal Dreamtime. Ages 5 & up.

Sun Mother Wakes the World: An Australian Creation Story by Diane Wolkstein. A beautiful retelling of an Aboriginal creation story. Ages 5 & up.

Stories from the Billabong by James Vance Marshall. Ten ancient Aboriginal legends from the Dreamtime, retold, explained and illustrated with Aboriginal Art. Ages 7 & up.

Mystery on the Great Barrier Reef by Carole Marsh. From "Around the World in 80 Mysteries." Ages 8 & up.

You Wouldn't Want to Be an 18th Century British Convict: A Trip to Australia You'd Rather Not Take by Meredith Costain. A fun non-fiction book about the life of British citizens convicted of minor crimes who were transported to Australia. Ages 8 & up.

Toad Rage by Morris Gleitzman. A comic Australian series about a toad campaigning to decrease roadkill. Ages 8 & up.

Not for Parents Australia: Everything You Ever Wanted to Know by Lonely Planet. Endless fun facts about the land down under. Ages 8 & up.

DON'T MISS WATCHING
(online)

Australian Rules Football or "footy." Imagine American football on an oval field with some hand dribbling, kicking to score, no throwing allowed and no protective equipment...you can't? You'll have to see it!
YOUTUBE SEARCH: Australian Rules Football

Australia's Natural Wonders See amazing videos about the Great Barrier Reef and Uluru. Lonely Planet and BBC have both on YouTube. **YOUTUBE SEARCH: Uluru Lonely Planet, Great Barrier Reef Lonely Planet**

Aboriginal Culture Learn about ancient Aboriginal beliefs in the "**Dreamtime**," when all the world was created through song. **YOUTUBE SEARCH: Aboriginal Dreamtime**

Australia's Deadly Animals Australia has a surprising number of deadly species as mentioned in this comic song by "Scared Weird Little Guys."
YOUTUBE SEARCH: deadly animals come Australia

Aussie Jingle Bells Don't miss funny Australian versions of Christmas carols like "Jingle Bells."
"Dashing though the bush, in a rusty Holden ute (truck), kicking up the dust, esky (cooler) in the boot (trunk). Kelpie (sheep dog) by my side, singin' Christmas songs, it's summertime and I am in my singlet (tank top), shorts and thongs (flip flops)! Oh jingle bells, jingle bells, jingle all the way! Christmas in Australia on a scorching summer day!"
YOUTUBE SEARCH: Aussie Jingle Bells

Australian Films Here are some Australia films that give a window to life Down Under:
Rabbit-Proof Fence (2003) PG: Aboriginal children try to make their way back to the family they were taken from
Storm Boy (1976) NR: Kid's film about a boy and a pelican
Crocodile Dundee (1986) PG-13: Stereotypical but fun
Australia (2008) PG-13: An Australian historical epic
Gallipoli (1981) PG: A classic about the tragic World War I battle that is commemorated on ANZAC Day

How to Make Aboriginal Dot Paintings

Dot painting is fun. With a little patience, anyone can create beautiful art with just paint, a pencil eraser and paper. Videos quickly teach the technique and may inspire you to create your own design.
YOUTUBE SEARCH: How to teach dot painting

EXPLORE A DOWN UNDER MAP OF THE WORLD!

Australia

Who says NORTH is UP and SOUTH is DOWN?

Why should Europe and Africa be in the center of a world map?

A world map is equally correct with the Southern Hemisphere on top and Australia in the middle.

Explore Map perspectives with these activities:

1. Try turning your own world map south side up and see how many places you can identify! Can you find your country? What about the bodies of water nearest to you?

2. Now try to identify the continents, oceans, Australia and its nearest neighbors. How many countries of the world can you recognize?

3. Take a map of your own country and turn it south side up. What cities can you identify from that new viewpoint? How would you describe the shape of the country from that perspective? What about the shape of your state?

 MAKE your own world or country map that uses a direction other than north as up! Print out blank "outline maps" from either wikimedia commons or worldatlas.com. Choose the cardinal direction you want to be at the top and then label your map with cities, rivers, mountains or whatever points of interest you choose.

Making a world map, you can also choose what place is at the center of your map. Print out a blank world map, cut out the continents and arrange them (as accurately as you can) to suit your chosen center and cardinal direction.

Did you know, historically maps were neither north or south side up?

Instead, the east was on top. Thus people would *orient* themselves to face the orient or east when reading a map. Facing the east is easy when the sun is visible as it rises in the east and sets in the west. So people can face toward or away from the sun to point themselves in the right direction.

Can you imagine our world map today with the east on top? What country would you place at the top of the map? What would be at the center of your map and why?

This world map dating from 1300 puts the east on top and Jerusalem in the middle. The top half of the map is Asia, the bottom right is Africa and the bottom left is Europe. The black in the center is the Mediterranean (running vertically) and other seas. Why aren't the Americas and Australia on this map? →

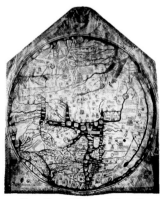

Hereford Mappa Mundi

B is for Brazil

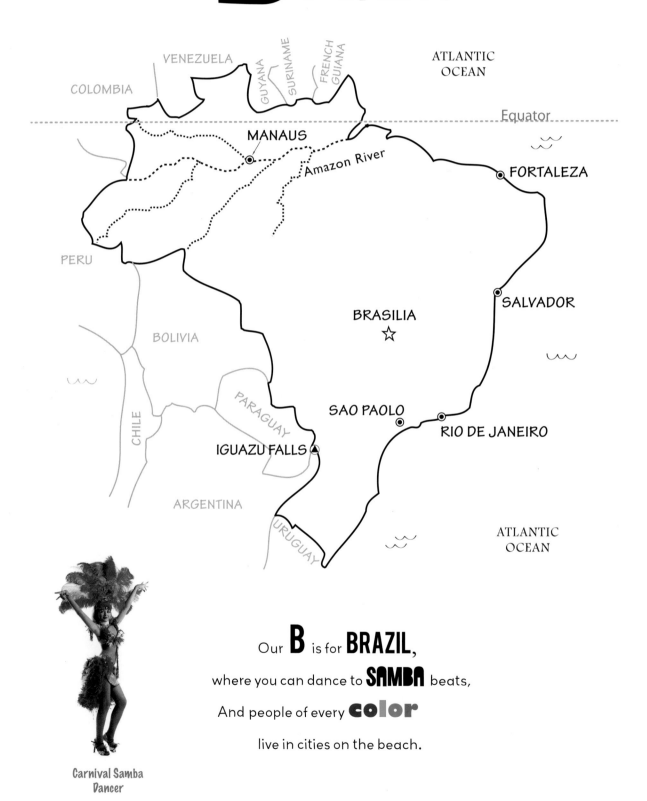

ATLANTIC OCEAN

VENEZUELA

COLOMBIA

GUYANA

SURINAME

FRENCH GUIANA

Equator

MANAUS

Amazon River

FORTALEZA

PERU

BOLIVIA

BRASILIA ☆

SALVADOR

CHILE

PARAGUAY

SAO PAOLO

RIO DE JANEIRO

IGUAZU FALLS ▲

ARGENTINA

URUGUAY

ATLANTIC OCEAN

Carnival Samba
Dancer

Our **B** is for **BRAZIL**,

where you can dance to **SAMBA** beats,

And people of every **color**

live in cities on the beach.

Bom dia!*

Toucan

Sucos

"Bom dia!" say the natives [bohm JEE-ah]

(for they speak in Portuguese).

"Um **suco**, por favor" [SU-coh]

is how to ask for "one juice, please!"

Once a colony where slaves

grew sugar and cigars

Brazil now mixes races

like the fruit at their **juice bars**.

Sugarcane

Guava

MANGO, **papaya**, GUAVA...

Indigenous, Latin and Black

All dance in the street for *Carnival*

and cheer at each football match.

But Brazil has more than **FOOTBALL**,

fruit and Carnival to boast.

Why this is where the **Amazon River**

flows from forest to coast!

Papaya

Futebol

The river and the forest both

are largest in all the globe,

And ten percent of species call

the **AMAZON** their home.

Amazon River

***Bom dia!** (bohm JEE-ah) means "Good day!"

Jaguar

Here **TOUCANS** caw with rainbow beaks,
pink river dolphins play,
And **SPIDER MONKEYS** swing from trees.
But WATCH OUT night and day –

For **VAMPIRE BATS** and **poisonous frogs**
and razor-toothed **PIRANHA**,
For silent **JAGUARS** on the prowl
and giant **ANACONDA**!

Luckily, these predators
aren't usually **people-eaters** –
Unlike **mosquitoes**, the Amazon's
most eager people-greeters.

With all the fruit and creatures here,
what DO Brazilians **EAT**?
A black bean stew with sausage
is their favorite savory *treat*!

FEIJOADA, served on rice with *greens*   [fay-JWAH-dah]
and **ORANGES** to the side,
Is favored lunch for Brasileiros   [brah-see-LAY-rohs, *Brazilians*]
living far and wide.

Pink River Dolphin

Poison Dart Frog

Mosquito

Anaconda

Feijoada

Sao Paolo

It's eaten by Sao Paolo's **huge**
and **HUSTLING** population,
And in **RIO** during **Carnival's**
most famous celebration.

Capoeira

It's fuel for Salvador's parties –
DANCING down the streets –
Or **CAPOEIRA**, a martial art [cah-poh-AY-rah]
with acrobatic feats.

So listen to the **sultry** sound
of **BOSSA NOVA** calling,
and let the music sway you –
you're past the point of stalling!

Iguazu Falls

Come see this land of **SAMBA**,
beaches, fruit and **Carnaval;**
Big **CITIES**, Amazonian splendor
and **Iguazu Falls**. [ee-GWAH-zu]

Football fans and **cafezinho** – [cah-fay-ZEEN-yo]
oh so sweet and hot!
Ahhhh… **BRAZIL,**
the **tropical melting pot.**

Cafezinho

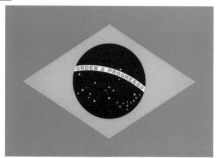

← The **Brazilian flag** has a blue disk with stars, which represents the constellations in the night sky over Rio de Janeiro in 1889 when Brazil declared itself to be a republic. Each of Brazil's **26 states** can point out its own particular star on the flag. The only star above the banner represents Pará, a large northern state that straddles the equator. Across the sky is a banner with their motto, "Ordem e Progresso" or "Order and Progress."

The name **BRAZIL** comes from brazil wood, a tree that Portuguese found in abundance when they first arrived in this land in 1500. Brazil wood or *pau do brasil* was found to produce a very valuable red dye used in making fine clothing. Portugal exported so much brazil wood from the region that it became known simply as Brazil. Today, brazil wood is used to make the bows of violins and other string instruments.

Amazon Rainforest

Local Name:
República Federativa do Brasil

Population: 203 million
(5th-largest country by population)

Capital: Brasilia

Largest Cities:
Sao Paolo, Rio de Janeiro, Salvador

Comparative Size:
Slightly smaller than the U.S.
(the 5th-largest country by area)

Ethnicity:
White 47%, brown (mixed) 43%, black 7%, Asian 1%, indigenous <1%

Language: Portuguese

Religion: Christian 89%
(Roman Catholic 65%, Protestant 23%), none 8%

Currency: Real

Where in the World Is Brazil?

GEOGRAPHICAL NOTES

◉ 80% of Brazilians live within 200 miles of the Atlantic Ocean.

◉ The Amazon Rainforest is largely preserved from human destruction by having few roads or cities.

◉ Brazil is the world's **5th-largest country**, both by land area and population.

◉ Brazil **borders** every South American country except Ecuador and Chile.

◉ Brazil is the **largest Portuguese-speaking country** in the world.

President Dilma Rousseff

Futebol Player, **Ronaldinho**

Giselle Bundchen, Supermodel

TV Celebrity, **Xuxa** (SHOO-shah)

Pelé, Football Icon

Samba Dancer

Indigenous Brazilian

Samba Dancer

← **Samba** is a Brazilian dance and musical style with both African and indigenous roots. Samba is famously performed during *Carnaval* (car-nah-VAL), which is known as the largest party in the world. Like Mardi Gras in the United States, **Carnival** is held each year before the beginning of Lent, the 40 days of fasting and prayer before Easter. ↓

←↑→What does a Brazilian look like?

In Brazil, races have been mixing since the Portuguese first arrived in 1500 and met Indigenous Brazilians. African slaves brought in to grow sugar cane were added to the mix beginning in 1551. The result is that most Brazilians are made up of some mix of European, African and Native American ancestry. Even Brazilians who identify themselves as white (branca) or black (preto) usually have some other race in their ancestry. About 43% of Brazilians identify themselves as "**pardo**" or "brown" and consider themselves too ethnically mixed to declare any one race. Purely **indigenous Brazilians** now make up less than 1% of the population, but a much larger percentage of the population has some indigenous DNA.

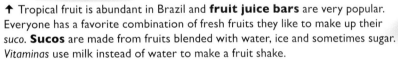
Papaya   Mango   Guava

↑ Tropical fruit is abundant in Brazil and **fruit juice bars** are very popular. Everyone has a favorite combination of fresh fruits they like to make up their *suco*. **Sucos** are made from fruits blended with water, ice and sometimes sugar. *Vitaminas* use milk instead of water to make a fruit shake.

Pelé

↑ There is nothing that Brazilians are more passionate about than **futebol**. Brazil has won numerous World Cups and one of their national heroes is Pelé, a futebol star. **Pelé** grew up in poverty and started to play professional soccer when he was only 16. He played for Brazil from 1956–1974 and scored more than 1,000 goals. Around the world, many fans rank Pelé as the best soccer player of all time. →

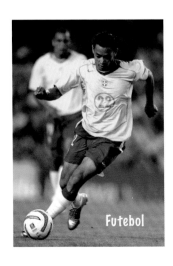
Futebol

Sugarcane

Sugarcane

↑ **Sugarcane** was Brazil's biggest crop and export from 1550–1700. Sugar, cotton and tobacco plantations imported hundreds of thousands of African slaves to farm crops here. In the 1700s, gold mining replaced sugar as the largest industry and importer of slaves to Brazil. By 1800, slaves made up half of the Brazilian population. Brazil became the last Western nation to abolish slavery in 1888. The nation is still the world's largest producer of sugarcane and Brazil has the world's largest population of African descent outside of Africa.

Amazon River

Toucan

Spider Monkey

← **Toucans** are known for their large, colorful beaks, which scientists believe help the birds cool off in hot weather.

← The **spider monkey** got its name from its long arms, legs and tail. It uses its tail as an extra limb to pick up things or hang from branches.

↑ The **Amazon River** is the largest river in the world and contains 20% of the world's river water. At some points, the Amazon is over five miles wide and it's not possible to see to the other side. The Amazon River is also one of the world's longest rivers, with a similar length to the Nile River.
The **Amazon Rainforest** spans five countries and is the largest rainforest in the world. It contains 10% of all the world's animal species.

The **pink river dolphin** is found only in South America. In Amazonian folklore, the dolphin turns into a beautiful man who charms women each night. ↓

Vampire Bat

Jaguars are the → largest cats in the Americas and the third largest in the world, after tigers and lions. They typically live in the rainforest and use their powerful jaws to kill their prey by biting through its skull and piercing the brain.

Jaguar

Pink River Dolphin

Poison dart frogs have toxic secretions on their skin that protect them from predators. Indigenous Brazilians once used these secretions to poison blow darts used for hunting. ↓

↑ **Vampire bats** hunt at night and drink the blood of large (often sleeping) animals. If a vampire bat bit you, they wouldn't be able to take enough blood to kill you. They can only drink about one ounce or an eighth cup per 20-minute feeding. **Mosquitoes** are much more likely to drink your blood in the Amazon.

Piranha

← Vampire bats, jaguars, piranhas and anacondas are not usually a danger to humans. Fried **piranha** is frequently eaten for dinner in the Amazon.

Poisonous Dart Frog

Anaconda

← **Anacondas** are some of the largest snakes in the world and can grow to over 22 feet in length. They are sometimes called "water boas" because they spend much of their time in the water. As nonvenomous snakes, they kill their prey by squeezing and suffocating it.

Feijoada

← **Feijoada** is the national dish of Brazil. A black bean stew made with many types of pork, it is traditionally served with rice, collard greens and orange slices. Savory but not spicy, it is Brazilian comfort food.

São Paulo

Rio de Janeiro or "River of January" used to be the capital of Brazil. Rio is famous for having a spectacular natural setting, the world's largest Carnival celebration and beautiful beaches like Ipanema and Copacabana. A large statue called "Christ the Redeemer" looks out over the city. ↓

Rio de Janeiro

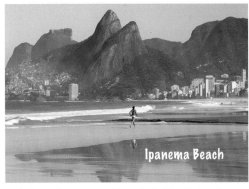
Ipanema Beach

↑ Ritzy **Ipanema Beach** in Rio de Janeiro became world famous with the bossa nova song, "The Girl from Ipanema." **Bossa nova** is a Brazilian musical style developed in the 1950s that was inspired by samba and jazz, and usually played on a classical guitar.

↑ **São Paulo** is one of the largest cities in the world, with over 11 million people. It is often compared to New York City because it is the business and financial capital of Brazil and home to many immigrant communities. For instance, São Paulo is home to the largest population of people of Japanese descent outside of Japan. São Paulo means "Saint Paul" in English.

Capoeira

Salvador da Bahia's Historic Center

Cafezinho

↑ **Capoeira** *(cah-poh-AY-rah)* is a martial art developed by slaves to look like a dance or game. With musical accompaniment and acrobatic moves, it fooled slave masters, who would not allow slaves to train to fight.

Salvador's Barra Beach

←↑ **Salvador da Bahia** is Brazil's third-largest city and the center of Afro-Brazilian culture. The city was once the capital of colonial Brazil and was the main port for slaves and sugarcane. The northeast still has the largest black population of any region in Brazil. Visiting Salvador, you can see capoeira, Bahian women in traditional dress and the festive lifestyle for which it is famous. Almost every night, there are parties in the city where people dance down the streets behind bands of samba drummers.

↑ **Cafezinho** is a small, very strong and sweet cup of coffee. Brazilians drink cafezinhos all day. They are symbols of hospitality and are always offered to guests.

Bahian Woman

Iguazu Falls is considered → one of the most spectacular waterfalls in the world. It flows from the Iguazu River and is located on the border between Argentina and Brazil.

Iguazu Falls

Listen to the SOUNDS of BRAZIL

Samba & Bossa Nova Samba and bossa nova are two musical styles that originated in Brazil. They can transport you to a Brazilian street party or a gorgeous tropical beach. **YOUTUBE SEARCH: samba macalena, bossa nova**

The Girl From Ipanema "The Girl from Ipanema" is a bossa nova classic written in 1962. The version performed by Stan Getz and João and Astrud Gilberto made bossa nova popular around the world and won the 1965 Grammy award. **YOUTUBE SEARCH: girl Ipanema**

Brazilian PORTUGUESE Portuguese is phonetically similar to Spanish but Brazilian Portuguese has some different consonant sounds. For instance, the letter "D" before an i or an e becomes like our "J." Also, rolled R's, used at the beginning of R words and when R is doubled (rr) become an "H." So Rio is actually pronounced "HEE-yo."

SPEAK Brazilian Portuguese!

Bom Dia!	Good Day!	*bohm JEE-ah*
Boa Tarde!	Good Afternoon!	*BOH-ah TAR-jay*
Obrigado:	Thank you *(used by males)*	*oh-bree-GAH-doh*
Obrigada:	Thank you *(used by females)*	*oh-bree-GAH-dah*
Por Favor:	Please	*por fah-VOR*
Tudo Bem?	How are you? *or All is well?*	*TU-doh BAYM*
Tudo Bem!	I'm fine! *or All is well!*	*TU-doh BAYM*
Te Amo.	I love you.	*tay AH-moh*
Legal!	Cool.	*lay-GAHL*
Lindo Maravilhoso! **Amazing!** *(Beautiful, Wonderful!)*		
	LEEN-doh mah-rah-vee-YOH-so	

RESEARCH:

Animals of the Amazon
Sloths, howler monkeys, capybara, anteaters, caiman, tarantulas, leaf-cutter ants, blue morpho butterflies - pick an animal that interests you - there are so many fascinating creatures to choose from!

Life of Pelé
There are many biographies of Pelé and other Brazilian futebol stars for kids; they provide insight on life in Brazil and Brazilian heroes.

MAKE: A Brazilian PINEAPPLE-MINT SUCO

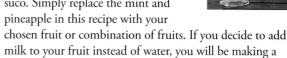

Feel free to use any ripe tropical fruit available to make a delicious Brazilian suco. Simply replace the mint and pineapple in this recipe with your chosen fruit or combination of fruits. If you decide to add milk to your fruit instead of water, you will be making a *vitamina*. This suco is very popular in Brazil.

1. Peel, core and cut up pineapple.
2. Combine all the ingredients in a blender and blend until smooth. Add more water if needed.
3. Taste and add sugar if needed. Serve immediately.

**½ fresh pineapple,
1 handful fresh mint
1 cup ice
1 cup water
Sugar to taste**

READ:

How the Night Came from the Sea: A Story of Brazil by Mary Joan Gerson. An African sea goddess brings rest to the world. Ages 6 & up.

The Great Snake: Stories from the Amazon by Sean Taylor. Take a trip down the Amazon and hear nine indigenous folktales. Ages 8 & up.

Keeper by Mal Peet. A journalist interviews World Cup soccer star "El Gato"in this novel about a mysterious Brazilian childhood. Ages 12 & up.

DON'T MISS WATCHING (online)

Capoeira Is it a sport? An art form? A martial art? A dance? Capoeira is amazingly athletic, acrobatic and beautiful to watch. **YOUTUBE SEARCH:** Capoeira

Carnival & Samba There are great documentaries about Brazilian *Carnaval* in Rio de Janeiro and what it's like to be a dancer in the parades. **YOUTUBE SEARCH:** Brazilian Carnaval history

Wonders of the Amazon Travel in a boat down the Amazon, see exotic plants and animals and visit indigenous peoples. **YOUTUBE SEARCH:** Amazon

Rio (2011) Rated G. Travel to Brazil with Blu, the macaw from Minnesota in this animated adventure film.

Have Your Own Carnival Parade!

To have your own Brazilian Carnival parade you need three things:

1. Music Music is the most important element. People play samba all year long in Brazil. Bands process through the streets regularly practicing their rhythms, and people dance behind them just for fun. Listen to some samba (see recommendations in the music section), and you might even want to make a ganza (see directions below) so you can play along. Practice playing before you parade to find your rhythm.

2. Dance Try out a "how to samba" video online. **YOUTUBE SEARCH: samba 4 minutes** There are several, including videos of men teaching samba – it's not just for women! Don't worry if you don't perfect your samba moves – as long as you get a feel for the rhythm and are having fun. Listening to a lot of samba can help you make up your own dance moves. Some paraders may prefer to be dancers, and some to play music.

3. Costumes Costumes are important because they help samba dancers really let loose and do things they might not do in their normal clothes... like dance down the street! For a costume, you can make a mask for yourself, wear face paint, Mardi Gras beads, or just your Halloween costume from last year. Scary costumes are great too – just imagine a samba-dancing monster coming your way! Carnival costumes are VERY diverse so you can't go wrong, as long as you have room to dance or play your instrument. The most important thing is to HAVE FUN! That's the whole point of Brazilian Carnival.

 # MAKE a Ganza and Play Samba!

Use a soda can to make your own samba shaker and play in a samba band.

A ganza is a Brazilian "rattle" that is frequently used to play samba. It is very easy to make a beautiful sounding ganza with only an empty soda can and rice!

Needed:
1 empty soda can
1 small handful rice
Tape
Samba music
Internet access

1. Rinse your can with water and dry it. Shake your can upside down to get out any extra liquid then set the can in the sun or some other warm place to dry.

2. Pour rice into your can. (If you discover your can is still a bit damp, you can always dry it further with the rice already inside.) Once you've added some rice, shake it and see if you like the sound. Experiment with adding and removing rice until it sounds the way you like it.

3. Tape over the opening.

4. Decorate (Optional) To decorate your ganza, cover it with stickers or colored tape.

5. Learn technique. Watch a YouTube video on "shaker technique." They give easy instructions to get you moving and sounding like a real percussionist!

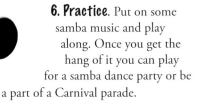

6. Practice. Put on some samba music and play along. Once you get the hang of it you can play for a samba dance party or be a part of a Carnival parade.

President Bush playing the ganza on a trip to Brazil.

There are many other easy shakers you can make! Experiment with things you have around your house like dried beans in a glass jar or cereal in a plastic bottle.

C is for China

RUSSIA

RUSSIA

KAZAKHSTAN

MONGOLIA

KYRGYZSTAN

Gobi
Desert

BEIJING ☆

Taklamakan
Desert

KOREAS

TAJ.

Yellow
Sea

PAKISTAN

Huang He (Yellow River)

TIBETAN
PLATEAU

Himalayan Mountains

Mekong

SHANGHAI

East China
Sea

Yangtze River

NEPAL

BHU.

INDIA

INDIA

GUANGZHOU

Taiwan

HONG KONG

BURMA

VIETNAM

LAOS

South China
Sea

Himalayas

China is our C,

an ancient **DRAGON** land,

of **HIMALAYAN** heights

and **Gobi Desert** sands,

Chinese Dragon

Kung Fu

Pipa

Of wet rice paddy farms

And giant cities teeming,

of **KUNG FU** classes, pipa bands

and yummy dumplings steaming!

We'll feast on them with CHOPSTICKS

then rice and noodle dishes,

Or crispy **Peking duck** —

it's all just so delicious!

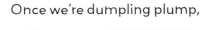

Peking Duck

Once we're dumpling plump,

let's **bike** around **BEIJING**,

China's bustling capital

(formerly called "**Peking**").

Forbidden City

We'll stroll the **FORBIDDEN CITY**

in Beijing's central ring.

It was home to mighty emperors

from dynasties MING and QING.

Near there, **Tiananmen Square,**

is where we'll surely spy

fierce **DRAGONS** on the prowl —

swooping through the sky!

Qing Emperor

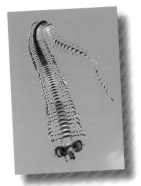

Dragon Kite

Great Wall of China

Below the locals watch them,

holding spools of twine.

They're flying **kites**, a Chinese sport

beloved since ancient times!

Next we'll travel north,

it's not too far at all

To hike along the heights

of China's long **GREAT WALL**.

Panda

From **TERRACOTTA WARRIORS**

to Shanghai's city lights

To **PANDAS** in the forest —

we'll visit tourist sites.

Terracotta
Warrior

And yet the greatest sight

within this ancient nation

Is China's many people —

ONE-FIFTH WORLD POPULATION!

A **billion**-plus Chinese

in eastern cities throng,

and skyscrapers grow like weeds

Crowds in Shanghai

in *Shanghai*, **Guangzhou**, and **Hong Kong.** [gwahng-JOH]

Hong Kong

Rice Farming

Camel in Gobi Desert

Or further west they dwell —
their homes near grassy **STEPPES**,
Or on rice paddy farms
the **Yangtze River** wets. [YANG-see]

In **HIMALAYAN** heights
or atop **Tibet's Plateau**,
Near **Gobi Desert** sands,
or the **Yellow River's** flow.

Yellow River

Chinese have been in China
for over **5,000** years.
With a civilization so old,
they've often been pioneers.

Porcelain
"Fine China"

They gave the world so much
that still today we use,
from **paper**, **printing** and **silk**
to new ideas and views —

Tea

Fireworks

MATCHES, *china*, **tea**
and **FIREWORKS** going **boom**.
And don't forget they first found
the **RABBIT IN THE MOON!**

Rabbit in the Moon

Chairman Mao

So don't be frightened by looming portraits

of former **Chairman Mao**,

But come and greet a new China

with a hearty **"NI HAO!"** [nee how]

This superpower of the East

will offer you quite a *feast*

Of history, landscapes, art...

and yummy food not least!

Ni Hao!*

*****Ni hao!** [nee-how] means "hello!" in Mandarin Chinese.

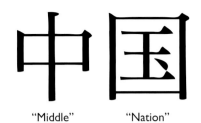

← The **Chinese flag** was adopted in 1949, the same year that China became a communist country. *(See Chairman Mao on page 37 for a definition of communism.)* The big yellow star represents the communist party that governs China. The four smaller stars represent the people of China: workers, farmers, intellectuals and business people.

中国

"Middle" "Nation"

China written in Chinese

China's name in Chinese is **ZHONGGUO** *[JONG gWOah]*, which roughly translates to "Central Nation" or "Middle Kingdom," reflecting an ancient view of their country as the center of civilization.

China's Provinces & Autonomous Regions

Official Name:
The People's Republic of China

Local Name: Zhongguo
(*CHONG gWOah*)

Population: 1.35 billion
(1,355,000,000)

Capital: Beijing

Largest Cities: Shanghai, Beijing, Tianjin, Guangzhou, Hong Kong

Comparative Size:
About the same size as the United States

Languages: Mandarin, Cantonese, Shanghainese and many other Chinese dialects

Religion: Buddhists 18%, Christians 5%, Muslims 2%, traditional beliefs 22%
(Officially, the nation is atheist.)

Currency: Renminbi
(RMB) or *yuan*

Where in the World is China?

GEOGRAPHICAL NOTES

◉ China has **22 provinces** and **five autonomous regions**. Autonomous regions (A.R.) were created to give minority ethnic groups like Mongols, Tibetans and Uygurs more independence. Some ethnic groups, like the Tibetans, would still like greater independence.

◉ There are four **administrative divisions** (in pink: Beijing, Tianjin, Shanghai and Chongqing) and two **special administrative regions** (Hong Kong and Macau). The Chinese consider Taiwan a 23rd province, though it is governed by a separate entity known as the "Republic of China."

← **Kung fu**, the word for all Chinese martial arts, began about 3,000 years ago. It is also referred to as *wushu* in China. Shaolin kung fu is a style that was developed at the Shaolin Monastery in Henan Province early in the 7th century. This style has become famous worldwide and was featured in the movie *Kung Fu Panda*. →

Shaolin Kung Fu

Canton Rice

Noodles

Dumplings

← **Dumplings** are similar to stuffed pasta. They are filled with minced meat and vegetables and then either steamed in bamboo baskets, boiled, or fried. So yummy!

↑ **Rice** was first grown and eaten in China over 8,000 years ago.
Noodles have been a staple of their → diet for over 4,000 years, and many claim that noodles and pasta originated in China.

Peking duck →
is the specialty of Beijing, China's capital city. (Beijing used to be called Peking by English speakers.) Originally served to emperors, Peking duck is famous for its crispy skin. Slices are wrapped up in thin pancakes with hoisin sauce and green onions.

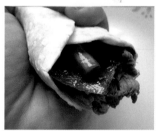

Forbidden City

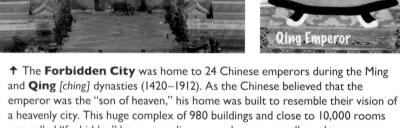

Qing Emperor

↑ The **Forbidden City** was home to 24 Chinese emperors during the Ming and **Qing** [ching] dynasties (1420–1912). As the Chinese believed that the emperor was the "son of heaven," his home was built to resemble their vision of a heavenly city. This huge complex of 980 buildings and close to 10,000 rooms was called "forbidden" because ordinary people were not allowed to enter.

Tiananmen Square

↑ Located in the center of Beijing, **Tiananmen Square** is the world's largest public square and can hold over one million people. Tiananmen means "Heaven's Gate," a reference to an entrance to the Forbidden City located at the square's north end. The Chinese National Museum and the Great Hall of the People (the national government building) are also located off the square.

↓ **Kite flying** is a favorite activity in Tiananmen Square. Chinese have been flying kites for over 2,500 years.

Dragon Kite

← **Dragons** have long been revered by the Chinese as symbols of strength, luck and power. Once used to represent the emperor, they became a symbol of China to the Western world.

Terra-cotta Army

Terra-cotta Warrior

The Great Wall of China

← **The Great Wall of China** is over 5,500 miles (8850 km) long, longer than as the US– Canada border from the Atlantic to the Pacific! The Great Wall was built to keep out invaders from the north. It is not continuous, but was built in several sections at different times ranging from the 5th century BCE to the 17th CE. Walking on top of the Great Wall can be a real workout as there are many hilly sections and a lot of steps. ↓

↑ Some 8,000 **terra-cotta warriors** were buried with Qin Shi Huang, the first Chinese emperor, in 210 BCE. Each soldier is unique and was created in order to protect Emperor Qin [chin] in the afterlife. They were rediscovered in 1974 by a group of Chinese farmers trying to dig a well in Shaanxi province. Over 700,000 workers created Qin's elaborate mausoleum. Beyond warriors, it contained 150 horses, acrobats and musicians, all held inside a model of his palace.

Qin Shi Huang united the → *"Warring States" into one undivided China and started the long reign of Chinese emperors with the Qin [chin] dynasty.*

Pandas

↑ **Giant Pandas** are an endangered species of bear found only in the mountains of central China in Sichuan, Gansu and Shaanxi provinces. They eat 20–30 pounds (9–14 kg) of bamboo everyday.

Walking the Great Wall

Hong Kong

↑ **Hong Kong** was a British colony until 1997 and still maintains its own government under China's "One Country, Two Systems" policy. With an incredibly dense population, Hong Kong's many high-rise buildings have made it known as the world's most vertical city.

↓ Known historically in the West as "Canton," **Guangzhou** [gwahng-joh] is the capital of Guangdong province. It is the largest city in southern China with a population of over 12 million people. In both Guangzhou and Hong Kong, the main language is Cantonese.

There are over 45 **cities** in China → with metropolitan populations of over 2 million people. In contrast, the United States has 22 metropolises with over 2 million people. Shanghai is China's largest city by population and there are more people living in its metropolitan area than in the entire state of Florida.

Shanghai

← The "New York City" of China, **Shanghai** is China's commercial and financial center and has a population of over 20 million people. At the mouth of the Yangtze River, Shanghai is also the world's busiest container port, serving as a key passageway for goods entering or exiting China.

Guangzhou

Yangtze River

← The **Yangtze River** is called *Chang Jiang* or "long river" in Chinese. It is the longest river in Asia and the third-longest river in the world. A third of China's people live along the Yangtze river basin. It flows from glaciers on the Tibetan plateau to empty into the sea at Shanghai.

Yellow River

↑ The **Yangtze River** valley was probably the site of the world's first cultivation of rice and remains China's rice-growing center. China is the world's largest producer of rice, which is their biggest crop. →

Farming Rice

Yellow River

↑ The **Yellow River** or *Huang He* is sometimes called the "Mother River" as it was the cradle of early Chinese civilization and ancient China's most prosperous region. But, due to its history of disastrous flooding, it is also called "China's Sorrow."

← The Yellow River gets its name from the yellow mud it carries in its waters, which is also a cause of its flooding. There is a famous Chinese saying, "When the Yellow River runs clear," which means "never." The Yellow River empties into the Yellow Sea.

Tibetan Plateau

←The **Tibetan Plateau** has been nicknamed the "Roof of the World" for its incredibly high altitude and relatively flat surface.

Containing the world's highest peaks, → the **Himalayas** soar east from Pakistan through China, India, Nepal and Bhutan. K2, the world's second-highest peak after Mt. Everest in Nepal, is located on the Pakistan–China border.

Himalayan Mountains

China has many **inventions** that have spread around the world. Some, such as **tea, silk** and **porcelain**, were important exports for many centuries and were traded with the West along the "Silk Road."

The secret of how to make → **porcelain** was known only in China for over 1,500 years. Europeans loved "fine china" but didn't learn how to make it until 1708.

Silk was discovered in China around 2700 BCE and is made from the cocoons of silk moths.

Porcelain

Gobi Desert

← The **Gobi Desert** is the fifth-largest desert on the planet, and along with the Taklamakan Desert, the only place you can still find wild camels. It extends from northern China to southern Mongolia and is a "cold desert," where it is not uncommon to see frost on the ground during the winter. The temperature can vary widely from -40°F (-40°C) in the winter to 122°F (50°C) in the summer. Most of the desert is not actually sandy but bare rock and gravel.

Tea was discovered in roughly the 10th century BCE in China and was originally drunk medicinally. It spread from China around the world and is now the most popular beverage worldwide (after plain water). It did not become popular in the British Isles (and American colonies) until the 18th century. →

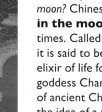

Tea

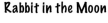

Silk

What do you see when you look at the moon? Chinese have seen a **rabbit in the moon** since ancient times. Called the "Jade Rabbit," it is said to be pounding an elixir of life for the moon goddess Chang'e. Like so much of ancient Chinese culture, the idea of a rabbit in the moon has spread through East Asia to Korea and Japan. →

Rabbit in the Moon

Chairman Mao

Chinese Dragon

→ Though imperial China and the emperor were associated with the **dragon**, China now prefers the **giant panda** as the international symbol of their country. Outside of Asia, dragons have a more fearsome image than they do in China. Whereas Europe has numerous stories of heroic knights slaying dragons, the Chinese have an expression about "hoping one's son becomes a dragon." Chinese may still refer to themselves as "descendents of the dragon," but they prefer the more internationally friendly image of the panda to signal that although they are "giants," it doesn't mean they are fearsome. ↓

Panda

↑ **Chairman Mao** is credited with making China a *communist* country. He governed China from 1949 until his death in 1972.

Communists want to create a society where no one is richer or more powerful than anyone else and everything is owned and shared by the community. In practice, many freedoms and human rights are sacrificed under communism because the government holds so much power over individuals. Mao was a dictator whose policies were responsible for many millions of deaths. Once a hero to the Chinese people, Mao's portrait was seen in homes and businesses everywhere. Now that China has changed and is becoming less communist, there are fewer Mao portraits to be seen. But, there is still a giant one hanging in Tiananmen Square and his face appears on their money. →

Fireworks

← **Fireworks** were invented in China in the 7th century along with "gunpowder." "Gunpowder" was used for fireworks and explosive devices for centuries before the invention of guns. Chinese first used fireworks for celebrations like Chinese New Year, when it is traditional to use lights and loud noises to scare away evil spirits.

100 中国人民银行 100 壹佰圓 XP38779600 100

Chinese Yuan

← The Renminbi, commonly called the **yuan** is the Chinese currency. The Chinese invented **paper** around 100 BCE and paper money (and **toilet paper**) around 600 CE. →

MANDARIN CHINESE
Written in Pinyin

Ni hao! *NEE howw*   Hello!

Ni hao ma?   How are you?
NEE howw MA?

Xie xie!   Thank you!
SHEay SHEay

Bu yong xie! You're welcome!
boo yong SHEay

Hao chi!   Delicious!
howw CHUH

Wo ai ni. *woh EYE nee*
       I love you.

Zai jian! *djai JEHN* Goodbye!

Written Chinese began its development over 3,000 years ago. Although Chinese characters have changed significantly since that time, many consider it to be the oldest writing system still in use. **Spoken Chinese** has many different "dialects," such as Mandarin and Cantonese, that are so different that their speakers can't understand one another. Written Chinese is much more uniform across the country. Mandarin is the world's most spoken language and the language spoken by 53% of the Chinese population. **Pinyin** (see left) is a system of spelling Mandarin Chinese with Roman letters that is used to help schoolchildren and foreigners learn how to pronounce Mandarin. Pinyin uses a similar alphabet to our own, but Q sounds like CH, X sounds like SH and Z sounds like DJ (hard J).

人	山	水	日	月	龙	女	男	子
people	mountain	water	sun	moon	dragon	woman	man	child

Listen to the SOUNDS of CHINA

Guzheng, Pipa, Erhu or Dizi

There are full orchestras of different traditional Chinese instruments, but these are the most popular and some of the most recognized sounds of China. The "12 Girls Band" is a popular group that plays traditional instruments. **YOUTUBE SEARCH:** guzheng, pipa, erhu, Chinese dizi, 12 Girls Band

Guzheng · Pipa · Erhu · Dizi

"Mo Li Hua" (Jasmine flower)

"Mo Li Hua" is a popular folk song written during the Qing Dynasty. Sung at the 2008 Beijing Olympics, it is often used to represent China to audiences abroad. **YOUTUBE SEARCH:** Mo Li Hua lyrics

Learn to sing the chorus of: "I Love You, China"

"I Love you China" or "Wo Ai Ni Zhongguo" is a song about China's beauties similar to "America the Beautiful." The chorus teaches you how to say "I love you" and "China" in Mandarin. The most famous version was sung by Ye Peiying in a 1979 movie. You can find a clip of her singing it with English subtitles. **YOUTUBE SEARCH:** Wo Ai Ni Zhongguo Ye Peiying

READ:

Chinese Folktales There are many wonderful Chinese folktales – your local library should have a wide selection. They are a great introduction to Chinese philosophy and values.

Moonbeams, Dumplings and Dragonboats: A Treasury of Chinese Holiday Tales, Activities and Recipes by Nina Simonds, Leslie Swartz. This book explores four different Chinese holidays through recipes, crafts and the folktales behind the customs. Ages 8 & up.

Beyond the Great Mountain: A Visual Poem about China, and **The Lost Horse: A Chinese Folktale** both by Ed Young. Ages 8 & up and ages 5 & up.

Little White Duck: A Childhood in China by Na Liu & Andres Martinez A graphic novel that follows a child in China after the death of Chairman Mao. Ages 9 & up.

Not for Parents: China by Lonely Planet. Filled with endless fun facts and photos. Ages 8 & up.

PLAY: Chopstick Challenge

Though you may already know how to use chopsticks, there is a "correct" way to use them in Chinese etiquette. For instance, you should hold them nearer to the top than to the food. Try watching an online video to practice your technique. Then, have a competition with a friend!

You'll need:
2 sets of chopsticks,
4 bowls
small items to put in the bowls
like dried beans, wrapped candy, paper clips – anything!
A clock or stopwatch

Put all the items in two of the bowls and leave two bowls empty. Each contender will have an empty and full bowl before them and a set of chopsticks. In a set amount of time (1–2 minutes), each player uses their chopsticks (correctly) to transfer as many items as they can. The winner has the largest number of items in their previously empty bowl when the time is up. This is an easy game to do with a large number of people, just use more bowls and chopsticks. Watching the competition is exciting too.
Variations: Put the bowls far apart so players have to carry the items further or run between the bowls.

DON'T MISS WATCHING (online)

Shaolin Kung Fu Shaolin kung fu practitioners can move in astonishing ways that seem contrary to the laws of physics! **YOUTUBE SEARCH: Real Shaolin kung fu**

Chinese Opera With gorgeously elaborate → costumes, stylized movements and music quite unlike any you have heard before, Chinese opera is fascinating. **YOUTUBE SEARCH: Beijing Opera**

School in China Visit a classroom in China and see how school life differs... and is exactly the same. **YOUTUBE SEARCH: China school**

Visit the Forbidden City, the Great Wall of China and the Terra-cotta Soldiers

Fabulous videos allow you to tour China's wonders and learn about its history. **YOUTUBE SEARCHES: Forbidden City, Great Wall, Terra-cotta soldiers**

Films Featuring China

Kung Fu Panda (2008) PG: The name says it all – a funny animated film that accurately depicts Chinese culture.
Shaolin Soccer (2004) NR, 9 & up: Chinese sports comedy

Learn how to Count to 10 on One Hand!

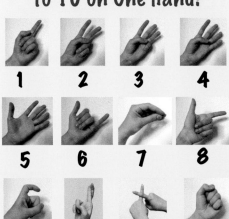

1 2 3 4

5 6 7 8

9 10 10 10 or 0

In China, there are single-hand gestures for numbers 1–10. Why do they use single–hand gestures for numbers? With the many different languages spoken in China, it can be easier to make sure you're understood with hand gestures. And if you are already carrying something in one hand at a crowded, noisy market, it's useful to be able to bargain with one. These gestures are also used to represent days of the week (1 is Monday, 2 is Tuesday…) and the months of the year, just as we can represent our months 1–12.

Memorize the hand gestures with a friend and then quiz each other with numbers and easy math. For larger numbers, like 36, people use the hand signs for 3 and then 6.

Learn how to Say 1-10 in Mandarin

1. YI (EE)
2. ER (AHr)
3. SAN (SUHN)
4. SI (SUH)
5. WU (WOHoh)
6. LIU (LEEoh)
7. QI (CHEE)
8. BA (BAH)
9. JIU (geeOH)
10. SHI (SHUH)

(Each number should be one syllable, which is why there are no dashes between the different vowel sounds.)

Write 1-10 in Chinese

For math and prices, Chinese write Arabic numerals like we do: 123456789. However, when they write the word for a number like "one" or "two," they use Chinese characters. With the characters below you can write numbers 1–99. Twelve is 十二. Twenty is 二十. Fifty is 五十. Ninety-nine is 九十九. Writing 100 and 1,000 require separate characters. One hundred is 百 and one thousand is 千. ***Can you write your age? And your parents' ages?***

Chinese Number		How to Write It & the Order of Strokes	Written in Pen or Pencil
1.	一	一	一
2.	二	二　二	二
3.	三	三　三　三	三
4.	四	四 四 四 四 四	四
5.	五	五 五 五 五	五
6.	六	六 六 六 六	六
7.	七	七 七	七
8.	八	八 八	八
9.	九	九 九	九
10.	十	十 十	十

ALL ABOUT CHINESE WRITING

1. Is Chinese written with an alphabet?

No. Chinese characters are not created from letters. This is very different from most languages used today. Korean writing, which may look similar to Chinese characters, is actually created from letters arranged in squares. Japanese uses some Chinese characters, but they also have syllabaries to spell out words phonetically. Chinese does use an alphabet called *pinyin* to help kids and foreigners learn to pronounce Chinese, but it isn't part of standard writing.

2. Are Chinese characters pictographs?

Is every character a picture symbol of a word? No. There are pictographic elements of Chinese writing, but there are also phonetic elements that tell you how the word sounds. Each character always represents one syllable. There are a couple hundred basic, one-syllable words that were originally pictographs and have been simplified to create "simple characters." Some examples are people, tree, sun or woman.

人 日 女 木

people "rén"   sun "rì"   woman "nǚ"   tree "mù"

These pictographs can be combined to create characters that symbolize more complex ideas. For instance, the sun character placed behind the tree character creates a third traditional character that means "east," as the east is where the sun rises. The sun character and the moon character together mean "bright" as they both are bright in the sky. And the word "good" or "hao" is made up of the characters "woman" and "child," referring to the goodness of the relationship between a mother and child.

東 明 好

east "dōng"   bright "míng"   good "hǎo"

3. What is phonetic about Chinese characters?

Phonics come in with an extensive use of near homonyms. Homonyms are words that sound alike, like "pear, pair and pare," "for, fore and four" or "blue and blew." In Chinese for example, the word for "fair weather" is qing (CHING). Qing is also the word for "blue/green" which is written:

青

blue/green "qīng"

To write "fair weather" → you would combine the sun character with the character for blue/green. The phonetic element (how it sounds) is on the right, and the subject area or "radical" is on the left. The entire character still fits into a square, as it is one syllable. These words do not sound the same though, they are only near homonyms as their tones are different. English also has words which are written the same way, but

晴

fair weather "qíng"

pronounced differently like "content" (the feeling) and "content" (the stuff contained). Chinese has many near homonyms. One popular example is "ma," which has many different meanings depending upon the tone in which it is said. If you just write the simple character "ma," it means horse. But "ma" also means mother. To write mother, the character for woman is put beside the horse character. "Ma" is also the word for scold. To write scold, you put two characters for mouth above the horse character.

马 妈 骂

horse "mǎ"   mother "mā"   scold "mà"

When Chinese people write mother or scold, they don't usually think about horses, the horse character just symbolizes the sound "ma" to them. The same way if you say your throat hurts and you're feeling "hoarse" you probably don't think about horses, even though it sounds the same.

4. How are foreign names written in Chinese?

Simple phonetic characters are also how Chinese write foreign names. For instance, to write Oklahoma, Alabama, Amazon or Himalayas they would use the "ma" character to represent that syllable in each word. Each word would be made up of as many characters as there are syllables in the word. Chinese pronunciation may need extra syllables for double consonants, for example: o-ka-la-ho-ma.

阿拉巴马 Alabama   奥克拉荷马 Oklahoma
亚马孙 Amazon   喜马拉雅山 Himalayas

5. How do you write America in Chinese?

America is called "Meiguo" (MAY-GWOH) in Chinese. "Mei" was chosen to sound like the 2nd syllable of America. Mei means "beautiful" or "admirable." Guo means "nation," just as in Zhongguo, or China. Another country name that ends in "guo" is "Yingguo" (YING-GWOH), which is the United Kingdom. "Ying" was chosen to sound like the "eng" in England. Ying means "heroic" or "brave" in Chinese. Canada, in contrast, has a much closer Chinese name, "Jianada."

美国 英国 加拿大

America "Meiguo"   United Kingdom "Yingguo"   Canada "Jianada"

6. What is pinyin?

Pinyin is a system developed to write Mandarin Chinese with Latin letters (like our own). Pinyin looks like our alphabet, but it also has marks above vowels to show their tone. Pinyin is used to help kids learn to read Chinese characters. It's also used to write Chinese names and places for foreigners. Pinyin can also be used to type Mandarin on computers. Special software converts the pinyin to Chinese characters.

MAKE YUMMY CHINESE DUMPLINGS!

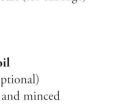

Dumplings or *jiaozi* [jeeow-ZUH] are popular all year long in China. In preparation for the Chinese New Year, many families get together to make lots of dumplings. They spend hours rolling out the dough and folding up the filling like little wrapped presents. Why make dumplings? Yes, they are so delicious, but you can probably find some at a local restaurant or grocery. But, if you have a couple hours to make dumplings from scratch, a partner to help, and some Chinese music, it is so much fun!

If there are dumpling wrappers (gyoza) at your grocery, use those instead of making your own. Making wrappers is not complex, but it's very time consuming, especially if you're new to it.

How to Make Dumpling Wrappers

1 cup sifted flour
¼ teaspoon salt
⅓ cup room temperature water

1. Sift flour and measure out a cup.

2. Add salt, mix, then add water, mix. The dough will be dry and hard to stick together.

3. Knead dough (helping it to stick together).

4. Allow the dough to rest for 15 minutes.

5. Make a hole in the center of the dough with your thumb, making a doughnut. Work the dough around the doughnut, making it bigger and bigger until as long as a necklace.

6. Break the necklace and roll dough against a flat surface with your fingers, making it smooth like a snake. It should be a bit larger than the diameter of a quarter.

7. Using a knife, cut the snake into pieces about the size of an egg yolk.

8. Take one piece, roll it around on a lightly floured surface until it is basically round. Then, flatten it with your palm. Using a small rolling pin and working out from the middle, roll out the dough, turning the dough as you work in a circle. Get the dough as thin as you can – this is where the work comes in! The goal is to have a roundish shape. Add more flour to your surface or rolling pin if needed. You can use a standard rolling pin, but a smaller one you can roll with one hand is much easier.

9. Repeat with other pieces. As you finish the dumpling wrappers, cover them with a damp paper towel so they won't dry out before you use them.

← *If you have a toy rolling pin or a small wooden dowel, either can enable you to roll with one hand and turn the dough with the other.*

How to Make Dumpling Filling

½ small cabbage (napa or green) chopped fine
½ lb. ground pork or other ground meat
1 teaspoon salt plus 1 tablespoon salt (for cabbage)
2 tablespoons soy sauce
3 green onions, chopped
2 cloves garlic, minced
1 ½ tablespoons sesame or olive oil
1 tablespoon rice wine or sake* (optional)
½ tablespoon fresh ginger, peeled and minced
1 clean dish towel

If you can't find rice wine, use pale sherry or apple juice.

1. Prepare cabbage. Dumpling cabbage needs to be chopped fine and then have the excess liquid taken out of it. You can chop it with a food processor – just stop before it's cabbage juice! Or, take 5 minutes to chop it by hand. (Get an adult with good knife skills to do it.) Put chopped cabbage in a bowl, add 1 tablespoon salt and mix. Allow it to sit for 30 minutes to draw out the water. Then place cabbage in a clean dish towel, wrap it up and squeeze it over a sink, you'll be surprised how much liquid will come out!

2. Put ground meat and cabbage into a bowl and add all the rest of the ingredients. Then mix it for several minutes until it is smooth and well blended. (If you wish to taste-test the filling before you make the dumplings, cook a small bit in a pan on the stove.)

Folding Dumplings

1. Take a dumpling wrapper, place a spoonful of filling in the center. Using your finger and a little water, dampen the outer ring of the dumpling wrapper.

2. Pinch the wrapper together around the filling, like a taco that meets at the top. Then bring the side flaps up to pinch to the top.

3. Pinch the corner flaps down together on either side – making one long line of pinched dough across the top.

4. Crimp the dough edge with your fingers – this helps to make sure that the dumpling is well-sealed.

Cooking Dumplings

1. Bring a large pot of water to a rolling boil.
2. Carefully add dumplings. (Lower them in with a sieve or a big spoon to avoid a splash.)
3. Cook for 6–8 minutes, stirring occasionally.
4. Remove from the water with a slotted spoon.
5. Serve with a dip like soy sauce mixed with water and sugar.

D is for Denmark

Our **D** is for **DENMARK,**

the home of the Danes –

A folk from the sea –

VIKING BLOOD in their veins!

Viking Ship

But in spite of their conquering,

seafaring past,

MODEST Danes are content

in a land not too vast.

North Sea

From the **BALTIC SEA** coast

to the **North Sea's** cool waters,

Danish children are taught

they're **NO BETTER THAN OTHERS.**

Little Mermaid

But those dear humble Danes

with their well-ordered brains,

They have much to be proud of

that they'll never name.

Copenhagen Summit
on Climate Change

Why this is the land

where the **Little Mermaid** came,

And Hans Christian Andersen

authored his fame!

Queen Margrethe II
"Daisy"

They have punctual **trains**

and world climate campaigns,

They invented toy **LEGOS**

and **Queen Daisy** reigns!

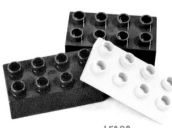

LEGOS

Wind Turbine

Bike Traffic Light

And in their flat plains,

filled with thick growing grains,

there are plenty of WINDMILLS

and BICYCLE LANES!

Happy Danes might complain

if it snows or it rains,

But inside they feel **hygge**, [HOO-guh]

in **COZY** domains.

Copenhagen

So come to the capital,

cool **COPENHAGEN**,

Once a fisherman's village

of **THOR**-praising pagans!

Thor

Though capital dwellers

still eat PICKLED HERRING,

Now their city's so modern

that you will be staring —

Not just at the clothes that

the Danes are out wearing,

But inside their homes

DESIGNED with such daring!

Pickled Herring

Egg Chair

Danish Designed Flatware

What tables! What chairs!

What KNIVES, FORKS and SPOONS!

All so sleek and delightful

in their light-filled rooms.

So *Velcommen* where Vikings [VELL-com]

in ships once embarked.

In this small Nordic land

you will have such a lark!

For despite what a player

in **Hamlet** remarks,

There is nothing that's rotten

in *charming* Denmark.

Shakespeare's Hamlet
Prince of Denmark

Viking

Velcommen!*

Velcommen! [VELL-com] means "welcome!" in Danish.

← Denmark's flag, the **Dannebrog**, is the world's oldest state flag still in use. According to legend, it descended from the heavens to help the Danes during a battle in 1219. Danes have loved their flag ever since and some even use tiny versions to decorate their Christmas trees. All other **Nordic countries** have modeled their flag on the Dannebrog.

Finland   Iceland   Norway   Sweden

The origins of the name **DENMARK** are unclear. One theory is that "Den" comes from an old Germanic word meaning "a low, flat land." "Mark" is thought to mean either "woodland" or "borderland."

Denmark and other Nordic Countries

Official Name:
Kingdom of Denmark

Local Name:
Kongeriget Danmark

Population: 5.5 million

Capital: Copenhagen

Largest Cities:
Copenhagen, Århus, Odense, Aalborg

Comparative Size:
Slightly less than twice the size of Massachusetts

Languages: Danish, Greenlandic, Faroese

Religion: Christian 84% (mostly Evangelical Lutheran), Muslim 4%, none 12%

Currency: Danish krone

Famous Exports:
Bacon, butter, windmills, furniture

Where in the World is Denmark?

GEOGRAPHICAL NOTES

◉ The **Kingdom of Denmark** includes the nation of Denmark and two autonomous (independent) territories: Greenland and the Faroe Islands. Both Greenland and the Faroe Islands govern their own local affairs but look to the larger Kingdom of Denmark for their currency, military and some international agreements.

◉ "Nordic" come from the word "north," and **Nordic countries** include Denmark, Sweden, Norway, Finland and Iceland. There are only three **Scandinavian countries**: Denmark, Norway and Sweden. Scandinavians are descendants of the Vikings.

Vikings

↑ **Vikings** were fierce sea-faring raiders who attacked and stole treasures from European coastal communities from the 9th to the 11th century. They used swift **longships**, powered by both sails and oars. Vikings were from **Scandinavia:** now Denmark, Norway and Sweden. →

How close is Denmark to Sweden? Just about 16 kilometers (10 miles) of water separate Copenhagen from the Swedish city of Malmö. Commuters can travel between them by taking the **Oresund Bridge**. Completed in 1999, it consists of a tunnel under the water, a man-made island and a suspension bridge. →

Oresund Bridge

Longship

Except for its southern border with Germany, Denmark is surrounded by water. The **North Sea** is to the west, the **Baltic Sea** to the east and between Denmark and Sweden and Norway there are two smaller bodies of water they identify as *Kattegat* and *Skagerrak*. Skagerrak got its name from the town of Skaggen on Denmark's northernmost tip. Kattegat means "cat's gate" as sailors said that the waters were so shallow, narrow and treacherous between Denmark and Sweden that only a cat could squeeze through. ↓

← Protecting the environment is very important to most Danes. This photo was taken during the Copenhagen Summit, a UN Conference addressing climate change held in Denmark in 2009.

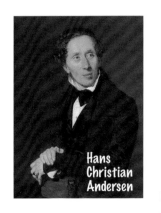

Hans Christian Andersen

North Sea

← **The Little Mermaid** was written by Danish author **Hans Christian Andersen**, who also wrote *The Ugly Duckling, The Emperor's New Clothes, The Princess and the Pea* and other fairy tales. The Little Mermaid statue is a beloved tourist attraction in Copenhagen harbor. ↓

Queen Margrethe

← Danes are known for their belief in modesty and equality (that *no one is better than the rest*), but they love their queen, **Margrethe II,** whom they affectionately call "Daisy." Queen Margrethe *(mar-GRAY-tah)* is the first female ruler of Denmark in over 600 years. She also has a career as an accomplished painter and illustrator.

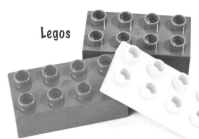

Legos

↑ **Legos** were first designed in the late 1940s by the LEGO toy company in Denmark. LEGO got their name from the Danish phrase "leg godt," which means "play well." The current brick design was not created until 1958, but all legos from that date on can interlock with the ones produced today.

Little Mermaid

Windmill

Copenhagen

Bicycling

↑ **Wind turbines** create about 20% of Denmark's electricity – more wind power than any other country. Denmark is also the world's largest producer of wind turbines. Wind turbines are a type of **windmill** that convert the wind into rotational energy. Windmills were originally used to mill grains into flour. ↓

Windmills on the Sea

↑ **Copenhagen** is a port city that is over 1,000 years old.

Denmark has ➜ no mountains so most of its rolling **plains** are used for farming grains like barley. Denmark's relative flatness also makes it an easy place to ride a bike.

Plains

↑ Biking everywhere is very popular in Denmark, so they have developed special **bike lanes** separated from the roads by a small median. This type of road is known worldwide as a "Copenhagen lane." ↓

Thor, the Norse god of ➜ thunder, was worshipped by Danes until the nation became Christian in the 10th century and rejected all *pagan* (non-Christian) gods. Thursday got its name from Thor (*Thor's day*), and Friday was named after Norse goddess Freya, who is mentioned in the Danish national anthem. (See anthem on page 50.)

Thor

Hyggelig Brothers

← Danes like for their homes and lives to create a feeling of **hygge** (HOO-guh). The closest translation for hygge is "coziness" but it means so much more in Denmark. The concept of hygge involves taking time to savor the little pleasures of life with others. It could mean candlelight, sharing food with family and close friends, gathering around a fire to visit, or making cookies with your grandmother. Hygge is feeling warm, contented and often close to others. Christmas is probably the most *hyggelig* (HOO-guh-lee) time of year in Denmark (and in the United States too!)
← Danes like to put real candles on the tree to light on Christmas Eve. Hygge is very important in a country that has a long, dark winter, and it may be one of the reasons that Danes are consistently ranked among the happiest people in the world.

Herring

← **Herring** is a fish that has been part of the diet in Denmark since Viking times. Now, it's served as a traditional first course to a meal.

Hyggelig Christmas

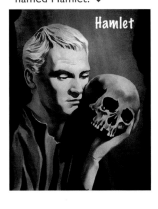

Egg Chair

Ant Chair

DENMARK 3.75

Danish Design

← **Danish design** is famous for its sleek simplicity and functional → elegance. Many designs like the Egg Chair (1958) and the Ant Chair (1952) by Arne Jacobsen have been copied around the world. The ant chair was part of a revolution in chair making as it could be mass produced and was light, compact and easily stackable. ↓

Modern Danish Architecture

"*Something is rotten in the state of Denmark*" is a famous line from **Hamlet**, a tragedy written by English playwright, William Shakespeare. The hero is a prince of Denmark named Hamlet. ↓

Hamlet

Smorrebrod

← **Smorrebrod**, or open-faced sandwiches, are a very popular lunch food in all of Scandinavia. Made on thin slices of buttered dark rye bread, smorrebrod have dozens of topping combinations.

Faroe Islands

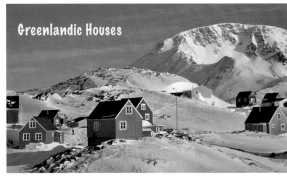
Greenlandic Houses

The **Faroe Islands** are part → of the Kingdom of Denmark. Located halfway between Scotland and Iceland, they have a population of 50,000. The Faroese people speak Faroese and are descendents of Scandinavians and Scotch-Irish.

Greenland
⭐ Nuuk

← **Greenland**, the world's ↑ largest island that is not a continent, is a self-governing province of Denmark. If Greenland were its own country, it would be the 12th largest in the world. But due to an ice sheet covering about 80% of their land, the population is only about 56,000. The native and official language is Greenlandic, but they also speak Danish. Greenland is known for having brightly painted houses and colorful traditional dress. These girls are wearing traditional dress in honor of their first day of school. →

Greenlandic Girls

SPEAK Danish!

Hej!	Hello!	high
	(sounds like our "Hi!")	
Velcommen!	Welcome!	VELL-comn
Tak!	Thank you!	tahk
Ja	Yes	yeh
Nej	No	nigh
Hygge	Coziness	HOO-guh
Farvel!	Goodbye!	fah-VELL
Hej Hej	Bye!	high high

Listen to the SOUNDS of DENMARK

"There Is a Lovely Land"

The Danish national anthem, "Der er et Yndigt Land" is sung with gusto at sporting events in Denmark. (Usually just the first stanza and the last four lines.) The English version below is not an exact translation, but it's close and keeps the rhyme and meter of the Danish. There are several online videos that play the anthem to scenes of Denmark.

*There is a lovely land
With spreading, shady beeches
Near Baltic's salty strand;
Near Baltic's salty strand;
Its hills and valleys gently fall,
Its ancient name is Denmark,
And it is Freya's hall
And it is Freya's hall*

*There in the ancient days
The armored Vikings rested
Between their bloody frays
Between their bloody frays
Then they went forth the foe to face,
Now found in stone-set barrows,
Their final resting place
Their final resting place*

*This land is still as fair,
The sea is blue around it,
And peace is cherished there.
And peace is cherished there.
Strong men and noble women still
Uphold their country's honour
With faithfulness and skill
With faithfulness and skill*

*Praise King and Fatherland
Bless every Dane at heart
For doing what he can
For doing what he can
Old Denmark will be true
As long as there are beeches
By a sea so blue
By a sea so blue*

DON'T MISS WATCHING
(online)

"MEET THE KIDS" The Danish government hosts an amazing website with animated videos explaining Danish culture. The address is: http://kids.denmark.dk
Or find it by searching: **"Denmark Meet the Kids"**

RESEARCH:

Vikings

Vikings never wore horns on their helmets, but they were fierce raiders and daring explorers. Find out how the Vikings lived, why they became so feared in the rest of Europe and how they crossed oceans in their narrow longships.

Norse Gods & Goddesses

Have you heard of **Thor**, god of thunder, or **Freya**, goddess of love, fertility, war and death? Thor used his mighty hammer to kill giants. Freya rode on a boar with golden bristles and drove around in a chariot pulled by cats. There are many fascinating stories about Norse gods who lived in a world with giants, dwarves, elves and sea serpents. Profile a favorite Norse god, including their powers, family and most famous exploits. Norse gods were worshipped by the Norsemen, the pre-Christian people of Scandinavia.

PLAY: Laenkfange

Laenkfange, or "Capturing Chains" is a popular game of tag played by Danish kids, teens and sometimes even adults. The person who is "it," the catcher, chases the other players until he or she touches one of them. The catcher then joins hands with the person tagged who is now also "it." Together, they continue the chase. Each new person that is tagged joins the group of catchers holding hands. Once the group grows to four people, it breaks into two groups who continue capturing other players until everyone playing is part of a chain. If you play with a large group, the chains will split many times (in order to never exceed 3 players running together), so there will be many groups of catchers running to capture all the remaining players.

READ:

D'Aulaires' Book of Norse Myths Explore stories of monsters, gods, gnomes, sprites and giants in this beautifully illustrated introduction to Norse mythology. Ages 7 & up.

Hans Christian Andersen Fairy Tales

Do you know "The Little Mermaid," "The Ugly Duckling," "Thumbelina," "The Little Match Girl," "The Snow Queen," "The Princess and the Pea," "The Emperor's New Clothes" and "The Steadfast Tin Soldier"? Reading the original tales might surprise you – often the stories have been changed. "The Ugly Duckling" has become Denmark's national bird, the mute swan.

BAKE Danish
Apple Cake

If you removed apples, potatoes, rye bread and herrings from the Danish diet, there would hardly be any recipes left. There are many versions of Danish apple cake. This is an easy one that is mostly apples.

9-inch square cake pan
⅓ cup butter
1 cup brown sugar
1 egg
½ cup buttermilk
1 teaspoon vanilla
1 ¼ cups flour
⅛ teaspoon salt
1 teaspoon baking soda

1 teaspoon cinnamon
2 cups apple peeled and diced

Topping: (optional)
½ apple cut into thin slices
chopped walnuts
dash of cinnamon
2 spoons of brown sugar
dash of salt

1. Preheat oven to 350⁰ and grease cake pan.

2. Cream butter and brown sugar (beat together until fluffy).

3. Add egg, buttermilk and vanilla; blend well

4. Add flour, salt, baking soda, and cinnamon; mix.

5. Fold in diced apples.

6. Spread mixture in greased cake pan.

7. Arrange sliced apple in design on the top.

8. In a separate bowl, mix together nuts, sugar, cinnamon and salt. Sprinkle over the top.

9. Bake for 40 minutes; let cool before serving.

10. The cake is delicious plain or served with a little ice cream or whipped cream.

MAKE Danish
Paper Heart Baskets

Danes like to make these red and white ornaments for their Christmas trees because it's such a *hyggelig* (cozy) activity. Of course you can make them anytime you want to give someone a little love.

Needed:
2 sheets of different colored paper (not thick, 8.5" x 11")
Scissors

Makes 4 paper heart baskets

1. Fold each piece of paper in half, then in half again in the same direction, keeping the paper's 8.5 inch width. You end up with a folded strip 8.5 x 2.75 inches.

2. Now turn and fold that shape in half, so that it is 4.25 x 2.75 inches wide.

3. Use your scissors to round off the short unfolded edge, creating a tall tombstone shape with the folded edge at the bottom.

4. Now trim the 2 sides off of your tombstones, making it slightly skinnier. You will be cutting the folded edges off the sides, but not the base. This creates 4 separate folded tombstones from each color page.

5. Take one tombstone of each color and stack together to make one tombstone. If one is larger than the other, trim its top until they are both the same size and shape. (Just don't trim off your bottom fold!)

6. Cut up from the folded side to make four approximately equal strips. Cut only until you reach the height where the tombstone starts to round in.

7. To weave the strips together, imagine one color has its strips labeled 1, 2, 3, 4 and the other A, B, C, D. First weave strip A. Take strip A and put it inside → of strip 1. Then put strip 2 inside of A. Then put A inside of strip 3. And finally put strip 4 inside of A. So A is going inside 1, outside 2, inside 3, outside 4.

8. Then start the same process to weave strip B. But in order to create a checkerboard effect, B will go outside 1, inside 2, outside 3, inside 4. So start by putting strip 1 inside B.

9. Once you're done weaving, you should be able to open

your basket and put things inside. If you can't, unweave it and try again. Make sure you are weaving inside-outside and not over-under. You can make a handle for your basket by cutting a long strip of paper and gluing it inside the top center of each heart.

After you've made one paper heart basket and learned how to weave them, you can experiment with cutting more strips, or strips of different widths (fat-thin-fat-thin) or strips that have wavy inside edges. →

E is for Ethiopia

Our **E** is in East Africa's Horn,

the land of **ETHIOPIA,**

A place so ANCIENT, history lovers

might call it their **utopia.**

Fossil Skeleton
of "Lucy"

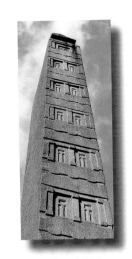

Axum's Stele
(soaring stone)

Church Painting

Queen of Sheba

Ethiopia in
Africa

How old is Ethiopia now,

and when did its story begin?

Why people have lived in *Abyssinia**

since the **DAWN OF MEN**:

From early human FOSSILS found

in Great Rift Valley bones,

To **KINGDOMS OF THE BIBLE**

and AXUM's soaring stones,

To emperors that claim descent

from Solomon and **Sheba,**

To being the second **Christian** country

(following Armenia).

And when Muslims feared persecution,

Mohammed sent them here.

His followers have lived here ever since –

for fourteen hundred years!

It's the only land NEVER COLONIZED,

in all of Africa's nations,

though they did endure five years

of Italian occupation.

*Ethiopian
Orthodox Priest*

*****Abyssinia** [ab-bis-SIN-nee-yah] is another name for Ethiopia.

Espresso

Roasting Coffee Beans as part
of Ethiopia's Coffee Ceermony

All that Italy left behind

was **pasta** and **espresso.**

Espresso still is much beloved,

the pasta somewhat less so.

But they didn't need an intro

to carbohydrates or caffeine

After all, this country first

discovered **COFFEE BEANS!**

And jumbo pancakes called **INJERA** [in-JAIR-ah]

serve as plates and forks.

They scoop up tasty stews and meats

(but never any pork!)

Injera with Wats (stews)

Here Christians and Muslims both abstain

from eating ham or bacon,

And if you think we'll find some here,

you're very much mistaken.

Many faiths and ethnic groups

have made this land **DIVERSE,**

And there are many languages

in which they all converse.

Scooping up Wats
with Injera

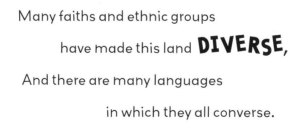

Girls in a Mosque Doorway

ግዕዝ

Geez Written in Geez

Axum's Stele

Tigray-Tigrinya speak Tigrinya,

Oromos speak Oromo,

Amharas speak **Amharic**

and there're many more I don't know.

Most are written in **GE'EZ,** [gay-EHZ]

a wavy alphabet,

But English is their second tongue

so you can come here yet!

Castle in Gonder

You'll stand in awe of Axum's stele [STEE-lee]

and the **BLUE NILE FALLS**.

You'll wander GONDER'S CASTLE

and HARAR'S medieval walls.

Blue Nile Falls

You'll climb the **SIMIEN MOUNTAINS**

where GELADAS gaze and chew. [JEHL-luh-duhs]

You'll see **Abyssinian Lions**

in the Addis Ababa Zoo.

You'll float to ISLAND MONASTERIES

on **Lake Tana's** shore.

You'll visit **Lalibela's churches,** [LAH-lee-BELL-lah]

carved from roof to floor.

Carved Rock
Church in Lalibella

Gelada

So come and say *Tadiyass* to [tah-DEE-yahss] this **cradle of mankind**.

Come visit Ethiopia,

a land unique through time.

Tadiyass!*

Akkam?*

Lion of Judah

* *Tadiyass* [tah-DEE-yahs] means "Hello" in Amharic.
* *Akkam* [AH-kahm] means "How are you?" in Oromo.

ኢትዮጵያ

Ethiopia written in its local form in the Ge'ez alphabet

Each letter is a syllable (i-te-yo-pe-ya). (Learn to write in Ge'ez on page 64.) Scholars speculate that the name **ETHIOPIA** came from the ancient Greek words for "sunburnt" referring to the darker skin of Ethiopians compared to Greeks. Ethiopia has also been traditionally called **Abyssinia** in English.

↑ The **Ethiopian flag** was the first to use the pan-African colors of red, yellow and green when it was designed in 1897. The colors became popular on other African flags as African nations gained their indepedence from colonial empires. The emblem in the middle was added in 1996 as directed by the new constitution. The blue disk represents peace, the star stands for the unity and diversity of Ethiopia's people and the rays represent prosperity.

Ethnic Regions in Ethiopia

Local Name: Itiyop'ya

Population: 97 million, the second largest country in Africa, the most populous land-locked country in the world

Capital: Addis Ababa

Comparative Size: Slightly less than twice the size of Texas, a bit larger than Egypt

Ethnicity: Oromo 34%, Amhara 27%, Somalie 6%, Tigraway 6%, Sidama 4%, many others 22%

Languages: Amharic, Oromo, Somalie, many others.

Religion: Christian 63% (Ethiopian Orthodox 43%, Protestant 19%), Islam 34%,

Currency: Ethiopian birr

Important Export: Coffee

Where in the World is Ethiopia?

GEOGRAPHICAL NOTES

◉ Ethiopia, Eritrea, Djibouti and Somalia are located in the **Horn of Africa,** Africa's eastern corner that points towards the Arabian Sea.

◉ Ethiopia is divided into nine regional states and two administrative cities (Addis Ababa and Dire Dawa). Each has its own flag and local government. The Tigray and Amhara states are largely Orthodox Christian, the Afar and Somali states are mostly Muslim and the Oromiya is mixed. In the Southwest, there are more than 45 different ethnic groups, which are predominantly Protestant Christians.

Three of the oldest human → **fossils** have been found in the Great Rift Valley in Ethiopia. "Lucy," "Selam" and "Ardi" are over 3 million years old and lived in an era when scientists believe that humankind was evolving from a more ape-like ancestor.

"Lucy" Rendering

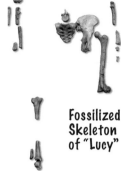

Fossilized Skeleton of "Lucy"

↑ *This is a rendering of what scientists think Lucy may have looked like 3 million years ago.*

"Makeda" Queen of Sheba

↑ Living in about the 10th century BCE, the **Queen of Sheba** is mentioned in the Bible as a ruler who visited King Solomon to learn from his wisdom. The Queen of Sheba is claimed as a historical ruler by both Yemen and Ethiopia. The countries are so close together that the Queen could have ruled over both areas. Alternatively, her descendants could have moved their capital or kingdom south from Yemen to Ethiopia at some point. Ethiopia claims that their long line of kings are direct descendants of Sheba and Solomon. The Queen's name was "Makeda," according to Ethiopians, and her child with Solomon was Menelik I, who founded Ethiopia's long dynasty of rulers. Ethiopia's last **emperor**, Haile Selassie, was deposed in 1974. There is also a small Jewish community from Ethiopia, called **Beta Israel**, who date their history back to the Queen of Sheba.

↑ *A crown worn by Ethiopian emperors*

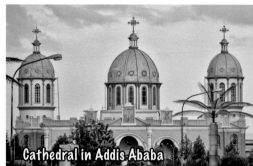

Orthodox Priest

Church Mural

← *Mural of Mary and Jesus in an Ethiopian Church*

← Ethiopia became a **Christian country** during the reign of King Ezana, early in the 4th century CE. Ethiopia and Georgia may be tied for the title of 2nd-oldest Christian country, both made it their state religion around 330 CE. Armenia was the first in 301 and the Roman Empire adopted Christianity as their official religion in 391. Today, about 62% of the nation is Christian. ↓

Cathedral in Addis Ababa

Stele in Axum

Stele in Axum

← During the Kingdom of Axum (100–700 CE), many **stele** were erected in Ethiopia to mark burial sites. Stele (*STEE-lee*) are tall, vertical monuments carved from a single stone, similar to Egyptian obelisks. The last stele was erected by King Ezana in the early 4th century, but many still stand in Axum. The grandest mark royal burial chambers and are carved with many stories of false windows and doors, like rock skyscrapers. →

Mosque

Mosque Doorway

← ↑ **Islam** has been in Abyssinia (another name for Ethiopia) since the time of the prophet Mohammed. Mohammed instructed a group of his followers to flee persecution in Mecca (Saudi Arabia) and seek refuge in the Christian Kingdom of Axum in 615. There have been Muslims in Ethiopia ever since and they make up 34% of the population today.

Ethiopia in
Africa

← Every country in Africa was once a colony of a European empire except for Ethiopia and Liberia. Liberia was founded by former American slaves in the 19th century, but Ethiopia has been independent since ancient times. This made Ethiopia a powerful symbol to other Africans and blacks when they were striving to gain independence and equal rights in the first half of the 20th century.

In Jamaica, a group of people called Rastafarians came to believe that Ethiopian Emperor **Haile Selassie** (reigning 1930–1974) was the → returned Christian messiah, coming to liberate blacks from white oppression and allow them to return to "Zion" (meaning Ethiopia or Africa). Selassie himself continued to be an Orthodox Christian all his life and Rastafarian beliefs never became popular in Ethiopia. Ethiopians do believe that Selassie and all their monarchs were direct descendents of King Solomon and the Queen of Sheba.

Haile Selassie

Coffee Ceremony

Injera

Teff

↑ **Coffee** was first discovered in Ethiopia over 500 years ago, and it is now their biggest export. The coffee ceremony is an important rite of hospitality. It starts with laying fresh grasses on the floor (even inside fancy buildings). Next, the coffee beans are roasted and then ground by hand, filling the air with the scent. Finally, the coffee is brewed. In a full ceremony, the same beans are brewed three times and everyone has three cups. Women typically perform the coffee ceremony, and in formal settings they wear a traditional coffee ceremony dress, which is white with colored embroidery. →

Coffee Ceremony

↑ **Injera**, the staple food in Ethiopia, is like a ↑ very large, thin, spongy pancake. Injera is made from **teff**, a grain that is widely grown in Ethiopia. Typically injera is served on a large metal plate and dishes are placed on top of it. Diners then tear off a piece of injera with their right hand and scoop up the dishes to eat. A plate of injera is frequently shared between friends or family. ↓

Eating Injera

Espresso

← **Italy** occupied Ethiopia for five years (1936–1941) but never managed to secure more than a small part of the country. You can still see the Italian influence, however, in the abundance of **espresso** machines throughout the country. Espresso has never replaced the coffee ceremony in popularity, but Ethiopians have learned to appreciate both. Pasta is also still served in Ethiopia, particularly to tourists, but it is not part of the daily diet.

NO PORK

← Ethiopians do not eat **pork** as both Ethiopia's Orthodox Christian Church and Islam forbid it. Orthodox believers also do not eat meat, eggs, fat or dairy on Wednesdays and Fridays to commemorate the death of Jesus Christ. As a result, there are many delicious vegan dishes in Ethiopia.

← Ethiopians are very **diverse** in terms of the languages they speak and their religion. From the more Christian highlands, to the largely Muslim east, to the many peoples in the "Southern Nations" of the southwest, all are proud Ethiopians. ↓ →

↑ Woven white shawls and headscarves are popular with both Muslim and Christian women.

School Girls in Harar

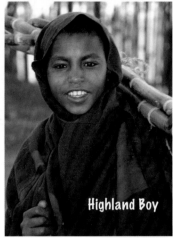

Highland Boy

Ethiopian students must learn English in elementary school to go to high school. High school and university are taught in English so that students from all parts of Ethiopia can go to school together and communicate. ↓

Priest Rowing on Lake Tana

Students

↑ **Lake Tana** is the source of the Blue Nile River and is not far from the **Blue Nile Falls**. The Blue Nile joins the White Nile in Khartoum, Sudan, to form the Nile River. There are several Ethiopian Orthodox Monasteries on the shores of Lake Tana, some of which are over 500 years old. ↓

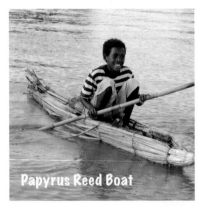

Papyrus Reed Boat

Fasildes' Castle

↑ Fishing is a large part of the economy around **Lake Tana** and fisherman still use the ancient **papyrus reed boats**, which are light, quick and easy to paddle on the water (and don't scare away the fish)!

Blue Nile Falls

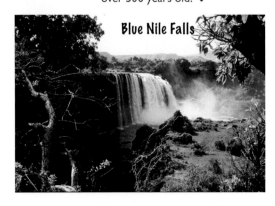

↑ The **Castle in Gonder** was built by Emperor Fasildes who reigned 1632–1667. He moved Ethiopia's capital to Gonder, where it continued to be until 1855. The large royal enclosure contains not just the castle but also a palace, library, bath house and churches. It was the home of Ethiopia's emperors until the capital was again moved several times in the late 1800s. Addis Ababa became the capital in 1887.

↓ Close relatives of baboons, **geladas** are the only primate that grazes on grasses as its main food source. They live exclusively in the Ethiopian Highlands and are concentrated in the Semien Mountains. The **Semien Mountains** in northwest Ethiopia are one of the few places in Africa where snow regularly falls. ↓

Geladas

Semien Mountains

Lalibela Church

Inside Church

↑ **Lalibela** is a small town in the mountains of northern Ethiopia that is famous for its 13 monolithic churches built between the 12th and 13th centuries. Monolithic means "one stone," that each church was carved out of the mountain from one huge piece of rock. To create the inside and outside of the churches, tons of stone had to be removed. Lalibela was built by King Lalibela in a layout to mimic the city of Jerusalem, which had been recently captured by Muslims. ↓ →

Through history, most **Ethiopian art** has been religious. Ethiopian churches are known for being covered with bright paintings outlined in black. The paintings are typically of saints and bible stories and the figures usually have huge almond eyes. This painting is of Ethiopia's patron saint, St. George, slaying a dragon. Ethiopia is depicted as the woman in the tree. →

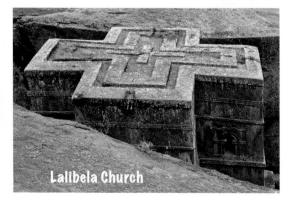

Lalibela Church

Abyssinian Lion

← Found only in Ethiopia, → **Abyssinian lions** are known for their black manes. Only about 1,000 remain in the wild. Lions are an important symbol of Ethiopia and appear on their coins.

The **Lion of Judah** was a symbol of the kings of Ethiopia. The lion was originally a symbol of the Israeli tribe of Judah, from which Solomon and Jesus were descended. As Ethiopians believe their kings were direct descendants of Solomon, they maintained their king was part of a long line of rulers descending from the ← tribe of Judah.

Lion of Judah

↑ Two views of the carved Church of Saint George, its roof is even with the surrounding ground. →

Addis Ababa

↑ Addis Ababa or "New Flower" is more than just the capital and largest city of Ethiopia. It is also the headquarters of the African Union, an organization of 54 African countries that meet with the mission to promote peace, prosperity and good governance on the continent. Located in the in the highlands of Ethiopia, Addis Ababa is the 4th-highest capital in the world.

Outside of cities, many people still live in **traditional homes** like this round adobe house with a thatched roof. Rounded walls have been shown to be much stronger in earthquakes. ↓

Traditional Home

Gebreselassie
Bekele

↑ Running is the most popular sport in Ethiopia and every morning you will see Ethiopians running through the streets. Ethiopia has had several world champion distance runners including Kenenisa Bekele and Haile Gebreselassie.

Rural Village

Highlands

Savannah

From warm savannah to cool green highlands to hot desert lands, Ethiopia has many **climates**. In the highlands, the weather is spring-like all year – with highs in the 70s°F (23°C) and lows in 40–50s°F (5–10°C). In the Afar Desert in the north of Ethiopia is an area known as Dallol, one of the hottest places on earth, which can regularly reach temperatures of 120°F (49°C).

Pelicans on Lake Tana

Farmer Plowing

↑ Most Ethiopians are **farmers** and use traditional methods to work the land. Their biggest crops are grains like wheat and teff, and their biggest export is coffee.

Afar Desert

Listen to the SOUNDS of ETHIOPIA

Krar Music

The *krar* is a traditional Ethiopian instrument, a six-string lyre. There are krar lessons and performers online and a special BBC segment on the group "Krar Collective." Other traditional instruments include a *masinko*, a one-string instrument played with a bow, and a *washint*, a highland flute. INTERNET SEARCH: BBC krar collective YOUTUBE SEARCH: krar, masinko, washint

A Teddy Afro Song

Teddy Afro, real name Tewodros Kassahun, is one of Ethiopia's most popular musicians. He has two songs about Ethiopia's world champion runners, "Haile, Haile" about Haile Gebreselassie and "Anbessa" about Kenenisa Bekele. "Yasteseryal" is a reggae song about Ethiopian unity and history. Its video (with real historical footage) can be graphic, but there are versions without footage. YOUTUBE SEARCH: anbessa, teddy afro haile gebreselassie (tribute to a legend), Yasteseryal

More Song Recommendations:

"Sela Bey" by Jacky Gosee, a mix of urban and traditional
"Gurumayle" by Gigi
"Fikiren Cheresew" by Aster Aweke, a love song
"Sewenwano" by Eden Gebreselassie, a popular Tigray song
"Sanyii Mootii" by Hachala Hundessa, a popular Oromo song
All can be found online with music videos.

DON'T MISS WATCHING (online)

Eskesta Dancing Eskesta originated in the Amhara region and means "shoulder dancing." Each ethnic group in Ethiopia has its own dances, so you can search "ethnic group name" plus "dance" to see examples. YOUTUBE SEARCH: Eskesta, Oromo dance

Haile Gebreselassie, King of the Kickdown A short biography. YOUTUBE SEARCH: King of the Kickdown

Tour Lalibela's Churches YOUTUBE SEARCH: Lalibela

Ethiopia's Ancient Kingdoms A fascinating BBC series "Lost Kingdoms of Africa" explores Ethiopia's ancient cities and if their kings were descendants of Solomon and Sheba. Available to stream on movie sites with clips on YouTube. YOUTUBE SEARCH: "Lost Kingdoms of Africa Ethiopia," "Ethiopia and the history not seen"

SPEAK AMHARIC!

Tadiyass! Hi!		*tah-DEE-yahss*
Selam! Hello!		*seh-LAHM*
Selamu? How are you?		*seh-LAH-moo*
Indemin neh? How are you?	(said to a male)	*in-DIM-in NEH*
Indemin nesh? How are you?	(to a female)	*in-DIM-in NESH*
Dehna Negn. I'm fine.		*deh-NAH-nay*
Ameseginalehugn! Thank you!		*AH-mah-say-guh-NAH-loh*
I'shee. Alright, okay.		*UH-shee*
Ai! Yes!		*eye or I*
Aow. No.		*ahhOW or OW*
Chow. Goodbye.		*chow*
Konjo Beautiful		*KON-joh*

← LEARN TO SPEAK SOME AMHARIC

Spoken by 25 million people, Amharic is the "working language" of the government of Ethiopia, used by about 30% of the population. Amharic is written in Ge'ez, which is an abugida script, meaning each "letter" is a whole syllable representing one consonant+vowel combination. For example, this Coca-Cola bottle with an Amharic label reads, *kola kola*, its name in Amharic. ↓

READ:

Fire from the Mountain by Jane Kurtz. A classic Ethiopian folktale of a brother and sister outwitting a greedy employer. Ages 4 & up.

Only a Pigeon by Jane Kurtz. Story of a boy raising pigeons in Addis Ababa. Ages 7 and up.

Saba: Under the Hyena's Foot by Jane Kurtz. From the "Girls of Many Lands" series, an exciting piece of historical fiction set in mid-19th-century Ethiopia. Ages 10 & up.

The Lion's Whiskers: An Ethiopian Tale by Nancy Raines Day. A new stepmother learns how to gain the love of her stepson by training a wild lion. Ages 5 & up.

When the World Began: Stories Collected in Ethiopia by Elizabeth Laird. Ages 9 & up.

Silly Mammo by Gebrebeorgis Yohannes. A comic tale of a boy Mammo, reminiscent of Amelia Bedelia. Ages 4 & up.

The Best Beekeeper in Lalibela by Cristina Kessler. A young girl keeps bees despite opposition. Ages 5 & up.

The Perfect Orange by Frank Araujo. A famous folktale about a child's gift to the king. Ages 3 & up.

Many books set in Ethiopia go in and out of print, check what is available at your public library.

LEARN HOW TO WRITE "LOVE" IN AMHARIC

The Ge'ez script was fully developed by the 4th century CE. It has 26 consonants and embellishments are added to each consonant to indicate what vowel follows. →

Love is pronounced *fiqir* in Amharic, the first letter is "fi," the second "qi" and the third "r." *Try writing love in Amharic yourself!*

በ	ቡ	ቢ	ባ	ቤ	ብ	ቦ
bä	bu	bi	ba	be	bə	bo
ወ	ዉ	ዊ	ዋ	ዌ	ው	ዎ
wä	wu	wi	wa	we	wə	wo

Two Ge'ez consonants, B and W, with vowel variations

Now try making an Amharic Valentine!

Want to write your name in Ge'ez?

Look online for a Ge'ez syllabary (a chart that shows every consonant combined with every vowel, showing all the syllables possible to write). Most names can be written in Ge'ez if you use their phonetic sounds, not their spellings. For example, Christine starts with the "k" sound, and Thomas starts with a "t" sound, not "th." For consonant blends, like "br" or "cl," use the sixth vowel column of the syllabary, (written Ə or ï) to write the first letter of the blend. Also use the sixth column if your name ends with a consonant. If your name starts with a vowel, start with the consonant ' (called 'Alf, a silent glottal stop.)

Search for the website "Amharic machine" for help writing your name.

Try to write each letter several times, then try the whole word in marker.

In rapid handwriting, it can look like this.

MAKE AN ETHIOPIAN ANGEL

Historically, most Ethiopian art has been religious, filling churches with brightly painted images. Their art is known for its simple lines, bright colors, big eyes and black outlines. This angel was inspired by the ceiling of a church in Gonder that is painted with 104 angel faces, each different. (Look at Ethiopian angel paintings online for inspiration. The Archangel Michael bearing a sword, or Saint George slaying the dragon are other possible ideas.) Paint your own angel, outlined in black, or try this cut-out paper angel. →

Detail of Angel Faces on the Ceiling of a Church in Gonder

Circle + egg = face

Background to eyes

Adding whites & then irises

Then add white dots and you're done!

Use these photos as inspiration or use the pattern and directions on the next page.

Draw in face, in pencil 1st

Cut many feathers with accordion fold

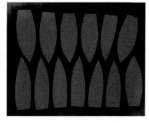

Glue feathers to black paper

Cut out with black outline, glue in place

ETHIOPIAN Angel Pattern: To use this pattern, either photocopy it twice on thick paper or trace it onto white paper. (The hair and face must be cut out separately.) Cut out all shapes and use them to outline the same shapes on colored paper.

1. **Cutting out hair and face:** Outline hair on black paper and the face on brown or tan paper; cut out.

2. **Cut out the eyes:** Cut out identical eyes by folding the paper to cut two sets of each part at once. Test how they look and trim if needed. Ideally, the irises meet the black eye outline on top and bottom. Wait to glue the eyes until after drawing the features.

3. **Drawing the features:** Lay out face with hair and eyes, leaving room for the nose. Using a pencil, lightly sketch in eyebrows and nose, and then the mouth and chin. When done, glue the pieces of the head together and trace over pencil in pen or marker.

4. **Cutting the feathers:** For feathers, fold paper accordion-style to cut out many feathers at once. Outline the shapes and cut.

5. **Adding black outlines:** Arrange feathers on two pieces of black paper, leaving space between each feather. Glue them down, then cut them out, leaving a black outline around each feather.

6. **Putting it together:** Glue head on a horizontal sheet of black paper with the top 1/4 of the head sticking above the page. Arrange small feathers on the paper around face, making a collar, and glue. Then, cut off any extra black paper from outside the collar of small feathers. Next, arrange long feathers behind the collar and glue.

7. **White dots:** Find white paper dots in a hole punch or paint them on. Put one on each small feather, and many on the longer feathers.

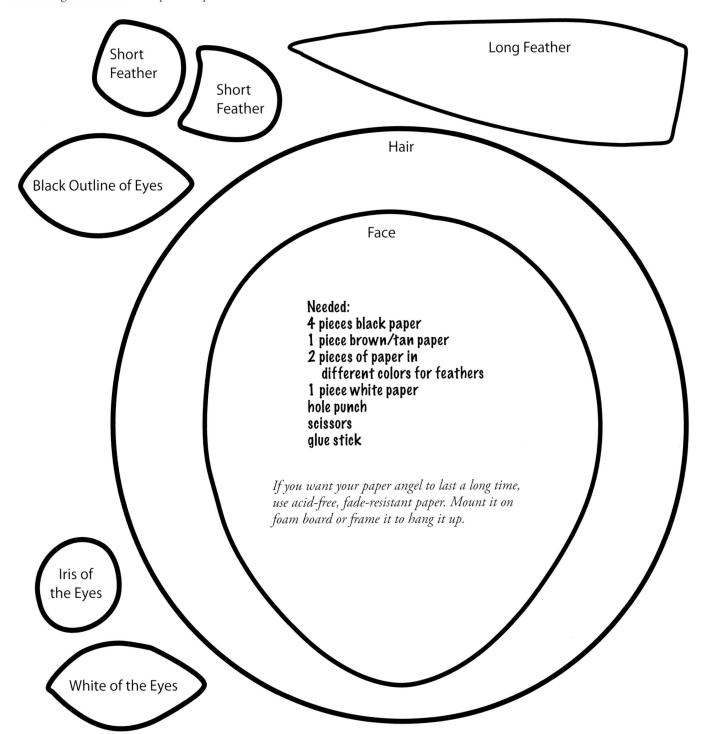

Short Feather

Short Feather

Long Feather

Black Outline of Eyes

Hair

Face

Needed:
4 pieces black paper
1 piece brown/tan paper
2 pieces of paper in
    different colors for feathers
1 piece white paper
hole punch
scissors
glue stick

If you want your paper angel to last a long time, use acid-free, fade-resistant paper. Mount it on foam board or frame it to hang it up.

Iris of the Eyes

White of the Eyes

MAKE ETHIOPIAN
NITER KIBBEH

Niter kibbeh is a spiced clarified butter that is a staple in Ethiopian cooking. Niter kibbeh, berbere (a spice mix) and injera are the three cornerstones of Ethiopian food. Niter kibbeh, unlike berbere, is not spicy hot, and it will keep in a pantry for several months. It makes vegetarian dishes heavenly!

1. Melt two sticks of butter on medium heat in a sauce pan.

2. Once butter has melted, add the rest of the ingredients and stir.

3. Wait for butter to begin to bubble slightly, turn down to the lowest simmer temperature (as low as you can go and still slowly produce bubbles.) Burning the butter would make the niter kibbeh bitter.

4. Let simmer for 45 minutes to an hour. Foamy milk solids should have turned golden brown by this point and dropped to the bottom of the pan.

5. Place a paper towel, cheese cloth or a coffee filter inside a sieve or colander. Place on top of a bowl.

6. Pour butter and spices through the paper-lined sieve and wait until all the clear butter has fallen into the bowl and only solids are left in your sieve.

7. Store niter kibbeh in a glass container; it can last months unrefrigerated.

1 cup butter* (2 sticks or ½ pound)
¼ onion, chopped thin
½ teaspoon cinnamon, or one cinnamon stick
2 cloves of garlic, chopped and smashed
¼ teaspoon ground cardamom, or 2 pods
1 inch ginger piece, peeled and cut into thin slices
½ teaspoon turmeric
⅛ teaspoon ground cloves or two cloves
¼ teaspoon fenugreek**

*Double the recipe if you already know you like niter kibbeh, less butter is lost straining a larger batch.
**Everyone makes niter kibbeh a little differently, don't worry if you don't have every spice.

MAKE ETHIOPIAN
Atakilt Wat

Atakilt wat is a heavenly stir-fry/stew made from cabbage, carrots and potatoes with niter kibbeh.

¼ cup niter kibbeh
1 large onion, chopped small
3 cloves garlic, crushed
1 inch piece of ginger
  peeled and minced
4 carrots, sliced thin
¾ teaspoon cumin
½ teaspoon turmeric
1 teaspoon salt, plus to taste
½ head cabbage, shredded
2–3 potatoes, peeled and diced
¼ teaspoon black pepper

1. Sauté chopped onion in niter kibbeh on medium heat until softened.

2. Add garlic, ginger and carrots and cook together for five minutes, stirring occasionally.

3. Add cumin, turmeric, salt and cabbage. Mix well and then cook for another 10 minutes, stirring occasionally.

4. Add potatoes, stir well and then cover dish, turn to medium low and allow to cook for 20–30 minutes, until potatoes lose their sharp edges when stirred.

5. Taste test, add more salt and pepper to taste.

6. Serve alone, or on fresh injera. This recipe is happy to sit around for a while cooling off while you make injera.

MAKE Substitute INJERA

Making injera without teff flour is like trying to make corn bread without cornmeal – not possible. Teff is expensive though and not widely available. There are non-teff recipes that try to replicate injera's sourdough taste with various methods, but they take a lot of time without great-tasting results. This is a quick, easy recipe for those without access to teff. It's not injera, but it has a similar spongy texture. Most importantly – it's very tasty with Ethiopian dishes!

2 cups whole wheat flour
1 cup all purpose flour
½ teaspoon baking soda
3 cups club soda

1. Mix dry ingredients, heat nonstick pan to medium heat.

2. Lightly brush the pan with oil. (Real injera uses a dry pan; so use very sparingly.)

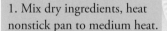

Scooping up a yummy bite with "substitute" injera!

3. Mix in club soda, stirring well. Batter should be thin.

4. Pour about ⅓ cup batter in pan while tilting and swirling the pan so batter spreads as thinly as possible.

5. Let injera cook for several minutes. Unlike pancakes, injera isn't flipped and doesn't burn. When no longer steaming, remove from pan with spatula, and stack on a plate.

6. To serve, spread injera on each plate, put wat on top and place the rest of injera (folded in half and rolled) on a plate for people to get extra during the meal.

7. To eat, tear off a piece and wrap around a bite of your wat. Finish the injera and your plate will be clean!

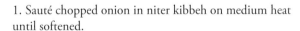
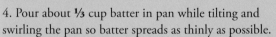

F is for
France

ENGLAND

Channel Tunnel

English Channel

BELGIUM

LILLE

LUXEMBOURG

Seine River

GERMANY

PARIS ☆

STRASBOURG

Loire River

SWITZERLAND

NANTES

ATLANTIC
OCEAN

LYON

Rhone River

ITALY

THE ALPS

BORDEAUX

TOULOUSE

MONACO

NICE

RIVIERA

THE PYRENEES

MARSEILLE

Corsica

SPAIN

*Mediterranean
Sea*

F is for **FRANCE.**

Ooh la la the romance!

For the French have a *passion*

for food, art and fashion.

Paris Fashion Week

The Alps

And the tourists! The **TOURISTS**!

They have the world's most,

From the heights of the **ALPS**

to the **Mediterranean** coast.

French Riviera

But many just visit

to tour gay *Paris* [pah-REE]

In the city of light,

there is so much to see!

Louvre Museum

Museums like the Louvre [LUU-vr]

and the Musée d'Orsay [mu-say dor-say]

Where there're works by Renoir, [rehn-WAH]

Matisse and Manet. [mah-TEE-S, mah-NAY]

Monet's **WATER LILIES**,

Rodin's **thinking man** [roh-DAN]

There's so much beauty here

you must see if you can!

Rodin's Thinker

Notre Dame

You must see the Cathedral

of NOTRE DAME, [NOH-tr DAHM]

The **ARC DE TRIOMPHE**

and the *River Seine*. [SEHN]

Seine River

Eiffel Tower

And you cannot forget

to reserve several hours

To go up to the top

of **EIFFEL'S** great tower!

Pain Au Chocolat

When your eyes are quite full,

and your belly is not,

Find a **boulangerie**

for **PAIN AU CHOCOLAT** [pan oh shoh-coh-lah]

Quiche

Or a quick slice of **quiche**, [keesh]

or a cream-filled **éclair.** [ay-CLAIR]

If you just can't decide,

get them all and then share!

éclair

Then go hop on a train

and head out to **VERSAILLES,** [ver-SIGH]

This most opulent palace

will **DAZZLE** your eyes.

Versaille

It was Louis XIV (the 14th)

who built it as **Roi.** * [rwah]

And he made it so grande

to say **L'ÉTAT, C'EST MOI!** [lay-TAH say mwah]

Louis XIV

* **Roi** [rwah] means king in French.
***L'état, c'est moi** means "The state (government), that's me."

Guillotine

It was also the home
of *Marie Antoinette,*

Up until revolution
removed her fair **tête**.

← (teht)

When **NAPOLEON** ruled,

he did not lose his head.

He was exiled to isles

when his empire was dead.

French history's exciting.

They like **REVOLUTION**!

Now **STRIKES** in the streets

have replaced **EXECUTIONS**.

Protester

Napoleon Bonaparte

Their passions extend

to their cheeses and wines,

Which are present at tables

whenever French dine.

From **Roquefort** and BRIE [rohk-fort, bree]

to *Bordeaux* and **CHAMPAGNE** [bor-DOH]

French wines and cheeses

are globally famed!

Champagne

So come to *fair France,*

land of passions galore,

Flaky **pastry** to taste

and great sights to enjoy.

So go now! Pack your bag!

Wish yourself **Bon Voyage**! [bon voy-YAHJJ]

And head off to go visit

the land of **FROMAGE.** [froh-MAHJJ]

Bon Appétit!*

Fromage (Cheese)

* **Bon Appétit** [BOHN ap-pay-TEE] means "good appetite" or "enjoy your meal" in French.

The name **FRANCE** comes from the Latin word "Francia," which means "land of the Franks." The Franks were a group of Germanic tribes whose first king, Clovis I, was crowned in 496 CE. Before being named Francia, the region was called "Gaul" and the word "Gallic" is still sometimes used as a synonym for "French."

← The **French Tricolor** was made the flag of France in 1794 during the French Revolution. *(See more about the French Revolution on page 75.)* Revolutionary fighters wore red and blue ribbons in their hats to represent the colors of Paris. White was added to represent all of France.

Map of the French Empire in 1946
(Not Including Islands in the Caribbean and Pacific)

Official Name:
The French Republic (République française)

Population: 66 million

Capital: Paris

Largest Cities: Paris, Marseille, Toulouse, Nice

Comparative Size: Slightly less than the size of Texas, the largest country in Western Europe

Language: French

Religion: Christian 63% (Roman Catholic), Muslim 7.5%, unaffiliated 28%

Currency: Euro

Famous Industries: Tourism, Luxury goods (perfume)

GEOGRAPHICAL NOTES

◉ **Why is French such a popular language?** Many countries that were once French colonies still use French as one of their official languages. Almost all French colonies had become independent nations by 1962.

◉ France still retains many overseas departments and territories like French Guiana in South America, French Polynesia in the Pacific and several islands in the Caribbean like Guadaloupe and Martinique.

Where in the World is France?

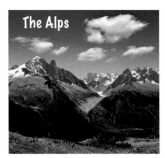
The Alps

French Riviera

Paris Fashion Week

⬆ There is more tourism to France than to any other country. There are many popular destinations including the Mediterranean, the **Alps** and Paris. The **French Riviera** or Côte d'Azur is the easternmost part of France's Mediterranean coast.

← France has been a **fashion** leader since the reign of Louis XIV when *la mode* at the French court influenced fashion all over Europe. Today there are many famous French fashion houses including Chanel, Dior, Gaultier, Givenchy, Hermes, Louis Vuitton and Yves St. Laurent. The annual Paris Fashion Week features designers from all around the globe.

Rodin's "The Thinker"

Renoir

Louvre

⬆ The **Louvre Museum** (Musée du Louvre) is the most visited art museum in the world. It is located in the center of Paris in what was once a palace for French Kings. It opened in 1793 during the French Revolution, when it was declared a place to hold the masterpieces of the nation (as opposed to its former use as a home to the king's treasures). The Louvre owns 35,000 pieces of art from Egyptian antiquities to paintings from the 19th century. *(Don't try to see it all at once!)* Its most popular attraction is Leonardo da Vinci's *Mona Lisa*. Its famous glass pyramid entrance was added in 1988.

← There are an incredible number of famous **French artists** including Cézanne, Monet, Manet, Renoir, Degas, Rodin and Matisse. Art is important in France, and the nation has been a center for many artistic movements and a home to many artists from other countries, including Picasso, Van Gogh and Chagall. ➔

Monet's Water Lilies

← Monet, Cézanne, Renoir and Degas were all **Impressionists**. Impressionism was an artistic movement that emerged in Paris in the late 19th century. It was the first "modern" artistic movement that shifted away from absolute realism to try and capture the light and feel of an instant. Many impressionist works can be found at the **Musée d'Orsay** in Paris.

The **Seine River** runs through the ➔ center of Paris, dividing the city into the Left Bank (*Rive Gauche*) and Right Bank (*Rive Droit*). The Left Bank is the southern side of the river, which used to be associated with artists, writers and philosophers living in Paris in the early 20th century.

Seine River, Paris

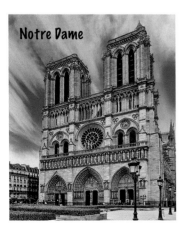
Notre Dame

← **Notre Dame de Paris** (Our Lady of Paris) is a Catholic cathedral and one of Paris's most famous sights. This church, built 1163–1345, is considered one of the best examples of Gothic architecture with its pointed arches, gargoyles and flying buttresses. It is the setting of *The Hunchback of Notre Dame* by Victor Hugo.

Arc de Triomphe

← The **Arc de Triomphe** or "Arch of Triumph" was commissioned by Napoleon Bonaparte in 1806 to commemorate victories of the French military. It is the largest triumphal arch in the world.

Eiffel Tower

Boulangerie

Pain au chocolat

← ↑ A **boulangerie** is a bakery that sells baguettes as well as other French breads and pastries. **Pain au chocolat** is like a flaky croissant filled with dark chocolate. A **quiche** is a savory pie made with eggs and cream. Boulangeries and pâtisseries (which serve mainly pastries) are found all over Paris and in every French city.

↑The **Eiffel Tower** was originally an entrance gateway for the 1889 World's Fair. Built by a company owned by engineer Gustave Eiffel, it was made of wrought iron plates riveted together into a lattice. The tower was the tallest building in the world for some time and a new achievement in the history of architecture. Originally, it was viewed as an eyesore by many in the French public, but it eventually became the beloved symbol of Paris that it is today.

Quiche

Éclair

Baguette

↑ Crunchy on the outside and light and chewy on the inside, **baguettes** are very important to the French and make up a significant part of their diet. As baguettes do not keep well, stopping by a boulangerie to pick up fresh baguettes is a part of daily life for most French families.

Gardens of Versailles

Versailles

Hall of Mirrors, Versailles

← ↑ One of the largest palaces in the world, the **Palace of Versailles** [ver-SIGH] has 2,300 rooms, 67 staircases, 6,000 paintings and 2,000 sculptures. **King Louis XIV** (the 14th) built Versailles to glorify his power and keep all the French nobility with him at court. He moved the French Court from the Louvre Palace to Versailles in 1682 to better control the French nobility, making himself an "absolute ruler" of France. King Louis is credited with saying, "L'état, c'est moi!" (which means, "I am the government.") as no one held any power but himself. →

Louis XIV

← **Marie Antoinette** was the French queen who famously lost her head in 1793 during the French Revolution. Marie was the wife of King Louis XVI (the 16th), who was also guillotined. Peasants who were starving due to bad harvests believed that the queen was indifferent to their suffering while she was living richly at Versailles. Later writers falsely accused her of remarking, "Let them eat cake," when told that poor people had no bread to eat.

The **guillotine** was → proposed by Dr. Joseph-Ignace Guillotine as a humane method of capital punishment. As gruesome as it looks, it delivers a quick death with less suffering than the previously common methods of execution. The guillotine was first used during the French Revolution, and it was the only method of execution in France until they abolished the death penalty in 1981.

Guillotine

The **French Revolution** was a movement toward ↑ democracy in France and away from the inequality of a nation ruled by a king and the nobility. It established France's **First Republic** (1792–1804) and embraced the modern idea that all people are equal under the law and that government should represent the will of the people. The motto of the French Revolution was "liberté, égalité, fraternité" or "liberty, equality, brotherhood." France has actually had several revolutions, including one in 1830 that is depicted above in the painting "Liberty Leading the People" by Eugene Delacroix. Each new revolution in France formed a new republic. France is currently governed by the **Fifth Republic**, which was formed in 1958. The Fifth Republic strengthened the French presidency. (Before it, they were governed by a frequently changing parliament and prime minister.) French people are still willing to take to the streets to demand that their rights and freedoms are respected. And if their government is no longer working for them, they are unafraid of another government revolution. If they decide to change their constitution again, it will create a Sixth Republic. ↓

French Cheeses

French Strikes

French Protester

↑ French **cheeses** are famous the world over and each region of France produces their own cheese. There are about 400 different types! Brie, Camembert, Roquefort and Cantal are some of the most famous French cheeses in the United States. Cheese is commonly eaten after the main course in France.

Napoleon

← **Napoleon Bonaparte** became the leader of France late in the French Revolution and then emperor of France (1804–1815). He is known as one of the best military leaders of all time. At the end of the French Revolution, the country was in chaos. There was fighting between political parties and with neighboring countries who opposed the revolutionary government. Napoleon emerged as a military hero when he regained French land that had been taken by the English. His army went on to conquer many neighboring countries, establishing a French Empire in Europe. Napoleon was finally stopped in his campaign to take Russia. France was invaded by European allies in 1814, and the monarchy was restored by putting the brother of King Louis XVI (the 16th) on the throne as King Louis XVIII (the 18th). Napoleon was exiled to the island of Elba. He escaped in 1815 and briefly rose to power again before he was finally defeated at the Battle of Waterloo. He was then exiled to the island of Helena, where he died five years later.

↓ France is one of the world's largest producers of **wine**. →
Just as each region of France produces its own kind of cheese, there are many regions that produce their own types of wine. Many wines have been named for the region or city that produces them, such as Champagne, Bordeaux and Burgundy. There are also many varieties of wine grapes that originate in France such as cabernet sauvignon, chardonnay and pinot noir. Similar sparkling wines are not allowed to use the name "champagne" unless they are from that region.

Champagne

Escargot

Escargot is a dish of cooked → snails that is a delicacy in France. Escargot means "snail" in French, and it is one of their more exotic appetizers. Escargot is frequently served in a rich garlic butter sauce.

↑ France is divided into 27 administrative regions. The 21 above and Corsica make up *Metropolitan France.* The five overseas are the Atlantic islands of Guadaloupe and Martinique, the Mediterranean islands of Reunion and Mayotte, and French Guiana in South America.

Lavender

← France is one of the world's top producers of **lavender** and sweet smelling fields of lavender are a common sight in the south of France. France is also a world center for perfume making and the word "perfume" comes from French.

Mont Saint-Michel is a rocky island located → off the coast of Normandy. Home to a hilltop monastery since 966 CE, it has been a popular tourist attraction for centuries. In medieval times, pilgrims reached Mont Saint-Michel by walking over a sandy path revealed at low tide. But when the tide comes in, it does so at a speed nearly impossible to outrun. Today, a dry causeway leads safely to the island.

Mont Saint-Michel

Coast of Normandy

← Off the English Channel, the cliffs of **Normandy** are famous in the United States because that was where Allied British, Canadian and American forces landed in 1944 on D-Day. D-Day was the invasion of France to remove Nazi German forces, which had occupied the country since 1940. "D-Day" is the largest amphibious (water to land) assault ever attempted. It was the turning point of World War II, and the Germans surrendered 11 months later.

SPEAK FRENCH!

French pronunciation is not easily transcribed. Use online resources like forvo.com to hear words pronounced correctly.

Bonjour! *BOHN-jju* **Good day!**

Salut! *sah-LU* **Hi! / Bye!**

Ca va? *sah-VAH?* **How are you?**

Ca va! *sah-VAH!* **I'm fine!**

S'il vous plaît **Please**
see vu play

Merci beaucoup!
MAIR-see boh-KU!
Thank you very much!

Je t'aime *juh TEHM* **I love you.**

J'aime le fromage. **I love cheese.**
JEHM luh fro-MAHJJ

Moi aussi! *mwah oh-SEE* **Me too!**

Quel domage! *kehl doh-MAHJJ*
What a shame! Too bad!

Bon voyage! Have a good trip!
bohn voy-AHJJ

(Map labels: North-Calais, Picardy, Normandy, Paris-Ile-de-France, Champagne-Ardenne, Lorraine, Alsace, Brittany, Pays-de-la-Loire, Centre, Burgundy, Franche-Comte, Poitou Charentes, Limousin, Auvergne, Rhone-Alps, Aquitaine, Midi-Pyrenees, Languedoc-Roussillon, Provence-Alps Cote D'Azur)

Listen to the
SOUNDS
of FRANCE

Edith Piaf The queen of French song. "La Vie en Rose" ("Life in Pink," meaning how the world appears to someone in love) and "Non, Je ne Regrette Rien" ("No, I Regret Nothing") are probably her two most famous songs.
YOUTUBE SEARCH: Edith Piaf

Ravel, Satie, Debussy Three of the most famous French composers. Try Ravel's "Bolero," Satie's "Gymnopedie" and Debussy's "Claire de Lune."

La Marseillaise The French national anthem is an example of the passionate attitude of revolution in France, "Tremble tyrants! ...Everyone is a soldier to fight you!"

Paris Combo Infectious French world music with influences from American jazz-swing, French chanson and rhythms from Roma and North Africa. Try "Moi, Mon Ame et Ma Conscience." **YOUTUBE SEARCH:** Paris Combo

MC Solaar A French rapper, his "Nouveau Western" has English subtitles on YouTube.
YOUTUBE SEARCH: MC Solaar Nouveau Western

PLAY: Escargot

Escargot or "Snail" is a combination of Monopoly and Hopscotch. Using chalk, a large spiral is drawn on the ground outside, divided into boxes spiraling inward. Each player tries to hop to the center of the spiral, hopping in squares from 1–20 (or 1 to any number), and then back out again, 20–1 using the following rules:
1. Hop only on one foot, the same foot throughout a turn, don't put the other foot down (except for in the center).
2. Hop in each square once, no double hopping for balance.
3. No hopping on the lines of the game board or outside it.
4. Players can rest in the center circle.

Breaking any of these rules will result in the end of a player's turn. If a player makes it all the way into the spiral, and then all the way back out again without breaking any rules, they are allowed to claim one square as their real estate. The player will mark that square with their initials and may use it to rest during their turn. No one else can hop in that square though, they have to hop over it. The game goes on until it is impossible to hop to the center due to the number of squares that players own. At that point, the winner is the player who owns the most squares.
TIP: Drawing the gameboard, make the boxes short and fat so that players can hop over them.

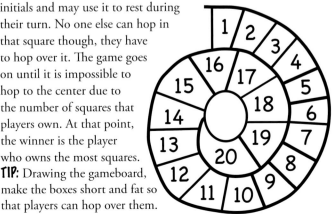

READ:

Asterix and Obelix Written by René Goscinny, illustrated by Albert Uderzo.
The first volume of this classic French graphic novel series came out in 1959 and new volumes are still being created today. It has been translated into many languages, which is impressive as the text is filled with puns and word play. Ages 9 & up.

The Little Prince by Antoine de Saint-Exupéry. A classic of world literature, as beloved by children as adults. The 1943 Katherine Woods translation is recommended over the newer one, which came out in 2001. Ages 9 & up.

Monet and the Impressionists for Kids: Their Lives and 21 Activities by Carol Sabbeth. A fun book for older kids, teens and adults that explores the first modern art movement, which was centered in France. Ages 9 & up.

DON'T MISS
WATCHING
(online)

The Red Balloon (1956) All Ages.
This classic of French cinema is a short film (34 minutes) about a boy and a red balloon that follows him around Paris. **YOUTUBE SEARCH: Red Balloon**

Un Monstre à Paris (2011) All Ages.
A charming animated tale that features songs from famous French musicians, Vanessa Paradis and –M–.

Introduction to the French Revolution
Khan Academy has a captivating history lesson on one of the biggest turning points in world history.
INTERNET SEARCH: Khan Academy French Revolution

Films based on the Classic Works of French Authors:

Victor Hugo: Victor Hugo probably never imagined his books set to song or turned into animated children's stories, but both films provide marvelous views of Paris and history.
The Hunchback of Notre Dame
Les Miserables

Alexandre Dumas: Dumas wrote some of the greatest adventure stories, filled with swashbuckling sword play.
The Count of Monte Cristo
The Three Musketeers

Jules Verne: One of the fathers of science fiction, Jules Verne's classic works have circled the globe.
20,000 Leagues Under the Sea
Around the World in 80 Days
Journey to the Center of the Earth

MAKE FRENCH
Quiche

A sort of savory custard pie, quiche is an easy and very versatile recipe. The quiche custard – made of eggs, cream, salt and nutmeg – doesn't change; but you can add many different types of meat, cheese and vegetables. There is a specific recipe below but feel free to use different fillings. Milk or cream can replace the half-and-half in this recipe. There is a guide to other fillings and modifications below.

1. Thaw pie crust on the counter for ten minutes then prick the crust several times with a fork so that it will not bubble while baking.

2. Preheat oven to 400° and put on some Edith Piaf.

3. Bake pie crust for 7–9 minutes, until it begins to brown, then set aside to cool. Turn oven down to 350°.

4. Cook bacon until firm; drain on paper towels.

5. Sauté chopped onion until translucent. Remove from heat and add well-drained, thawed spinach and mix. (Squeeze extra liquid out of spinach before using.) Add half of shredded cheese and crumble the bacon into the mixture and set aside.

6. Beat eggs, then add half-and-half, salt and nutmeg. Beat until frothy.

7. Take cooled pie crust and put the rest of the cheese on bottom; then add the filling; then pour in the custard mixture.

8. Bake on top of a cookie sheet at 350° for 40–50 minutes, or until the sides are set but the center is still a bit wobbly. (It will set as it cools, an overcooked quiche can get rubbery.)

9. Serve warm or at room temperature, ideally with a fresh green salad.

1 (frozen) pie crust

Filling
5 pieces bacon, cooked and crumbled
½ package frozen spinach, thawed and drained
1 sweet yellow onion, chopped small
1 cup Gruyère (or other) **cheese**, shredded

Quiche custard
3 eggs
1½ cups half-and-half (or milk or cream)
1 teaspoon salt
dash nutmeg

GUIDE TO QUICHE MODIFICATIONS

Fillings: The originally famous *Quiche Lorraine* added only bacon and onion to the custard mixture and did not include cheese. Today in France, there are as many different fillings for quiche as there are toppings for pizza. Here are some popular ones: **ham, bacon, mushrooms, spinach, onion,**

garlic, asparagus, broccoli, leeks, tomato. The most important thing is that ingredients need to be mostly dry and usually not raw. Extra liquid can make a quiche soupy. Spinach or broccoli need to be lightly sautéed until wilted. Onion and mushrooms also need to be sautéed in advance – onions until translucent, mushrooms until shrunken. Use no more than 1–2 cups of dry ingredients (not including cheese).

Pastry crust: Make your own pastry crust or buy a pie crust at the store. The traditional quiche crust has straight vertical sides instead of the slanted sides of a pie. Either way, the taste and ingredients are the same. It is more challenging to achieve the straight sides, but there are videos online of chef Julia Child making *Quiche Lorraine* that show how to make a perfect quiche crust if you feel ambitious. You can also make **crustless quiches** – just add an extra egg and 2 tablespoons flour to the quiche custard recipe and use a well-buttered cake pan when you bake it. There are gluten-free recipes online.

Cheese: Gruyere cheese is the probably the most popular cheese in French quiches, but any cheese could work including cheddar, Swiss, Gouda, Parmesan, feta, etc. Recipes usually use between one and two cups shredded, but cheese is optional, so feel free to use as much or little as you like.

G is for Ghana

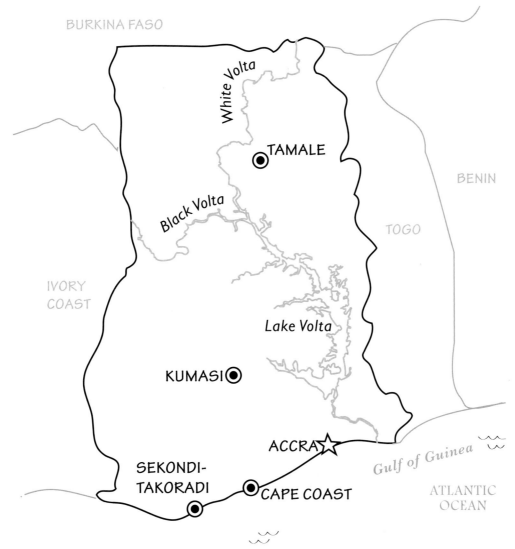

BURKINA FASO

White Volta

TAMALE

BENIN

Black Volta

TOGO

IVORY COAST

Lake Volta

KUMASI

ACCRA

Gulf of Guinea

SEKONDI-TAKORADI

CAPE COAST

ATLANTIC OCEAN

Cocoa Beans

Our **G** is for **GHANA**

where cocoa beans grow,

Bright **KENTE CLOTH'S** made

and the children all know –

Kente Cloth

Of **anansi** the spider,

a trickster who's clever,

The hero of folktales

for almost forever.

Anansi

Once called the **GOLD COAST**,

this West African land

Has rainforest, grasslands

and coastal beach sands.

Gold Coast Stamp

It was here the **ASHANTI'S**

great empire once ruled,

And their king is still reigning

from his **golden stool**.

Ashanti Flag
with Golden Stool

Europe's empires sought GOLD,

ivory and **SLAVES**

When they came to this coast

to conquer and trade.

The Asantehene,
(Ashanti King)

The **British** took over

(once the slave trade had ended)

And formed here a nation

of ethnic groups blended:

Combining the **Mole-Dagbon**, [moh-lay dahg-bon]

the ***AKAN***, [ah-KAHN]

The **EWE**, the **Ga-Dangme**, [EH-weh, gah dahng-may]

and the GUAN. [gwahn]

Independence Arch

These people with languages

and customs diverse

All became British subjects,

learning English to converse.

In **1957**,

they gained **INDEPENDENCE**

And **Civil Rights** leaders

were there in attendance –

Martin Luther King Jr.
attended Ghana's
Independence Ceremony

To see the black Africans

first to regain

Their rights to self-govern

their own land again.

Kwame Nkrumah
Ghana's First President

They became the **BLACK STAR**

and all Africa's hope

That the continent soon

would be in the same boat.

Black Star on Ghana's Flag

Ghanaian Beach

Ghanaians are **PROUD**

of their history and nation,

Their **BEAUTIFUL BEACHES,**

and diverse population,

Their **Hiplife** musicians,*

mixing rap and Highlife,

Their **FANTASY COFFINS**

celebrating each life,

Lion Coffin

Rolls of Kente

Their fabrics like **KENTE**

and **ADINKRA**-stamped cloth,*

From which tailors make clothing

so stylish and soft,

Their foods, which are savory

with plenty of spice,

Like their **GROUND PEANUT SOUP,***

or their **RED JOLLOF RICE,**

Jollof Rice

Adinkra Symbols
Stamped on Fabric

Their open air markets

where haggling over **cedis**

Can only come after

exchanging *warm greetings.*

100 Cedi Coin
Featuring Cocoa

*Find out more about hiplife music, adinkra symbols and a recipe for peanut butter soup in the Ghana activity pages.

So come now **_Obruni_***

your welcome is waiting.

With people so friendly,

there's no hesitating!

Go hop on a plane

from wherever you are,

Visit Ghana to meet

this shining **BLACK STAR**.

Akwaaba!**

***_Obruni_** means "foreigner" in Twi and is used affectionately to call to visitors in Ghana.
****_Akwaaba_** means "Welcome!" in Twi.

← Ghana was the first country to adopt the "Pan-African" colors of red, green and gold on their flag, modeling it after the flag of Ethiopia. These colors went on to be used in many other African flags. Red symbolized the blood of those who died in the struggle for independence, gold represents the mineral wealth of the country and green represents the country's green forests and natural resources. The **black star** represents Ghana as the "lodestar (or guiding star) of African freedom," a reference to Ghana being the first country in Sub-Saharan Africa to gain its independence in 1957. (Liberia and Ethiopia were never part of European empires and thus always independent.) Ghana's football team is nicknamed the "Black Stars" after the flag.

Ghana in West Africa

Official Name:
Republic of Ghana

Population: 26 million

Capital: Accra

Largest Cities: Accra, Kumasi, Tamale, Secondi-Takoradi

Comparative Size:
Slightly smaller than Oregon

Ethnicity: Akan (Ashanti & Fanti) 45%, Mole-Dagbon 15%, Ewe 12%, Ga-Danme 7%, Guan 4%, others 8%

Languages: Asante (also called **Twi**), Ewe, Boron, Fanti, Dagomba, Dangme & many others.

Official Language: English

Religion: Christianity 75%, Islam 16%, traditional 5%, none 4%

Currency: Ghana cedi

Important Exports:
Gold, cocoa

Where in the World is Ghana?

GEOGRAPHICAL NOTES

◉ **GHANA** was named after the medieval West African **Ghana Empire**, which ruled from before 830 to 1250 CE and was located in modern-day Mali and Mauritania (not in Ghana). The Ghana Empire was wealthy due to trade in gold and salt across the Saharan Desert. Some Ghanaian peoples are believed to be descended from those of the Ghana Empire, but the name was chosen in 1957 to reflect the nation's new independence from the British Empire and their own African identity.

Cocoa Farmer

Cocoa Pods with Beans Inside

Cocoa, Chocolate & Nibs

↑ **Cocoa beans**, from which we make chocolate, are one of Ghana's largest exports. Although cocoa beans originally come from the Americas, the majority of today's cocoa is produced in West Africa. Cocoa beans are dried, roasted, cracked and deshelled to produce "nibs." These nibs can be ground to produce chocolate liqueur or processed to separate into cocoa and cocoa butter. Dark chocolate is generally made with chocolate liqueur plus cocoa butter and sugar.

Asantehene

Ashanti Flag

↑ The **Ashanti** (also spelled Ashante → or Asante) are the largest ethnic group in Ghana. Along with the Fanti and other subgroups, they make up the **Akan** people, which are 45% of Ghana's population. The Ashanti king is the Asantehene, who sits on a **golden stool**. The golden stool is a symbol of the king and is featured on the Ashanti flag.

Anansi

↑ **Anansi** is a trickster character in Ashanti folktales who may have been the first "spider man." He is depicted as a man in some stories and as a spider in others. There are so many stories of Anansi, that folktales are called "spider tales" or Anansesem in Asante language. Anansi was transported across the Atlantic by African slaves, and his tales exist across the Caribbean and in America, where they are sometimes called "Aunt Nancy" tales. Storytelling is incredibly important in Ghana where traditions, history and values are passed down through stories.

Rolls of Kente

Royalty wearing kente at Ghana's independence celebration

Elmina Castle

↑ **Elimina Castle** was the first European settlement on the southern "Gold Coast" of West Africa. Built by the Portuguese in 1482, it became one of several castles along the coast that were used as trade ports for gold and later slaves going to the New World.

Weaving Kente

↑ **Kente cloth** is handwoven by the Ashanti and Ewe people of Ghana and has become one of Africa's most famous textiles. Once reserved for royalty, kente is still used only for very special occasions. It is woven in 4-inch-wide strips, which are then sewn together. Making kente takes a very long time and the fabric is expensive. Kente weavers are traditionally men who have trained from a young age. There are over 300 different kente patterns, and each has its own meaning taken from history, proverbs, religion or folktales.

Slave dungeons are still intact in many and were the last places many Africans saw before their journey to the Americas. The door into the dungeons at Cape Coast Castle was called the **"Door of No Return"** until it was renamed the "Door of Return" in honor of those who return to Africa to see their heritage.

Gold Coast Stamp

← The **Gold Coast** was a British colony from 1874 to 1957. It was named the Gold Coast by Europeans centuries before due to the large amounts of gold available for trade there. The court of the Ashanti king was full of beautiful gold → ornaments, like this large "**soul washer's badge**" worn by the man responsible for the ritual purification of the Asantehene's soul. Ghana still produces a large amount of gold for export.

The **Independence Arch** in Ghana's capital, → Accra, is inscribed with their national motto, "**Freedom and Justice**." and the year of their independence, 1957.

Independence Arch

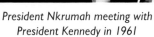

↑ Ghanaian **students** study both English and a local language at school. For upper level students, all classes are in English. English enables Ghanaians of every ethnic group to communicate with each other and with people from around the world.

↓ **Martin Luther King Jr**. said, "Ghana tells us that the forces of the universe are on the side of justice," and Ghana "reminds us of the fact that a nation or a people can break loose from oppression without violence."

In 1957, Ghana became the first country in Sub-Saharan Africa to win its **independence**. Every African country but Ethiopia and Liberia had been the colony of a European empire. Like Ghana, the 13 American colonies had been part of the British Empire before declaring their own independence in 1776. When Ghana gained its independence from the British Empire in 1957, it was greeted as a turning point in black history around the world. It was said that "freedom first rang for blacks in Ghana." In the United States, the Civil Rights Movement had recently gained national attention when Rosa Parks refused to give up her seat on a bus in 1955, starting the Montgomery Bus Boycott. ← **Martin Luther King Jr.** and other African American leaders traveled to Ghana to be present at their independence ceremony and spoke about Ghana's new freedom in the United States. Ghana did lead the way for other countries. By 1968, most countries in Africa had gained their independence. And in the United States, both the Civil Rights Act and the Voting Rights Act had been passed.

← **Kwame Nkrumah** was the first president of Ghana and a leader in their struggle for liberation. He attended universities in the United States and London, getting several degrees, before returning to his native Ghana to work for Ghanaian independence and Pan-African unity. →

Kwame Nkrumah

President Nkrumah meeting with President Kennedy in 1961

What's the difference between a tribe, a nation and an ethnic group?

There's not really a difference in Africa. Many scholars complain that "tribe" is used only when referring to non-European peoples. We don't say that the English, Scottish and Welsh are "tribes," within the United Kingdom. Instead they are separate "nations" of people who each have their own culture, history and language, even though they are currently all part of the United Kingdom. Spain also has several ethnolinguistic groups with their own language, culture and history that they describe as "nationalities," not as tribes. (See U is for UK and S is for Spain for more details.) Similarly, the Ashanti people have their own language, history, royal family and customs. When there are several "nations" within one country (which is the case with most countries in Africa), "ethnic group" can be a less confusing term to use, as the word nation can also mean "country." (For instance, the United Nations is a group of countries, not ethnic groups.) There are hundreds of ethnic groups in Africa; about 50 of them have one million people or more and about 15 have more than 10 million people in them. Many ethnic groups are spread over more than one country. For instance, the Ewe people of Ghana also live in Togo and Benin.

Fantasy Coffins

Lion Coffin

← In Ghana, craftsmen carve **fantasy coffins** to represent the life of the person who has died. If you loved to travel, you could be buried in an airplane. A successful businessman might be buried in a Mercedes. If you loved Coca-Cola, or sold it, you could be buried in a coke bottle. A fisherman might choose a fish or a boat. A great leader might be buried in a lion, and a wonderful mother and grandmother in a hen. There are infinite possibilities. → *What would you want to be buried in?*

Tailor-made Clothing

Making Adinkra Cloth

← **Adinkra symbols** can convey ideas, history or popular proverbs. Used to decorate cloth, pottery, architecture, websites and signage, they originated with Akan peoples in Ivory Coast and Ghana. Each symbol has a complex meaning and can't be condensed to the one-word labels below. The first symbol, labeled "God," actually means "Gye Nyame" or "Except God" (I fear none). Adinkra-stamped cloth was originally worn only by royalty and spiritual leaders, but is now worn by everyone. There are over 50 Adinkra symbols, and new ones are still being made. Adinkra cloth is still usually produced by hand, but there are machine-made versions. ↓

Tailor

↑ Want to get some new **clothes** in Ghana? → First you must go to the market and select your fabric. Then you go to see your tailor. He (or she) will have designs for you to choose from or you can just describe what you want. (Anyone can be a fashion designer in Ghana, if you can dream up the clothing, a tailor will be willing to make it for you.) After taking your measurements, it can be a day to a week before your new clothes are ready for you to try on. For special events like weddings, graduations or other celebrations, large groups may get something made from the same fabric or even a special fabric commissioned for the event.

GOD   Adinkra Symbols   WISDOM

ADAPTABILITY   HUMILITY

JEALOUSY   HOPE

Jollof Rice

← **Jollof rice** is a savory tomato-infused rice dish that is popular across West Africa. Chicken, jollof rice and salad are a common offering at restaurants in Ghana.

Cedis (SEE-dees) are the currency in → Ghana. Cedi is the Akan word for cowry shell, which was once a currency here. Whenever buying something, it is polite to first greet the seller and ask how they are, how is their family and how is business. It is also courteous to give and receive items using your right hand.

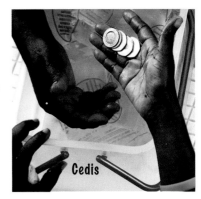

Cedis

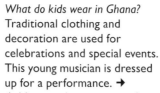

What do kids wear in Ghana? Traditional clothing and decoration are used for celebrations and special events. This young musician is dressed up for a performance. →

← Most students wear uniforms to school. ↓

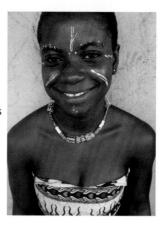

Fishing on the Volta River

↑ **Lake Volta** was made from the Volta River by the Akosombo Dam, which was completed in 1965. The lake is the largest reservoir of water by surface area in the world and the fourth-largest in terms of volume. The dam provides much of Ghana's electricity. ↓

Running to School

Biking to School

Fishing on Lake Volta

↑ Walking, running or riding a bike are all commons ways to get to school in Ghana. →

← Kids in Ghana use their heads to carry things the easiest way. People often use a coil of fabric on their heads to help balance things. →

Why do people in Africa (and many other places) carry things on their head?

The short answer is that it is easier and better for their backs. Carrying anything a long distance, it is much easier to carry it on your head than to hold it with your arms or carry it on your back. There is less strain on your arms, hands, shoulders and back and it doesn't misalign your spine. Carrying things on your head requires that you use good posture and distributes the weight so you can carry a heavy load much farther.

Practicality and ease is also why many babies are wrapped close to their mothers' backs. Not only does it keep the baby happy to be right beside its mother, it allows the mother to do all the work she needs to during the day, leaving both arms free. The baby stays safe, and the mother doesn't strain her arms or back or risk the baby getting too close to anything dangerous like cooking fires.

TRY IT YOURSELF! If you want to try carrying something on your own head, start small. Without experience, you could hurt your neck with something too heavy. Use a piece of fabric wrapped in a coil on your head to help balance something there without having to hold it.

The Original Hands-Free Baby Carrier

Listen to the SOUNDS of GHANA

Hiplife

Hiplife is a mix of highlife, hip hop and reggae.
Suggested songs with online music videos:
Nana Boroo's "Ahayede" also spelled "Eha Ye De"
Praye's "Shordy" or "Kesu"(no video, only mp3)
Castro's "African Girls"
Nkasai's "Tuabodom"
Dunsin's "Oye Adie Yie"

Highlife Music

Originating in Ghana, Nigeria and Sierra Leone, highlife
began mixing brass, guitars and African rhythms in the
1950s and continues making mellow, infectious dance tunes
today. Suggested online:
E. T. Mensah's "Ghana Freedom" (about independence)
Rambler's Dance Band's ""Agyanka Dabre"
Daddy Lumba's "Mpempem,"
**"Ghana Special: Modern Highlife, Afro Sounds and
Ghanaian Blues 1968-1981"** a compilation album which
features classic Ghanaian highlife and blues

Talking Drums

Originating in West Africa, the talking drum was a form
of mass communication to send messages throughout a
village and even to neighboring villages. It is still used
today in more rural areas and in traditional festivals. The
drums mimic the sounds of human speech and particular
rhythms are widely understood to convey various messages.
YOUTUBE SEARCH: talking drum Ghana

DONT MISS WATCHING (online)

Making Kente & Adinkra Cloth

Visit Bonwire and see master weavers in action.
YOUTUBE SEARCH: weaving kente, Adinkra stamping

Azonto Dancing Azonto is a Ghanaian dance craze that
has spread to many countries. BBC News has a segment on
Azonto taking over the world and *The Guardian* has a video
of Ghanaian youth showing off their best Azonto moves.
There are hundreds of Azonto videos. YOUTUBE SEARCH:
Guardian Azonto Ghanaian Youth, Azonto BBC, Azonto Fuse,
Azonto Dance Tutorial Ghana

Families of Ghana From a video series about life in other
countries, it follows two Ghanaian children, one from the
city and one from the country, through a typical day. There
are trailers on YouTube and your library might have a copy.
YOUTUBE SEARCH: families of Ghana

READ:

ANANSI stories: You can probably find many at
your local library, here are a couple favorites:
A Story, a Story by Gail Haley. The tale of how
Anansi brought stories to the world. Ages 5 & up.

The Pot of Wisdom: Ananse Stories by Adwoa Badoe. A
collection of ten classic Anansi tales. Ages 7 & up.

Nii Kwei's Day: From Dawn to Dusk in a Ghanaian City
by Carolyn McNamara and Francis Provencal. Ages 5 & up.

Spider Weaver: A Legend of Kente Cloth by Margaret
Musgrove. A traditional tale of how kente weavers were first
inspired by the intricate design of a spider's web. Ages 4 & up.

Master Weaver from Ghana by Gilbert Ahiagble and
Louise Meyer. A true story with photos of a master weaver
passing on the art of weaving kente to his son. Ages 7 & up.

One Hen by Katie Smith Milway. Based on a true story, a
Ghanaian boy starts his own highly successful chicken farm
from one hen, which enables him to go to school. Ages 8 & up.

Abina and the Important Men by Trevor Getz and Liz
Clarke. A historical graphic novel from the Gold Coast
about a real woman who was enslaved, escaped and took
her former master to court in 1876. Ages 12 & up.

PLAY: Ampe

Ampe is like a whole body game of "**Rock, Paper, Scissors.**"
Two players face one another and jump up into the air
putting one leg out in front of them when they land. For
one player, landing with the same foot forward as their
opponent means a win. For the other player,
landing with the opposite foot forward
means a win. Players decide in advance
who wins with the same side and with
the opposite. When they jump, they
clap twice, the first clap while they
are airborn and the second clap when
they land simultaneously with one leg
forward. Sometimes a bounce then jump
is used to get in the same rhythm. The
winner of each jump gets a point.

TWO-PLAYER: The first person to win 10 points wins.

INDIVIDUAL PLAY IN A GROUP: Players stand in a semi-
circle and one player faces the group as a challenger. A
challenger always wins with the same foot forward as their
opponent. They play the first person in the semi-circle, and
if they win a point, they keep playing the rest of the players
until they lose. Whoever beats them gets to be the next
challenger who plays the next person in line.

TIP: For technique, watch ampe being played online!

MAKE GHANAIAN
Groundnut Soup

Groundnut Soup (or peanut butter soup) is a popular meal for Sunday dinner in Ghana. It's so creamy-spicy-savory yummy! This recipe is a very Americanized one (they do not use jars of salsa in Ghana), but the ingredients are the same: tomato, onion, peanut butter, ginger, peppers, chicken. And the results are just as heavenly delicious.

1. Put on some Ghanaian Highlife or Hiplife music to set the mood. In soup pot, sauté onion, ginger and cayenne in oil until the onion softens.

2. Add chicken thighs and stir to coat fully with onion mixture, allow to cook for a couple minutes, turning the chicken over midway.

3. Add salsa, stir. Then add one bouillon cube and one cup water, bring it to a steady simmer.

4. Once it's simmering, add one more cup water, stir, then take out one cup of broth out and put in a separate smaller pot.

5. Add peanut butter to broth in smaller pot and mix until fully combined. (Ghanaians use their fingers for this.)

6. Put peanut butter broth mixture on medium low heat and continually stir to avoid burning it. Eventually, the peanut butter will start to "fall apart" with the oil separating out and pooling on top and the peanut paste losing its consistency. This may take 10 minutes.

7. Once it starts to separate, add one more half cup broth from the chicken pot, stir, then add the whole peanut butter broth to the soup.

8. Simmer soup for 40 minutes or longer, until chicken becomes tender enough to be easily pulled apart and shredded. Turn off the heat.

9. Removing one piece of chicken at a time, use two forks to shred the chicken into bite-size pieces on a plate, then add back to the soup.

10. Add more water and bouillon if more broth is needed – it should be soupy, not a thick stew. In Ghana, Maggi bouillon cubes are popular, but any brand of large soft bouillon cubes may be easily crumbled into the soup in proportion to the liquid added. Rewarm soup, stir and taste test.

11. Serve warm with a mound of rice (or fufu) and a side of greens.

1 onion, diced into small pieces
1 teaspoon fresh ginger, peeled and chopped fine
¼ teaspoon cayenne pepper (optional, to taste)
2–4 tablespoon oil
1 lb boneless, skinless chicken thighs
1 bottle mild salsa 12–16 oz (salsa with tomatoes, peppers, and onions, no herbs)
1–2 large chicken bouillon cubes (Knorr or Maggi brand)
¾ cup peanut butter (natural, no sugar)

Optional Modifications:

Add vegetables: There are many different vegetables that Ghanaians may add to groundnut soup; some of the most popular ones are okra, mushrooms or greens. Other possibilities include sweet potatoes, eggplant, green peas or bell peppers.

More/Less Spicy: Use diced tomatoes instead of salsa if you want the dish to have no heat. To make it hotter, dice a couple of hot peppers to add in with the onions, *or* use hotter salsa.

Vegetarian: Replace the chicken with sweet potatoes and greens.

More Ghanaian: Use a whole chicken, chopped into pieces with skin and bones intact. Serve soup with a piece of chicken and a mound of rice or fufu in each bowl.

Shredding the chicken with forks. In Ghana, chicken pieces are served whole in the soup. This version shreds the chicken as you would for a gumbo to make it easier to spoon up.

Eat like a Ghanaian!

In Ghana, most dishes are eaten with the fingers of the right hand from a communal plate. Usually sticky rice, fufu or another carbohydrate is pinched off and then dipped in sauce or soup. There are plenty of spoons and forks for tourists, but you might like to try eating your groundnut soup with your right hand. Ghanaians always wash their hands thoroughly before and after eating. In fact, in restaurants, materials to wash your hands are the first thing that comes to the table.

 MAKE ADINKRA STAMPS!

1. Pick a symbol below and trace it on a piece of thin paper. (Notebook paper works. Alternatively, photocopy this page, or print symbols from adinkra.org.)

2. Cut out the shape and then outline it on your sheet of foam.

3. Cut out the Adinkra shape from foam. Smaller sewing scissors are ideal for any twisty parts. Bend your shape in half in order to cut into the center.

Trace shape on paper ➜ *Cut out paper shape* ➜ *Outline shape on foam* ➜ *Cut out foam shape.*

4. Glue your foam Adinkra symbol onto card stock paper, ensuring that all the edges are glued down. Press on it to make sure no glue seeps out. Clean up any extra glue.

5. Cut out the card stock around the Adinkra stamp, close to the outside edges.

6. Glue another piece of card stock on the back of your first, then cut out again. The stamp backing is now two pieces of card stock thick. This base is strong enough to last indefinitely without warping, but is still flexible.

7. Allow to dry completely, then put clear packing tape on the back of your stamp. Now, it's protected from water damage and ready to stamp.

8. Find a stamping base or make one. A wooden block works well as a handle for your stamp, but anything that can fit in your hand and has a solid flat surface would do. The stamping surface should be near the size of your stamp, not much bigger or smaller. You will use it to press down forcefully on the entire area of your stamp.

Materials:
1 sheet of card stock (thick paper)
1 sheet of white paper (thin)
1 craft foam sheet
Tape (clear packing tape)
Glue (Elmer's or Craft)
Scissors (smaller is easier)
Wooden block or shipping box cardboard.

Make your own stamp base!

If you don't have a ready base around the house, you can make a one out of cardboard. Cut out four equal-size squares of card board that are not much bigger than your stamp. Tape the cardboard together with packing tape. Press down on the corners and outside edges of your square, making them collapse slightly. This curved shape will make sure paint stays off your base. Add clear packing tape to the rest of the surface, making it waterproof on all sides. Then tape a strip of thick paper on the flat back side to make a loop handle. The handle makes it easier to pick your stamp up from the fabric without smearing paint. ↓

The **crocodile** ➜ represents adaptability as crocodiles can live on land or in water. An adaptable person can go anywhere.

↑ **"Except God"**
Meaning, "I fear none except God."

↑ A Good Omen
"That which removes bad luck"

← The **spider's web** represents wisdom and creativity.

Want more symbols to choose from? Go to www.adinkra.org

STAMP ADINKRA ON FABRIC

How to use your new foam Adinkra stamps:

1. Attach stamp to a base with a loop of tape. This makes it easy to change stamps on one base.

2. Lay out fabric on a flat surface. Paint may bleed through the fabric, so put a protective covering underneath. Avoid corrugated cardboard (too bumpy) or newspapers that can stain the fabric.

4. Squeeze some fabric paint into a pan, and thin it with a few drops of water. It should be thicker than water, thinner than gel. If your symbol wants to stick to the fabric, it's too thick/dry.

5. Use paintbrush to paint your foam stamp. The brush makes sure than every bit of foam is covered, and it can remove extra paint from interior crevices if any accumulates there.

6. Place stamp down onto the fabric, then press down firmly on the entire area. Rock your base slightly from side to side and press firmly, pushing the foam stamp into the fabric. Don't rush, it may take a few seconds to fully transfer the paint.

7. Pull up stamp and see how it looks. Don't aim for perfection, the charm of hand stamping is in variation. If there are any large unpainted spots in the stamped symbol, touch them up with your paint brush. Use watery paint for touch ups or they will dry darker. Repaint the stamp before each stamping.

6. Don't shift fabric until the stamps dry. Unless your fabric is very thick, there will be paint on the surface below and it may smear if you move the fabric before it dries.

7. Use fabric to make something. You could frame a section of your fabric, or you could make a pillow, or a wall hanging, etc.

ALTERNATIVE Adinkra Craft: Instead of stamping Adinkra on fabric, blow up your favorite Adinkra symbol to a large size, trace it onto fabric, then paint it in. Adinkra symbols are used in Ghanaian architecture, signs and websites. The symbols don't need to be stamped and can be painted instead.

NEEDED:
Fabric Paint
Paint Brush
Fabric
Adinkra Stamps

WHAT MIGHT YOUR NAME BE IN GHANA?

Born on a:	Boys' Names with variations*	Girls' Names with variations*
Monday	Kwadwó, Kojo, Jojo	Adwoa, Adjua, Ajwoba, Adjoa
Tuesday	Kwabena, Ebo Komla, Kobina	Abena Abla, Abrema
Wednesday	Kwaku, Koku, Kaku, Kuuku	Akua Akuba, Aku, Ekua
Thursday	Yaw, Yao, Yaba, Ekow, Kwaw	Yaa, Araba, Ayawa, Baaba, Yaaba, Aba
Friday	Kofi, Fiifi, Yoofi, Koffi	Afua Afí, Efia, Efua
Saturday	Kwame Ato, Komi	Ama, Ame, Amba, Ameyo
Sunday	Akwasí, Kwesi, Siisi, Kosi	Akosua, Akosi, Así, Akosiwa, Esi, Kwasiba

There are many more variations not listed here.

Among the Akan people, children are frequently given names based upon the day of the week they are born and their birth order. In a naming ceremony when they are eight days old, children are also given an "ideal name," usually the name of a beloved relative, like a grandparent, who should be their ideal in life. The first president of Ghana, **Kwame Nkruma**, was named for being born on a Saturday (Kwame) and as the ninth child (Nkrumah). Former secretary general of the U.N., **Kofi Atta Annan,** was named for being born on a Friday (Kofi) and as a twin (Atta). This naming practice is popular around Ghana and with some other peoples in West Africa.

What might your name be if you had been born in Ghana?
Research online to learn about more Akan names!

BIRTH ORDER NAMES male/ female (if different)

1st child: Píèsíe	**8th child:** Bótwe
2nd child: Manu/ Máanu	**9th child:** Ákron(m),Nkruma
3rd child: Mensa/ Mansa	**10th child:** Badú/ Badúwa
4th child: Anan/ Anané	**Born after long wait for**
5th child: Num/ Anum	**children:** Nyamekye (gift of God)
6th child: Nsia	**Twin:** Ata/ Ataa
7th child: Asón/ Nsowaa	**Born after twins:** Tawia

H is for Haiti

BAHAMAS & Florida

CUBA

ATLANTIC OCEAN

CAP-HAITIEN

GONAIVES

DOMINICAN REPUBLIC

PORT-AU-PRINCE

JACMEL

JAMAICA

PUERTO RICO

Caribbean Sea

On the Caribbean island

of **HISPANIOLA,**

(Where life is as bright

as a box of **Crayola**)

Lies Haiti beside

its Dominican neighbors,

Two nations, one island

with two distinct flavors.

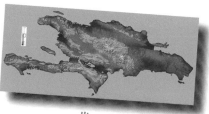

Hispaniola

**Eske
ou pale
Kreyòl?**

Do you speak Haitian Creole?

Their neighbors speak Spanish,

"Hablan Español," [ah-BLAHN ay-spahn-YOHL]

But Haitians prefer to **PALE** [pah-LAY]

in **KREYÒL.** [kree-YOHL]

In Kreyòl they say, "How are you?"

"Sak pase?" [SAHK pah-SAY]

The response is, "I'm burning!"

which is **"MAP BOULE!"** [MAHP boo-LAY]

Though the tropical weather's

quite hot at midday,

Haitians really just mean

that life's going okay.

Columbus

Canoe

When **Columbus** arrived

in **1492,**

This was home to the Tainos, [TIE-nohs]

who rode in **canoes.** *

Hammock

They slept in cool **hammocks** *

and bounced rubber balls.

They ate **barbecued** meats

and saw **HURRICANE** squalls.

Taino Chief Anacoana

* *Canoe, hammock, barbecue* and *hurricane* were all originally Taino words.

Smallpox

But they did not survive

the arrival of Spain,

Whose diseases destroyed them

until none remained.

Cotton

Then French **buccaneers**

claimed the land here for France,

And a colony formed

to grow tropical plants.

Sugarcane

It was named "*Saint Domingue*" [san doh-MING]

and the French brought in **SLAVES**

To grow SUGARCANE, cotton

and coffee they craved.

Coffee

They exported their crops,

and the colony came

To be **RICHER** than any

in all French domain.

By then, slaves outnumbered

the French **TEN TO ONE,**

So they fought for their freedom

until it was won.

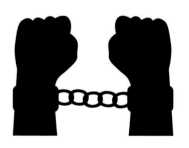

Slave Rebellion

In **1804**

they became a new nation

The **first black republic** –

a brand new creation!

Haitian Coat of Arms

"AYITI" or "*mountainous land*"

it was named.

(The Tainos before them

had called it the same.)

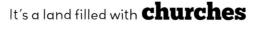

It's a land filled with **churches**

and **VODOU** practitioners,

Where music called **KOMPAS**

calls out to its listeners

Citadelle Laferrière

To sway hips and to dance

all throughout Haiti's hills,

where a **CITADELLE** rises

and ***waterfalls*** spill.

Bassin Bleu Waterfall

Port-au-Prince is the capital,

where you can ride

On a colorful **TAP TAP**

to see sights citywide:

Tap Tap

Cap Haitian Cathedral

Beaded Vodou Flag

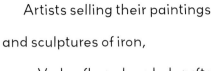

Artists selling their paintings

and sculptures of iron,

Vodou flags, beaded crafts –

all in bustling environs.

Gourde

There are churches and museums

and markets galore,

Where you'll spend all your **gourdes**

till you're too hungry for –

Griot

Fried pork that's called **griot** [gree-yoh]

or kabrit (goat meat).

That's all served with a hot sauce

that's called **Ti Malice.** [tee mah-LEES-s]

Ti Malice

And of course there's the staple

of **BEANS AND WHITE RICE**,

For dessert, **pain patate** [pah pah-TAHT]

has a sweet touch of spice!

Sweet Potato
"Pain Patate"

So come get a taste

of this nation's sweet flavor;

From **beaches** to culture

there's so much to savor.

Haiti's Caribbean Blue Water

Though Haiti has suffered

from poverty's bane,

through **HURRICANES**, **earthquakes**

and **DICTATORS'** reigns,

Its history is one

of survival and **PRIDE**

In their strength and their spirit

of **JOY** nationwide.

This Caribbean **black pearl**

still remains a rare treasure,

Our **H** is for **HAITI**,

where smiles are forever.

**Black Pearl
Haiti's Nickname**

Bonjou!*

**Sea Angel Sculpture Made By
Haitian Artist**

*__Bonjou__ [bon-JJU] means "Hello" in Kreyòl.

The **Haitian coat of arms** is in the center of their flag. A royal palm tree symbolizes their independence. → It is topped with the "cap of liberty" symbolizing how their freedom from slavery came from their independence. The band of weapons surrounding the palm is their determination to defend that independence. Their motto at the bottom is "La union fait la force" meaning "unity makes strength."

HAITI comes from the Taino word, "Ayiti," meaning "mountainous land." The Taino were the native peoples living in Hispaniola and other parts of the Caribbean when Columbus arrived.

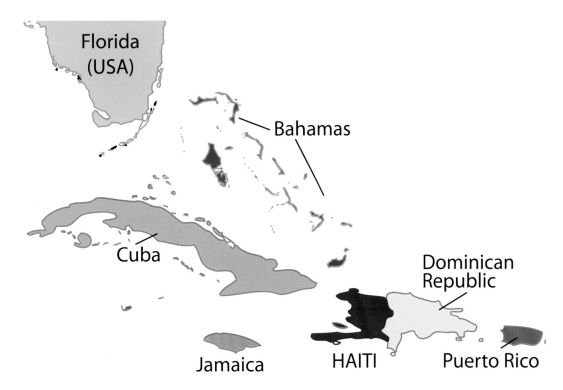

Haiti and Its Neighbors

Official Name:
Republic of Haiti

Population: 10 million

Capital: Port-Au-Prince

Largest Cities:
Port-au-Prince, Jacmel, Cap-Haitian

Comparative Size:
Slightly smaller than Maryland

Ethnicity: Black 95%, mulatto and white 5%

Language: Creole, French

Religion: Christian 96% (Mainly Roman Catholic), Vodou is also practiced by about half of the population

Currency:
Haitian gourde

Where in the World is Haiti?

GEOGRAPHICAL NOTES

◉ Haiti and the Dominican Republic share the island of **Hispaniola**.

◉ Hispaniola, Cuba, Jamaica and Puerto Rico make up a group of islands called the **Greater Antilles**, which contain 90% of the land in the **Caribbean** or the "West Indies."

◉ The **West Indies** are a string of islands located between the Caribbean Sea and the Atlantic Ocean that stretch from Florida to Venezuela. They were named the "West Indies" because when Columbus first landed here in 1492, he thought he had reached the "Indies," or the Pacific islands of Asia.

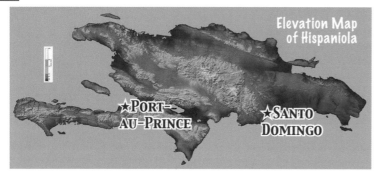

Elevation Map of Hispaniola

★PORT-AU-PRINCE ★SANTO DOMINGO

↑ Columbus encountered the island of **Hispaniola** on his first voyage to the Americas in 1492. There he met **Taino** people whom he described as peaceful and happy. He called them "Indians" as he believed he had reached islands off the coast of South Asia.

← The western third of **Hispaniola** is the Republic of Haiti, and the rest of the island makes up the Dominican Republic. The **Dominican Republic** was once a Spanish colony called "Santo Domingo," which is now the name of their capital. Haiti was colonized by the French and called "Saint Domingue." Though both nations are mountainous, Haiti has much less flat land than the Dominican Republic. ↓

Haiti's Hills

Canoe

Hammock

↑ *Did you know you speak Taino?* The Taino language gave us the words **hammock, hurricane, barbecue, tobacco** and **canoe**. The Taino slept in hammocks, barbecued meat and used canoes to get around the island. They also played a game similar to basketball with two teams, a bouncy ball and a rectangular court. →

Taino Chief Anacaona

Dominican girls dressed up as Taino for a festival. Taino lived on many islands in the Caribbean including Cuba and Puerto Rico. Many people in the Caribbean claim some Taino ancestry. ↓

↑ The native Taino people had no resistance to the epidemic diseases of Europe such as **smallpox**, influenza and typhus. Between 80–90% of the population of Taino died within 25 years of Columbus's arrival. Later famines and enforced servitude eventually wiped out the entire population. Some Taino had intermarried with Europeans and Africans; their descendants live on.

Smallpox

Eske ou pale Kreyòl?

Do you speak Haitian Creole?

↑ Haiti has two **official languages**: French and Haitian Creole or *Kreyòl*. Traditionally, most Haitians spoke **Kreyòl** but were taught in French at school. French was also the language used for newspapers and official documents. Kreyòl is the descendent of a marriage between French and several West African languages. Today, it is becoming more common in schools to learn in Kreyòl first and then learn French as a separate language. →

Student

Caribbean Blue Waters

↑ Haiti's climate is **tropical**. At sea level, Port-au-Prince has average temperatures that range from 73°–88°F (23°–31°C) in January and 77°–95°F (25–35°C) in July. Up in Haiti's hills, the weather is usually about 10°F cooler.

Saint Domingue became France's richest foreign holding due to its exports of sugarcane, indigo, cotton and coffee. They brought thousands of African slaves to farm huge plantations of these crops. The conditions were incredibly grim – the average slave lived only 30 years. However, Saint Domingue continued to grow its slave population until its ratio of slaves to free people was more than ten to one. Slaves in rebellion eventually overthrew their French masters and former slaves declared their own republic. →

Indigo

Coffee

Sugarcane

Cotton

Toussaint Louverture → was the leader of the Haitian Revolution, successfully freeing slaves, pushing out the French and later British forces, and eventually fighting the Spanish to take over all of Hispaniola. He reconciled with France when they abolished slavery in the French Empire and became governor of the French protectorate of Saint Domingue. But France sought to regain full control of Saint Domingue and they betrayed Louverture, kidnapping him in 1802 and taking him to a French prison, where he died.

The **Marron Inconnu →** or the "unknown runaway slave" is a monument near the National Palace in Port-au-Prince. The slave is depicted with a broken chain at his ankle, a machete in his hand and blowing a conch shell as a call to arms for all slaves to fight together for freedom and independence. Haiti is the only example of a nation formed from a successful slave rebellion.

San Souci Palace

← Palais San Souci was a huge palace surrounded by gardens built by Henri Christophe. Now lying in ruins, it was once termed the "Versailles of the Caribbean."

← Jean Jacques Dessalines was the first leader of independent Haiti. After Louverture was taken to prison in France, Dessalines lead Haitian forces in successfully defending the land from an invasion by Napoleon's army and declared Haiti's full independence from France in 1804. He named himself Emperor Jaques I of Haiti. Dessalines was assassinated by rivals in 1806.

Dessalines

Henri Christophe was the first and only king of Haiti. After Dessalines was killed, Haiti became split between two governments: in the south, a republic run by Alexandre Pétion, and in the north, a kingdom ruled by Christophe. Elected president in 1807, Christophe made himself King Henry I of Haiti in 1811 and established a hereditary European-style monarchy in which his son would be the next king. He built Citadel Laferrière and Palace San Souci, as well as six chateaux and seven other palaces. He also created a Haitian nobility with princes, dukes, barons and knights. (cont.→)

King Henry I

(← cont.) His reign was not entirely popular, and after King Henry and his son died in 1820, the Haitian monarchy ended. President **Alexandre Pétion** tried for a more egalitarian form of government in the south, but his republic struggled economically. He famously provided vital support to fellow revolutionary, Simon Bolivar, (on the condition that he abolish slavery) as he led many South American nations to independence from Spain. After the death of King Henry, northern Haiti and southern Haiti were reunited under President Boyer, the successor to Pétion.

President Pétion

Almost all Haitians are **Christians**, with 80% of the population Catholic ➔ and 16% Protestant. About half of the population also practices Vodou. **Vodou** is a religion brought over with slaves from West Africa and then melded with Christian beliefs. Vodou believes that the world is filled with spirits. In the visible world, there are human spirits. But in the invisible world there are spirits of ancestors, angels, the recently deceased and Iwa. **Lwa** are spirits given power by the one almighty god, *Bondye* (meaning "good God"). Bondye is unreachable by humans, so believers appeal to his servants, the Iwa, for aid. There are dozens of Iwa responsible for agriculture, love, health, death, etc. Lwa became associated with various saints once the population converted to Christianity. During Vodou religious ceremonies, Iwa may briefly possess a believer in order to give a message to humans. The most well-known Iwa is Papa Legba, who is the gatekeeper to the spirit world. He is called on at the beginning of each Vodou ceremony to ask permission to communicate with the spirits.

Cap-Haitian Cathedral

Vodou Flag

↑ *Vodou drapo flags depict Iwa using their symbols. This drapo flag represents Loko Atison, the Iwa of Vodou priests, plants and healing.*

Sculpture

Bassin Bleu

← In its hills, Haiti has a number of **waterfalls** where visitors can swim. *Bassin Bleu* is a site with several falls that is famous for its blue water made by naturally occurring minerals in its pools.

← *Haitian artists are famous for their metal sculptures and those made from recycled items. This is a sea angel made from a recycled steel drum.*

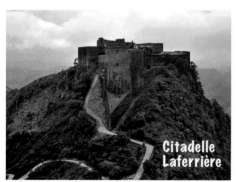

Tap tap

↑ **Tap taps** are the most popular way to ➔ get around in Haiti. They are private buses decorated with colorful pictures and slogans. Tap taps have a driver and an assistant who calls out the route and collects money from passengers. When passengers want to get off, they just "tap tap" on the metal body of the bus, so the driver will know to stop. Tap taps have set routes but not set schedules; they only take off when they are full of passengers. They let people off and pick up more passengers on their way.

Tap tap

Gourdes, or *goud* in Kreyòl, are the currency in Haiti. This 250 gourde note (*desan sekant goud*) features Jean Jacques Dessalines, the first leader of independent Haiti. The 20 gourde coin features Francoise Mackendall, the leader of a slave rebellion. Each gourde can be divided into 100 centimes, or *santim* in Kreyòl. ↓

Citadelle Laferrière

← In order to defend Haiti from French invasion (and the reenslavement of its people), Henri Christophe began work on **Citadelle Laferrière** in 1805, just after Haiti won its independence. A feat of military architecture, it is the largest fortress in the Americas, with walls over 130 feet high and 365 cannons. It was designed with water cisterns and a food storage capacity able to house up to 5,000 people for a full year. Located 28 kilometers from Cap Haitian, it sits atop a 3,000 foot peak, so you can see the Atlantic Ocean (and possible invaders) from its high walls. Citadelle Laferrière was never tested by invasion but stands as a symbol of Haiti's fight for independence and freedom.

Griot

← **Pork griot** is a favorite dish in Haiti. Pork cubes are marinated for hours in citrus, boiled until tender and then pan fried. It is usually served with fried smashed plantains, rice and beans and a spicy cabbage salad known as *pikliz*.

Pain Patate

← This **sweet potato desert** is actually called *pain patate* [pan pah-TAHT] in Haiti or "sweet potato bread." Made with sweet potato, banana, condensed milk, coconut milk and spices, it's delicious!

Ti Malice is the most → popular condiment in Haiti. A savory, sour, hot sauce, it can be served warm over meat, fish or rice. The sauce is named for a trickster character, Ti Malice, who didn't want to share his food so he covered it with hot sauce. But his friend Bouki loved the sauce most of all and couldn't resist it.

Ti Malice

Though Haiti has had more than its share of → natural disasters and hardships, the **Haitian spirit** remains strong and joyful. It is not that Haitians are accepting of life's difficulties; they know that like their founding fathers, they must struggle to overcome the conditions that oppress the Haitian people. But Haitians do not believe that these hardships are a reason to stop celebrating the joys of life – family, friendship, faith, music, dance, art and folklore.

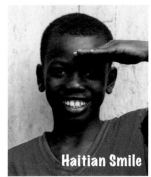
Haitian Smile

After the Earthquake

← *Haiti's National Palace before and after the earthquake. Much larger than the White House, it is home to the president of Haiti and presidential offices.* ↓

↑ The **2010 Earthquake** in Haiti killed over 200,000 people and destroyed much of southern Haiti's infrastructure, especially in the cities of Port-au-Prince and Jacmel. Rebuilding these cities with new earthquake-resistant homes, businesses and government buildings will be a priority for the Haitian government for many years. →

National Palace

← Walking to school though the bustling streets of Cap-Haitian, passing by motorcycle taxis and food stands. Almost all Haitian students wear school uniforms.

Cap-Haitian Students

Why is Haiti a "poor" country?
Before its independence, Saint Domingue was the richest of all French colonies due to its large slave plantations that cheaply grew tobacco, sugarcane, indigo, cotton and coffee and exported them for a large profit. Today, Haiti is the poorest country in the Western Hemisphere. Why? While there is not one simple answer, the international community played a large role in making Haiti poor. After its independence, other countries refused to recognize Haiti or trade with it, fearing Haiti's example was a danger to their own slave-based societies. Haiti's export-driven economy was at a standstill. Haiti was even blockaded by French ships, making it impossible to trade. This continued until 1825 when Haiti agreed to French demands to be paid for their "lost property." Essentially, Haitians had to pay for their own freedom from slavery and the cost was extremely high. Haiti was forced to borrow from a French bank a sum of 90 million francs (equal to $12.7 billion today). The interest rates were very high, and Haiti did not finish paying off this debt until 1947. This severe financial strain on the small Haitian government took money that could have otherwise been used for roads, schools and rebuilding the Haitian economy. This is just one of multiple incidents in which the international community caused Haiti economic hardship.

Listen to the SOUNDS of HAITI

Compas Music

Suggested Songs:

"Ooh La La," by **Sweet Micky**, also known today as Haitian President Michel Martelly. This is the biggest hit from the 1980s for this singer turned president.

"Vive Kompa Direk" by Nemours Jean Baptiste, the father of Haitian Compas.

DON'T MISS WATCHING (online)

Haitian Gestures There are many unique Haitian hand gestures that are essential to nonverbal communication there. Haiti Hub has fun videos that teach the gestures. **YOUTUBE SEARCH:** Haiti gestures

Haiti Tap Tap There are several short documentaries that will take you on a ride on a Haitian tap tap and let you see how they are decorated. **YOUTUBE SEARCH:** Haiti tap tap

Haitian Revolution History Lesson Khan Academy has a wonderful video about the Haitian Revolution and its connection to the French Revolution and world history. It introduces all of Haiti's founding fathers. **YOUTUBE SEARCH:** Haitian Revolution Khan Academy

Have a Haitian Storytelling Party!

Krik? **Krak!**

In Haiti, when someone wants to tell a story, they say, **"Krik?"** and if their their audience wants to hear it, they respond **"Krak!"** In the evenings, friends and family get together to visit and they tell stories to entertain each other. Everyone tells stories, from young to old. Some stories are so popular that their teller may be asked to tell them again and again over the years, each time a little differently.

Read Diane Wolkstein's collection of Haitian folktales (in the READ section) and pick one to tell yourself. Or, pick a story you already know and love. First, try retelling the story in your own words. Then practice, and make it your own by adding in details, hand gestures, dramatic pauses, sound effects or funny facial expressions to make the story fun.

SPEAK HAITIAN KREYÓL!

Bonjou!	Good day	Bon-JU
Bonswa!	Good evening!	Bon-SWAH
Mesi	Thank you	MEH-see
Merite	You're welcome	MAIR-ee-tay
Souple	Please	SU-play
Komon ou ye?	How are you?	COM-mon oo yeh
Sak pase?	What's up? (slang)	sahk pah-SAY
Map Boule	I'm fine	mahp boo-LAY

Dye mon, gen mon. Beyond the mountains, more mountains.
Behind each challenge, there will always be more challenges.

Tout moun, se moun. Everyone is someone.
Every person deserves to be treated as a fellow human being.

Si travay te bon bagay, moun rich la pran-l lontan.
If work were such a good thing, rich people would've taken it long ago.

Bondye bon. God is good. *God willing. God's will is good.*

READ:

Tap-Tap by Karen Lynn Williams. Sasifi proudly walks to the market with her mother, but she longs to ride on a tap tap. Ages 5 & up.

Eight Days: A Story of Haiti by Edwidge Danticat. Trapped in the rubble of Haiti's 2010 earthquake, a small boy imagines he is playing his favorite games with his friends and family. A beautiful story about the power of imagination. Ages 5 & up.

Sélavi: That Is Life: A Haitian Story of Hope by Youme Landowne. A homeless boy in Port-au-Prince finds a community of street kids and a home. Ages 6 & up.

The Magic Orange Tree and Other Haitian Folktales by Diane Wolkstein. A collection of 27 folktales and how they were told by Haitians storytellers. Ages 7 & up.

Behind the Mountains by Edwidge Danticat. Told as a diary filled with Kreyòl and daily Haitian life, a young Haitian girl immigrates to the US. Ages 10 & up.

Anacaona: Golden Flower, Haiti 1490 by Edwidge Danticat. From the Royal Diaries series, a Taino princess survives the arrival of the Spanish in Hispaniola. Ages 9 & up.

A Taste of Salt: A Story of Modern Haiti by Frances Temple. Two teenagers tell of growing up in the firestorm of Haitian politics and working for change. Sprinkled with Kreyòl, the book is both captivating and brutally honest. Ages 12 & up.

MAKE HAITIAN
Pain Patate

Though called "sweet potato bread," pain patate has more of the texture of a dessert bar. Haitians use white sweet potatoes called *boniatos*, but orange sweet potatoes or yams also work. Sweet, spicy and just heavenly – it can be served warm or cold, with whipped cream, ice cream or just plain.

2 lbs. sweet potatoes, peeled & shredded
1 ripe banana
¾ cup brown sugar
2 teaspoons cinnamon
½ teaspoon salt
1 teaspoon nutmeg
1 teaspoon vanilla extract
1 teaspoon ginger (freshly grated or ground)
¼ teaspoon ground clove or 3 cloves crushed
Zest of 1 lemon or lime
1 can coconut milk
1 can evaporated milk (unsweetened)
⅓ cup raisins (optional)
½ cup shredded coconut (optional)

1. Use a vegetable peeler to peel the sweet potatoes.

2. Use a food processor to shred the potatoes or grate them by hand for a very good workout. Place them in a mixing bowl.

3. Preheat oven to 375°.

4. Add ripe banana to potatoes and mash together, mixing fully.

5. Add remaining ingredients, one by one, making sure to stir each one in as you go.

6. Butter a 9 x 13 inch pan generously.

7. Pour in mixture and bake for 90 minutes or until a toothpick inserted in the center comes out clean.

MAKE A Haitian Sequined Art Flag

Drapo flags were originally made to represent Vodou lwa in rituals. (See page 102.) However, the global market for Haitian beaded flags has grown so much that artists have started to produce flags that are purely art with no religious theme. Try making your own flag. Any theme or color background will do – a city skyline, under the sea, an animal, a king.

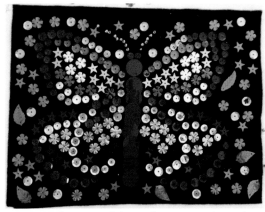

A combination of glue and sewing can be used. The butterfly's beaded antenna were easier to sew.

METHOD: Drapo flags are sewn and if you have a lot of time and dexterity you can actually sew your sequins or beads in place. The easiest method with sequins is to use glue, putting a big dot of glue on the fabric, then adding the sequin on top. Once you have all of the sequins in place, leave your flag to dry overnight before you move it. Beaded parts are best done sewing 1–2 beads per stitch.

MATERIALS: Glue: Elmer's glue works fine, as does glitter glue and tackier craft glue. **Sequins:** Larger sequins are useful for covering a larger canvas. If you use smaller sequins, you might want to work with a smaller piece of fabric. **Flag Material:** For a fabric flag, use a 13 x 9 inch piece of felt of any color. Or, use thick stock colored paper.

STEPS: Lightly outline a simple design in pencil or chalk, then cover it in sequins. Once you've laid out your design, glue down the sequins.

OTHER POSSIBILITIES:

Combine glitter paint with sequins. Rather than cover the whole surface with sequins, use them only as embellishment.

Use recycled materials: Haitian art is known for recycling materials to make art. Metal bottle caps or aluminum can tabs are possibilities to replace sequins – look through your recycling and see what you find!

Outline a basic design first in pencil or chalk

MATERIALS:
sequins
glue
13 x 9 inch felt or
  card stock paper

Optional Materials:
craft gems
glitter pens/ paint
beads
dowel to hang flag

I is for India

PAKISTAN

Indus River

CHINA

HIMALAYAS

NEPAL

BHUTAN

NEW ☆ DELHI

Ganges River

BANGLADESH

▲ Taj Mahal

◉ AHMEDABAD

KOLKATA (CALCUTTA)* ◉

BURMA (MYANMAR)

Arabian Sea

MUMBAI (BOMBAY)* ◉

Bay of Bengal

HYDERABAD ◉

The State of GOA ◎

BENGALURU (BANGALORE)* ◉

◉ CHENNAI (MADRAS)*

SRI LANKA

INDIAN OCEAN

*The former English names of cities are written in parentheses.

Asian Elephant

Bengal Tiger

Our I is incredible **INDIA,**

a subcontinent teeming with life.

Here religions and languages multiplied,

making **DIVERSITY** rife.

Here where forests have *TIGERS* and **ELEPHANTS,**

and cities grow sweet MANGO trees,

We'll be welcomed with palms pressed together

and cups of milky spice tea.

Chai

Namaste

Here we'll hike in the high **HiMALAYAS**

and visit a village remote.

We'll sun on Goa's fine beaches

then down the **GANGES** we'll float.

We'll pretzel our bodies with YOGa

and listen to long chants of **O-O-O-O-om.**

We will find so much to enthrall us,

wherever we wander and roam!

Yoga

Autorickshaw

In the cities we'll eat **spicy curries,**

then ride on an **autorickshaw.**

We'll see monkeys and cows on the roadside

and tourists just staring in awe.

Indipop Star Miss Pooja

For India **floods** the senses

with colors and smells strong and sweet,

the sway of hypnotic music

and **Indipop's** blaring beat.

There are people, **PEOPLE** everywhere,

walking down city streets,

Filling the trains and buses –

there's rarely an empty seat!

Crowded Train Platform

Ganesh

For soon they will overtake China,

and by their size they'll be known.

India today is the nation

that one in six people call home!

Here are temples to Hindu deities,

like the elephant-headed **GANESH**, [guh-NAYSH]

Shiva, the **COSMIC DANCER**,

or **KRISHNA**, the prince with blue flesh.

Dancing Shiva

Krishna

There are so many gods and goddesses

for every power and need –

they make one higher power called **BRAHMAN**,

one infinite being supreme.

Sikh Man

India's also the birthplace

of **Buddhists**, **Sikhs** and **Jains**, [seeks]

With the third-largest **Muslim** population

found in any domain.

Jamii Masjid Mosque
in Delhi

And the Christians here date their history

to **52 CE**.

(Today, there are as many here

as in Portugal, Ireland and Greece!)

The official language of India

differs from state to state.

With over 20 in usage,

there's no shortage of words to translate.

Church in Kerala

Their mother tongues number in hundreds,

and no two are close to the same.

But **ENGLISH** is almost everywhere,

on street signs, billboards and shop names.

Sign in a Bangalore
Museum

The culture and food vary widely

in each of their **28 STATES.**

But they all like to eat with their right hand

from food on their very own plate.

Thali

To the south they eat **RICE** at most mealtimes;

in the north they are fonder of **BREAD**.

But they all like to eat lunchtime **thalis**, [THAH-lees]

and their *sweet tooth* must often be fed.

From the INDUS RIVER CIVILIZATION

to the time of **BUDDHISM'S BIRTH**,

From the reign of the MUGHAL EMPIRE

to the **LARGEST DEMOCRACY ON EARTH**,

Statue from Indus
River Civilization

Buddha

Indian history stretches

over **7,000 YEARS**.

There are too many heights and achievements

to summarize them here.

But I must mention **Gandhi**, their founder,

called **MAHATMA**, which means "**GREAT SOUL.**"

In the forming of modern India,

no one played a larger role.

The Red Fort
A Mughal Palace

Through **NONVIOLENT PROTEST**, he ended

the British Empire's rule.

He taught the world that violence

is not our only tool.

Gandhi

Bollywood Star
Aishwarya Rai

So dance your way to **Mumbai,** [moom-BIGH]

where **BOLLYWOOD** movies are made.

Then go feast your eyes in **Chennai,** [chin-NIGH]

where **SARIS** in rainbows parade.

And you must tour the TAJ MAHAL,

which is sure to awe and delight.

It's as ornate as India's essence,

its flavors, sounds and sights.

Taj Mahal

Namaste!*

*__Namaste__ [nah-MAH-stay] is a Hindi greeting meaning "I bow to the divine in you."

India has two official names within the country: India and Bharat. →
INDIA, its English name, comes from the Indus River. The Indus River is also the source of the word Hindu, India's dominant religion, and Hindi, its most spoken language. **Bharat** is the nation's name in Hindi.

India or *Bharat* written in Hindi

↑ India's flag
was adopted in 1947 when they won their independence from the British Empire. The saffron stripe represents courage and sacrifice, the white is for purity and truth, and the green is for fertility and faith. In the center is the Ashoka Chakra or the "Wheel of Dharma," which represents the rule of virtue and the eternal wheel of law.

Official Name:
Republic of India

Local Name:
Bharat or India

Population: 1.2 billion

Capital: New Delhi

Largest Cities:
Mumbai, Delhi, Bangalore, Hyderabad, Ahmedabad

Comparative Size:
The 7th-largest country, slightly more than a third the size of the United States

Languages: Hindi, Bengali, Telugu, Marathi, Tamil, Urdu, Gujarati, Kannada, Mayalayam, Oriya, Punjabi, Assamese, Kashmiri, Sindhi and Sanskrit

Religion: Hindu 80%, Muslim 14%, Christian 2.5%, Sikh 2%

Currency: Indian rupee

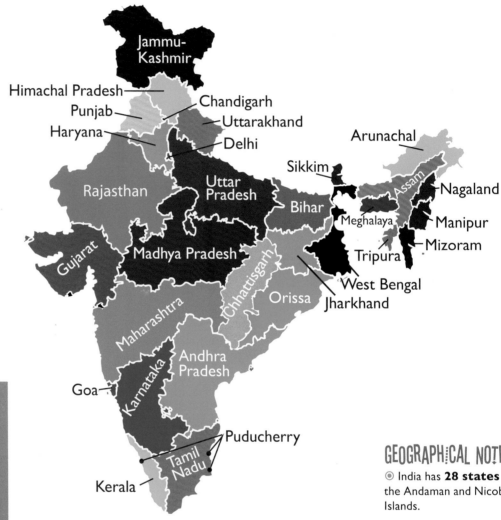

Indian States

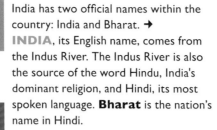

Where in the World is India?

GEOGRAPHICAL NOTES

◉ India has **28 states** and the Andaman and Nicobar Islands.

◉ Prior to **Partition** in 1947, India included the land that is now Pakistan and Bangladesh, two predominantly Muslim countries.

◉ Many Indian cities have **changed their names** since India gained its independence in 1947. (The old names are included in parentheses on the map page 106.) The new names typically have a more Indian origin or pronunciation, as opposed to the names used by the British and Portuguese Empires.

Map of Languages in India

Kashmiri
Punjabi
Khasi &Garo
Ao
Nissi & Daffla
Mizo

Oriya
Bengali
Assamese
Manipuri

Hindi
Gujarati
Marathi
Konkani
Telugu

Kannada
Malayalam
Tamil

The **Royal Bengal Tiger** is India's national animal. Though endangered, there are over 2,000 in the wild of India. The greatest concentration is found in the foothills of the Himalayas in India and Nepal. Tigers are the world's largest cats, and most of the world's tigers live in India. ➜

Bengal Tiger

Asian Elephant

← India is home to more **Asian elephants** than any other country with over 20,000 left in the wild. Asian elephants are smaller than African elephants and have smaller ears. Elephants are a popular part of Indian culture, appearing in festivals and religious ceremonies.

↑ There are over **400 languages** spoken in India. Thirty of them have more than one million speakers each. Hindi is the most widely used native language, spoken by about 40% of the population. English and Hindi are the official languages of the union of Indian states, but each state has its own official languages. Some Indians who are not native Hindi speakers prefer English as a second language. English is widely spoken in all parts of India.

Mango Tree

← The **mango** originates in India and is India's national fruit. Mangoes are now grown in tropical countries around the world, but India is still the largest producer. Mangoes are used both ripe and unripe to make chutneys (salsas), pickles, jellies, mango lassi and hundreds of other dishes.

Chai

Tea or **chai** is the favorite beverage ↑ in India. It is traditionally made with black tea, milk, sugar and a mix of spices like ginger, cardamom, cinnamon, cloves and pepper. It is called *masala chai,* which means mixed-spice tea. Chai is served from morning to evening and is commonly offered to guests.

Cricket

Namaste

↑ **Cricket** was brought to India by the British. It is now the most popular sport in India, and the nation has won several world championships, including the Cricket World Cup. Traditional cricket games called "test matches" can last several days.

← "Namaste" (nah-MAH-stay) is a popular greeting in Hindi. It means, "I bow to the divine in you," which is a traditional salutation among Hindus. It is customary to press your palms together and bow your head slightly when saying it. *Can you say Namaste properly?*

Himalayas

Goa's beaches on the Arabian Sea are very ➔ popular for holidays in India. Goa was formerly a Portuguese overseas territory called "Portuguese India." As a result, there is a mix of Portuguese and Indian architecture there, including many churches. About 25% of all Goans are Christian.

Beach in Goa

← The **Himalayan Mountains** contain all the world's peaks above 8,000 feet. The Himalayas run along India's border with Nepal, China and Bhutan.

The **Ganges River,** or *Ganga* as it is known ➔ in Hindi, is sacred to Hindus. A bath in the Ganges River is believed to remove all sins. Many Hindus make a pilgrimage to visit the Ganges at **Varanasi,** one of Hinduism's most holy cities. The Ganges is also thought of as the "mother of India"; its delta is one of the most fertile and densely populated areas on Earth. The Ganges River originates in the Himalayas and empties at the Bay of Bengal near Kolkata.

Ganges River

Varanasi

Yoga

Om, *ohm* or *aum* is a sacred syllable used in Hinduism, ➔ Sikhism, Buddhism and Jainism. Om has many different meanings. In Hinduism, om is believed to have been the first sound, the first vibration from which the world was created. Before om, there was nothing. Om has continued uninterrupted in the eternal vibration of the universe, its creation, movement and destruction. To chant "om" is to recognize the presence of God, the divine vibration, in all things including oneself. Om is usually chanted before and after reading Hindu scripture. Yoga practitioners also may chant "om" at the beginning and end of practice to recognize they are one with the movement of all creation. The om symbol often represents Hinduism in the same way that a cross represents Christianity.

OM written in Hindi

↑ **Yoga** is an ancient Hindu philosophy that uses mental and physical exercises to center the spirit and free it from the material world with the goal of union with the divine. The physical practice of yoga has become a popular form of exercise around the world and is known for helping people to become more flexible, strong, relaxed, focused and energetic.

Peacock

← The **peacock** or peafowl is the national bird of India, and it can be seen roaming wild in the countryside. Only the male is called a peacock and has such elaborate plumage. He uses it to attract female peahens.

The **lotus** is the national flower of India. It is a symbol of purity and known for growing up out of the mud but remaining unstained. ↓

Jasmine

← It is popular for women in southern India to wear strings of fresh **jasmine** blossoms in their hair. Besides being beautiful for many hours, the wonderful scent of jasmine follows them everywhere they go.

Lotus

← **Curry** is a term first used by the British to describe savory South Asian dishes made with a mix of spices. The word curry probably comes from the Tamil word *kari,* which means "sauce."

← Cycle rickshaws or pedicabs are available in most Indian cities. They are not very fast, but they are quiet and very pleasant if you are going a short distance or are not in a great hurry.

Autorickshaw taxis are the quickest and easiest way to get around most Indian cities. They are better at weaving through bad traffic than cars and their natural air conditioning keeps you comfortable. ↓

When British colonialists wanted to take Indian recipes back to Britain, Indians developed spice mixes they could take with them called "curry powder." **Curry powder** can include turmeric, cumin, cayenne pepper, coriander, cardamom, ginger, fenugreek, mustard and other spices. Today, Indians have adopted the term "curry." But, the recipes for chicken, fish or vegetable curry vary widely from state to state and even family to family. →

Curry Powder

Autorickshaw

Sitar

Indian popular music or **Indipop** has many different styles that reflect a mix of classical and folk Indian music with modern musical genres like hip hop and R&B. Often it uses classical Indian instruments like the **sitar**. One style that has become popular worldwide is **Bhangra**. Bhangra dancing originated in the state of Punjab in India. Bhangra music originated with Pujabi immigrants to the United Kingdom. There are now Indian Bhangra artists like Miss Pooja who are popular around the world. ↓

Cow on a City Street

Monkeys in Delhi

← Why are **cows** and **monkeys** allowed to roam around Indian cities? Within Hinduism, the cow, the elephant and the monkey are sacred, so hurting them is avoided if possible. Many people even feed them in honor of the gods. Many Hindus are vegetarians, but even those that eat meat are less likely to eat beef. Cows are seen as the mother of civilization. Their milk provided a steady diet of yogurt, cheese and the protein needed for a settled life. Cows also helped to till fields for farming, and their dung was used for fertilizer and as fuel for fires. Lord Krishna, a Hindu god, was a cowherd, and cows are also not killed out of respect for him. There is a monkey god named Hanuman, and the god Ganesh has the head of an elephant. As symbols of the divine, all are treated with respect.

Miss Pooja

Indian traffic is noisy due to lots → of horn blowing. It is considered polite to let cars beside you know that you are there by honking the horn. Similarly, if drivers wish to pass someone, they honk to let them know they're coming. Many trucks encourage this practice with signs on the back reading "**Horn OK Please**." They believe this practice helps to prevent car accidents.

Crowded Train Platform

← It is estimated that India's population will exceed China's in 2025, making India the world's largest nation. Currently, Indians make up about 18% of world population.

Unlike Christianity, Islam or Judaism, → there is not one special day of the week for going to **Hindu temples**. The Hindu calendar has many special days that follow the cycle of the moon. Hindus may pray or *make puja* at home, in sacred places like the Ganges River or at temples. ↓

Hindu Temple

Ganesh, the god with an elephant head, is one of the most popular gods in the Hindu pantheon. He is known as the "Remover of Obstacles" and "Lord of Beginnings and Obstacles." Many people ask Ganesh for his blessing whenever they are starting any new business, project or stage in life. He is known for being able to remove obstacles and also for being able to place obstacles in front of those who need to be stopped. ↓

Offerings Prayers on the Ganges

Krishna is an incarnation of the god Vishnu, and a very popular member of the Hindu pantheon. (For more about Vishnu, see "Hinduism Q & A" on page 123.) Krishna is traditionally depicted with blue flesh and often he is playing the flute or dancing. Krishna is seen as a model of divine love and joy. Through love of ← Krishna (God), believers are able to overcome all pain and sin. ↓

Ganesh

Krishna

Krishna & Radhika

Shiva is frequently depicted → as Nataraja or "lord of the dance." He dances on top of the demon of ignorance, whirling in a circle with his hair spinning out. In his right hand is the kettle drum of creation, in his left hand is the fire of destruction. The second right hand has the palm up facing out in a "stop" sign, symbolizing "fear not," protection and peace. The last hand is pointing down toward the raised left foot, symbolizing liberation from the cycle of death and rebirth.

Shiva Nataraja

← Why are Hindu gods often represented with many arms or heads?
Each arm usually represents a different power of that god. The point of depicting a god with four or even twelve arms is not that the god necessarily has that many limbs but that they simultaneously hold that many powers. Many faces may represent a god's many roles or incarnations.

Jama Masjid (Friday Mosque) in Delhi

← **Muslims** have a long and glorious history in India. They were the founders of the **Mughal Empire**, which ruled much of India and Pakistan in the 16th to 17th centuries, and was responsible for building the Taj Mahal and other beautiful palaces, mosques and forts. Before Pakistan and Bangladesh divided themselves from India to create separate Muslim countries during Partition (1947), Muslims made up 25% of India's population. Today, Muslims are just 13%. Muslim Indians generally greet each other with some variant of "salaam" or "peace."

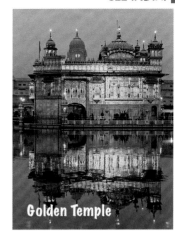

Golden Temple

Though **Christians** →
are only 2% of the Indian population, there are as many Christians in India as in the nations of Portugal, Ireland and Greece combined. Indians were some of the first people to convert to Christianity with the arrival of the Apostle Thomas, also known as "doubting Thomas" in the Bible.

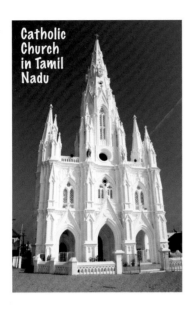

Catholic Church in Tamil Nadu

Sikh Man

← The **Sikh religion** was ↑ founded in late 15th century and one of its most important shrines is the Golden Temple in Amritsar, India. Sikhs are known for not cutting their hair in order to reject human vanity. The men wear a turban in order to tie up their long hair. Sikhs believe in tolerance for other religions, equality among all men, universal brotherhood and one supreme god. Sikhs should "work diligently and honestly, meditate on God's holy name and share the fruits of their labor with others." Sikhs make up the majority of the population in the state of Punjab.

Lotus Temple

← The **Baha'i** faith believes in the unity of all religions and of all mankind before one God. There are about 2 million Baha'i in India, more than in any other country. Their **Lotus Temple** near Delhi is one of India's most visited tourist sites.

Just as the Middle East was the birthplace of Judaism, Christianity and Islam, India is the birthplace of Hinduism, Buddhism, Sikhism and Jainism, which are all called **Dharmic** Religions.

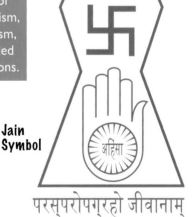

Jain Symbol

परस्परोपग्रहो जीवानाम्

Siddhartha Gautama, or **Buddha,** was →
born between the 6th and 4th century BCE in Lumbini, Nepal. He gained enlightenment in Bihar State in India. For the rest of his life, he spread his teachings in northeastern India and southern Nepal. Buddhism teaches that life is full of suffering caused by desire and delusion. Enlightenment frees people from the ignorance and delusions that create desires; thus enabling them to escape from the cycle of death and rebirth and to reunite with the divine.

Buddha Statue

The **Jain** religion believes in ↑ nonviolence to all living things (this includes being vegetarian), truthfulness, overcoming worldly desires and respect for other religions and viewpoints.
The swastika is an ancient religious symbol in India for Hindus, Jains and Buddhist; it signifies, "to be good."

Thali

A **thali** (THAH-lee) is a plate with a selection of many different dishes with rice and/or bread in the center. Thalis are very popular for lunch in restaurants all over India because they offer a fun variety of foods and flavors. Generally, you can order either a vegetarian or nonvegetarian thali, as about a third of all Indians are vegetarian. Indian food is eaten using only the tips of the fingers of your **right hand**, although spoons are used to eat soups. Sauces are generally poured over rice or scooped up with bread. Unlike in Africa or the Middle East, where sharing platters of food is the norm, each person eats only from their **own plate** as sharing from one plate is considered unhygienic.

Thali

The **Red Fort** or *Lal Qila* was the home of Mughal emperors from 1648 to 1857. Emperor Shah Jahan (who was also responsible for the Taj Mahal and the Jami Masjid) built the Red Fort when he moved his capital from Agra to Delhi. At its height, the Mughal Empire ruled over all of India and sought to create a united nation of Muslims and Hindus. The Mughals still ruled over parts of northern India until they were exiled by the British in 1857. The Mughals are descendents of the Mongols of Central Asia.

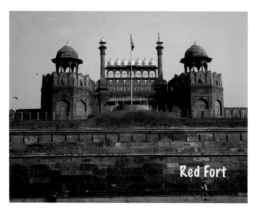

Red Fort

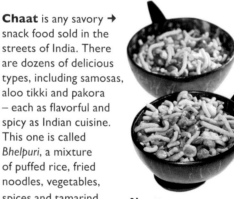

First Decimal Numerals

↑ Indian mathematicians were the first to use a ten numeral system of writing numbers – the decimal numeral system. Through only ten numerals, 0–9, any number could be written. Hindu-Arabic numerals are the basis of the numerals and mathematics we use today. They have long been termed simply "Arabic numerals," as it was Arab traders who first brought them to Europe.

Chaat is any savory snack food sold in the streets of India. There are dozens of delicious types, including samosas, aloo tikki and pakora – each as flavorful and spicy as Indian cuisine. This one is called *Bhelpuri*, a mixture of puffed rice, fried noodles, vegetables, spices and tamarind.

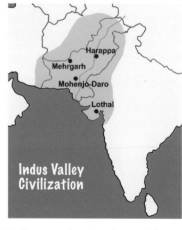

Chaat

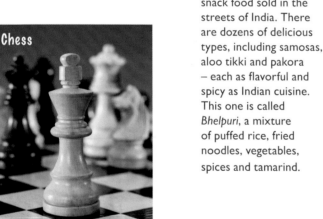

Chess

↑ The game of **chess** first appeared in India in about 600 CE and was originally called *chaturanga*. From India, the game spread to the Middle East and then to Europe and is today played around the world. In the original Indian version of the game, all of the pieces (other than the king) had different names. For example, the queen was the king's minister, the bishop was an elephant or camel, the rook was a boat, the knight was a horse and the pawn was an army.

Indus Valley Civilization

Ancient Indus Valley Statue

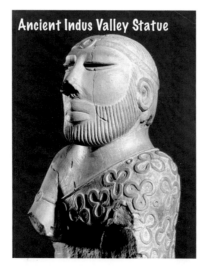

The **Indus River Valley** was the site of one of ↑ the three oldest urban civilizations in the world. (The other two were Mesopotamia and Ancient Egypt.) The Indus Valley Civilization (3300–1300 BCE) covered the largest geographic area of the three. The two largest cities of the city were Mohenjo-Daro and Harappa, which are located in modern day Pakistan. The Indus Valley had the first urban sanitation system. Citizens lived in brick, one or two-story homes and got their water from either private or neighborhood wells. Homes had their own bathrooms with clay pipes that sent wastewater to covered drains that lined major city streets. In Mohenjo-Daro are the remains of what was either a large public pool or a bathhouse. The Indus Valley Civilization also had its own writing system, which has yet to be fully deciphered.

← The "Priest-King" found at Mohenjo-Daro from the Indus Valley civilization dated roughly 2600–2000 BCE.

Gandhi

← Mohandas Gandhi (1869–1948) was the leader of India's independence movement from the British Empire. He pioneered the use of nonviolent protests to demand that Indians be allowed to rule themselves. He was known for being able to bring together Muslims, Hindus, men, women and people of every caste in unity as Indians. He said he preferred nonviolent responses to violence because "an eye for an eye only ends up making the world blind." Indians affectionately called Gandhi "Bapu," or father as the father of their nation, and he was deemed "Mahatma" or "great soul" due to his virtue, self-sacrifice and love for others of all castes and religions. Civil rights leaders from around the world, including Martin Luther King Jr. and Nelson Mandela, were greatly influenced by Gandhi's philosophy.

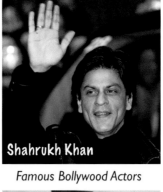
Shahrukh Khan

Famous Bollywood Actors

Aishwarya Rai

← Bollywood is a name for the Hindi movie industry based in Mumbai, a city formerly called Bombay. Outside India, Bollywood is frequently used as a nickname for the entire Indian film industry, but there are many other cities and languages in which Indian films are produced. Together, the Indian film industry is the largest in the world, producing more films per year than any other country. Bollywood movies are known for using dance and songs in their storytelling, as well as elaborate costumes and sets. The typical Indian film is 2.5–3 hours long, so there is usually an intermission in the middle.

Sari

While most Indian men wear Western clothing on a daily basis, most Indian women prefer more traditional Indian dress like **saris, salwar kameez** and **gaghra cholis.**

Salwar Kameez

↑ Women have been wearing **saris** here since 600 BCE. Saris are wrapped from one piece of fabric that is 4–9 meters (13–30 feet) long and are worn over an underskirt and a small coordinated blouse called a *choli*. Cholis typically expose the midriff, which can be a helpful cooling mechanism in hot weather.

The **salwar kameez** was first worn **↑** in the north of the country, particularly Punjab state, and is also called a "Punjabi suit." They are made from a long tunic (kameez), coordinating pants cinched with a drawstring (salwar/ pyjama), and a scarf. Salwar kameez have become increasingly popular all over India for both men and women as they are so comfortable and easy to wear.

Last, the **ghagra choli**, is a **→** blouse (choli), long skirt (ghagra/ lehenga) and scarf that was originally worn by women of Rajasthan and Gujarat.

Ghagra Choli

Mumbai

↑ Mumbai (formerly Bombay) is India's biggest and richest city as well as its commercial and entertainment capital. It is also one of the world's largest cities with over 20 million people living in the metropolitan area. Mumbai's deep natural harbor makes it a major port on the Arabian Sea.

Taj Mahal

↑ The **Taj Mahal** is considered by many to be the most beautiful building in the world. Built (1632-1648) by Mughal Emperor Shah Jahan, it was designed to be a mausoleum for his wife and also became his own tomb. The Taj Mahal is made of carved white marble inlaid with designs in semi-precious stones. The millions of tourists who visit the Taj Mahal every year are all barefoot, both in respect for the tombs and so as not to scratch and dirty the marble.

Listen to the SOUNDS of INDIA

Jana Gana Mana

The national anthem, written and composed by Indian Nobel laureate Rabindrath Tagore, is actually a hymn of praise to God. It begins, "You are the ruler of the minds of all people," then says that God's name is sung with praise throughout India. It ends, "Maker of India's destiny; Victory, victory, victory to thee." A bit like "God Bless America," which asks for God's blessings "from the mountains, to the prairies, to the oceans, white with foam." But "Jana Mana Gana" instead says that God's name "echoes in the hills of the Vindhyas and Himalayas, mingles in the music of Yamuna and Ganga and is chanted by the waves of the Indian Ocean." **YOUTUBE SEARCH:** Jana Gana Mana

Mile Sur Mera Tumhara

Roughly translated as "We All Sing to the Same Tune" or "My Song Is Your Song," "Mile Sur Mera Tumhara" is a song about Indian unity that was recorded in 1988. Sung in Hindi and 13 other Indian languages, the song features stars, musical styles and cultures from all over India. A patriotic song celebrating India's diversity, it is still very popular and played on national holidays. A newer, much longer version came out in 2010, but it was criticized as being less diverse than the original. **YOUTUBE SEARCH:** Mile Sur Mera Tumhara

Sarangi and Sitar

Both Indian instruments are used in classical music from northern India (called Hindustani Music) and in some modern Indian styles including bhangra. The sarangi is a bowed string instrument, something like a violin but with a very different sound. The sitar is a tall plucked string instrument with a long hollow neck. Ravi Shankar (1920–2012), frequently called "Pandit," meaning teacher or scholar, was the most famous sitar player and his daughter Anoushka continues the tradition. There are many other traditional Instruments you might enjoy hearing, including the **tabla** (drums), **pungi** and **jal tarang** (ceramic bowls filled with water). **YOUTUBE SEARCH:** sarangi Sultan Khan, sitar, Ravi Anoushka Shankar raag khamaj, tabla, pungi Rajasthan

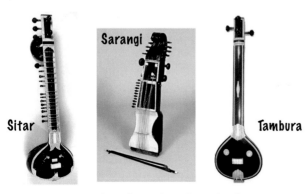

Sitar, Sarangi, and Tambura: three classical Indian string instruments with very different sounds and styles

SOUNDS of INDIA continued...

Tambura & Carnatic Music

Carnatic music is classical music from the south of India. Carnatic music is primarily vocal, and the singer is usually accompanied by a violin, drum and a drone instrument, traditionally a tambura (also spelled tanpura). The drone is a constant throughout the piece and the violin frequently echoes the melody sung. Singing Carnatic music takes many years of training to learn the intricate melodies passed down for hundreds of years. **YOUTUBE SEARCH:** tambura, Yesudas Maha Ganapathim

Filmi Filmi or Film music is the most popular type of music in India, accounting for the vast majority of all music sales. Here are a few recommendations:
"Why This Kolaveri Di?" from the Tamil film *3*
"Chaiyya Chaiyya" from the Hindi film *Dil Se*
"Nuvvastanante" from the Telugu film *Varsham*
"Joy Dugga Thakur" from the Bengali film *Khiladi*
"Om Hindu Guruthu" from the Kannada film *Rajahuli*
"Bellam Belaga" from the Kannada film *Brindavana*
"Sadda Dil Vi Tu" from the Malayalam film *ABCD*
YOUTUBE SEARCH: film name + song name

Other Recommendations:

Miss Pooja's "Menu Tere Jeya" (Punjabi Bhangra)
iQ Guju Bhai's "Gold" (Gujurati Hip Hop)

DON'T MISS WATCHING (online)

How to Play Cricket

Learn the basics of the sport Indians are obsessed with. **YOUTUBE SEARCH:** how to play cricket

The Story of India A six-hour BBC documentary introducing 4,000 years of Indian history with gorgeous cinematography and fascinating stories all the way through. Even watching a small part of the whole is worthwhile. Available to stream or on DVD. PBS also offers program lesson plans. **YOUTUBE SEARCH:** story India

Timeless India Created by India's Ministry of Tourism, "Timeless India" tours many of India's wonders in 24 minutes. Designed more to intrigue the viewer with fascinating scenes than to explain them, it highlights India's vastness. **YOUTUBE SEARCH:** Timeless India.

Welcome to India A 2012 BBC documentary that explores working-class life in modern India in 3 episodes, each an hour long. **YOUTUBE SEARCH:** welcome India

DON'T MISS WATCHING continued...

Bollywood Movies There are an abundance of Bollywood movies with English subtitles, both for kids and adults. *Om Shanti Om* is a 2007 Bollywood extravaganza, with tragedy, romance, humor, a makeover, reincarnation and, of course, several song and dance routines. It has over 40 of Bollywood's biggest stars and makes fun of the industry. Available to stream or on DVD.

Holi Festival See India's most colorful holiday. The Hindu festival of Holi celebrates love, joy, spring and the victory of good over evil with this festival of colors. Watch as all ages hurl colored powders and liquids at one another; no one is immune to becoming a rainbow of different dyes.
YOUTUBE SEARCH: Holi India

Tour the Taj Mahal See India's most famous site and why many consider it the most beautiful building on earth.
YOUTUBE SEARCH: Taj Mahal India

Ramayana There are multiple animated movies that tell the story of the Ramayana, the most famous Indian epic. Rama, his wife, Sita, and their friend Hanuman must fight against the demon, Ravanna, in this action-packed story that is over 2,400 years old. **YOUTUBE SEARCH:** Ramayana

Classical Indian Dance There are many different styles of classical dance coming from different areas and ethnic groups in India. Here are a few of the most well-known styles: **Bharatnatyam** (originating as a South Indian temple dance), **Kathak** (a storytelling dance from North India), **Kathakali** (a form of theater from Kerala with very elaborate makeup and costumes), **Odissi** (from northern India, particularly Orissa), **Manipuri** (from Manipur), **Sattriya** (from Assam), **Kuchipudi** (from Andhra Pradesh).
YOUTUBE SEARCH: (dance style name) dance

Learn How to Make Kolam & Rangoli!

See kolam, the daily folk art made each morning in front of many homes in India. Designs are made with rice powder or chalk to welcome the gods and visitors. Each kolam will be washed away, and a new one is made the next day. Watch the technique, and then try making your own with chalk!
YOUTUBE SEARCH: Friday Kolam Lakshmi, kolam, rangoli

← *Kolam*

Rangoli →

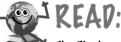

READ:

The Elephant's Friend and Other Tales from Ancient India by Marcia Williams. A collection of short folktales. Ages 5 & up.

Indian Tales by Shenaaz Nanji. A tour around India through traditional tales. Ages 5 & up.

The Little Book of Hindu Deities by Sanjay Patel. Cute cartoon drawings and short introductions to all the major Indian gods and goddesses. Ages 8 & up.

Ramayana: Divine Loophole by Sanjay Patel. A gorgeous introduction to one of India's best known epics. Ages 8 & up.

Rama and the Demon King: An Ancient Tale from India by Jessica Souhani. A tale from the Ramayana, Ages 5 & up.

Gandhi : A March to the Sea by Alice McGinty. A picture book chronicling Gandhi's famous march to the sea to protest British rule and their ban on salt production. Ages 8 & up.

Conch Bearer by Chitra Banerjee Divakaruni. This fantasy series sends a boy on a quest across India with a magic conch shell. Ages 10 & up.

Boys without Names by Kashmira Sheth. Boys fight to escape from their prison, a sweatshop. Ages 9 & up.

No Ordinary Day by Deborah Ellis. The captivating story of a girl who leaves the abuse of a small village to make her way on the streets of Kolkata. Ages 10 & up.

Books by Uma Krishnaswami including:
The Grand Plan to Fix Everything Dini loves Bollywood movies. When her family moves to India for a couple of years, she schemes to meet her favorite star in this comic adventure. Age 9 & up.
Monsoon A child awaits the joyful arrival of monsoon season. Ages 5 & up.
The Happiest Tree: A Yoga Story Ages 5 & up.
Shower of Gold: Girls and Women in the Stories of India Ages 10 & up.

The Gifts of Wali Dad: A Tale of India and Pakistan by Aaron Shepard. A charming Punjabi tale. Ages 7 & up.

One Grain of Rice: A Mathematical Folktale by Demi. With illustrations inspired by Indian miniature paintings, a story of using math to outwit a greedy raja. Ages 5 & up.

Going to School in India by Lisa Haydlauff. From city classrooms to desert tents to train platforms, see all the different places children attend class in India. Ages 8 & up.

The Savage Fortress by Sarwat Chadda. A fantasy adventure series in which a 13 year-old boy must save the world from the demons of Hindu mythology. Ages 12 & up.

MAKE INDIAN
Mango Lassi

Yogurt, mango, ice and sugar. One of the easiest recipes ever, and so deliciously refreshing. Some recipes use more yogurt or more mango, but this one uses equal amounts of both. Experiment and decide what you like best. Sugar should always be added to taste as some mangoes are sweeter than others.

1. Remove skin and seed from mango with this easy method: Cut the two widest sides off of the mango, slicing close to the seed to remove the mangoes "cheeks." Then cut a criss-cross checkerboard in the cheeks, cutting through the flesh but not the skin. Flip the skin inside out and easily pop mango cubes off the skin with your knife.
2. Put all ingredients in blender and blend until smooth. Add sugar to taste and a pinch of cardamom if you like.

2 ripe mangoes
2 cups plain yogurt
1–2 cups ice
sugar to taste

PLAY: KABADDI

Kabaddi is a form of team tag that originated in India and is popular all over South Asia – there is even a Kabaddi World Cup! Kabaddi has two teams of 3–12 players each. It is played on a rectangular field divided in two; each team owns one half of the field.

RULES: Teams take turns. On a turn, a team sends one player over to the other side on a "raid." The raider attempts to tag one or more people with his hand or foot then run back to his own side, all without taking a breath. The raider must chant "kabaddi-kabaddi-kabaddi-kabaddi," (KAH-bah-dee) throughout his time on the other team's side to prove he is not breathing. The defending team attempts to catch the raider and keep him from returning to his own side before he runs out of breath. If the raider is captured and/or takes a breath, he is out. If he makes it back safely to his own side without taking a breath, then anyone he tagged is out. The other team may immediately begin their turn once the raider has returned to his own side.

POINTS: A team gets a point for each player on the other team that goes out. They also get to "revive" one of their own players who is out, for every player on the other team that they get out.

OTHER WAYS TO GO OUT: Anyone on either team who steps off the field or on the out-of-bounds line is out. An exception is made during a struggle between a captured raider and the opposing team, as long as leaving the field is unintentional and a result of the struggle. During a struggle, raider and captors are not allowed to hurt one another

(kick, bite, pinch) or they will be put out. Similarly, no one is allowed to push anyone out of bounds.

TIME: Official games have two 20 minute halves, with 5 minutes in between for the players to rest and change sides. Unofficial play can last as long as you want.

PLAYING FIELD: A regulation game takes place on a field that is 10 x 12.5 meters or 33 x 41 feet (close to the size of half a basketball court). Fields much larger or smaller (your backyard) would also work as long as the midfield line and the playing field boundaries are clearly marked with chalk, rope or tape.

VARIATIONS: There are many variations in kabbadi rules, often made to suit the available field or players. Make your own modifications or research online for official regulations.

A raider attempts to tag someone with her hand or foot without being captured or stopping the chant "kabaddi, kabaddi." The opposing team hovers, ready to avoid or capture her.

Hinduism Q & A

How old is Hinduism?

Hinduism is often called the "oldest living religion." Many of its practices date back between 4,000 and 5,000 years.

What are the central beliefs of Hinduism?

Hindus believe in reincarnation, karma and one supreme being, Brahman. The goal of Hindus is to be liberated from the cycle of life, death and rebirth (reincarnation) and to be reunited with God or Brahman. Bad karma is what separates living souls (atman) from Brahman.

What is karma?

Karma is the principle that what you do, good or bad, comes back to you. If you do good in the world, you have good karma and good things come to you either in this life or in the next. When you do bad things, you gain bad karma and bad things come to you.

Do Hindus believe in souls?

Yes, according to Hinduism, all living things (including plants and animals) have a soul (atman), which is the eternal and the true self. The body is simply a vessel for the atman which may struggle to be released and reunited with God over the course of many lives. Some describe the atman as "Brahman in a pot" (the body); essentially every soul is a small part of God.

How do you stop being reincarnated?

Liberation from the cycle of life, death and rebirth is called *moksha*. To acquire moksha or salvation, a person must realize that their true self, their soul or atman, is identical to Brahman, the divine. To do this, they must dispel the illusion of the self. There are many paths to reaching this stage of enlightenment including serving God (Brahman), through good deeds (karma), realizing/ understanding God, meditation on God and worshipping and loving God.

What are the Hindu scriptures?

The oldest Hindu scriptures are the Vedas, which contain hymns of praise to God, directions for priests on performing rituals and prayers and guidance for everyone on worship and meditation. The final part of the Vedas is called the Upanishads, which discusses the mystical beliefs and philosophy of Hinduism.

The Bhagavad Gita is another Hindu scripture and part of the world's longest epic poem *Mahabharata*. The Bhagavad Gita is a conversation between a warrior prince and his charioteer, who is actually Lord Krishna. About to go into battle against his cousins and friends in a civil war, the prince does not want to fight. Lord Krishna explains to him his duty as a warrior, that death does not kill any soul, that there are many paths to salvation and his greatest loyalty must be to God.

Do Hindus believe in many gods or just one?

Hinduism has only one supreme being, Brahman, who is a formless universal soul. You cannot see Brahman or hear Brahman, there are no stories about Brahman who is infinite, without boundaries, without beginning or end. Without a physical or visual presence, Brahman, or God, can be very difficult for humans to comprehend. Hindus solve this problem through avatars.

What is an avatar?

Avatars are physical, visual manifestations of Brahman or God. Each Hindu deity or "god" is an avatar that shows one aspect of Brahman. Their stories depict different understandings of God. There are three main avatars, the Trimurti, or Hindu trinity, to which most Hindu gods are related. They are: Brahma, the creator; Vishnu, the preserver; and Shiva, the destroyer and judge. Each member of the Trimurti has a consort or wife, which make up the Trivedi: Sarawati, goddess of wisdom; Lakshmi, goddess of wealth; and Parvati, goddess of love and devotion. Other gods are either family members of the Trimurti-Trivedi unions or they are incarnations of the gods themselves. The god Ganesh is the son of Shiva and his consort Parvati. Lord Krishna is one of Vishnu's many incarnations. (Gods can be reincarnated too.)

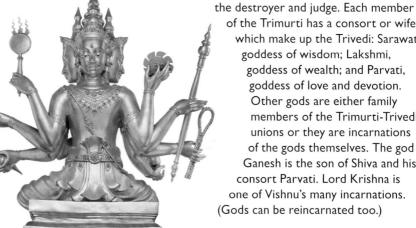

The Trimurti: Brahma, Vishnu and Shiva

How do Hindus select which gods to worship?

Each family has a shrine in their home to a particular god or gods and will teach their children how to pray (make puja) there. In that way, frequently one god will be particularly honored by a family over many generations. This does not keep Hindus from going to temples of other gods or choosing other gods to worship also. As all gods are a manifestation of Brahman, worshipping any of them is acceptable.

Who is the leader of Hinduism?

Although there are Hindu priests, there are no central leaders in Hinduism, and thus no one set of beliefs or practices. Faith is passed on through families, who may each have particular gods or goddesses that they usually pray to. The lack of any centralized authority has allowed Hinduism to become incredibly diverse in terms of its beliefs and practices. *For that reason, this description of Hinduism does not describe all Hindus' beliefs.*

J is for Japan

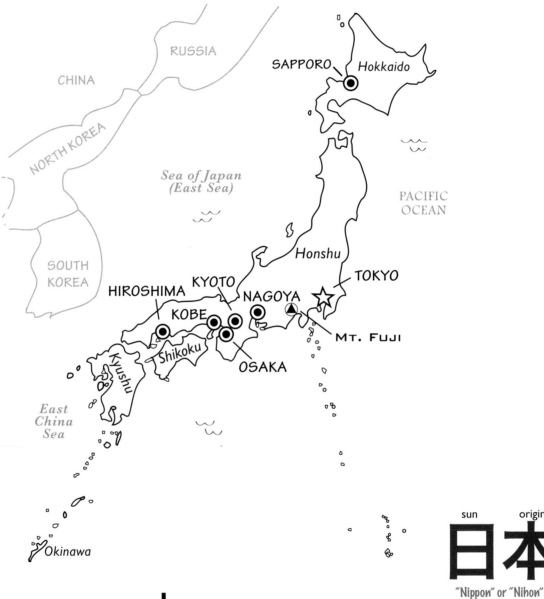

RUSSIA

CHINA

NORTH KOREA

Sea of Japan
(East Sea)

SOUTH
KOREA

SAPPORO ·Hokkaido

PACIFIC
OCEAN

Honshu

TOKYO

HIROSHIMA KYOTO

NAGOYA

KOBE

MT. FUJI

Shikoku

OSAKA

Kyushu

East
China
Sea

Okinawa

sun   origin

日本

"Nippon" or "Nihon"
"Land of the Rising Sun"

For our **J** we will jump to **JAPAN,**

which is natively known as **NIPPON,**

And written in characters meaning,

the *"LAND OF THE RISING SUN."*

And being far east of the East,

And near where the DATELINE is crossed,

They can greet the sunrise near first,

"Ohayo Gozaimasu!" [o-high-yo go-zigh-mah-ss]

Sunrise in the Hija Mountains

More than 3,000 mountainous islands

make up this nation of shores,

But most Japanese live in cities

in one of the largest four.

Hokkaido

Honshu

Shikoku

Kyushu

In the center is HONSHU, the mainland,

where the capital **Tokyo** lies.

Hokkaido, **Shikoku** and **Kyushu**

are the other three, smaller in size.

Zen Garden

Bullet Trains

They all have got **SUPER-FAST RAILWAYS,**

zen gardens and old **SHINTO** shrines.

Their fish markets bustle with buyers

and the **SUSHI** they make is divine.

As a principal seafaring nation,

Japan's food often comes from the sea.

They eat **SEAWEED** and fish almost daily,

along with white rice and hot tea.

Fish Market

Sushi

Bento Box

Miso soup is a favorite for breakfast.

Bento boxes make for a fun lunch.

(They're so cute in their artful arrangement,

they're almost too pretty to munch!)

Miso Soup

But if we speak of the **"JAPANESE DIET,"**

that's their governing parliament's name.

It's the voice of the Japanese people

(though their **emperor's** family still reigns).

Emperor Akihito

Japanese love all natural beauty;

to each season, they're greatly attuned.

There's a spring celebration **"Hanami,"**

where they watch all the **cherry trees bloom.**

Cherry Blossoms

It's the land that produced the FIRST NOVEL,

and the art form of writing **HAIKU.**

Now all ages read comic book *MANGA*

and watch cartoon **ANIME** too.

Anime

In a nation once governed by **SHOGUNS,**

when warrior **SAMURAI** ruled,

There are legally now almost no guns

and police go to martial arts school.

No Guns

Japanese are extremely well-mannered,

and their etiquette seems quite complex.

But don't fear, as a **GAIJIN** or foreigner, [guy-jin]

they will know you mean no disrespect.

House Slippers &
Tatami Mat

Honda's ASIMO

Just smile and do not lose your temper,

in houses please **TAKE OFF YOUR SHOES,**

Show respect to officials and elders,

then watch them and do as they do.

So come to this land of **MOUNT FUJI,**

volcanoes and **mist-shrouded hills,**

Futuristic big cities and **ROBOTS,**

and traditional martial art skills.

Karate

We'll try on a **Silky Kimono**

and go see a **SUMO MatCH** won.

Then we'll go out to sing **KARAOKE**

in this land of the **rising sun.**

Kimono

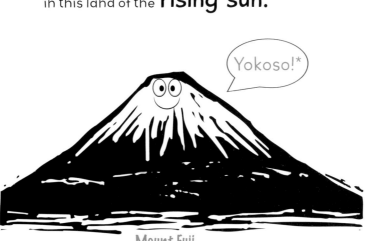

Yokoso!*

Mount Fuji

*_Yokoso_ [YOH-koh-soh] means "Welcome!" in Japanese.

← The **Japanese flag** is called Hinomaru and it features a red sun in its center, representing Japan as the "land of the rising sun." Japan's name in Japanese is **NIPPON** or "Nihon," which means "the sun's origin." (You might recognize the Chinese character for sun → in its name.) Japan got its name because it is located east of the Asian continent and the sun rises in the east. As Japan is located near the International Date Line, it is one of the first countries in the world to see the sunrise each day. *Can you write Japan in Japanese?*

Japan or "Nippon"
written in Japanese

Traditionally, → Japanese is written in vertical columns starting at the top right of the page, with each new column formed to the left. Today, Japanese can be written both in the Western style (horizontal, left to right) and in the traditional way. Most newspapers and books are written in the traditional way, and open from what we consider the "back."

Hokkaido

Honshu

Shikoku

Kyushu

Japan's Four Main Islands

Local Name:
Nippon *or* Nihon

Population: 127 million

Capital: Tokyo

Largest Cities: Tokyo, Yokohama, Osaka, Nagoya Sapporo, Kobe, Kyoto

Comparative Size: Slightly smaller than California, a bit larger than Germany

Language: Japanese

Religion: Shintoism 84%, Buddhism 71% (many follow both), Christianity 2%

Currency: Yen

Important Exports: Automobiles, electronics

GEOGRAPHICAL NOTES

◉ Japan has **four main islands** with the majority of their population living on **Honshu**, the largest. There are over 3,000 islands in the Japanese archipelago (island chain), but only a few are inhabited.

◉ Far to the south, **Okinawa** is the island with the fifth-largest population. It is home to beautiful beaches, an incredibly long-lived population and a US military base.

Where in the World is Japan?

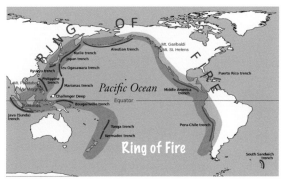

Ring of Fire

International Dateline

+one day   −one day

Japan   Hawaii

The **International Date Line →** is an imaginary line that runs through the middle of the Pacific Ocean, marking the point where a new day begins. To the east of the line, it is one day before the west of the line. As a result, Hawaiians in the middle of the Pacific greet Sunday morning only a few hours before the Japanese greet Monday morning.

↑ Japan is located on the **Pacific Ring of Fire**, a location that is known for volcanoes, mountain chains and seismic activity (earthquakes). About 90% of the world's earthquakes occur in the Pacific Ring of Fire. Japan has 10% of the world's volcanoes and frequently has earthquakes. Japanese buildings are designed to withstand earthquakes; and in school, children have earthquake drills to prepare them for what to do in an emergency. With mountainous terrain covering about 75% of Japan, there is relatively little land for farming or cities.

Yokohama

← Yokohama is Japan's second-largest city. It is located in Greater Tokyo, also known as the National Capital Region. **Greater Tokyo** is one huge metropolitan area with over 35 million people. It is the most populous metropolis in the world. **↓**

Crowds in Greater Tokyo

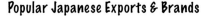

← Tokyo is Japan's capital and largest city. Tokyo means eastern (*to*) capital (*kyo*). Tokyo became the capital in 1868. It was formerly a fishing village called *Edo*. Today, Tokyo is one of the finance capitals of the world, along with New York, London and Hong Kong.

← Signs in Japan are frequently **vertical**, in part due to space restrictions but mainly because that is how Japanese is traditionally written, from top to bottom.

Tokyo

Popular Japanese Exports & Brands

Japan is a nation with a large population and **few natural resources**. **↑** They can't extract precious metals or fossil fuels from their soil, and only about 20% of Japanese land is useful for farming. In order to have enough food and raw materials to support their economy, they must import goods (buy them from other countries). For that reason, the Japanese economy is focused on creating goods for **export** (to sell to other countries). Japan creates high-technology goods like **cars, cameras, watches** and **video games** for export, in order to import raw materials like coal, natural gas and food. Japan's many brands are known worldwide, and chances are there are Japanese brands and products in your home. ***Do you own any of these brands?* →**

HONDA   CITIZEN
LEXUS   mazda
Nintendo®   NISSAN
OLYMPUS   Panasonic
SEGA®   Canon   SEIKO
SHARP   SONY   SUBARU
Nikon   SUZUKI   TOSHIBA
HITACHI   TOYOTA   YAMAHA

High-speed Rail

新幹線
Shinkansen

↑ **Shinkansen** is a network of high-speed bullet trains connecting Japan's major cities. These bullet trains can go 150–185 mph (240–300 km/h). The island of Shikoku does not have Shinkansen service (or large cities), but its express trains can travel at speeds of up to 80 mph (130 km/h). Japan was the first country to build special lines for high-speed travel, and its high-speed train lines are the busiest in the world.

Zen gardens are also called rock gardens. Rocks, gravel, moss and pruned shrubs are arranged to create a miniature landscape. The pebbles might be raked to represent ripples or rivers of water. The large rocks are like small mountains. Zen Buddhist monasteries started using rock gardens (which already existed in Japan) as aids for meditation in the 14th century. Gardens are considered works of art in Japan. ↓

Zen Garden

Shinto Shrine

↑ **Shinto** is the native religion of Japan. Shinto is "the way of spirits." These spirits, called *kami*, are the divine spark found in nature and all living things. Shinto shrines are homes for kami, and through rituals Shinto practitioners can achieve purity and live at one with the kami. Shinto is known for its reverence for nature, physical cleanliness and their traditional festivals celebrated throughout the year and throughout one's life. Most Japanese practice both Buddhism and Shinto, even though they do not consider themselves to be religious. Many are married in a Shinto ceremony and have their business or home blessed by a Shinto priest. Their funerals, however, are usually Buddhist ceremonies. The entrances to Shinto temples is always two vertical posts crossed by two horizontal beams.

Fish Market

↑ As an island nation, **seafood** is abundant in Japan. There are many different recipes for fish, everything from fried fish to fish sushi. **Sushi** is cooked rice seasoned with rice vinegar and molded into a variety of one-bite shapes. Sushi has a variety of toppings including raw meat or raw fish (called sashimi) and/or vegetables. Sushi is now popular around the world, particularly sushi rolls, which outside of Japan typically contain raw fish and are wrapped with toasted seaweed. ↓

Miso Soup

Miso soup and white rice ↑ are a traditional Japanese breakfast. Miso soup can have many different ingredients but it always has miso paste. Miso paste is made from fermented rice, barley and/or soy with salt and fungus. Miso has lots of protein, fiber and beneficial bacteria.

Bento

← **Bento** boxes are single-serving meals in a box. ↑ They usually contain rice, protein and pickled or cooked vegetables. Typically, bentos are arranged in a pleasing manner, as the Japanese believe that the eye is first to taste a meal. Bentos can even use food to create pictures or characters. Bentos are prepared at home to take to school or work, and they can be ordered in a restaurant or bought from bento shops or convenience stores. →

Sushi

Bento

Bento

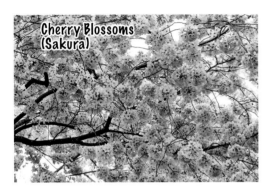
Japanese Diet Chamber

← The **Japanese Diet** or *Kokkai* is their governing legislature. Japan is a constitutional monarchy with a democratically elected legislature and a prime minister selected by that legislature

Emperor Akihito is the 125th emperor to reign → over Japan in a line of rulers dating back to 660 BCE. Though the emperor's role today is purely ceremonial, the royal family is a symbol of Japanese culture and unity. Emperor Akihito (born 1933, reigning since 1989) is the world's only monarch currently using the title "emperor." His title in Japanese is *tenno* or "heavenly sovereign." ↓

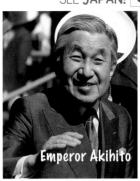
Emperor Akihito

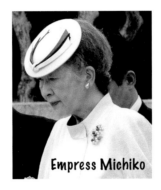
Empress Michiko

← Emperor Akihito and Empress Michiko on their wedding day in 1959. Their son, Prince Naruhito, will be the next emperor.

Ikebana

Cherry Blossoms (Sakura)

↑ **Hanami** is a spring festival in which people gather under blossoming cherry trees to picnic and celebrate the arrival of spring. The delicate cherry blossoms, called *sakura,* are admired for the beauty of their short (1–2 week) lifespan. Japanese culture is very attuned to the seasons and nature. Japan has four roughly equal seasons, and there are holidays and festivals year-round to welcome and celebrate each.

← **Ikebana** is the Japanese art of arranging flowers. It is considered as artistic as painting and a way to commune with nature for both women and men. Having a little bit of nature inside your home is important in Japan, and many homes have fresh flower arrangements throughout the year. Ikebana looks very different from Western flower arrangements; there is a focus on simplicity, natural lines, asymmetry and negative space.

Scene from the Tale of Genji

← Written in the 11th century, **The Tale of Genji** is considered by many scholars as the world's oldest novel. Its author was a noble woman, Murasaki Shikibu, who described life at the emperor's court and the romantic adventures of Prince Genji.

Anime, short for "animation," is the word for → Japanese animated films or cartoons. Anime is considered to be an art form that can be directed toward people of any age. Some anime films are intended for exclusively adult audiences.

Manga is the word for Japanese comic books, which are considered works of literature and are read by all ages in Japan. Just like with regular books, some are created for children and some for adults. Manga is known for characters drawn with huge eyes. Manga, like most Japanese books, is read from "back to front," meaning they read from the right cover to the left. →

Anime Character

Manga Eyes

Reading Manga

Samurai

↑ Samurai were Japanese knights. They were a class of warriors that ruled over Japan from the 12th century until the Meiji Restoration in 1868, which gave governing power back to the emperor. They reigned in a military dictatorship called a *shogunate*. Aristocratic samurai, called *bushi*, developed their own code of conduct called Bushido, which is still reflected in Japanese values today. Bushido or the "way of the samurai" emphasizes honesty, bravery, loyalty, respect and honor unto death. Samurai culture made both the tea ceremony and ikebana popular in Japan.

Ninja were almost the opposite of samurai – they had no code of conduct or concern for honor. They were spies, assassins and saboteurs for hire. They specialized in covert operations, which meant that they often arrived at night, wearing all black so that they would not be detected. ↓

Ninja

Karate

← Karate, judo, aikido and jujitsu are all Japanese martial arts. Karate, meaning "open hand," uses kicks, punches, elbow strikes and "knife hands," but never weapons. **Judo, jujitsu** and **aikido** occasionally use weapons, but they are not the focus of training. There are also weapon-based martial arts like *kendo*, the Japanese art of fencing.

Japan has some of the strictest **gun laws →** of any democratic nation. Individuals cannot own handguns and gaining the license to buy a hunting rifle is a long and difficult process. Even most police do not usually carry a gun, they train in using judo and kendo instead. There is almost no gun violence in Japan.

Tea Ceremony

← The tea ceremony is a ritual of preparing and serving powdered green tea called *macha*. It was developed by Zen Buddhist monks in the 13th century as a way to show reverence for the routine, daily tasks and interactions of life. The grace, care and attention with which the simple ceremony is performed are what make it an art.

Indoor School Shoes

In Japan and many Asian countries, it is considered polite to **remove your shoes** when entering someone's house. In the house, you keep on your socks, and slippers may be provided. To walk on traditional tatami mats, people remove their slippers and walk with only socks or bare feet. →

← At school, students also have soft **indoor shoes**, which they change into once they arrive in order not to track in dirt with their street shoes.

Indoor Slippers & Tatami Mat

Bowing

← Bowing is the Japanese handshake and greeting. **→** It can be used to say hello, goodbye, thank you, I'm sorry, welcome and congratulations. It has one advantage over handshakes in that it avoids spreading germs. Men bow with their hands at their sides, while women bring their hands together in front of their legs. It is polite to make a deeper bow to show your respect to those older than you or in a position of authority. Deeper bows may also be used to emphasize the message of welcome, respect or apology. In general the person of lower rank, the student, child or employee should bow lower and longer. Slight bobs may be used for casual greetings. *Can you bow as the Japanese do?*

Bowing

Hokusai's Mount Fuji

← **Mount Fuji** is the highest mountain in Japan → and is sometimes used as a symbol of Japan. It is considered one of Japan's three "holy mountains," and it often appears in their art. Two famous 19th-century artists, Ando Hiroshige and Katsushika Hokusai, each completed a set of woodblock prints called "36 Views of Mount Fuji." Climbing Mount Fuji is a popular activity for Japanese people and tourists. A well-known Japanese saying is: "Anybody would be a fool not to climb Mount Fuji once, but a fool to do so twice." It is most popular to ascend at night to reach the peak at sunrise. Mount Fuji is an active volcano that last erupted in 1708. →

Hiroshige's Mt. Fuji

Robot

Sumo Wrestling

← **Sumo wrestling** is an ancient form of Japanese wrestling. Wrestlers win when they force their opponent to either step out of the ring or touch the floor with any part of their body other then their feet. Sumo wrestlers live and train together, following a special diet. They often start training at 15 or 16 years of age.

↑ Japan has been the country doing the most research into making **robots** that can behave like humans or animals. ASIMO (above) was made by Honda and can run, climb stairs and talk. Sony created a robotic dog called AIBO that sees, walks and obeys voice commands.

Karaoke first became popular in Japan in the late 1970s among Japanese businessmen and has since spread around the world. There are even karaoke coaches in Japan who can help you perfect your performance. →

Kimono

Kimono

Sapporo Snow Festival

↑ **Sapporo** is the largest Japanese city not located on the island of Honshu. On the northernmost island, Hokkaido, their winter brings lots of snow, and the Sapporo Snow Festival is famous for its enormous snow sculptures.

Yukata

← ↑ **Kimono** is traditional Japanese dress for men, women or children. Kimono are long T-shaped robes with wide sleeves. They are tied up with sashes called *obi* and worn over a complete under robe that keeps the kimono clean. There are so many layers and accessories to properly wear a kimono that there are kimono dressers you can hire to help you dress for formal occasions. Women typically wear a kimono for the coming of age ceremony held the year they turn 20. Less formal and easier to wash, an unlined cotton kimono called a **yukata** is popular in the summer months for festivals.

Listen to the SOUNDS of JAPAN

Shamisen

The shamisen looks somewhat like a square banjo without frets. It's typically played with a large hand-held pick. You might also enjoy the **koto**, **hocchiku** and **shakuhachi**. For modern popular shamisen music, try the Yoshida Brothers.

YOUTUBE SEARCH: shamisen, koto, hocchiku, shakuhachi, Yoshida Brothers

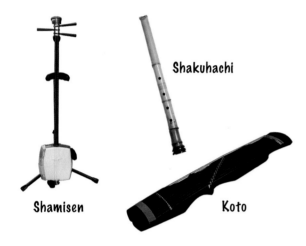

Shakuhachi

Shamisen

Koto

Kimigayo

Japan's national anthem is one of the shortest national anthems in the world, as well as one of the most poetic. Its words mean, "May your reign continue for a thousand, eight thousand generations, until the pebbles grow into boulders lush with moss."

Jpop

Japanese popular music includes many different styles from jazzy blues to rock to hip hop to bubble gum pop. Here is a small selection of artists and songs:

Namie Amuro's "Baby Don't Cry"

Asian Kung-Fu Generation's "Well Then, See You Again Tomorrow"

Perfume's "Spending All My Time"

Ikimono Gakari's "Hoshi"

Shiina Ringo's "Tsumi to Batsu"

Momoiro Clover Z's "Neo Stargate"

Aiko (anything)

M-Flo's "All I Want Is You" or "The Love Bug"

Yuzu's "Land"

Radwimp's "Oshakashama," "Order Made" or "Dada"

B'z's "Juice"

Alice Nine's "Rainbow"

Crystal Kay's "Girlfriend" or "Forever"

Daichi Miura's "Inside Your Head"

READ:

There is a wide selection of books reflecting Japanese culture, from folktales to samurai adventures to manga series from Japan. This is just a small sample, check your local library.

I Live in Tokyo by Mari Takabayashi. A year of food and festivities for a child living in Tokyo. Ages 4 & up.

Japan: Over 40 Activities to Experience Japan – Past and Present by Debbi Michiko Florence. Ages 8 & up.

Wabi Sabi by Mark Reibstein. A Japanese cat searches for the meaning of his name, "Wabi Sabi," a Buddhist concept of beauty in ordinary things. Ages 7 & up.

Tsunami! by Kimiko Kajikawa. A heroic old man must sacrifice to save his village from a big wave. Ages 4 & up.

Real Samurai: Over 20 true stories about the knights of old Japan by Stephen Turnbull. Ages 8 & up.

Sword of the Samurai: Adventure Stories from Japan by Eric Kimmel. Ages 9 & up.

Sisters of the Sword by Kimiko Kajikawa. Girls disguised as boys train to be samurai. Ages 10 & up.

Hachiko Waits by Leslea Newman. The true story of the loyal love of a dog, famous throughout Japan. Ages 8 & up.

Sadako and the Thousand Paper Cranes by Eleanor Coerr. The true story of Sadako, a girl with "atom bomb sickness" who tried to make 1,000 origami cranes in order to make herself well. Ages 8 & up.

Hiroshima: A Novella by Lawrence Yep. Powerfully realistic – a child's account of surviving an atom bomb. Ages 9 & up.

Moonshadow: Rise of the Ninja by Simon Higgins. Moonshadow is part of the shogun's secret service in this action-adventure set in medieval Japan. Ages 10 & up.

MANGA

Yotsuba by Kiyohiko Azuma. A comedy about the daily life of a strange child, Yotsuba. Ages 7 & up.

Kyuma by Shunsin Maeda. A ninja baseball adventure. Ages 7 & up.

Chi's Sweet Home by Konata Konami. A lost kitten finds a home with a family not allowed to have pets. Ages 8 & up.

Astro Boy by Osamu Tezuka. A classic superhero comic. Ages 8 & up.

Pokemon Adventures by Jidenori Kusaka. Ages 9 & up.

Cardcaptor Sakura by CLAMP. Sukura is a magical girl who must save the world. Ages 9 & up.

MAKE JAPANESE
Okonomiyaki

Okonomiyaki, sometimes called a "Japanese pancake," is a popular street food in Japan that is like a cross between a pancake and a spring roll. Filled with cabbage, cooked meat and any vegetable, it is an easy and infinitely variable recipe. Okonomiyaki are fun to decorate and always delicious, whether made with your favorite meats and vegetables or just whatever leftovers are in the refrigerator.

1. Chop fillings. Cut cabbage into thin ribbons, omitting core. Cut other vegetables and meats to be small; mix together. (Pancake will steam for about 10 minutes, don't include any vegetable too large to cook in that time frame. Drain juicy vegetables well.)

2. Mix batter. Whisk eggs and cold water, then add flour and salt. Beat until smooth.

3. Combine batter and fillings. Pour batter over filling ingredients; mix well.

4. Prepare pans. Get out 1 or 2 non-stick frying pans with lids. (You can cook in two pans simultaneously.) Put one tablespoon oil into each pan and raise to medium heat.

6. Pour pancakes. Mix batter and vegetables again, then scoop into pans to make pancakes (no more than 6 inches across). One in a small pan or many in a larger.

7. Shape pancakes. Flatten cabbage down with the back of spatula, and pull in the sides, compacting and giving pancakes a flat surface on the top and rounded edges.

8. Steam. Cover with lid and turn heat to medium low. Steam for 10 minutes.

9. Flip. Remove lid, and use a spatula to lift up the pancake and check that the bottom has browned. If browned, flip the pancake in the pan to brown the other side.

10. Flatten and brown. Immediately after flipping, use the back of spatula to press down again on the pancake, compacting it further. Let it cooked uncovered until bottom browns and then slide from pan onto a plate.

11. Cover with your favorite condiments. In Japan they use squeeze bottles and make fancy designs on their okonomiyaki. Chuno sauce and mayonnaise are two of the most popular condiments used together. Kids sometimes use condiments and slices of cheese or dried seaweed to make faces or pictures on their okonomiyaki.

Modification:
On a Griddle/ Many at Once: It is possible to cook okonomiyaki without steaming the pancake in a covered pan. To do so, keep your cabbage and vegetables finely chopped, and make pancakes thinner, about ½ inch in height, and then cook like an American pancake. Watch until air bubbles start to pop in the center of your pancake, then flip, frequently pressing down on the pancake with the back of your spatula until it is done.

Filling
⅓ of a head of cabbage, cut into thin ribbons, about 3 cups shredded

1–1½ cup other vegetables, such as shredded carrots, corn, peppers, green onion, finely sliced mushrooms, fresh herbs or any leftover in the refrigerator

½–1 cup meat (precooked) like ham, bacon, beef or sausage

Batter
2 eggs
½ cup cold water
1 cup all-purpose flour
½ teaspoon salt

2 tablespoons oil

Topping/ Condiment Possibilities
chuno sauce (ingredients below)
mayonnaise, ketchup, hot sauce, fresh herbs, dried bonito shavings, dried green seaweed, pickled ginger or any other condiment!

To make chuno sauce:
2 tablespoons ketchup
1 tablespoon Worcester sauce
1 teaspoon soy sauce

← *Cabbage with shredded carrots, green onion, green peas and bacon.*

Filling

Poured and Shaped

Flipped

Three in one large pan

↑ *Woodblock prints from Katsushika Hokusai's (1760–1849)* **36 Views of Mount Fuji** ↓

✳ ART PROJECT:

Celebrating nature and the changing seasons is an important part of Japanese culture and there are many sets of art about the four seasons. Study Hiroshige's and Hokusai's famous prints of Mount Fuji. (To find all their images and more information, see "36 Views of Mount Fuji" on Wikipedia.) Choose one landmark or object in nature and have it appear in four art pieces about the seasons. Select something in your daily scenery like your house, school, a bench, a bridge or even your dog. The art pieces can be paintings, drawings or any media that inspires you. Look at photos of all four seasons in your location as a reminder of what the seasons actually look like. If you can't find photos of each season, try to capture four different types of weather (like rain, sun, clouds and wind) or four different times of day (daybreak, noon, dusk, nighttime). The landmark must appear in each artwork, but it does not have to be the focus or appear from the same perspective.

↑ *Woodblock prints from Katsushika Hokusai's (1760–1849)* **36 Views of Mount Fuji** ↓

SPEAK JAPANESE! 日本語

Part of Speaking Japanese is PAUSING.
When having a conversation in Japan, it is polite to be silent for a brief period after someone tells you something, pausing to show consideration for their words.

Ohayo Gozaimasu.
oh-high-yo go-zigh-mas-ss

Good Morning.
おはようございます。

Konnichiwa!
koh-nee-chee-wah

Good Afternoon!
今日は

Konbanwa!
kohn-bahn-wah

Good Evening!
こんばんは。

Ogenki desuka?
'gehn-kee dess-kah

How Are you?
お元気ですか？

Genki desu.
'gehn-kee deh-ss

I'm fine.
元気です。

Maa-maa desu.
mah-mah deh-ss

I'm so-so.
まあまあです。

Anatawa?
ah-nah-tah-wah

And you?
あなたは？

Arigatou!
ah-ree-gah-toh

Thank you!
ありがとう！

Sayonara.
sigh-yoh-nah-rah

Goodbye.
さようなら！

Saru mo ki kara ochiru. Even monkeys fall from trees.
(Even experts make mistakes.) 猿も木から落ちる。

👁 DON'T MISS WATCHING
(online)

Anime Watch a Japanese animated movie or television show, also known as Anime. Some suggestions are:

Spirited Away (PG)

Kiki's Delivery Service (G)

My Neighbor Totoro (G)

Dragon Ball Z (PG-TV) Ages 8 & up for violence.

Hikaru No Go (PG-TV)

Castle in the Sky (PG) Ages 10 & up for violence.

All available to stream online, with trailers on YouTube.

Tea Ceremony Watch the carefully choreographed Japanese tea ceremony, developed during the reign of the samurai. **YOUTUBE SEARCH:** Japanese tea ceremony

Sumo Wrestling There are many wonderful Sumo documentaries, including two short ones by National Geographic. **YOUTUBE SEARCH:** Sumo

Cool Japan: Japanese Calligraphy NHK (The Japanese Broadcasting Company) has a show called "Cool Japan" that explores Japanese culture with an international audience. **YOUTUBE SEARCH:** Cool Japan Calligraphy

What Not to Do in Japan There are many YouTube videos about Japanese etiquette, but this one covers the biggest no-no's and how they relate to the Japanese outlook on life. **YOUTUBE SEARCH:** What not to do Japan

MAKE An Origami Water Bomb!

Materials: Paper

(Origami paper, colored paper, or wrapping paper)

1. Start with a square piece of paper.
To make a square from a rectangular sheet of paper, fold down one corner so that edges meet, making a right triangle. Cut off the extra paper, unfold the right triangle for a perfect square.

2. Make an X of folds.
Fold square in half diagonally. Unfold, and fold along the other diagonal. Unfold, and you will have an x of creases on the square.

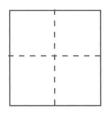

3. Make a + of folds.
Turn paper over to fold on the other side. Fold square in half horizontally. Unfold and then fold in half vertically, making a cross of folds. Unfold.

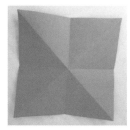

4. You should end up with this. (+) Cross folds are down, diagonal folds (X) are up.

5. Bring + cross folds together, letting x folds flare out. Then bring two flared-out flaps together on either side, making a triangle. Press down on triangle to keep it folded.

6. Put triangle on a flat surface, fold down flap corners to meet in the middle, making a diamond.

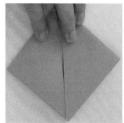

7. Flip and do the same on the other side.

 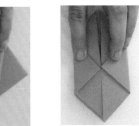

8. Fold up either side of the diamond to meet at the line down the middle.

9. Flip and do the same on the other side

10. Fold up bottom flap to fold the triangle in half.

11. Put finger in side flap to make room to fold paper inside it.

12. Fold triangle into the open flap.

13. Follow the same steps (10–12) for the opposite bottom flap and the two on the other side.

14. Time to inflate your balloon. Open flat sides to an X formation. Blow into open top of the balloon with your mouth.

15. Leave origami ball as a paper balloon, or fill it with water to use as a water bomb. Bombs tend to drip, so fill outside and throw soon after. Unlike water balloons, water bombs always explode on contact.

K is for Kazakhstan

RUSSIA

RUSSIA

ASTANA ☆

QARAGHANDY ◉
(KARAGANDA)

ALTAI MTS

Aral Sea

CHINA

ALMATY ◉

SHYMKENT ◉

TIAN SHAN
MOUNTAINS

Caspian Sea

UZBEKISTAN

KYRGYZSTAN

TURKMENISTAN

TAJIKISTAN

Shepherd

Our **K** is in Central Asia,

the land of the cowboy **Kazakhs,** [kah- ZAHKS]

A once nomadic people

who roamed on the range with their flocks.

Steppe

"**Kazakh**" in ancient Turkish

means independent and free,

And the **STEPPES** on which they wandered [steps]

are as open and wide as the sea.

As the world's *largest landlocked nation*,

and the NINTH LARGEST out of them all,

Kazakhstan's size is impressive,

but their number of people is **small.**

Yurt

Kazakhs used to wander as nomads

in portable homes called **YURtS,**

Large tents made of camel's wool felt,

with carpets to keep out the dirt.

Kazakh Carpet

"**CAMELS?**" you may ask with wonder,

"Don't they live amongst desert sands?"

But the Bactrian (two-humped) camel

is native to dry steppe lands.

The Kazakhs also kept other animals,

like cattle, sheep and goats,

But the **HORSE** was always their favorite,

that they used and loved the most.

Bactrian Camel

Horse

The horse was first tamed and employed
over **five thousand years** ago here –
Used for food, transportation and sports,
and of course, to make **horse milk beer**.

"Kumis" Fermented
Horse Milk

It's horse meat that's boiled to make **Beshbarmak**,
Kazakhstan's national dish.
Served up on wide doughy noodles,
I've heard that it's quite *delish*.

Beshbarmak

And their **marathon horse races** here
are much longer than most that you'll find.
Their traditional tracks are a mile long,
and they go around thirty times!

Horse Racing

There's also a contest for riders
that measures their skill on a steed.
They have to **pick up a handkerchief**,
while galloping at full speed!

Golden Eagle Hunter

Beyond horses they're known for hunting
with **GOLDEN EAGLES** and hounds.
Both animals' speed and vision
can quickly find food to take down.

Yurt

So many nomadic traditions

are still alive here today.

At festivals, you'll see a **YURT**,

and the horse games are all still played.

Altai Mountains

But Kazakhs are no longer nomads,

and their country is not only steppe.

To the east are snow-capped MOUNTAINS

and the **Caspian Sea's** to the west.

Caspian Sea

Their country is rich in resources

with wealth lying under the soil.

They have coal and **mineral deposits**

and loads of gas and oil.

Coal Mining

There are cities with skyscrapers looming,

like **Almaty** where apples are from, [al-MAH-tee]

Or **ASTANA**, the newly made capital, [ah-SHAH-nah]

that has lately become –

Apples

The home of fantastical buildings

like the fabulous **KHAN SHATYR,** [kahn shah-TEER]

The largest tent in the world,

with draping walls that are clear.

Khan Shatyr

Bayterek, A Monument
in Astana

New buildings reflect a new country,

finally spreading its wings,

Finding its own identity

from history, hopes and dreams.

Kazakhs spent most of their history

under foreign rule.

From GENGHIS KHAN to the **Soviets**,

the times have often been cruel.

Genghis Khan

It was part of the Mongol Empire –

the famous Golden Horde,

Which swept across Central Asia,

destroying with fire and sword.

Russian Empire
Coat of Arms

They were part of the *Russian Empire*

and the Soviet Union as well,

And in those times many Russians

came to this country to dwell.

Kazakhstan's
Soviet Flag

Kazakhstan gained **INDEPENDENCE**
in **1991**.

When the Soviet Union dissolved,

the time for their nation had come.

So come now and wander to Kazakhstan,

and ride out a horse on the steppe,

visit towns on the old **SILK ROAD**

and feel free where adventure's still kept!

Horses on the Steppe

Salem!*

Salem [sah-LEM] means "hello," or literally "peace."

Қазақстан

Kazakhstan Written in its Local Form in the Cyrillic Alphabet

Can you write it yourself? See page 247 to learn how to read and write Cyrillic.

↑ Kazakhstan's flag was adopted in 1992 after they declared their independence from the Soviet Union in 1991. The blue color stands for their endless sky, as well as the peace and unity of all Kazakhstan's people. The sun represents wealth and abundance and its rays are shaped like grain, formerly a source of their prosperity. The golden steppe eagle represents freedom and was an important hunter in their nomadic history. The decorative line to the left is their national ornamental pattern called "horns of the ram."

Kazakhstan in Central Asia or the "Stans"

Official Name:
Republic of Kazakhstan

Local Name:
Qazaqstan (Қазақстан)

Population: 17.9 million

Capital: Astana

Largest Cities: Almaty, Astana, Karaganda

Comparative Size: 9th-largest country, slightly less than four times the size of Texas

Ethnicity: Kazakh 64%, Russian 24%

Language: Kazakh, Russian

Religion: Muslim 70%, Christian 25%, unaffiliated 4%

Currency: Tenge

Important Exports: Oil, coal, precious metals

Where in the World is Kazakhstan?

GEOGRAPHICAL NOTES

◉ Central Asia is filled with countries ending in "**stan**," which simply means "land of." **KAZAKHSTAN** is the land of the Kazakh people just as Afghanistan is land of the Afghans, Uzbekistan is land of the Uzbeks and Tajikistan is the land of the Tajiks. One exception is Pakistan, which means "land of the pure."

◉ Central Asia is historically associated with nomadic peoples and the overland **Silk Road**. The region was a crossroads between Europe, India and East Asia.

Chaban (Shepherd)

↑ Traditionally, Kazakhs were **nomadic shepherds** (called *chaban*), who followed their flocks moving their portable homes (yurts) to wherever there were good pastures. There are still shepherds today in Kazakhstan, but most people are settled in cities. There is also widespread farming, which was developed during Soviet times.

Yurt Roof Crossbeams

Kazakh Coat of Arms

Yurt on the Steppe

↑ A **yurt** is the traditional Kazakh home. A yurt is a tent constructed from a wooden frame and felt cloth. It is easy to disassemble and pack, making the Kazakh's nomadic lifestyle possible.

← The yurt is such a large part of Kazakh culture that the crossbeams from the yurt's roof are the central symbol on Kazakhstan's national **coat of arms**. Today, shepherds only use yurts seasonally and keep permanent houses for the rest of the year. But you will still see yurts set up at Kazakh festivals.

Bactrian Camels

Kazakh Carpet

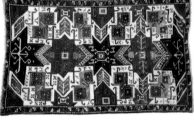

← Yurts can be bright, cozy and colorful inside, with hangings on the wall and carpets on the floor. ↓

Inside a Yurt

↑ **Bactrian camels** are native to the dry steppes of Central Asia. First domesticated in roughly 2500 BCE, they were beasts of burden and provided milk, wool, meat and as beasts of burden. Nicknamed the "ships of the desert," camels can carry 350–500 lbs (159–227 kg) in weight and go long periods without food or water. The Bactrian camel is shorter, hairier and stronger than Arabian camels. Its two humps of fat store extra calories and help keep the camel warm during harsh winters, as does its long hair. Though Bactrian camels can go four or five days without drinking water, they can also drink up to 80 liters of water in one day. The only remaining wild Bactrian camels are in the Gobi Desert in China and Mongolia. →

Camel in Winter

Horses on the Steppe

← A **steppe** is an ecoregion that has grasses but no trees. It is too wet to be a desert and too dry to become a forest. Like the American prairie, the steppe can be used for both growing grains and grazing animals.

Kumis

← Kazakhstan's national drink is **kumis**, fermented horse's milk. Mildly alcoholic, kumis has a very strong flavor. As it is fairly difficult to milk horses, cow's milk is often mixed in when manufacturing kumis on a large scale.

Beshbarmak

Horse Racing

↑ **Beshbarmak** is Kazakhstan's national dish. It is horse meat on wide, doughy noodles with parsley and cilantro on top. Beshbarmak literally means "five fingers" (besh barmak), as it was traditionally eaten using the right hand. This dish is so good, you'll use all five fingers to eat it — not just a polite three.

Horses were first domesticated → in Central Asia, probably in Kazakhstan in 4000–3500 BCE. They are still such a popular part of the culture that it is said that many children learn to ride before they learn to walk. Many people have a framed photo of their horse in their home or office. ↓

Boy Riding

↑ Traditional **horse races** or *baiga* are popular at festivals, and usually the competitors are boys riding bareback. Horses race on a mile-long course around the steppe, circling 30 times. It is a race of endurance rather than speed. Many competitors will drop out before the end, and a horse may drop dead from over-exerting itself.

Girl Riding

Kuuz Kuu

↑ **Kuuz kuu** or "capture the girl" is a traditional game on horseback where a young man chases a young woman. The woman attempts to escape through speed and using her whip to beat him back. If he doesn't capture her within a predetermined time or distance, she rewards him with more whipping. If he does capture her, he wins a kiss.

Kokpar

← **Kokpar** is another game on horseback that is somewhat similar to polo. However, instead of moving a ball toward a goal with a mallet, each team in kokpar attempts to move a headless goat carcass to a goal by carrying it. It is basically a game of "steal the goat."

Golden Eagle Hunter

← **Hunting with birds** (falconry) and hounds has been in Central Asia since the Bronze Age, and the practice is associated with traditional nomadic life on the steppes. Falconry typically takes place in the winter when foxes and rabbits have the softest, thickest coats of fur. Hunting supplemented the protein in their winter diet and provided furs to keep them warm. **Malakhai hats** are traditional fur hats with ear flaps that keep you warm in even the harshest winter weather. ↓ →

Boy with His Falcon Hunter

↑ Training a **golden eagle** takes extreme patience, skill and commitment. Only months of work and some sleepless nights will make an eagle both attached to their owner and willing to hunt for them. The eagle and its trainer will be together throughout the eagle's life, which may last up to 30 years. Hunting with golden eagles is considered an art form in Kazakhstan.

КАЗАКСТАН · KAZAKHSTAN
100.00

Children may be taught how to ↑ capture, care for and train a smaller bird like a **falcon**. Once they have mastered falconry and reached their teens, they may attempt to train a golden eagle, which is the largest and most powerful raptor.

Golden Eagle Hunting

← The **golden eagle** is a symbol of Kazakhstan and appears on their flag. They are symbols of strength, independence and freedom. Even a trained golden eagle maintains its independence and only works as a partner with its master.

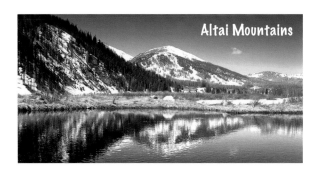

Altai Mountains

↑ The Tian Shan and the **Altai Mountains** in Kazakhstan run along its eastern border with Russia, Kyrgyzstan and China.

The **Caspian Sea** is the world's largest → lake. It is one of only a few "lake-seas," which are salty but have no outlet to another sea or ocean. The Caspian Sea hosts many oil platforms as well as sturgeon that are fished for their caviar.

Caspian Sea

The **Aral Sea** is another lake-sea bordering Kazakhstan. It has shrunk significantly since the Soviets diverted the rivers that fed the Aral Sea for agricultural purposes. ↓

Kazakhstan has tremendous **natural resources** to mine: including oil, coal, natural gas, and minerals such as uranium, copper and zinc. ↓

Dried-up Area in the Aral Sea

Oil Drilling

Coal Mining

Presidential Palace in Astana

← **Astana** became the capital of Kazakhstan in 1997. Much colder, less populated and more isolated than the former capital, Almaty, many Kazakhs were skeptical of the change. Since becoming the capital, it has been filled with interesting new buildings and architecture. It is the second-coldest capital in the world after Ulaanbatar, Mongolia.

Almaty

Bayterek is a ➔ monument and observation tower in central Astana that has become a symbol of the city. Its design is based on a traditional folktale in which the magic bird of happiness, Samruk, laid a golden egg in the crevice of a branch of the "tree of life." From the top of the tower, you can look out over all the interesting new skyscrapers of Astana.

Bayterek

↑ **Almaty** is Kazakhstan's largest city and former capital. Located in the south by the Tian Shan Mountains, Almaty has a warmer climate and is a great place to go for skiing. The name "Almaty" is said to mean "full of apples" ← as the region is where the earliest apples first grew.

Khan Shatyr Beach

Genghis Khan

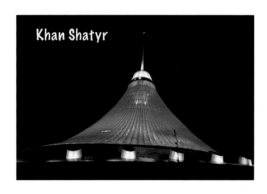

Khan Shatyr

← The **Khan Shatyr** is a huge indoor park, ↑ shopping center and entertainment complex in Astana that was constructed by the government as a refuge against their harsh winters. In a space as large as ten football stadiums, it holds an amusement park, canals, a beach, a monorail and many shops and restaurants. Its clear walls capture heat and let in natural light so that in Astana's extreme winters, when temperatures can go below -20°F (-28.9°C), residents can still get out of the house, go for a stroll or relax on the beach.

↑ Genghis Khan created the **Mongol Empire** (13th–14th centuries CE), the largest contiguous empire in history. It was split into four parts and divided among his sons. The northwest part of his empire, including much of western Kazakhstan and southern Russia, was called the "Golden Horde," and eastern Kazakhstan became part of "Chatagai." The Mongols conquered new territory with incredible speed, using warriors on horseback who were excellent archers. The Mongols also used sweeping terror – murdering whole villages, setting towns on fire, etc. Millions died. The rule of the Mongols was fairly benign, however, and included tolerance for other religions, support for trade, no taxes for the poor and very little crime. The Mongols were the first to unite Kazakhstan with Russia, an association that would return with the Russian Empire and not be fully broken until 1991.

Russian Empire Coat of Arms

← The **Russian Empire** ruled increasing areas of Kazakhstan from 1731 to 1917. Becoming a part of the Russian Empire was the first blow to the Kazakhs' nomadic lifestyle. By 1917, half a million Russian farms were in the north and east of the country, cutting off valuable land for grazing and access to important water sources. After the Russian Empire dissolved, the Soviet Union soon stepped in to its place.

During Soviet → times Kazakhstan was the site of the Soviet space program and home to the largest space launch center in the world, the **Baikonur Cosmodrome**. Still today, the Russian government leases the cosmodrome as their center for space exploration.

Baikonur Cosmodrome

From 1920 to 1991, Kazakhstan was a part of the **Soviet Union**. *(See page 244 for more information about the Soviet Union.)* Soviets continued some of the policies of the Russian Empire, including moving many Russians to Kazakhstan to farm. An effort to force nomadic Kazakhs into collective farming in the 1930s resulted in widespread famine, where up to 40% of the Kazakh population died. As part of a "Virgin Lands" campaign begun in 1953, vast tracts of grazing land were turned to farming grains. The population was decimated during Soviet years, and with the arrival of so many Russians, the Kazakhs became a minority in their own land. The Soviet Union supported the use of Russian as the language of unity for all Soviets. And so, by 1991, many more people in Kazakhstan were fluent in Russian than in Kazakh. Today, Kazakhs are again in the majority and Kazakh language is growing in use. →

Soviet Socialist Republic of Kazakhstan Flag

Mosque in Astana

↑ Kazakhs have traditionally been **Muslims** since the 9th century. During Soviet times, all religion was discouraged, strictly controlled and kept out of public life. Since independence, there has been a resurgence of religious practice. New mosques are being built like the Khazret Sultan Mosque (above), which is the largest mosque in Central Asia.

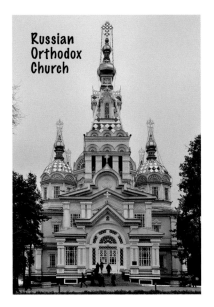
Russian Orthodox Church

← Since independence, many Russians have left Kazakhstan, significantly reducing the number of **Christians** in the country. The government, however, has supported the construction of new churches, wishing to support religious freedom and diversity. The government has even constructed a **Palace of Peace and Reconciliation**, which hosts international conferences of religious leaders seeking to establish peace and understanding between religions of the world. ↓

Palace of Peace & Reconciliation

Traditional Dress

Traditional Dress

←↑ **Traditional dress** in Kazakhstan usually has outer garments made of velvet (or other rich material) embroidered with a design. In colder weather, hats and outerwear are traditionally made with various animal furs, which are uniquely able to protect people from subzero temperatures. →

Kazakh Skullcap

Traditional Dress

Listen to the SOUNDS of KAZAKHSTAN

Listen to a:
Dombra The dombra is Kazakhstan's national instrument. It has two strings and a long neck with 7–10 frets to alter the pitch. In particular, the song "Adai" is a famous Kazakh classic. For rock dombra music, try listening to the band Aldaspan. And for a mix of pop and traditional Kazakh music, try Makpal Dihanbaeva.
YOUTUBE SEARCH: Azai kazakh music, Aldaspan, Kazakh dombra, Makpal Dihanbaeva

READ:

Tales Told in Tents: Stories from Central Asia

by Sally Pomme Clayton. A picture book of short folktales from Central Asia, featuring a Kazakh classic about a wily trickster. Ages 7 & up.

PLAY: Baiga

Baiga, or "horse race," is a race between teams of two players, a horse and rider. The horse must extend his hands down behind him. His teammate, the rider, will stand behind him and hold his hands. They will run together, holding hands this way during the race. All the teams will assemble at a starting line for the race to begin. Teams are not allowed to let go of their teammate's hands or get in another team's way. Somewhat similar to a three-legged race, the key is coordination between the horse and rider so that they don't fall down or release hands. At the finish line, the rider must jump in the air to retrieve a handkerchief hanging from a stick or high on a wall. The first team to get the handkerchief wins.

PLAY: Jebeshkek Bukender

Jebeshkek Bukender, or "Sticky Tree Stumps" is a tag game played with a large group. Three or four players are designated as "sticky tree stumps" and they kneel on the ground, spaced far apart. The other players run around a large defined space while the sticky tree stumps stick out their arms and try to touch them without moving from where they are planted. (They can keep just one knee on the ground to reach further.) Anyone they tag becomes another "sticky tree stump," planting themselves in the ground and trying to catch the rest of the players.

DON'T MISS WATCHING (online)

Welcome to Kazakhstan

Kazakhstan's tourism bureau has created many gorgeous videos of Kazakh scenery and culture. **YOUTUBE SEARCH:** Kazakhtan Heart of Eurasia

Kara Jorga

or Qara Zhorga, a traditional Kazakh dance. There are plenty of Kazakh music videos on YouTube demonstrating the Kara Jorga in traditional costumes.
YOUTUBE SEARCH: kara jorga, qara jorga

Hunting with Golden Eagles

Go hunting with a Kazakh falconer and his golden eagle on horseback. See how the art of falconry brought Kazakh nomads food and warm furs during long winters.
YOUTUBE SEARCH: golden eagle hunting

Assembling a Yurt

If you've ever spend a chilly night camping in a tent, you might wonder how yurts are made into such cozy homes, capable of keeping out all the elements on the windy steppe. Watch one being assembled and then take a tour inside.
YOUTUBE SEARCH: yurt assembly, inside kazakh yurt

PLAY: "Eger"

"Eger," or "If," is a noncompetitive game for a large group that can be played in a classroom. The teacher or leader of the game loudly says "IF," then a player whispers to the leader a condition – any condition whether possible or impossible. "If it rains all day," "If clouds are made of cotton candy," "If we never do homework again." Then the leader says loudly "THEN" and another player announces a result, "We'll all go live at the sea." "We'll discover cats are aliens" "I'll go live in Paris." "There will be an epic battle." The leader then announces loudly the entire sentence, putting together the "if" and "then" statements for usually silly or funny results. "If clouds are made of cotton candy, we'll all go live at the sea" "If a monster comes to town, we'll discover cats are aliens." Making up a condition or a result about other players is not allowed.

PLAY: Tasimaldau

Tasimaldau or "Crossing Over" is a competitive game between two blindfolded players. Four chairs are set up, two for each player. The chairs are spaced 10–12 feet (3–4 meters) apart. Each player is assigned two of the chairs. On one of their chairs, five spoons are placed. Each player must transfer their five spoons, one by one, while blindfolded, to their other chair (and not their opponent's chair). The player who correctly transfers his spoons first, wins. This is a fun game to play as a relay in teams.

Visit www.australiatozimbabwe.com for links to online activities.

 # MAKE KAZAKH
Baurasaki

Baurasaki is a type of fried bread that is popularly served at celebratory meals, for breakfast, and when breaking Ramadan fasts. It is frequently strewn around the table at feasts. It can be sprinkled with sugar to eat as a treat.

1 package dry active yeast
¼ cup warm water
2 cups flour
2 teaspoons sugar
2¹/₂ teaspoons salt
1 egg
1 tablespoon soft butter
¼ cup yogurt

1–2 cups vegetable oil
for frying

1. Mix water and yeast in a small bowl. Mix the rest of ingredients in a mixing bowl, adding yeast and water last.
2. Knead dough to fully combine.
3. Cover with a cloth and let sit for 30 minutes.
4. Heat oil to medium high heat in a wide, shallow pan.
5. Roll a tablespoon of dough into a ball in your hands.
6. Gently lower dough into hot oil and fry until golden brown, turning over as each side browns.
7. Remove from oil with tongs or a slotted spoon and drain on paper towels.
8. (Optional) Roll lightly in sugar.

SPEAK KAZAKH!

Salemetsizbe! **Hello!**
sah-lem-EHT-suhz-beh

Salem! **Hi!** (informal)
sah-LEM

Kaleniz kalai? **How are you?**
kah-luh-NUHZ kah-LAI

Zhaksi **Good**
jahk-SUH

Zhaman **Bad**
jah-MAHN

Rakhmet! **Thank you!**
rah-k-met

At **Horse**
AHT

Dos **Friend**
DOHS

Dossyz Omir bos.

Without friends, the world is empty.
doh-suhz oh-meer bohs

Koshpeli **Nomad**
koh-sh-peh-lee

Oz ulem, ken saradat boz ulem.

East or west, home is best.

Sau Bolynyz! Good bye!
SOW bohl- luh-NUHZ

Traditionally, Kazakh teacups are small bowls with no handles. Today, mugs and Western teacups are also used.

MAKE KAZAKH
Chai

The Kazakhs like to drink a milky black tea flavored with cardamom and fennel. Kazakhs use loose black tea instead of tea bags. They combine water with tea, fennel and cardamom, bring almost to a boil, simmer for three minutes, then add milk and simmer for 2 more minutes, then strain the tea. If you have loose tea, use 1 teaspoon tea per cup of water. This recipe uses tea bags, which are more widely available.

2 teaspoons fennel
8 cardamom pods
or ³/₄ teaspoon ground cardamom
6 cups of water
6 black tea bags (with or without caffeine)
2 cups milk
Sugar and/or salt to taste (optional)

← Kazakh language
is currently written in Cyrillic, the same as Russian. However, there is discussion of potentially switching to a Latin alphabet in the coming years. Kazakh can be written in Latin letters, but spellings have not been standardized.

1. Crush fennel and cardamom lightly, add to water and bring to a boil.
2. Turn down to simmer, add tea bags and allow to steep for 3 minutes.
3. Add milk and bring back to a simmer.
4. Strain tea and serve, adding sugar (or salt) to taste.

Some Kazakhs like to add a little salt to their tea.
Others may also add pepper, butter or a type of Kazakh sour cream know as kaymak.

L is for Lebanon

SYRIA

LEBANON MOUNTAINS

Bekaa Valley

ANTI-LEBANON MOUNTAINS

TRIPOLI

Mediterranean Sea

BYBLOS (JUBAYL)

BAALBECK

BEIRUT

ZAHLEH

SYRIA

SIDON

TYRE

ISRAEL

Mediterranean Sea

Lebanon lies on the *Mediterranean,*

In **Levant,** its easternmost shore. [leh-VANT]

Here civilization has thrived for millennia,

Since biblical times and before!

Phoenician Ship

Here ancient **Phoenicians** were maritime traders;

These businessmen ruled the seas!

They sold rich purple clothing,

Blown glass and fine sewing

And wood from their tall **cedar trees**.

Cedar of Lebanon

The Phoenicians brought us the **ALPHABET**,

The **PHONETICAL** spelling of words,

And alphabetical order,

(In which this book's contents occur).

Their letters spread all through their empire,

To Carthage and distant trade ports.

First the Greeks, then the Romans

Made it their own, and

That's ABC's history in short.

' B G D H W Z Ḥ Ṭ Y K L M N S ' P Ṣ Q R Š T

Phoenician
Alphabet

Lebanese are still **entrepreneurial**,

Still impeccably styled and dressed,

And they're still spreading letters and writing,

As the Arab world's top printing press.

Their official language is **Arabic**

(With English and French mixed in).

So everywhere you hear:

"Thanks! Merci, kteer!" *

With **"Yalla, bye!"** said at the end.

Books in Arabic

*__Merci__ is French for "thank you." __Kteer__ is Arabic for friend. __Yalla__ is Arabic for "let's go" or "alright."

Beirut

Cafes in Beirut

Beachside **Beirut** is their capital city,

Cosmopolitan, artsy and chic. [sheek]

With outdoor cafes and beautiful people,

It has a *Parisian* mystique.

Most other big cities are all on the coastline:

Tripoli, Sidon and Tyre.

All were seaports Phoenician –

Quite ancient, though each one

Is younger than Byblos by far. [BIB-blohs]

What makes people here

So urbane and worldly –

Multilingual world traders at ease?

It has to do with the **LEBANON MOUNTAINS**,

Which drop right down to the sea.

These strategic seaports

At the crossroads of continents

Through hist'ry have been much desired.

Their great *sophistication*

Is due to a location

That many empires have acquired.

Beirut Fashion Show

Lebanon Mountains

Roman Ruins
in Baalbeck

EGYPTIAN, **Assyrian** rulers invaded,

BABYLONIANS, PERSIANS and GREEKS

The ROMAN and **Byzantine** Empires took over,

Then ARABS, **Crusaders** came each.

The **Ottoman Turks** were the last to hold them,

Before the mandate of FRANCE.

In **1943**

They were finally free

As a nation alone to advance.

Crusader Sea Castle

Church and Mosque
in Beirut

Lebanese are of several religious persuasions,

Some **Christians**, some **Muslims,** some **Druze.**

But whatever their faith,

In one thing they're united,

Their love for the voice of FAIRUZ.

In this region of conflict

Her voice rings out clearly,

Throughout all the Arab world's streets.

And though fierce **CIVIL WAR**

Came to Lebanon's door,

In her music they all can agree.

Fairuz

Baba Ghanoush

Hummus

Falafel

Fattoush

Lebanese people now live the world over.

They call many continents home.

There are more of them settled

Outside of their nation

Than those who now live in their own.

And with them they brought

Tasty foods from their homeland,

Like **HUMMOUS** and **baba ghanoush**.

There's **falafel in pita**

And salads you'll eat

Like **tabbouleh** and minty **FATTOUSH**.

Lebanon measures remarkably **skinny**,

Just twenty to fifty miles wide.

And if you compare it

To states in the US,

It's about **Connecticut's size**.

But Lebanon's smallness is really a virtue,

For nothing is too far away.

You can **ski** on the slopes

And then *swim* on the coast,

All within an exhausting spring day.

Ski Slopes

So pack up your swimsuit

And maybe your ski gear –

Your most stylish clothing as well.

You will want to look good

For Beirut's chic cafes –

When you'll rest isn't easy to tell.

For **Crusader-built Castles**

And ruins of the Romans

Will make you get up to explore

All the sights Lebanese

Like their famed **CEDAR TREES**

In a landscape of mountains and shore.

Crusader Castle

Roman Temple to Bacchus

Hi! Kifak? Ça va?*

*A common greeting in Lebanon combining English, Arabic and French.
Kifak? means, "How are you?" in Arabic. **Ca va?** means "How's it going? " in French.

→ The **Lebanese flag** was adopted in 1943 when Lebanon gained independence from France. The red represents the blood sacrificed in the struggle for independence and the white represents peace, purity and the snow on the top of the Lebanon Mountains. The cedar tree represents immortality and the famous cedars of Lebanon mentioned in the Bible. "The righteous flourish like a palm tree and grow like a cedar in Lebanon." Psalm 92:12

Lebanon or Lubnan written in Arabic

The name **LEBANON** or "Lubnan" dates back to about 2000 BCE. It means "white land," which probably refers to the snow that stays on top of the Lebanon Mountains most of the year.

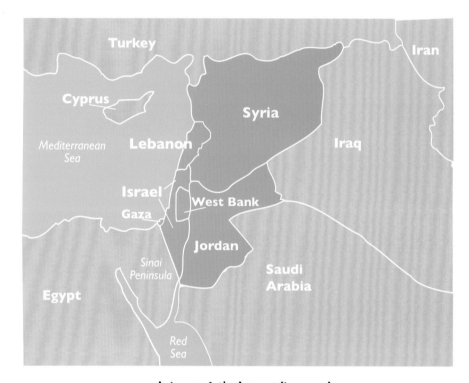

Lebanon & the Levant (in green)

Official Name: Republic of Lebanon

Local Name: Lubnan

Population: 5.8 million

Capital: Beirut

Largest Cities: Beirut, Tripoli, Zahleh, Sidon

Comparative Size: About the size of Connecticut

Ethnicity: Arab 95%, Armenian 4%

Language: Arabic, French, English, Armenian

Religion: 61% Muslim, 38% Christian

Currency: Lebanese pound

Important Industries: Banking, tourism

Where in the World is Lebanon?

GEOGRAPHICAL NOTES

◉ Lebanon is part of the **Levant**, the eastern coast of the Mediterranean in between Turkey and Egypt. Levant comes from the French word *levant,* which means rising, referring to the east, where the sun rises. Levant was a term used for the eastern Mediterranean (sometimes including Turkey and Greece) since the time of the Crusades.

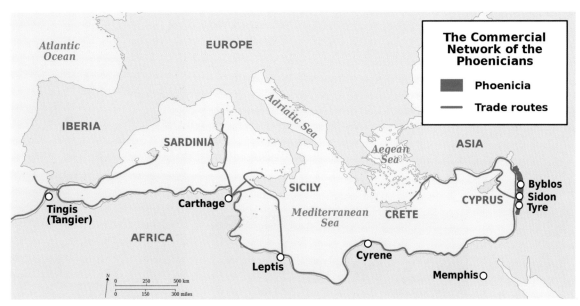

The Commercial
Network of the
Phoenicians

◼ Phoenicia
— Trade routes

← The Phoenician Empire had two capitals: **Byblos** (1200–1000 BCE) and **Tyre** (1000–333 BCE). Tyre was conquered by Alexander the Great in 332. However, from 650 to 146 BCE, the center of Phoenician trade was in **Carthage**. Carthage was defeated by the Roman Republic during the Punic Wars (*Punic* comes from word Phoenician). Carthage today is a suburb of Tunis, Tunisia.

Phoenician Ship

←↑ The **Phoenician Empire** did not exist in order to conquer peoples or take over lands. Instead, they were interested in gaining new markets for their goods. By gaining access to ports all around the Mediterranean, they both sold their own goods and were the middlemen for goods being traded in the region. The Phoenicians were famous first for selling expensive purple dye, which they extracted from the shell of the Murex snail. The name Phoenicia comes from the Greek word for purple, *phoinios*.

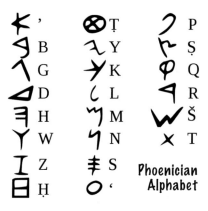
Phoenician Alphabet

↑ The **Phoenician alphabet** was the first completely "phonetic" system of writing, meaning each letter stood for only one sound. In fact, the words "phonics" and "phonetic" come from Phoenician. Other writing systems (Egyptian hieroglyphics, Sumerian cuneiform and Chinese characters) all had pictorial elements or symbols that stood for entire syllables. The Phoenician alphabet was the grandfather of almost every alphabet in use today, including Greek, Hebrew, Arabic and Roman (our alphabet).

The **cedars of Lebanon** → were one of the most famous Phoenician exports, highly prized for their scent, strength and size. Phoenicians used the cedars to build their ships and biblical King Solomon used them to build his temple. Today, the cedars are the country's best-known symbol, appearing on the Lebanese flag. There are relatively few full-sized cedars left, but national parks conserve the majestic ones that remain.

Cedar of Lebanon

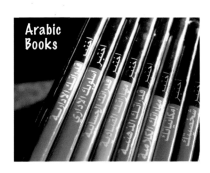
Arabic Books

← Historically, Lebanon and Egypt have been the countries that publish the most **books in Arabic**. As Lebanon is a small country, the majority of their books are for export to the rest of the Arab world. There used to be an expression in the region, "Egypt writes, Lebanon publishes and Iraq reads." Reading, writing and publishing are more evenly spread to other countries today, but Lebanon still plays a leading role in publishing for the Arab World. →

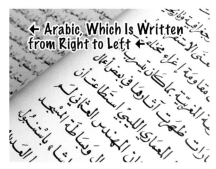
← Arabic, Which Is Written from Right to Left ←

Beirut

Beirut is Lebanon's cosmopolitan capital. It has often been termed the "Paris of the Middle East" for its fashionable people, outdoor cafes, wrought iron balconies, vibrant nightlife and many tourists. Lebanon itself was once thought of as the "Switzerland of the Middle East," as it was the banking center in the region, multilingual and mountainous. Lebanese love to be well-dressed, from those who wear the latest runway fashions to those in more traditional Muslim attire. →

Beirut Fashion Show

Outdoor Cafe in Beirut

Nejmeh Square

↑ **Nejmeh Square** or Place D'etoile is the central square in downtown Beirut. Home to the Lebanese Parliament and a Rolex clock tower, it's a popular gathering place in the city.

Occupied since 5000 BCE, **Byblos** may be the oldest continually inhabited city in the world. Byblos was the Greek name for the Phoenician city of Gebal. The Phoenicians used Byblos as the center for trading papyrus paper, and due to that fact, *biblos* became the Greek name for papyrus, and *biblion* their word for scroll or book. In fact, the English words "Bible" and "bibliography" come from this same root. Today, the modern Arabic name for ← Byblos is Jubayl.

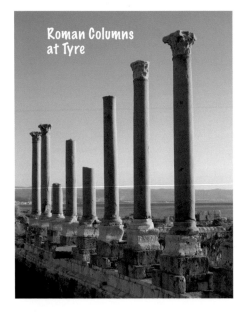
Roman Columns at Tyre

Byblos

← ↓ The Phoenician ↑ seaport cities: **Tripoli, Sidon, Tyre** and **Byblos** later became Roman cities and Crusader cities, and the historical remains of each era can still be found in each. →

Tripoli's Coastline

The **Lebanon Mountains** → are probably the source of Lebanon's name. Lubnan means white (lub) land (nan), which is believed to refer to the peaks of the mountains that remain snow capped most of the year. The mountains shield the coast from eastern desert attacks making the ports ideal for trade.

Lebanon Mountains

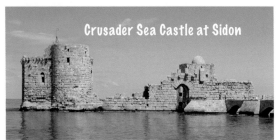
Crusader Sea Castle at Sidon

The Lebanese population is made up of many **religious groups**: Muslims (Sunni and Shi'a), Christians (Maronite, Greek Orthodox and Greek Catholic) and Druze.

Religious Groups in Lebanon

- Sunni (27%)
- Shi'a (27%)
- Maronite Christians (21%)
- Greek Orthodox (8%)
- Druze (5%)
- Greek Catholics (5%)
- Other Christians (7%)

Statistics Source: CIA World Factbook

As the shift in religious populations is a very sensitive issue in Lebanon (and one cause for the Lebanese Civil War), a national census has not been taken since 1932. Thus, these numbers are only estimates.

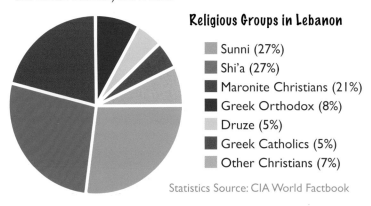

Church & Mosque in Beirut

↑ Lebanon's long history is mainly one of peaceful coexistence of people of many religions. Churches and mosques are built side by side, just as people have lived and worked side by side for millennia. Friendships between people of different religions are common.

What caused the Lebanese Civil War?

When Lebanon won its independence from the French in 1943, it was decided that the government would share power between religious groups. The president would be Christian, the prime minister would be Sunni Muslim, and the speaker of the National Assembly would be Shi'a Muslim. At the time of independence, there were roughly equal numbers of Christians and Muslims in Lebanon. That changed over time, particularly after the state of Israel came into being in 1948. Palestinian refugees began to flood southern Lebanon from neighboring Israel and eventually made up 10% of the Lebanese population. The Palestinian Liberation Organization (or PLO) set itself up in the south of the country and built a militia to attempt to retake land from Israel. The PLO came to have a decisive influence on politics in Lebanon, and other political parties began to build their own military groups to regain power. These militias are mainly who fought in the civil war, though outside countries (Syria, Israel and the United States) got involved in an attempt to end the war. Israel in particular wanted to end attacks made by the PLO onto Israeli soil. In the end, foreign intervention did as much to prolong the war as to end it.

← A building in Beirut still riddled with bullet holes from **Lebanon's Civil War** (1975–1990). Beirut was divided by a "Green Line" into opposing sides. Some buildings along the Green Line have been left standing and unrepaired as a testament to the destruction of the war.

Bullet holes from the Lebanese Civil War

Fairuz is the stage name for Nouhad Haddad, → a Lebanese singer who is incredibly popular throughout the Arab world. Fairuz means "turquoise" in Arabic. She is a Christian, but her music is beloved by people of all religions. During the civil war, Fairuz would not take sides and refused to leave Lebanon, even as many of her countrymen fled abroad. She stopped giving concerts in Lebanon during the war but continued in other countries, singing songs like "I love you, Lebanon," which speaks of the beauty of a united country. She became a symbol of Lebanese unity.

Fairuz

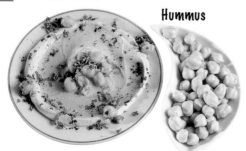

Hummus

Baba Ghanoush

Lebanese people who live around the world have made many foods from the Levant internationally popular. Many times their food is served at "Mediterranean" or "Middle Eastern" restaurants.

Baba ghanoush is a dip made → with eggplant, spices and olive oil.

↑ **Hummus** is a dip made with chickpeas (garbanzo beans), lemon, garlic and sesame tahini. It has been eaten for millennia in the Levant.

Falafel are fried patties made of → either ground chickpeas or fava beans. Served in pita bread, it is a favorite fast food in the Middle East. Falafel may be originally from Egypt, but it is now popular throughout the region.

Falafel in Pita

Fattoush

← **Tabbouleh** is a salad made from bulgur wheat, tomatoes, parsley and mint. In Lebanon, there is more parsley than wheat in the dish.

↑ **Fattoush** is a salad that was originally made with leftover stale pita bread plus vegetables. Today, the salad usually has either toasted or fried pita bread, tomatoes, cucumber, parsley, mint, green onion and sumac.

Tabbouleh

The **Lebanese diaspora** (those Lebanese who live outside of Lebanon) is estimated to be between 12 and 15 million people, at least double the population of Lebanon itself. The countries with the largest Lebanese populations are as follow:

1. Brazil (10 million estimate)
2. United States (3.3 million estimate)
3. Argentina (1.5 million)

The diaspora has made Lebanese food popular around the world.

← Rima Fakih, who is originally from Lebanon, was Miss America in 2010.

Author and poet **Khalil Gibran** may be the most famous Lebanese American in history. →

Mediterranean Coast

↑ As the Lebanon Mountains run close to the coast, it's possible to ski in the mountains and swim in the Mediterranean Sea in the same day. →

Ski Slopes in the Lebanon Mountains

Roman Temple to Bacchus

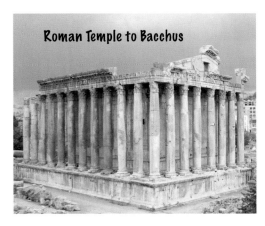

Lebanon has been growing grapes in the Bekaa Valley since before the Romans began worshipping Bacchus, god of wine, there.

Bekaa Valley

↑ **Baalbeck** is a town in the Bekaa Valley and the site of remarkably intact Roman ruins. During Roman times it was known as *Heliopolis* or the "city of the sun," and it was a religious center for the empire. It had three of the largest Roman temples, which honored the gods Jupiter (king of the gods and the god of the sky and thunder), Venus (goddess of love and beauty) and Bacchus (god of wine). The temple to Jupiter was the largest temple in the Roman Empire, and the temple to Bacchus (god of wine) is one of the best preserved Roman temples anywhere today. At Roman temples, animals could be sacrificed on an open-air altar. ➜

Roman Columns at Baalbeck

↑ The **Bekaa Valley** is a fertile region between Lebanon's two mountains. Once a source of grain for the Roman Empire, it remains an important agricultural region in Lebanon, growing grapes, citrus fruits, wheat, barley, apples, tomatoes, cucumbers, olives, sugar beets and tobacco. There are many wine-making vineyards in the Bekaa Valley. The valley's largest city is Zahleh.

Crusader Castle in Byblos

There were several **Crusades** between 1095 and 1291 CE ↑ ➜ when men from Western Europe traveled to the "Holy Land" (the lands where Jesus Christ lived and died) in an attempt to put the land in Christian hands. The Holy Land (mostly modern day Israel) was and is a very important pilgrimage site for Christians, Muslims and Jews. The Christian Byzantine Empire had once held all of the Levant, but Seljuk Turks were taking over the region and Jerusalem had been in Muslim hands since 636. The Crusaders succeeded for a time and Lebanon was held by Crusader kingdoms for over 150 years. There remain several Crusader castles built by medieval knights that you can tour today.

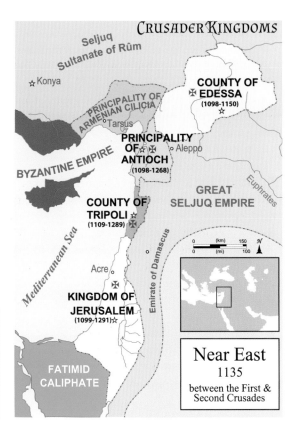

CRUSADER KINGDOMS

Seljuq Sultanate of Rûm

☆ Konya

PRINCIPALITY OF ARMENIAN CILICIA

☆ Tarsus

COUNTY OF EDESSA (1098-1150)

BYZANTINE EMPIRE

PRINCIPALITY OF ANTIOCH (1098-1268)

● Aleppo

GREAT SELJUQ EMPIRE

Euphrates

COUNTY OF TRIPOLI (1109-1289)

Mediterranean Sea

Emirate of Damascus

Acre ☆

KINGDOM OF JERUSALEM (1099-1291)

FATIMID CALIPHATE

Near East
1135
between the First & Second Crusades

Listen to the SOUNDS of LEBANON

Fairuz

Suggested songs: "Habbaytek Bel Saif," "Nassam Alayna," "Bahebak Ya Libnan" ("I Love You, Lebanon"). You can listen to the last with English subtitles on YouTube. **YOUTUBE SEARCH:** Fairuz + song name, Bahebak Ya Libnan English

Mijwiz

Also spelled "mejwez" and "mejwiz," a double piped flute used in traditional Lebanese music, including Dabke dance music. Its distinctive wail takes you straight to the Levant. **YOUTUBE SEARCH:** Mijwiz

mijwiz

Lebanese Pop

Suggested songs:
"Mashy Haddy" by **Nancy Ajram**
"Kifak Enta" by **Myriam Fares**
"Yana Yana" by **Sabah** and **Rola**
YOUTUBE SEARCH: Mashy Haddy, Kifak Enta, Yana Yana

DON'T MISS WATCHING (online)

How to Dabke Dabke is a form of line dancing that is very popular at weddings, parties and festivals all over the Levant. Dancers all hold hands, making one long line, which may circle around the room. Dabke dancing is not hard to learn, and if you can get a good group (at least 7 people) it is really fun. Make sure you dance to Lebanese dabke music.
YOUTUBE SEARCH: how to dabke, Lebanon dabke

Phoenician History Discovery Channel's Secrets of Archaeology program has a 24-minute episode, "Sailing with the Phoenicians." National Geographic has an 54-minute episode from its Ancient Civilizations series called "Quest for the Phoenicians." Both explore Phoenician civilization and the rise of their empire to rule the seas. Available to stream on Amazon and with clips on YouTube.
YOUTUBE SEARCH: Sailing Phoenicians, Quest Phoenicians

What Caused the Lebanese Civil War?
A short motion graphic created by artist Simon Howe covers the causes of the war in under two minutes.
YOUTUBE SEARCH: what caused Lebanese civil war

READ:

A Game for Swallows: To Die, To Leave, To Return by Zeina Abirached. A touching graphic novel memoir about growing up during the Lebanese Civil War. Ages 10 & up.

Oranges in a No Man's Land by Elizabeth Laird. Ten-year-old Ayesha must cross a war zone to get medicine for her grandmother during the Lebanese Civil War. Ages 10 & up.

FIND YOUR FAVORITE LEBANESE PROVERB!

He who took the donkey up to the roof should bring it down.

Let trouble alone and it will let you alone.

Lower your voice and strengthen your argument. *(Note: Lebanese still love to debate at all volumes.)*

Lock your door rather than suspect your neighbor.

When you come back from a journey, bring your family something, though it be only a stone.

He who wants the honey should endure the stings.

Love overlooks defects; hatred magnifies them.

A polite devil is more agreeable than a rude saint.

If anyone is not willing to accept your point of view, try to see his point of view.

If the camel saw his hump, he would fall and break his neck. *(Focusing on your own imperfections can keep you from achieving your potential.)*

SPEAK LEBANESE:

Though Arabic is the official language of Lebanon, French and English are so widespread that Lebanese slang is known for mixing French, English and Arabic.
Here are some examples:

Bonjour Habibti. Hello my dear. *French + Arabic*
Habibi (for men) and Habibti (for women) are two common endearments that literally mean "my love."

Thanks, merci, kteer! Thank you very much!
English + French + Arabic

Yalla bye! Alright bye! *Arabic+ English*
Yalla means, "let's go" or "come on" in Arabic.

MAKE LEBANESE
Tabouli

Tabouli is a delicious green salad of herbs, tomato and a little bulgur or cracked wheat. Some recipes include garlic and some onion; you can choose one or use both. Lebanese cooks pride themselves on tabouli that is mostly herbs with little wheat.

1. Pour boiling water over bulgur wheat and one pinch salt. Stir and cover, allow to sit for one hour or according to package directions.
2. Using kitchen scissors, cut up leaves of mint and parsley,.
3. Remove tomatoes' core and seeds, dice the remaining red flesh. Peel cucumber and dice white flesh, removing seeds. Chop onion small.
4. Mince garlic and mix with oil. Combine with tomato, cucumbers chopped herbs and onion.
5. Add bulgur wheat, stir and salt to taste.
6. Serve in lettuce leaves or with pita chips.

Modification: Use quinoa instead of wheat for a gluten-free tabouli.

¼ cup bulgur wheat, finer ground
¼ cup boiling water
1 bunch fresh mint
2 bunches fresh, flat leaved parsley
4 ripe tomatoes (medium-large)
1 cucumber
¼ sweet yellow onion (optional)
¼ cup olive oil
2 cloves garlic, minced

1 can of small chickpeas, rinsed
(also called garbanzo)
4 tablespoons sesame tahini
(stir tahini before measuring)
4 tablespoons lemon juice
2 tablespoons water
½ teaspoon salt
1–2 cloves garlic, crushed
2 tablespoons olive oil
Toppings: Parsley, paprika, olive oil

MAKE LEBANESE
Hummus

The best recipe for hummus is as contested in the Levant as the best recipe for chili in Texas. Though recipes vary, some ingredients are constants: chickpeas, sesame tahini, lemon juice, salt, garlic and a drizzling of olive oil on top. Others are optional, like yogurt, cumin and toppings like parsley and paprika. The preferred proportion of tahini to chickpeas is as individual as the proportion of peanut butter to jelly in a PBJ sandwich. Should olive oil also go in the hummus, or only be served on top? Must chickpeas be peeled? Is a half-cup of plain yogurt the key to creamy hummus or a heinous crime? Should hummus be served warm, cool or at room temperature? Form your own opinion on the great hummus debate by experimenting and seeing what you like best. This recipe has the basics. Taste after making it and add more tahini, salt, garlic or lemon, as you desire. You can also put some to the side to experiment with adding yogurt or cumin. Once you've got your favorite flavor, garnish with olive oil, parsley and paprika for a pretty effect.

1. Place all ingredients in a food processor or blender. Blend for several minutes until creamy. For blenders, put in liquids first, and expect to scrape down the sides several times. Add more water as needed.

Modifications:

From dried chickpeas: Use ½ cup of dried chick peas for this recipe. Cover with at least 2 cups water mixed with 1 teaspoon of baking soda. Soak overnight, change water, soak for at least one more hour and rinse. Boil in a pot with water and 1 teaspoon of baking soda (no salt) for 60–90 minutes until peas are very soft; drain and use.

For sensitive tummies: To make a creamy hummus that is easier to digest, rinse canned chickpeas well, removing loose skins by rubbing handfuls between your fingers. Then gently boil for 15 minutes in a pot with water and one teaspoon baking soda. Rinse in cold water and remove any additional skins that have come loose; then put in blender and proceed with recipe. Skinned chickpeas make for a super creamy hummus and are part of most traditional recipes in Lebanon.

M is for Mexico

UNITED STATES

California

TIJUANA ◉

Arizona

New Mexico

Texas

BAJA PENINSULA

SIERRA MADRE OCCIDENTAL

MONTERREY ◉

SIERRA MADRE ORIENTAL

Gulf of Mexico

CANCUN ◉

GUADALAJARA ◉

MEXICO CITY ☆

YUCATAN PENINSULA

PACIFIC OCEAN

OAXACA ◉

SIERRA MADRE DEL SUR

GUATAMALA

BELIZE

Sombrero

M is for **Mexico**,

land of the Mayas,

the Aztecs, sombreros

and beautiful playas. [PLY-ahs]

Caribbean Playa (Beach)

Cape Gopher Snake

Tortoise

The most populous country

that speaks **Español**,

It is striped with three mountains

and has mucho SOL.

So **reptiles** like tortoises,

lizards and snakes

Love to live in this nation

with **thirty-one states**.

Desert

There are DESERTS, wild JUNGLES

and *FORESTS* of pine,

Marshy WETLANDS, **savannah**

and BEACHES so fine.

Rainforest

MESTIZO'S the race

that most Mexican's claim,

A mixture of natives

and Spanish who came.

La Malinche, Mother of
the First Mestizo

They conquered the AZTECS

and MAYANS who ruled

Over cities and empires

advanced and well schooled.

Mayan Pyramid at
Chichen Itza

To build **PYRAMIDS** soaring

the Mayans used math,

They wrote hieroglyphics

and took steamy baths.

Mayan Hieroglyphics

Their accurate CALENDARS

followed the stars.

They had bustling cities

without any cars.

Mayan Calendar

The Aztecs consumed

many foods that were yummy

And completely unknown

to the rest of the world's tummies.

Avocados

They had chocolate, PEPPERS,

tomatoes and **MAIZE**,

AVOCADOS, *vanilla*

and TURKEYS they raised.

Peppers

Tomatoes

Vanilla Beans

Aztecs also built

one of the world's largest cities,

In a lake on an island –

now isn't that pretty?

Turkey

It was **MEXICO CITY**,

the capital now,

North America's

largest big city or town.

Mexico City

Now **twenty percent**

of the country lives near

This city that's thrived

more than **SIX** hundred years.

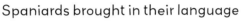
Quetzacoatl
"Feathered Serpent"

Spaniards brought in their language

and drained off the lake.

They ended all prayers

to the **feathered sky snake**.

Now Mexicans pray

to **Jesús**, and they love [hay-SOOS]

His mother who visited

them from above.

We can see her,

Our Lady of Guadalupe, [gwah-dah-lu-pay]

If we travel

to **MEXICO CITY** today.

Our Lady of
Guadalupe

There we'll spy **AZTEC TEMPLES**

and *museums galore*.

We'll stroll open-air markets

'till we're hungry and sore.

Museum of Bellas Artes

We'll eat **MOLE POBLANO** [MOH-lay poh-BLAH-noh]

(that's chocolate-sauced meat).

With hot chilies and nuts,

it's a savory treat!

Mole Poblano

So let's pick up some **Pesos**,

we'll need some dinero. [dee-NAY-roh]

In **Guadalajara**

we'll buy a **SOMBRERO.**

We'll need it for learning

their famous hat dance,

When we'll hear **MARIACHI** play music

and prance.

Mexican Hat Dance
"El Jarabe Tapatio"

Mariachi

In **OAXACA** we'll shop [wah-HAH-cah]

for some native-made crafts,

See the *world's largest tree*

and then take a **STEAM BATH.**

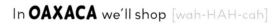

Oaxacan Craft

M5

We'll snack on **fried grasshoppers**,

tacos, burritos,

TAMALES and corn,

till we end up gorditos! [gor-DEE-toh-s, *little fatties*]

Fried Grasshoppers

Tamales

Pack your Spanish, your swimsuit,

sunglasses and **vamos!** * [BAH-moh-s, *Let's go!*]

Let's go see our neighbors

and the sights **Mexicanos!** [may-hee-CAH-no-s]

¡Bienvenidos Gringos!*

*__Bienvenidos Gringos__ [bee-AYN-bay-NEE-dohs GREEN-gohs] means "Welcome English speakers!"

← With minor changes, **Mexico's flag** has been the same since their independence from Spain in 1821. In the center is the Mexican coat of arms, → which comes from the Aztec's symbol for their capitol, Mexico-Tenochitlan. According to Aztec mythology, their leader was told in a dream that they should look for the sign of an eagle holding a snake on a cactus and found their city there. The place they first saw this symbol became their capital.

Mexican States

Official Name:
The United States of Mexico

Local Name:
Los Estados Unidos Mexicanos

Population: 120 million
(11th-largest country)

Capital: Mexico City

Largest Metropolitan Areas: Mexico City, Guadalajara, Monterrey

Comparative Size:
14th-largest country, about 25% of the size of the continental United States

Ethnicity: Mestizo 60%, Amerindian 30%, white 9%

Language: Spanish

Religion: Christianity 95% (Roman Catholic 85%, Protestant 10%)

Currency: Mexican peso

Important Industry:
Manufacturing

GEOGRAPHICAL NOTES

◉ Mexico is the world's **largest Spanish-speaking country**, with double the population of the second largest Spanish-speaking country, Spain.

◉ Mexico has **thirty-one states** and one federal district.

◉ **MEXICO** got its name from the Aztecs, who called themselves the "**Mexica**." The Aztec's capital, **Mexico-Tenochtitlan**, is still the capital today.

◉ México is pronounced **MAY-hee-coh** in Spanish.

Where in the World is Mexico?

MEXICO'S MANY CLIMATES

Desert

Rainforest

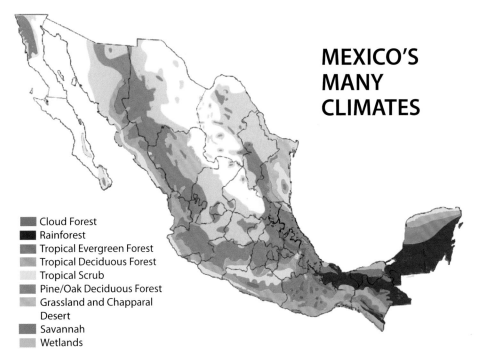

- Cloud Forest
- Rainforest
- Tropical Evergreen Forest
- Tropical Deciduous Forest
- Tropical Scrub
- Pine/Oak Deciduous Forest
- Grassland and Chapparal Desert
- Savannah
- Wetlands

↑ Because the US–Mexico border is largely desert, it's easy for Americans to think of Mexico as being hot and dry. But in reality, the **climate** varies widely, with cooler temperatures in the mountains, large forested areas, coastal wetlands and rainforest. In the highlands, like in Mexico City, there are spring-like temperatures all year long.

Cape Gopher Snake

Tortoise

Wetland

Sea Turtle

↑ Mexico's immense coastline is home to many tropical animals like sea turtles and iguanas. →

Mexico competes with Australia for the title of the country with the most **reptiles**. Its variety of sunny climates, from desert to wetlands to rainforest, provides every type of warm habitat they enjoy.

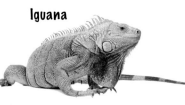

Iguana

Cloud Forest

Chaparral

Edge of the Forest in the State of Mexico

← About one-third of Mexico is **forested**, which is equal to the percent of forested land in the United States. Rainforests are mainly near the Atlantic coast and pine and oak forests are in the mountains. On the Pacific coast there are many tropical deciduous forests, also known as dry forests.

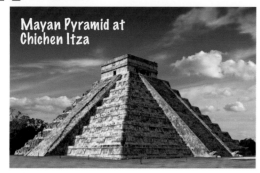

Mayan Pyramid at Chichen Itza

↑ Unlike the Egyptian **pyramids** used as tombs for pharaohs, Mayan and Aztec pyramids were usually active religious buildings. On top of their pyramids, Mayans built a shrine to a god. Steps to the top allowed priests to "ascend to the heavens" to offer prayers and sacrifices. The pyramid from the Mayan city of Chichen Itza has 365 steps, one for each day of the year. The pyramid below was topped by a temple so sacred that no one was allowed to touch it; thus the stairs were built too steep to climb. ↓

Mayan Ruins

Aztecs introduced the world to many foods. When Europeans arrived in the Americas they were unfamiliar with **tomatoes, chili peppers**, **vanilla**, **avocado**, turkeys, squash, pumpkins, potatoes, **chocolate,** corn (**maize**) and pinto, kidney and black beans. These foods, many of which originate in Mexico, are now eaten the world over. Take a look in your pantry and refrigerator; which foods have Aztec ingredients?

The Mayan and Aztec diet was based on the "**three sisters**": corn, squash and beans. The three crops grew well together in the same field. The beans provided the soil with nutrients (nitrogen) for the corn and squash. The corn provided stalks for the beans to grow up and shade for the squash to grow under. The leaves of the squash created a rough hairy ground cover that protected the plants from weeds and animal foragers. Aztecs also raised **turkeys** for meat and eggs, and hunted local game. **Cocoa beans** were so valuable they were used as money in Aztec society. The beans made a caffeinated beverage drunk only by the royalty and nobles.

Mayan Calendar

Cocoa Beans

Maize

↑ Due to their knowledge of astronomy, the Mayans knew that a solar year was 365 days long. The **Mayan Calendar** included that concept of a year (eighteen 20-day months plus five unlucky days), as well as a 260-day ceremonial or religious year (thirteen 20-day months). Mayan Calendar rounds represented exactly 52 solar years and 73 ceremonial years. Once that time frame is up, the calendar begins again.

← Mayans created the first written language in the Americas dating back to at least 300 BCE. **Mayan writing** generally used one symbol per syllable or per word. The squares to the left have combined many symbols so that each square represents a word, or even a phrase. Many Mayan words could be written in two ways: either with a picture symbol, or phonetically (by its sound), which made it very difficult for scholars to decipher. The Spanish burned most Mayan writings, believing that destroying records of their culture would make it easier to convert them to Christianity. Today only four Mayan codices (books) remain. After burning and outlawing texts, knowledge of how to read it disappeared. Only recently have scholars been able to read Mayan with any accuracy.

Mayan Writing

Detail from Diego Rivera's mural "The Great Tenochtitlan"

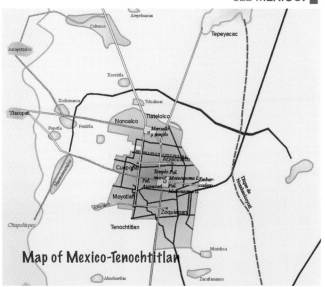

Map of Mexico-Tenochtitlan

↑ **Mexico-Tenochtitlan** was the capital of the Aztec Empire. It was a beautiful island-city founded in 1325 in the middle of lake Texcoco. The Aztecs created floating gardens, *chinampas*, to farm crops on the lake. They built an aqueduct to bring in fresh water from the mountains. Three major causeways connected the city to the mainland and each had a drawbridge that could be raised for defensive purposes. In the center of the city was a huge pyramid. Mexico-Tenochtitlan had a population of 200,000 people and was larger than any European city at that time. When the Spanish arrived, they were impressed by its wide boulevards, cleanliness, fine homes, huge markets and many canals that reminded them of Venice, Italy.

Xochimilco Canals

The Spanish, and later Mexican governments, drained ↑ most of the lakes surrounding Mexico City (due to persistent flooding). However, there are still some **canals** to the south, in the neighborhood of Xochimilco. Here, it's popular to take boat rides along the canals as the Aztecs once did and to visit the chinampas (floating gardens).

Mexico City

Quetzacoatl

↑ **Mexico City** today is one of the world's largest cities. Located in the mountains, it has spring-like temperatures throughout the year. One-fifth of all Mexicans live in or near Mexico City. With over 20 million people in the metropolitan area, many consider it the largest metropolis in the Americas.

Quetzacoatl

← ↑ **Quetzacoatl** is one of the most famous gods of pre-Christian Mexico. A feathered serpent, Quetzacoatl was the god of the morning star who gave mankind the calendar, books and maize. In one story, he created the human race from the bones of past races and his own blood. Another legend says that Quetzacoatl was an enlightened priest-king who outlawed human sacrifice. His enemy was the god Tezcatlipoca, who through trickery sent him off into exile. Quetzacoatl sailed off to the east, and it was believed that he would return in his calendar year, "One Reed." When the Spaniards arrived in their ships in Mexico, it was during "One Reed" and they later claimed that the Aztec king Montezuma was at first unsure if they were the return of Quetzacoatl.

Virgin of Guadalupe

Our Lady of Guadalupe is an image of the Virgin Mary that is believed to be miraculous. According to legend, a native peasant named Juan Diego was wandering on a hill outside of Mexico City in 1531 when the Virgin Mary appeared to him to say that she wished for a church to be built there. Juan Diego told the Spanish archbishop, who then sent him back to the hill to ask for a sign. The Virgin Mary told him to pick flowers for the archbishop, and though it was December, Juan Diego filled his cloak with roses. When he delivered the roses to the archbishop, the image of the Virgin Mary had appeared inside his cloak. The basilica that holds the image is visited by millions each year.

Father Hidalgo

Father Miguel Hidalgo was a priest and the father of Mexico's independence from Spain. A Mexican of Spanish descent, Father Hidalgo was troubled by the great poverty in his church in Dolores, which was due in part to Spain's colonial policies. In 1810, he gathered the people of his town and called for them to unite to fight Spanish rule. Mestizos, Indians and Mexican-born Spanish were asked to join under the name of Our Lady of Guadalupe to create a new nation. This call to arms that started the Mexican War for Independence is called the "Grito de Dolores." Hidalgo's cry for independence is actually reenacted every year by the current Mexican President on its anniversary, September 16, which is Mexico's Independence Day. Father Hidalgo was executed by Spanish authorities in 1811, but Mexico went on to gain its independence in 1821.

La Malinche (mah-LEEN-chay) is the most famous and controversial figure in Mexican History. A native Mexican, she served as a translator for Spanish Conquistador Hernán Cortés to communicate with the Aztecs and other indigenous groups. With her help, Cortés was able to conquer the Aztecs. Their son, Martin, is thought of as the first **mestizo**, or person of mixed Spanish and native Mexican descent. Today, 60% of the country is mestizo and Mexican culture has both Spanish and Amerindian roots. In this way, La Malinche is the mother of Mexican culture, but she has also been accused of betraying native Mexicans to the Spanish.

La Malinche & Hernán Cortés

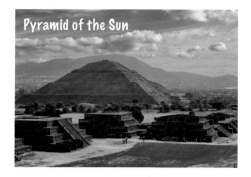
Pyramid of the Sun

The **Pyramid of the Sun** is in Teotihuacan, an archaeological site about 30 miles from Mexico City. Built between 100 BCE and 250 CE, it is the third-largest pyramid in the world and a ruin from an unknown civilization before the Aztecs. It is an example of one of the many other great Mexican civilizations including the Olmecs, Toltecs, Mixtecs and Zapotecs.

Zócalo

Zócalo is the central plaza in Mexico City and the largest public square in the Western Hemisphere. A central gathering place for people since Aztec times, it is bordered by the Cathedral, the National Palace and the Aztec's Templo Mayor.

Mexico City claims to have more **museums** than any city in the world — art, anthropology, history, culture — there are so many to see!

Museum of the Palace of Fine Arts

Mole Poblano

Sometimes called the national dish of Mexico, **mole poblano** is a sauce for chicken or other meats that is made from chocolate, nuts, peppers and other spices. Mole sauce is savory, not sweet, and has 20 different ingredients, giving it a very complex flavor.

Sombrero

← **Sombreros** are practical hats for dry, intensely sunny climates. Providing enough shade to cool and protect its wearer from the sun, sombreros were originally used by Mexican cowboys and horse riders. Today, they have become symbols of Mexican culture.

Arbol del Tule

← **Arbol del Tule** is a tree in Oaxaca that has the world's thickest trunk, measuring 30 ft (9 m) wide. It is a Montezuma cypress, estimated to be over 1,400 years old.

Mariachi have become the most famous type of Mexican musicians. Originally, they were strolling street musicians dressed in traditional clothing who played festive folk music perfect for celebrations. Mariachi bands typically include vihuela and guitarron (both string instruments similar to guitars), as well as violins and/or trumpets. Some people think the word mariachi came from "marriage," as they frequently play at weddings. →

Mariachi

Temazcal (Steam Bath)

Steam baths or *temazcal* were ↑ used by the Aztecs for health and purification. They also bathed themselves with water and soap on a daily basis, which shocked the Spanish when they arrived. At that time Europeans rarely bathed, as they thought it could cause illness.

Mexican Hat Dance

↑The **Mexican hat dance** or the *Jarabe Tapatio*, is a folk dance that tells the story of a courtship. Danced in traditional costumes, the men dress up as charros, or horsemen, and the women wear wide skirts with embroidered blouses. The couples dance playfully around one another to lively music. The woman first rejects the man, then the man throws down his hat and they dance around it. When she moves to pick up his hat, he kicks his leg over her head, symbolizing that he has won his lady. The Mexican hat dance has become a symbol of Mexico and most children learn how to dance it in school.

Oaxacan Craft

← **Oaxaca** (wah-HAH-ka) is famous as a center for indigenous culture and for handicrafts like this carved wooden sculpture. Oaxaca is home to many native groups including Zapotecs and Mixtecs.

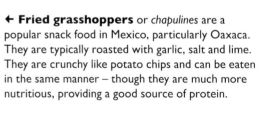

Fried Grasshoppers

← **Fried grasshoppers** or *chapulines* are a popular snack food in Mexico, particularly Oaxaca. They are typically roasted with garlic, salt and lime. They are crunchy like potato chips and can be eaten in the same manner – though they are much more nutritious, providing a good source of protein.

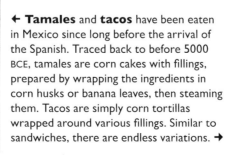

Tamales

Tacos

← **Tamales** and **tacos** have been eaten in Mexico since long before the arrival of the Spanish. Traced back to before 5000 BCE, tamales are corn cakes with fillings, prepared by wrapping the ingredients in corn husks or banana leaves, then steaming them. Tacos are simply corn tortillas wrapped around various fillings. Similar to sandwiches, there are endless variations. →

With **gorgeous beaches** on the Pacific Ocean, the Gulf of Mexico and the Caribbean Sea, Mexico's coastline is a popular vacation destination. Both for its beaches and ancient Native American ruins, Mexico has become the number one country visited by American tourists, and it is the most popular tourist destination in Latin America. ➔

Pacific Beach near Puerto Vallarta

Caribbean Beach near Tulum

Oregon
Idaho
Wyoming
Nevada
Utah
Mexican Cession 1848
California
Colorado
PACIFIC OCEAN
Arizona
New Mexico
Gadsden Purchase 1853

← Did you know that the southwest of the United States was once a part of Mexico? Almost a third of US land was once part of the Spanish colony of "New Spain." In 1819, Spain gave up Florida to the United States in exchange for uncontested rights to Texas. When Mexico gained its independence from Spain in 1821, their territory included all the land from Texas west to California. Mexico lost the land to the United States during the **Mexican-American War** (1846–1848). The war was sparked by the United States annexing Texas (making it part of the United States) in 1845. Texas had declared its independence from Mexico as "The Republic of Texas" in 1936, and Texans largely favored becoming a part of the United States. But, as Mexico had never recognized Texan independence, it fought the United States in an attempt to regain the territory. When Mexico lost, it also lost all of the land west of Texas to the Pacific, roughly half of Mexico's territory at the time. Many Mexicans who lived in this territory remained and became Americans. And many former Mexican cities like Los Angeles, San Diego and Santa Fe kept their Spanish names.

Mexican Americans make up 10% of the US population. Sixty percent of all Mexican Americans live in Texas or California. Some famous Mexican Americans include actress Salma Hayek, comedian George Lopez, actress and singer Selena Gomez and civil rights leader Cesar Chavez. ➔

Salma Hayek

Cesar Chavez is probably the most famous Mexican American in history. He worked to end the abuse and exploitation of migrant farm workers in California and across the United States. A child of migrant farm workers, he spent his childhood moving around Arizona and California, rarely able to attend school. Eventually, he became a farm worker himself and the cofounder of the National Farm Workers Association, which worked to ensure better pay and safer working conditions for migrant workers. A civil rights leader who believed in nonviolence, Chavez performed fasts where he would not eat for over 20 days in order to draw national attention to the injustices faced by migrant workers. ➔

"ONCE SOCIAL CHANGE BEGINS, IT CANNOT BE REVERSED. YOU CANNOT UNEDUCATE THE PERSON WHO HAS LEARNED TO READ. YOU CANNOT HUMILIATE THE PERSON WHO FEELS PRIDE. YOU CANNOT OPPRESS THE PEOPLE WHO AREN'T AFRAID ANYMORE."

CESAR CHAVEZ DAY MARCH 31, 2010

Listen to the
SOUNDS
of MEXICO

Learn to sing the chorus of:

Cielito Lindo

"Cielito Lindo" is a Mexican *ranchera* song known best by its chorus, which begins: "Ay, ay, ay, ay, canta no llores." The chorus means "Don't cry, sing! Because singing gladdens hearts." "Cielito lindo" literally means "pretty little heaven" and is a term of endearment. **YOUTUBE SEARCH:** Cielito Lindo lyrics English

Marcha de Zacatecas

A rousing patriotic song, nearly as popular as the national anthem. It's hard not to start marching when you hear it.
YOUTUBE SEARCH: Marcha de Zacatecas

Mariachi

Mariachi is not a style of music but a type of band that plays traditional Mexican music. Mariachi always wear costumes and play the vihuela and guitarron. Bands usually also include a trumpet or violin.

guitarron

vihuela

Favorite Mariachi songs: "El Rey," "Cielito Lindo," "Las Mañanitas" (the Mexican birthday song), "El Jarabe Tapatío" (Mexican hat dance song), "Viva Mexico!" and "Mexico Lindo y Querido."
YOUTUBE SEARCH: mariachi + song name

Norteño Music

A norteño band typically has a button accordion, a bajo sexto (similar to a guitar, but with twice the number of strings) and frequently a double bass, drum set and a saxophone. Norteño (northern) music is popular on both sides of the US–Mexico border. Try **Ramon Ayala**'s "Un Rinconcito en el Cielo" or "Chaparra de mi Amor."

Banda Music

Banda music was developed in Sinaloa state after an influx of German immigrants settled there. It mixes the brass instruments and rhythm of polka with Mexican music for a fun, festive combination.
Try **Banda Carnaval**'s "Y Te Vas"or "Fiesta A Himara" or "Cahuetes, Pistaches" by **Banda Sinaloense**.

READ:

Horse Hooves and Chicken Feet: Mexican Folktales by Neil Phillip. Traditional folktales filled with magic, humor and Catholic beliefs reflect Mexican culture. Ages 9 & up.

The Woman Who Outshone the Sun by Alejandro Cruz Martinez. A folktale about tolerance based on a legend of the Zapotec Indians of Oaxaca. Ages 5 & up.

El Cucuy: A Bogeyman Cuento in English and Spanish by Joe Hayes. Discover the terrifying bogeyman of Mexico and much of the Hispanic world. Ages 6 & up.

Mexico: 40 Activities to Experience Mexico Past and Present by Susan Milord. Ages 8 & up.

The First Tortilla: A Bilingual Story by Rudolfo Anaya. A folktale about the origin of tortillas. Ages 9 & up.

Lucha Libre: The Man in the Silver Mask by Xavier Garza. Carlitos attends his first Lucha Libre wrestling match in Mexico City. Ages 7 & up.

Playing Lotería by Rene Colato Lainez. Discover Loteria, an elaborate Mexican Bingo that brings an American boy and his Mexican abuela together. Ages 6 & up.

Diego Rivera: His World and Ours by Duncan Tonatiuh. An introduction to the artist and inspiration to make your own murals. Ages 5 & up.

Frida Kahlo: The Artist Who Painted Herself by Margaret Frith. Discover Frida's daring art and life. Ages 8 & up.

Frida Kahlo and Diego Rivera: Their Lives and Ideas, 24 Activities by Carol Sabbeth. Ages 10 & up.

Esperanza Rising by Pamela Muñoz Ryan. Set during the Depression, Esperanza must leave her life as the daughter of a rich Mexican rancher, emigrate to the US and become a migrant farm worker to save her mom. Ages 10 & up.

Aztec Food Safari

Go on safari in your kitchen to see if you can find Aztec foods! Which Aztec foods do you eat? What foods in your kitchen would Aztecs not have had access to? And what foods did the rest of the world not have before coming to the Americas? (See "P is for Peru" for information about potatoes.) Which foods combine American and "Old World" ingredients? After your safari, make an Aztec meal. Soft corn tortillas are an easy base with beans, tomatoes, guacamole and peppers as possibilities to go on top. There would not be any dairy products – but that is true of many Mexican recipes even today, which are quite different from cheesier Tex-Mex foods.

DON'T MISS WATCHING
(online)

The Mexican Hat Dance

El Jarabe Tapatio, known to Americans as the "Mexican Hat Dance," has become a symbol of Mexico. There are several similar dances from different regions, but the Jarabe Tapatio is from Guadalajara. **YOUTUBE SEARCH: Jarabe Tapatio**

La Leyenda de la Llorona

Translated as "The Legend of the Weeping Woman," this fun 2011 animated film puts kids in the middle of Mexican folklore. It's available on DVD in English or Spanish, or to stream in Spanish with English subtitles. Also from the same animation studio, *La Leyenda de la Nahuala* (2007) is about celebrating the Day of the Dead. It's available on DVD with English subtitles. See trailers on YouTube, stream it on Netflix or buy DVDs on Amazon.

Day of the Dead Celebrations

Unlike its US counterpart, Halloween, El Día de los Muertos is a time for Mexican families to honor and "visit" with their relatives who have passed away. Graves are decorated and offerings are made to invite spirits to visit with their family. Travel Channel and BBC both have short documentaries about the holiday. **YOUTUBE SEARCH: Day of the Dead Mexico**

SPEAK SPANISH!

Hola!	Hello!	*OH-lah*
Buenos días!	Good day!	*BWAY-nohs DEE-ahs*
Buenos tardes!	Good afternoon!	*BWAY-nohs TAR-days*
Cómo está?	How are you?	*COH-moh ays-TAH?*
Bien, y usted?	Well, and you?	*bee-AYN ee oo-STAYD?*
Por favor.	Please.	*POR fah-VOR*
Gracias.	Thank you.	*GRAH-see-ahs*
De nada.	You're welcome.	*day NAH-dah*
Me encanta guacamole.	I love guacamole.	*may ayn-CAHN-tah gwah-cah-MOH-lay*
Me gusta viajar.	I like to travel.	*may GOO-stah bee-ah-HAR*
No me gusta pelear.	I don't like fighting.	*no may GOO-stah pay-lay-AR*
Le gusta bailar?	Do you like to dance?	*lay GOO-stah bigh-LAR*
Te amo.	I love you.	*tay AH-moh*
Dígame.	Tell me.	*DEE-gah-may*
Diga. (Hello on the phone)	Speak.	*DEE-gah*
Hasta luego.	See you later.	*AH-stah loo-AY-goh*
Adiós.	Goodbye.	*ah-dee-OHS*

MAKE MEXICAN
Guacamole

Guacamole comes from the Aztec word for "avocado sauce." Aztecs did not originally use onion or garlic, as they were not available in the Americas, so you can omit those altogether if you'd like your guacamole to contain only the original Aztec ingredients. But in modern day Mexico, most guacamole includes one or both. This recipe can be scaled up or down depending on how many avocados you want to use.

1. Chop up tomato, onion and pepper and put in a bowl.
2. Cut avocado in half, remove seed and scoop flesh into bowl.
3. Using a fork, mash avocado into other ingredients.
4. Add salt, cilantro and lime*, and stir.

*If you would like to save this guacamole to eat later, mix half of your lime juice in, then squeeze the rest over the top of the guacamole and cover with plastic wrap or waxed paper, laying it directly on the guacamole, allowing no air to touch its surface. Store in the refrigerator. This will keep your guacamole from spoiling, as it can brown quickly when exposed to the air.

¼ **large tomato,** seeds removed, chopped
1–2 tablespoons minced onion
¼ **jalapeño pepper, minced**
1 avocado, ripe and soft
½ **teaspoon salt**
1–2 tablespoons cilantro, chopped (to taste)
Juice of ¼ lime

MAKE PAPEL PICADO

Papel picado or "perforated paper" is a folk art in Mexico that is commonly used as decorations for festivals, celebrations and religious holidays. Mexican artists actually use special chisels and a hammer, a design pattern and a stack of tissue paper to cut out 40 or more pieces of papel picado at one time.

METHOD: There are two ways to make papel picado. You can fold the paper and cut it with scissors as you would when making a "paper snowflake." That method is beautiful and quick – just remember to leave a band of paper at the top that can be folded over so that it may be strung up. There are even templates online for using the "snowflake method" to make folded papel picado into pictures like a skull or a cat's face.

The other method is to use an exacto knife to cut a design into a stack of tissue paper. This method, described below, is more time consuming, but it creates an entire string of papel picado at one time. And, it allows you to create a picture, write words or make whatever image you can dream up. There are amazing papel picado templates online. Check them out to get a few ideas before you start.

WORKSPACE: Create a cardboard workspace, by stacking at least two pieces of shipping box cardboard and taping them together. Stack twelve pieces of tissue paper, of at least two colors, on top of the workspace and put a plain piece of paper on top with your design. Staple paper and tissue to the cardboard in the four corners to secure it during cutting.

DESIGN: Sketch out a design idea on a piece of paper, you don't have to follow it exactly. Choose a simple design and keep in mind that it is easier to cut straight lines than curves. Each cut must not be too wide or it will make the paper below it sag. Make sure you leave ¾ inch of paper at the top that can be folded over to hang it from a line.

CUTTING: When using the exacto knife, you will want to slice all the way down into the first layer of cardboard in order to cut through all the tissue. Cut out the full design, then remove staples and use scissors to cut off the extra tissue paper borders outside of your design.

HANGING: Fold over and crease each piece of tissue paper at the top. Then line them all up, keeping a half inch between each piece of tissue paper. Run a thread through the fold of the entire line of papel picado. Thin some liquid glue with water, then use a cotton swab to wipe watery glue into the crease. Then press down on fold to stick. Allow to dry and you're ready to hang your papel picado!

Rough design outline stapled over a stack of tissue paper into cardboard workspace

Using exacto knife to cut through paper and tissue down to cardboard. You may decide on a simpler design.

Completed cutout before removing staples and tissue paper border

With top folded over and glued to string to hang in a line.

PAPER SNOWFLAKE METHOD: Here are some examples of what you can create with the snowflake method of making papel picado. You can make 2–3 at one time. Look online as there are many patterns to make pictures of skulls or other shapes with the "snowflake method."

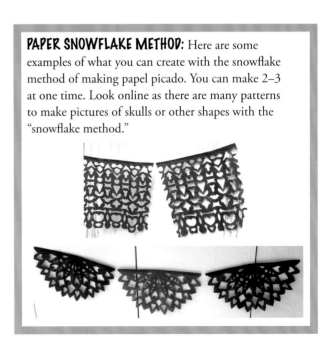

N is for Nigeria

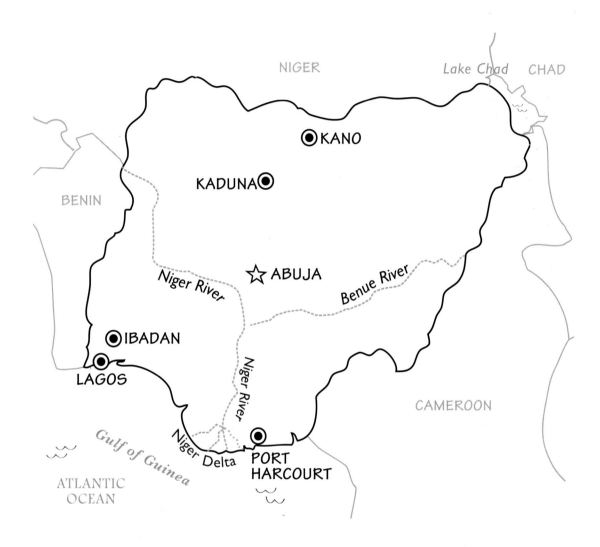

Our **N** is Nigeria,

a fast-growing nation

called **AFRICA'S GIANT**

for its huge population.

Map of the Traditional Homelands
of the Largest Ethnic Groups

Benué River

Kwa Falls in
Southast Nigeria

Nigerians are

quite diverse as a people.

With **500 languages,**

most are bilingual.

Fishing on the Niger River

But English unites

this country with roots

From **250**

distinct ethnic groups.

There are **Hausa**, Fulani,   [HOW-sah, foo-LAH-nee]

Yoruba, Igbo,   [YOR-roo-bah, EE-boh]

Ijaw, Kanuri,   [EE-jaw, kah-NUR-ree]

Tiv, Ibibio.   [tiv, ih-bih-BEE-yo]

Rivers Niger and Benué [NIGH-jur, BEN-way]

divide it in three,

Into northern **savannah,**

WET west and southeast.

The Igbo and **YORUBA**

mostly live down

In the green, humid south

where **rainforests** are found.

School in Southwest
Nigeria

Lagos

And there, you'll find **LAGOS**
(Nigeria's **New York**),
And most of the **Christians**
and dishes with **pork.**

Hausa Farmer

The **Fulani** and Hausa
live mostly on top,
Where many Raise Cattle
or tend to grain crops.

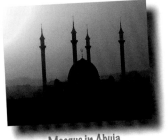

Mosque in Abuja
During Harmattan

Their faith is Islam,
their weather is **DRY**
And **HARMATTAN** winds [HAR-mah-tahn]
can darken the sky.

Though **climate,**
religion and **languages** change,
Across all Nigeria
some things stay the same.

Nollywood Star

Green Eagles
Football Player

They love to watch movies
All **NOLLYWOOD MADE,**
And they root for the **EAGLES**
When football is played.

Fried Plantains

Cassava

They eat cassava garri

and *fried **sweet** plantains*.

They eat **black-eyed pea** dishes

– too many to name!

Black Eyed Peas

They spend **NAIRA** on clothes

to look good for their friends.

They learn English in school

but most speak some **PIDGIN.**

Naira

"How you dey?" they may greet you,

(Are you doing well?).

"Make I yarn!" they will say

if they've something to tell.

King Sunny Adé

In the south you'll hear **JUJU,**

King Sunny Adé,

Fela Kuti's **afrobeat,**

gospel and reggae.

In the north, they listen

to **GRIOTS** sing praise;   [gree-ohs]

But everywhere POP and

HIP HOP   are played.

Rapper D'banj

They read Chinua Achebe's book, [CHIN-wah ah-CHEH-bay]

THINGS FALL APART,

Poems of Wole Soyinka [WOH-lay shoy-YINK-kah]

and study great art –

Benin Bronze

BENIN BRONZES, **Nok sculptures** –

masterworks of mankind,

Made by **Ancestor Kingdoms**

with cultures refined.

Nok Sculpture

Long before Britain came

there were great kingdoms here,

But there was no **"NIGERIA"**

Until Brits appeared.

It was in **1914**

that Britain united

The land of Nigeria,

its borders decided.

Colonial Flag of Nigeria

And in **1960**

they gained **INDEPENDENCE,**

And kept up their union,

through wars waged within it.

And soon it was known

as a land rich in **OIL**,

and drilling for petrol

brought wealth from their soil.

But **DIVERSITY** still

is this land's greatest worth.

Oh **Nigeria**,

largest black nation on earth.

You are welcome to Naija!*

**Edo Mask of Queen Idia
From the Kingdom of Benin
16th Century**

**Mask from Nok Culture
in Kaduna, 500–50 BCE**

Igbo Mask

*__Naija__ [NIGH-jah] is a nickname for Nigeria.

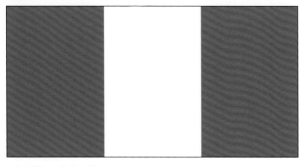

The name **NIGERIA** comes from the Niger *(NIGH-jur)* River, which flows through the countries of Guinea, Mali, Niger and Nigeria. The Niger River has many different names in different languages. Its English name probably came from the Tuareg language, in which the river is called *egereou **n-iger**eouen* or "river of rivers." Europeans first encountered the river in Timbuktu, Mali, trading with Tuareg businessmen. The European version was probably also influenced by a Latin word, *niger*, which means black. Although the Niger River isn't black, the people who live along it were very dark skinned to Europeans. **Naija** is a popular nickname for Nigeria, it is also sometimes spelled **9ja**.

↑ **Nigeria's flag** was adopted in 1960 when it gained independence from the British Empire. The green bands represent the forest and abundant natural resources of Nigeria, and the white band represents peace.

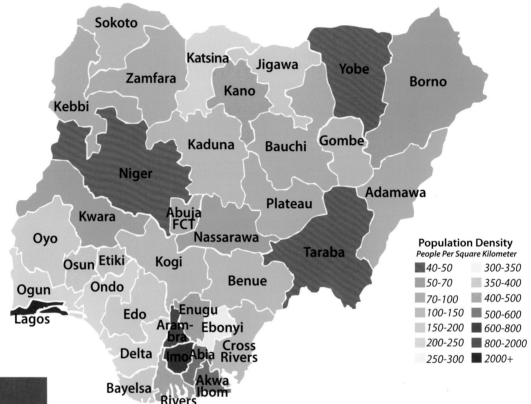

Nigerian States and Population Density

Population Density
People Per Square Kilometer

40-50	300-350
50-70	350-400
70-100	400-500
100-150	500-600
150-200	600-800
200-250	800-2000
250-300	2000+

Official Name: Federal Republic of Nigeria

Population: 177 million

Capital: Abuja

Largest Cities: Lagos, Kano, Ibadan, Kaduna

Comparative Size: Slightly more than twice the size of California, a bit smaller than Egypt

Ethnicity: Hausa & Fulani 29%, Yoruba 21%, Igbo 18%, Ijaw 10%, Kanuri 4%, Ibibio 3.5%, Tiv 2.5%, over 250 ethnic groups in total

Language: English (official), Hausa, Yoruba, Igbo, Fulani and more than 500 other languages.

Religion: Muslim 49%, Christian 49%

Currency: Nigerian naira

Key Export: Oil

Where in the World is Nigeria?

GEOGRAPHICAL NOTES

◉ Nigeria has the **largest population** of any country in Africa. It has over half the population of the United States but is growing at a much faster rate. Nigeria is currently the seventh-largest country in the world, but it is projected to be the fourth-largest country in the world by 2050, right behind the third-largest country, the United States.

◉ Nigeria has **36 states** and one federal capital territory, Abuja. Abuja was a planned city that became the capital in 1991. The former capital, **Lagos**, is the largest city in Sub-Saharan Africa.

Ethno-Linguistic Map of Nigeria

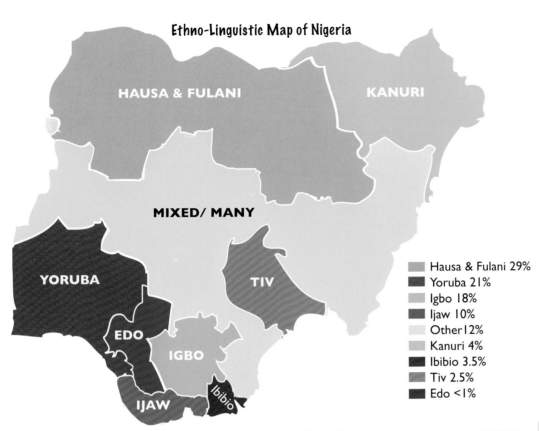

HAUSA & FULANI

KANURI

MIXED/ MANY

YORUBA

TIV

EDO

IGBO

IJAW

Ibibio

Hausa & Fulani 29%
Yoruba 21%
Igbo 18%
Ijaw 10%
Other 12%
Kanuri 4%
Ibibio 3.5%
Tiv 2.5%
Edo <1%

← Nigeria has over **250 ethnic groups** and more than 500 languages. Though Nigerians move freely about the country, this map shows the traditional locations of the largest ethnic groups and where they still make up a dominant part of the population.

The "Middle Belt" is the most diverse part of Nigeria, where many ethnic groups live and where religions and climates from the North and South meet and mix.

Though there are more than 500 different local languages in Nigeria, everyone learns **English** in school, so that is the main language of government, business, news and signage. About 45% of Nigerians are multilingual and speak more than two languages.

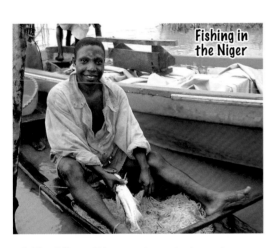

Fishing in the Niger

↑ The **Niger River** is the main river of West Africa and the third-longest river on the continent (after the Nile River and the Congo River). The Niger River floods each year and is used for irrigating farmland in each country it flows through. Fishing is very important along the river and the Niger River Delta is the source of most of Nigeria's oil wealth. ↓

Niger River   SAHARA DESERT

MALI   Niger River Basin

Timbuktu

NIGER

Bamako   Niamey

GUINEA

BENIN   NIGERIA

ATLANTIC OCEAN

Gulf of Guinea

School in Ondo State

Abeokuta, Ogun State

Lagos

Kwa Falls, Cross River State

← ↑ Lush green southern Nigeria has **rainforests**, waterfalls and marshes. Lagos, Nigeria's biggest city (and the biggest city in Sub-Saharan Africa), is on the coast and gets on average 72 in (183 cm) of rain per year, more than any major American city. There are two rainy seasons in Southern Nigeria: April– July and October–November.

Igbo Bride and Groom

← **Traditional dress** varies among each ethnic group in Nigeria, but all like to dress up in the same fabric for special events like weddings and festivals. →

Yoruba Drummers

Lagos

↑ **Lagos** is like New York City in that it is Nigeria's largest city and its financial center. It is also a port city filled with immigrants from all over Nigeria and West Africa.

Nigeria is → roughly half **Christian** and half **Muslim**. Christians tend to live in the south of Nigeria and Muslims in the north. Christians are Catholic, Anglican, Protestant, Evangelical or members of local churches.

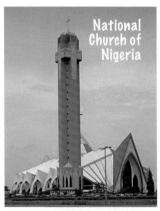

National Church of Nigeria

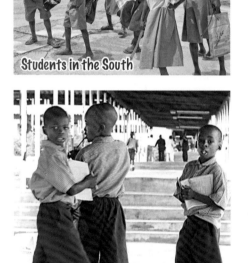

Students in the South

Students in the North

←↑ **Students** in Nigeria wear uniforms and learn in English in school. The style of uniform changes around the country, as does the local language in which they are also taught. Though students learn standard English in school, a type of Nigerian English known as "Pidgin" (or "Brokin") is spoken informally in marketplaces and around towns throughout Nigeria. ↓

Northern Nigeria was converted to Islam 1100–1600 CE. There are also many Muslims in southwest Nigeria among the Yoruba. Yoruba people, like Nigerians as a whole, are roughly 50% Christian and 50% Muslim. ↓

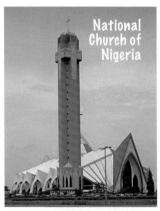

Nigerian Nun

Students in the South

Students in the North

Mosque in Abuja

↑ This photo of a mosque in Abuja was probably taken during **Harmattan**, a time during the dry season when winds come down from the Sahara Desert filling the air with a fine layer of dust. The air stays hazy and cooler during Harmattan, a season that affects all of West Africa south of the Sahara Desert.

↓ As you go north, Nigeria gradually gets drier. **Northern Nigeria** becomes a grassland then a dry savannah. The grassland provides a large area suitable for grazing animals or growing grain crops.

Hausa Farmer

Hausa Griot

↑ **Griots** are traditional musicians, poets, historians and storytellers. They sing praise songs and tell stories passed down for generations.

← **Nollywood** is the name of Nigeria's local film industry, the second largest in the world after the Indian film industries in terms of the number of films made per year. Nigerians prefer their own films to foreign productions. Films go immediately to DVDs that are sold in markets and watched at home. Nigerian films are popular in many African countries.

Fried Plantains

↑ **Fried plantains** are a popular side dish in Nigeria.

Cassava

← Nigeria is the world's largest producer of **cassava**, a tropical crop that is a staple food in many parts of Africa, Asia and South America. Cassava, which is also called manioc and yucca, is as versatile as potatoes, it can be mashed, boiled, fried, and made into flour. It makes many food products including tapioca, fufu, garri and cassava flour. Garri is a staple food in Nigeria. It is made from cassava chips that have been allowed to ferment and then are dried in the sun and ground into granules. Cassava can grow in poor soil, even under drought conditions. However, cassava must be properly prepared as it is poisonous raw.

Nollywood Star

Actress Ufuoma Ejenobor

Black-eyed Peas

Akara

← **Naira**

↑ *Did you know that* **black-eyed peas** *originally come from Africa?* They were brought to the United States through the slave trade. They are usually called cowpeas in Nigeria, and they are made into many types of dishes. There are black-eyed pea fritters called *akara* and there's black-eyed pea spoon bread called *moi moi*. (See a recipe for akara on page 195.) →

The **naira** is ↑ Nigeria's currency. A naira can be divided into 100 *kobo*. The naira sign (used like a dollar sign) is an N with two horizontal lines through it. ↓

₦5

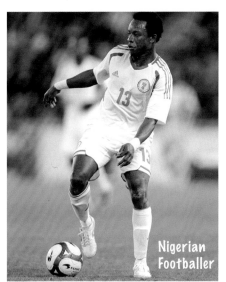
Nigerian Footballer

← **Football** (or soccer) is the most popular sport in Nigeria. The national men's team is the Super Eagles (formerly called the Green Eagles) which regularly goes to the FIFA World Cup. The women's national team, the Super Falcons, has dominated and typically won the African Women's Championship.

Nigerian Football Fans

Femi Kuti

Fela Kuti (1938–1997) was a musical pioneer who created a new style of music called **Afrobeat**, which mixes American jazz and funk with traditional Yoruba music and Nigerian highlife music. Afrobeat music gained a worldwide following, and Fela Kuti used his fame to promote human rights in Nigeria.

← His sons, **Femi Kuti** and Seun Kuti, continue to make Afrobeat music today.

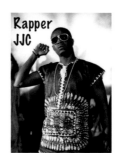
Rapper JJC

← **Hip hop** is as popular → in Nigeria as it is in the United States, and Nigerian artists as well as Americans are popular on the radio.

← *Rapper JJC, part of the Nigerian diaspora in the UK.*

Rapper D'banj →

D'banj

Sunny Adé

← **"King" Sunny Adé** is a star of **juju** music. Mixing traditional Yoruba polyrhythms with steel guitar, keyboard and talking drums, juju is a mellow, infectious dance music.

Traditional Music → and dancing are still passed down and performed in each ethnic and religious community. These Jarawa musicians are performing for a celebration in Plateau State.

These drummers are participating in *Qadirriyyah Maukib*, an Islamic festival in Kano. ↓

← **Wole Soyinka**, a Nigerian poet and playwright, was the first African to win a Nobel Prize in Literature in 1986. A political activist, many of his plays used humor and satire to criticize oppressive governments and corrupt people in society.

Wole Soyinka

Chinua Achebe's book, *Things Fall Apart,* is a classic of world literature and the first African novel to become internationally known. Published in 1958, it tells the story of European colonialism from an African viewpoint. Set in an Igbo village, the destruction of traditional culture makes "things fall apart" for Igbo individuals who are caught between the values and beliefs they were raised with and a new foreign world view that claims those values are wrong. Achebe challenges the idea that European empires brought progress to Africa by capturing both the sophistication of Igbo culture and the destructive effect of colonialism on individuals and traditional society. →

Chinua Achebe

Drummers in Kano

The **Nok culture** thrived in → Nigeria between 500 BCE and 200 CE. Little is know about the society beyond the many beautiful terra-cotta sculptures and iron tools that have been excavated from sites in central Nigeria. The sculptures can be as large as life size and frequently display elaborate hair and jewelry. It is thought that the Nok people may have been ancestors to the Yoruba as there are some similarities in their artistic styles. →

Nok Sculpture

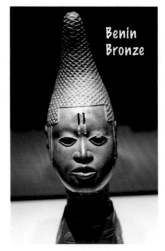
Benin Bronze

← **Benin bronzes** are cast metal sculptures that are considered masterpieces of world art. They were created by the Kingdom of Benin, which ruled in Nigeria from the 13th to the 19th century before being defeated by the British Empire. The British took most of the bronzes from the king's or *oba's* palace and brought them back to Britain. When Europeans first saw them in museums, they were shocked. They couldn't believe that Africans they viewed as "uncivilized" had made such beautiful, technically superior art.

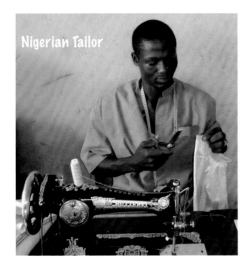

Nigerian Tailor

← Big occasion or party coming up? In Nigeria, you *→* and your friends or family might decide to all have clothing made in the same fabric for the event. This tradition, called "***aso-ebi***" by the Yoruba, is common at parties, weddings and funerals. At weddings, the family and friends of the bride may wear one fabric and the groom's family another. Getting your clothes "tailor-made" is still the standard in Nigeria. *↓*

Boys at a Party

Igbo Ladies at a Wedding

Nigeria has abundant **oil** and **natural gas**. Their largest export is petroleum and they are estimated to have the tenth-largest oil reserves in the world. The majority of government revenue comes from oil production, Nigeria's largest industry. *→*

The **Niger River Delta** is the vast marshy land where the river splits into several branches before it meets the ocean. It is also the site of almost all of Nigeria's rich oil resources. *↓*

Oil Rig & Ship near Lagos

Not only is Nigeria the **world's largest black country**, it has nearly double the population of the next largest country in Africa. One in four Africans is Nigerian, and almost one in five people of African descent is Nigerian. For comparison, there are roughly 41 million African Americans in the United States. In Brazil, there are 14 million people who identify themselves as black, and another 82 million mixed-race Brazilians who claim some African heritage. *↓*

Largest Countries in Africa*

1. Nigeria	177 million
2. Ethiopia	97 million
3. Egypt	87 million
4. D.R. Congo	77 million
5. South Africa	50 million
6. Tanzania	48 million
7. Kenya	45 million
8. Algeria	39 million
9. Uganda	36 million
10. Sudan	35 million

*2014, CIA World Factbook

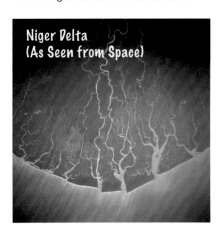

Niger Delta
(As Seen from Space)

Bush Elephant

*← Nigeria's national parks are home to many **wild animals** including elephants, monkeys, lions and hippos. ↓*

Mona Monkeys

Picking up groceries in Nigeria typically means going to an **outdoor market**. There are street-side vendors, walking sellers, convenience stores and a few supermarkets, but for a major shopping expedition, a large outdoor market, or partially covered market like this one, is the place to go to find the best selection and price for virtually anything. Shoppers must bargain with vendors to decide on a price for all goods and services. *→*

Lekki Market in Lagos

Listen to the SOUNDS of NIGERIA

All suggestions available on YouTube.

Highlife Highlife combines African rhythms with guitars, horns and influences from jazz.
Try: "Sweet Mother" by **Prince Nico Mbarga**
"Osondi Owendi" by **Chief Stephen Osita Osadebe**
"Ada Ada" by **Flavour**

Juju Popular music using the "talking drum" and Yoruba percussion as a base. Also try Afro-juju, a style made popular by Shina Peters that mixes juju and Afrobeat.
Try: "Iba Foluwa Ajo-Ajo Kodabi Ile" by **Ebenezer Obey**
"Oro Towo Baseti" by **King Sunny Ade**
"Ijo Shina" by **Shina Peters**.

Afrobeat is a mixture of jazz, funk and Nigerian highlife.
Try: **Fela Kuti**'s "Shakara," "Zombie"or "Water No Get Enemy"
Femi Kuti's "Truth Don Die," **Wizkid**'s "Jaiye Jaiye"
Lagbaja's "Konko Below"

Nigerian Hip Hop
Wizkid's "Pakurumo," **Olamide**'s "Young Erikina"
Ice Prince's "Aboki," **Soultan Abdul**'s "Aboki Party"

Other Suggestions:
Banky W's "Yes/No" (R&B)
Onyeka Onwenu's "Onye Bu Nwannem" (Gospel)
Lynxx's "Fine Lady" featuring Wizkid
JJC's "We Are Africans" Naija Remix
2Face Idibia's "African Queen"
D'banj's "Fall in Love"
Chidinma's "Kedike"
Adam Zango's "Duniya Tazo Karshe" (Hausa Pop)
Mamman Shata's "Lafiya Zaki" (Hausa Griot)

READ:

Anna Hibiscus by Atinuke.
Written by a Nigerian author and set in "Africa," Anna Hibiscus is a sort of "Ramona Quimby" of Africa. A short chapter book with illustrations, it is a captivating introduction to African family values for all ages. Ages 5 & up.

Master Man: A Tall Tale of Nigeria by Aaron Shepard.
With comic book color and action, boastful Shadusa learns to be careful of his claims. Ages 5 & up.

Ikenna Goes to Nigeria by Ifeoma Onyefulu.
Ikenna goes from London to visit his extended family in Nigeria. A photo essay showing a real child experiencing Nigerian life and culture. Ages 5 & up.

Here Comes Our Bride: An African Wedding Story by Ifeoma Onyefulu. A photo essay from a child's perspective of all the traditions of a Nigerian wedding. Ages 5 & up.

Why the Sun and Moon Live in the Sky by Elphinstone Dayrell. A folktale about Nigerian hospitality. Ages 4 & up.

Beat the Story Drum Pum Pum by Ashley Bryan.
Five rhythmically told Nigerian folktales with woodcut illustrations. Ages 8 & up.

Chike and the River by Chinua Achebe. Young Chike leaves his village and family and sets off on an adventure to cross the Niger River and go live with his uncle. Ages 9 & up.

How the Leopard Got His Claws by Chinua Achebe. A fable and allegory about Nigerian society. Ages 9 & up.

The Girl Who Married a Ghost and Other Tall Tales from Nigeria by Ifeoma Onyefulu. Ages 7 & up.

SPEAK NIGERIAN PIDGIN ENGLISH!

How you dey? How body? How are you?
I dey fine.   I'm fine.
Body dey inside cloth.   I'm still clothed.
 A pitiful response to "How body?" meaning, "Could be worse."
Wetin? What? Dey: To be, is, are, am
Wetin dey?   What's happening?
How now? How Far? How are you? Hi!/ Hello
I no know. I don't know.
I no sabi. I don't understand.
Sabi sabi Know it all
Wahala Problem, trouble *Why you dey give me wahala?*
Vex Upset
I no gree. I don't agree.

Go Slow Traffic jam
Chop Eat
Abeg Please
Na so? Isn't that so?
Abi? Isn't it?
Gi mi. Give it to me.
Eh eh. No.
Silpass Slippers, known in the US as flip-flops
Distin This thing, that thing
Small small: very small   *Doubling words means very.*
Bad bad bad bad Very, very bad
Dem send you? Have you been sent to torment me?

Wetin dey?

Visit www.australiatozimbabwe.com for links to online activities.

MAKE NIGERIAN
AKARA (Black-eyed Pea Fritters)

A little like hashbrowns made of black-eyed peas, akara make a tasty breakfast, snack or side dish.

1. **SOAK:** Soak black-eyed peas for at least 8 hours, placing them in a large mixing bowl full of hot water. (Peas will greatly expand during soak.)
2. **BLEND:** Drain and rinse peas, then place in food processor with egg, onion, salt and pepper. Blend until peas are finely grained, but not smooth.
4. **ADD WATER:** Add water, and blend. Mixture should be "fluffy," easy to pick up in soft but cohesive spoonfuls, a bit like oatmeal.
5. **HEAT OIL:** In frying pan, add enough oil to create a depth of about 1/4–1/2 inch. Heat to medium heat.
6. **FRY:** Add a spoonful of mixture to pan, flattening slightly. Using a separate metal spoon, drizzle a little hot oil from the pan over the top of the fritter. (This "sets" the top to stay together well when you flip it.)
7. **FLIP:** Using a spatula, flip when golden brown and fry the other side equally. Oil should be too shallow to splash. But, use your spoon in conjunction with the spatula to gently lower the fritter back into the pan.
8. **DRAIN:** Remove to a plate covered in paper towels to drain. Cook as many fritters at once as your pan will allow, leaving room to flip them.
9. **SEASON & SERVE:** Add salt if needed (like hashbrowns). Serve with hot sauce, tomato relish or ketchup.

1 food processor

1 cup dried black-eyed peas, soaked overnight

1 egg

1 medium onion, chopped into quarters

1 teaspoon salt

½ teaspoon chopped hot pepper (optional, or ¼ teaspoon cayenne/ black pepper to taste)

3–4 tablespoons water

¼–½ cup vegetable oil for frying

DON'T MISS
WATCHING
(online)

Benin Bronzes Open University and BBC have great short documentaries about the history and artistry of the Benin Bronzes, stolen from the palace of the Kingdom of Benin by the British.
YOUTUBE SEARCH: Benin Bronzes

Wole Soyinka Reading His Poetry The Nobel Prize channel has a video of Wole Soyinka reading his poem, "Lost Poems."
YOUTUBE SEARCH: Nobel Soyinka read poem

We Are Nigerians: Journey to Amalgamation

This 15-minute documentary covers Nigerian history from ancient times until the nation was made one and "amalgamated" in 1914. It creates a single national story from the experiences of many nations brought together. Also great is the song "This Land," celebrating the 100th anniversary of Nigeria's Amalgamation. **YOUTUBE SEARCH:** Nigerian Amalgamation, This Land Celebrating 100 Years of Nigeria

Nollywood Journeyman Pictures has a wonderful short documentary about Nollywood's unique method of making movies.
YOUTUBE SEARCH: Journeyman Nollywood

The Benin Bronzes were cast in a copper-rich alloy of bronze. Artists created intricate clay molds, fired them and then poured in the hot metal. There were nearly 900 Benin Bronzes, most of them plaques on the palace wall of the Oba (King) of the Kingdom of Benin.

O is for Oman

For our **O** we must look to Arabia

and its easternmost nation, **OMAN!**

Find it southeast of Saudi Arabia

and across its own gulf from Iran.

Dates

It's a land of sweet *dates* and **dishdashas,** [dish-DAH-shas]

of wooden DHOWS sailing the seas, [dows]

Of **FRANKINCENSE** wafting around you,

of desert and **coconut** trees.

Boys Wearing
Dishdashas

It's a nation of fortifications,

over five hundred **castles** and **forts.**

They were built to protect their interior

and many strategic seaports.

Dhow

Oman has a history longer

than any Arabian state.

Independent since **1744,**

one family has managed their fate.

Frankincense, Typically
Burned as Incense

Their nation's a **SULTANATE** still;

it's one of the few left on earth.

But their sultan is known for reforming,

and his reign's been a time of rebirth.

Fort

To advance to the future, Oman

has invested in saving their past.

Oil profits preserve their traditions,

while developing growth that will last.

Sultan Qaboos
Bin Said Al Said

Omani Empire

In their past is a glorious **EMPIRE,**

built upon maritime trade.

In their seafaring **DHOWS** they went sailing,

crossing oceans their fortunes were made.

Dhow on the Beach

From Persia and India's coastline,

they sailed to **East Africa's** shores.

They held several coastal port cities,

and brought their own culture ashore.

In Kenya's **MOMBASA** and **LAMU,**

Tanzania's port **Dar-es-Salaam,**

They traded in gold, spices and slaves

and spread their own form of Islam.

Omani Boy

In Oman you will still hear **SWAHILI,**

from descendents of those who lived there.

But mostly they're **ARABIC** speakers

and so they are sure to declare –

"As-Salaamu Alaikum!" and offer [ah-sah-LAH-moo ah-LIGH-koom]

you qahwa (that's coffee) and dates

And sweet ***halwa,*** a heavenly candy,

just try not to eat the whole plate!

Qawah Pot

As-salaamu alaikum literally means "peace be upon you" and is equivalent to "hello!"

Muscat's White
Architecture

Once you've fueled up on caffeine and sugar

and satisfied all of your thirst,

Let's head out to explore their fair nation,

we'll start in their capital first.

Gate into Muscat

MUSCAT is gorgeous and humid,

a traditional white-washed Gulf port.

It has no tall skyscraper buildings,

but many historical forts.

Sultan's Palace

The sultan lives here in his **PALACE**,

and museums and markets abound.

The mountains stand tall as a backdrop

and hills divide neighborhood grounds.

From Muscat we'll sail to *Musandam*, [mu-SAN-dam]

its "fjords" on the **Strait of Hormuz**.

On its shore are the Hajar Mountains,

in the water huge oil tankers cruise.

Sailing in Musandam

Frankincense Tree

Far to the south is **SALALAH**,

where most the world's *frankincense* grows.

It's a port lined with white sandy beaches,

fresh fruit stands and **coconut** groves.

Dune Bashing

Outside of the cities the desert

will call you to trek and see sights,

To drive over **DUNES** like a race car,

to swim in a **Wadi's** green light.

So come see this sultanate's splendor,

their traditions preserved with great pride.

As Arabia's *perfumed oasis,*

Oman is like no place worldwide.

Wadi

As-salaamu Alaikum!*

Loggerhead Sea Turtle**

*__As-salaamu Alaikum__ [ah-sah-LAH-moo ah-LIGH-kum] means "Peace be upon you" in Arabic.
**Oman has the largest concentration of loggerhead sea turtle nests of anywhere in the world.

No one is quite sure where → the name **OMAN** came from, but locally the name is actually 'Uman, and its full name is the Saltanat 'Uman, or the Sultanate of Oman. Oman is one of the few sultanates (lands ruled by a sultan) left on earth.

Oman or "Uman" written in Arabic

↑ The **Omani flag** was adopted in 1970 when the current sultan came to power. The white band represents peace and prosperity, green is for the fertility of the land and red represents the battles against foreign invaders. On the mast is the national symbol of Oman, which is also the symbol of the ruling Al Busaidi Dynasty. It is two swords crossed behind a traditional curved dagger called a khanjar.

Omani Empire 1856

Official Name: Sultanate of Oman

Population: 3.2 million

Capital: Muscat

Largest Cities: Muscat, Salalah, Suhar

Comparative Size: Slightly smaller than Kansas, slightly bigger than Italy

Ethnicity: Arab, Baluchi, South Asian, African

Language: Arabic

Religion: Ibadi Muslim 75% other Muslims 11%, Christians 6.5%, Hindus 5.5%

Currency: Omani rial

Important Export: Oil

Where in the World is Oman?

GEOGRAPHICAL NOTES

◉ Oman has the longest **Indian Ocean coastline** of any nation on the Arabian Peninsula and sits at the entrance to the Persian Gulf.

◉ Oman has been described as a nation **"between two seas,"** with the ocean on one side and a sea of sand on the other (the Rub al-Khali Desert) isolating it from other nations.

◉ Oman used its ocean access to create a trading empire on the Indian Ocean. The **Omani Empire** was at its height from around 1700 to 1856. In 1856, the empire was divided in two among the sultan's two sons. The African portion of the empire became the Sultanate of Zanzibar.

Dates

Date Palm Trees

The **dishdasha** is the traditional dress for Omani men and is still worn on a daily basis. A dishdasha is an ankle length, long-sleeved tunic with a tassel attached to the collar. Traditionally, the tassel would carry the scent of perfume. Dishdashas come in any color, but white is the most popular, particularly in the summer. Dishdashas are perfect for keeping Omani men cool, comfortable and protected from the sun. ⬇

← ↑ Sugar-sweet **dates** are the most important crop in Oman and have grown there for thousands of years. When you are welcomed to an Omani home, it is traditional to be offered coffee and dates. Date palm trees grow exclusively in and near deserts and are popular across Arabia and North Africa.

Boys in Dishdashas

Dhow Cruising near Musandam

The **Rub al-Khali** or the "Empty Quarter" is an extremely dry desert covering most of the southeast of the Arabian Peninsula, including Oman's interior. ⬇

Rub al-Khali

↑ Wooden **dhows** are the traditional sailing vessels in Oman. Oman used dhows to create a maritime trading empire that stretched from ports on the northwest coast of India to the coast of East Africa in the 18th and 19th centuries. Dhows are still used today as fishing vessels and as recreational boats for both locals and tourists. They have become a symbol of Omani culture and history. ⬇

Dhow

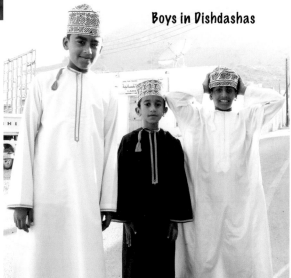
Al-Rustaq Fort

↑ Oman has a large number of forts and **castles** built to protect the interior of the country from invaders.

Sultan Qaboos Bin Said Al Said → is one of the last remaining sultans in the world. He has ruled Oman since a coup in 1970 when he took over from his father. Although he is an absolute ruler, with complete control of the government, he is popular with his people, whose quality of life has risen steadily during his reign. When he came to power, there were only a few paved roads and schools in Oman and now every Omani city has plenty of both. He goes on frequent tours of his kingdom in which Omani citizens are invited to speak with him personally about their needs. He has used Oman's oil wealth to preserve their culture and traditional industries, while developing modern infrastructure, improving education and diversifying the economy, preparing for when their oil will run out. Sultan Qaboos has allowed parliamentary elections in the country with women voting and standing for public office. The sultan has increasingly allowed the parliament more independent power.

Sultan Qaboos Bin Said

Oman has the oldest independent government on the Arabian Peninsula. It has been ruled by the Al Bu Said family since 1750 and became a trading empire stretching from Gwadar in Pakistan to the east coast of Africa, trading in spices, incense, copper, slaves and ivory. Slavery in the Omani Empire differed from that in the Americas in that many slaves were concubines who married their master. Their children were born free and became part of the family. In 1850, the sultan moved his throne to **Zanzibar**, an island off the coast of what is today Tanzania. Eventually the empire split in two with separate sultans of Oman and Zanzibar. But you can still tour the palace in Zanzibar and see the influence of Omani culture on the coast of East Africa. ↓

Palace in Zanzibar

← *Barghash Bin Said, Sultan of Zanzibar 1870–1888*

↑ Sultan Qaboos is on Oman's money, the **Omani rial**. This note is worth 100 baisa. (There are 1000 baisa in one rial.) This note features Oman's falaj irrigation system; find out about it on page 205.

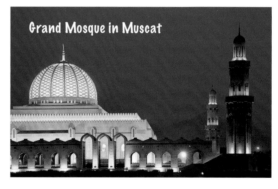

Grand Mosque in Muscat

← Oman has its own form of Islam called **Ibadhism**, which is distinct from Sunni and Shi'a Islam. Ibadhi Islam is also the main religion in Zanzibar, Tanzania, and there are small Ibadhi populations in East and North Africa.

Girl in Fancy Traditional Dress

← Traditional dress for women in Oman is colorful and → ornate with a long tunic, trousers and a scarf used as a head covering. Fancy forms of traditional dress are still worn at social celebrations. Today many Omani women wear the black abaya over their clothes in public, as is the fashion in most Persian Gulf countries. The style of black abaya changes every season and they may be decorated with fancy embroidery or crystals. In the capital, Muscat, businesswomen may be seen in suits, and many women wear colorful outfits of long skirts, long-sleeved shirts and head scarves. ↓

Women in Black Abayas and Veils

← ↑ *Woman from the Royal Calvary wearing traditional dress.*
← *The black abaya is popular with many women in public.*

Omani Boy

Just as you can still see the influence of Oman in East Africa, you can see the descendants of East Africans in Oman. Many of these Omanis are descendents of Swahili traders in Oman's East Africa Empire. They moved to Oman and intermarried with Arab Omanis. There are many descendants of Oman's East African Empire in Oman today and they are frequently called Zanzibaris. Many families speak Swahili, the language of trade on the coast of East Africa.

Boys at a Camel Race

Kummas

Beyond the dishdasha, Omani males wear either a hat called a *kumma* or a turban in order to protect their heads from the sun. For more formal occasions, their dishdasha is belted and a ceremonial dagger called a **khanjar** is tucked into the belt.

khanjar

It is traditional to offer guests coffee with something sweet, usually dates or halwa. Halwa is an Omani treat with the consistency of soft fudge. It is flavored with saffron, cardamom and rosewater and has pistachios and cashews mixed in.

Arabian Coffeepot

Sultan's Palace

Sultan Qaboos hosts foreign leaders at his **Al Alam Palace** in Muscat. Al Alam Palace, or "Flag Palace" is in the heart of Muscat but the Sultan rarely stays there.

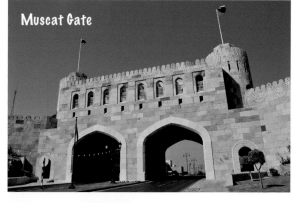

Muscat Gate

Traditional Architecture

Unlike its neighbors on the Persian Gulf, Oman has not used its oil wealth to build fanciful skyscrapers or artificial islands. Oman's capital, Muscat, has maintained its beautiful **traditional architecture** of fortress walls and whitewashed buildings. This reflects the sultan's policy of preserving Oman's culture while developing its economy.

On a hill looking over Muscat stands a huge statue of a frankincense burner. It honors Oman's long history of frankincense production and their custom of burning it to welcome guests.

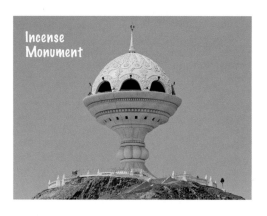

Incense Monument

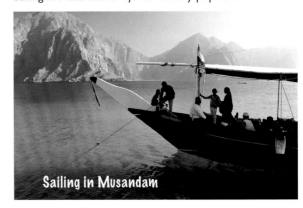

Oil Tanker

Musandam is very mountainous and has small waterways that run into the cliffs of the coastline, resembling the fjords found in Norway and Sweden. Sailing in Musandam's "fjords" is very popular. ↓

Strait of Hormuz

↑ The **Strait of Hormuz** is the curved waterway connecting the Persian Gulf to the Gulf of Oman and the Arabian Sea. It is the only way for oil tankers to leave the Persian Gulf to transport oil around the world. Oman holds the tip of land jutting into the strait known as Musandam. Iran shares control of the Straight of Hormuz with Oman.

Sailing in Musandam

Salalah in Monsoon

↑ **Salalah** catches some of India's monsoon weather in July and August in a season called **khareef**. Clouds of fog roll in from the Indian Ocean (Arabian Sea) and the land turns green. Tourists from the rest of Oman and neighboring countries come to Salalah during khareef to escape the summer heat and enjoy the humidity, rain and greenery. ↓

Boswellia Tree (Frankincense)

Frankincense

Dune Bashing

↑ **Dune bashing** is popular for thrill seekers in Arabia. A sort of desert roller coaster, it requires an SUV and a lot of experience driving on sand to not get stuck and to keep the car upright.

← **Frankincense** is resin from the boswellia tree that has been used to make incense and perfume since ancient times. Oman is one of the leading producers of frankincense, known for producing the highest quality in the world.

Arab Tourists in Oman for Monsoon

How do you live and farm in a country →
with no rivers? Oman transports water from underground aquifers using a system called **falaj**. A falaj has a deep well in a mountainside, then a gently sloping tunnel that runs from the well to the water's destination. The tunnel is mostly underground to keep the water from evaporating in the sun. There are aflaj (the plural of falaj) over 1,000 years old that are still in use in Oman.

Falaj Waterway

Wadi

↑ A **wadi** is a seasonal streambed around which oases form in the desert. Many wadis flow only after it rains.

Listen to the SOUNDS of OMAN

Omani Khaliji Music Oman's version of the music popular around the Persian Gulf.
YOUTUBE SEARCH: Oman Khaliji traditional

Al Bar'ah Traditional music from Dhofar. Oman is the only Persian Gulf country in which men and women, old and young, participate together in traditional folk music.
YOUTUBE SEARCH: Oman al Bar'ah

"Oman" A music video tribute to Oman sung by girls in traditional dress. **YOUTUBE SEARCH:** Oman Mahbooba

READ:

The Turtle of Oman by Naomi Shihab Nye. A novel about a boy who travels around Oman to say goodbye to his homeland before moving to the United States. Ages 8 & up.

DON'T MISS WATCHING (online)

Tour Oman Rough Guides TV, Unravel Travel, Travelguru tv, Expoza Travel and other YouTube travel channels tour Oman's top tourist sites. There is also one run by the Sultanate called "Oman Tourism." "This is America" with Dennis Wholey also explores Oman. **YOUTUBE SEARCH:** (YouTube channel recommended above) + Oman, Oman Tourism, This is America Oman

Oman's Frankincense The Travel Channel tours Dhofar and its ancient industry harvesting and exporting frankincense. **YOUTUBE SEARCH:** Oman frankincense

Royal Cavalry of Oman See the majestic riders and horses perform. **YOUTUBE SEARCH:** Oman royal cavalry

How to Wrap a Masarh (Omani turban)
YOUTUBE SEARCH: Oman wrap masarh

MAKE OMANI

Swayweih

Swayweih is a sweet breakfast food made from pasta, eggs and coconut. A similar recipe called *balaleet* is popular in the United Arab Emirates. As sweet and savory as cinnamon rolls, swayweih has a similar spicy, sweet and buttery taste.

1. Break vermicelli pasta into small segments. Put a big handful of pasta into a large plastic bag to keep if from flying in all directions as it is broken. Reach your hands into the bag to break it. Swayweih pasta is generally ½ inch long, but 1-2 inches long will still work. Break and measure until you have two cups.

2. Put a medium-sized pot of water on to boil.

3. In a large pan, saute onions in 2 tablespoons of butter on medium heat until onions brown around the edges. Remove onion from the pan and set aside.

4. Scramble eggs, breaking them into the same pan. Sprinkle with salt and constantly stir and break them up while they cook. Remove eggs from the pan.

5. Cook Pasta. Once water is boiling, add a tablespoon of salt and broken vermicelli. Boil, occasionally stirring until it is *cooked but still firm*. It is easy to overcook vermicelli and turn it into mush, so immediately drain it when it is done. Use the vermicelli package directions as a guide and start checking when it is one minute less than their minimal time.

6. Sauté sugar, spices, eggs and coconut. After draining pasta, immediately add 2 tablespoons of butter to the pan along with spices, onion, coconut, sugar, salt (¼ teaspoon or to taste) and eggs. Sauté together for a minute.

7. Add pasta to the pan, stir well and allow it to cook for a couple minutes more. Taste-test to see if it needs more salt.

8. Serve immediately. Makes 3–4 large servings.

2 cups vermicelli pasta, broken into 1-inch pieces
½ cup sweet yellow onion, chopped small
4 tablespoons butter
3 eggs
1 tablespoon salt, plus salt to taste
2 teaspoons cardamom
pinch of saffron (optional)
⅓ cup sugar
⅓ cup dried shredded coconut

Visit www.australiatozimbabwe.com for links to online activities.

WRITE In ARABIC!

← اب ت ث ج ح خ د ذ ر ز س ش ص ض ط ظ ع غ ف ق ك ل م ن و ه ي

Arabic has 28 letters. Above they are in order, starting from the right.

Cursive Direction: Arabic is written in cursive, **← لعام منختما to معام** ←

Changing Letters: The letters change their form if they are located at the beginning of the word, in the middle or the end. (Similar to the different ways that we write uppercase and lowercase letters.) Most letters are joined in cursive, but the red letters on the chart do not connect to the following letter. The next letter (to the left) must use either the isolated or beginning form. For example, the "a" in Oman doesn't connect to the "n." As the "n" is the last letter in the word, it uses the isolated form.

عُمان

Oman written in Arabic

عُمان (short vowel, a glottal stop)

Vowels: The Arabic alphabet doesn't typically write short vowels like the "a" in can, the "e" in beg, the "i" in bit, the "o" in sob or the "u" in put. Instead, the reader can usually guess those vowel sounds.

Cn you read 'nglsh wthout those vowls?

Arabic does write long vowels like the "ee" in free, or the "u" in true.

There are diacritical marks (markings above or below the letter) that can be optionally used to signify which short vowel is used. The little loop (و) above Uman, signifies a short "u." Diacritical markings are used when a certain pronunciation is important, as with the name of a country. All copies of the Muslim holy book, the Qu'ran, are written with diacritical markers to ensure correct pronunciation and interpretation.

← Similar Consonants: In the chart, capitalized English letters signal that the Arabic sound is pronounced strongly. The "th" is the sound in "this." The "TH" is the sound in "thing." B is also used to write the sounds "v" and "p."

ARABIC ALPHABET CHART

letter isolated	end of a word	middle	beginning
a ا	ا	ا	ا
b ب	ب	ﺒ	ﺑ
t ت	ت	ﺘ	ﺗ
TH ث	ث	ﺜ	ﺛ
j ج	ج	ﺠ	ﺟ
H ح	ح	ﺤ	ﺣ
kh خ	خ	ﺨ	ﺧ
d د	ﺪ	ﺪ	د
th ذ	ﺬ	ﺬ	ذ
r ر	ﺮ	ﺮ	ر
z ز	ﺰ	ﺰ	ز
s س	ﺲ	ﺴ	ﺳ
sh ش	ﺶ	ﺸ	ﺷ
Ss ص	ﺺ	ﺼ	ﺻ
D ض	ﺾ	ﺿ	ﺿ
T ط	ط	ﻂ	ﻃ
Z ظ	ظ	ﻆ	ﻇ
glottal stop ع	ﻊ	ﻌ	ﻋ
gh غ	ﻎ	ﻐ	ﻏ
f ف	ﻒ	ﻔ	ﻓ
q ق	ﻖ	ﻘ	ﻗ
k ك	ﻚ	ﻜ	ﻛ
L ل	ﻞ	ﻠ	ﻟ
m م	ﻢ	ﻤ	ﻣ
n ن	ﻦ	ﻨ	ﻧ
h ه	ﻪ	ﻬ	ﻫ
w/u و	و	و	و
y/i/ ee/ay ي	ﻲ	ﻴ	ﻳ

TRY WRITING "SALAAM" IN ARABIC!

Salaam is a greeting meaning "peace." The letters are s-l-a-m as the first "a" is soft. The "l" and "a" have a special combination shape, the "a" becoming slanted to separate it from the "l."

م =m   ا =a   ل =l   س =s

سلام سِلام

Now try to write your own name in Arabic. You can check your answer online. There are websites that will write your name in Arabic. Once you've written your name, try the names of family and friends!

INTERNET SEARCH: write your name in Arabic

P is for Peru

P is for **PERU,**

Where the Inca Empire grew

Until it was defeated

In **1532.**

Tawantinsuyu
(Inca Empire)

Condor

Pizarro

The Inca's great empire

was based in Peru.

It was named the "four regions,"

"TAWANTINSUYU."

In the **ANDES** they lived,

making **terraced** hillsides,

Where they first grew **POTATOES**

up where **CONDORS** glide.

They built **ROADS** through the mountains

to cloud level cities

And temples to worship

their sun god named **INTI.**

When *Pizarro* came here

in **1532**,

He conquered the Incas

and Spain took Peru.

They brought **churches** and **HORSES**,

taking silver and gold.

They brought people, the Spanish,

whose culture took hold.

Potatoes

Inti

Church in Lima

Quechua Traditional
Clothing

But the Incas' descendents

still live in Peru.

They speak **Quechua** and say, [keh-chwa]

"Allillanchu?" to you. [ah-yil-YAHN-chu]

And **Native Americans**

still number much greater

Than all other people

who came here much later.

Andes Mountains

The **Andes** divide

Peru's land into three

Distinct regions and cultures

from **JUNGLE** to **sea.**

First there's the **coast,**

which is arid and dry,

where Spanish colonials

settled and thrived.

Coast of Lima

The capital, **LIMA,**

is located here

Where it's **CLOUDY,** though rain

is quite scarce through the year.

Government Palace in Lima

Ceviche

Beside cobblestone streets

And Spanish-style churches

You'll find high-rises, museums

And boutiques for splurges.

On the coastline **ceviche's** [say-VEE-chay]

the best thing to eat,

Raw fish "cooked" in lime –

it's a national treat.

Inca Rainbow Flag

And then there's the MOUNTAINS

where the **RAINBOW FLAG** flies.

It's a sign of the Incas,

whose culture resides

Cusco Cathedral

In **CUSCO**, their capital

once long ago.

Here the tourists now flock

with their backpacks in tow.

To see **Machu Picchu**,

they'll hike for some days –

To a city once hidden

in mountaintop haze.

Machu Picchu

Alpaca

They'll see **LLAMAS, alpacas,**

Vicuñas, **guanacos,** [bee-COO-nyahs, gwah-NAH-cohs]

All Andean camels

with fur good for **ponchos.**

Vicuña

The air here is thin

so you'll need **COCA TEA**

(it helps with altitude

sickness you see).

Coca Tea

When you're feeling fine

you might like to try **cuy** — [KWEE]

because guinea pig here

is a delicacy!

Roasted Cuy

The last region is largest

of all in Peru.

It's **la selva** [SAYL-bah]

(the Amazon Jungle to you).

House on the
Amazon River

In the forest, the cities

and people are sparse.

There are not many roads

for the driving of cars.

Iquitos Traffic

Here's the world's largest city

unreachable by road.

It's **Iquitos,** a port [ee-KEE-tohs]

on the Amazon's flow.

Juane

Here you'll feast on fat **juanes** [HWAH-nays]

and tropical fruit,

And then go take a cruise

to see **monkeys** so cute.

So go get your backpack

and come to Peru.

In this land of the Inca

there's so much to do!

Emperor Tamarin

Reed Boat

You can ride a reed boat

on the **world's highest lake,**

Then go out to eat

an alpaca meat steak,

Wash it down with florescent

and sweet **INCA KOLA,**

Then climb in the Andes

and tell llamas "Hola!"

Inca Kola

Lake Titicaca

Corn Varieties

Try dozens of types of

potatoes and corn,

See the number one place

BOWLER HATS are still worn.

Nature, hist'ry and food,

it's the place to go to.

Grab your poncho and come –

our P is **Peru!**

Bowler Hat

Allillanchu!*

Llama

* ***Allillanchu*** [ah yihl-YAHN-choo] means "Hello" and "How are you?" in Quechua.

← **Peru's flag** was adopted in 1825 when they won their independence from Spain. In the center is their coat of arms. On the top left is their national animal, the vicuña, a type of mountain camelid (similar to a llama) found only in the Andes. It symbolizes the unique wildlife of Peru. On the right is a cinchona tree, symbolizing Peru's plant life. The cinchona tree is used to make quinine, a powerful medicine against malaria that the Incas first discovered. Below is a cornucopia with gold coins spilling out, symbolizing Peru's mineral wealth.

PERU was given its name by Spanish explorers, but its exact origin is uncertain. One theory is that Spanish explorers met a local ruler, Birú, in Panama, the southernmost nation in Central America. At that time, Panama was the furthest south that Spaniards had been in the Americas. So when they continued south down the west coast of South America, they thought of everything to the south as "Biru's," which was also spelled "Viru," "Beru," and "Peru." When Spaniards planned to take over this area from the Incas, they planned the "conquest of Peru."

IQUITOS

TRUJILLO

LIMA

CUSCO

AREQUIPA

Coastal Desert & Scrub
Mountain Grasses & Scrub
Mountain Rainforest
Tropical Rainforest

Climate & Vegetation in Peru

Official Name:
Republic of Peru

Population: 30 million

Capital: Lima

Largest Cities: Lima, Arequipa, Trujillo

Comparative Size: Slightly smaller than Alaska, the 20th-largest country

Ethnicity: Amerindian 45%, Mestizo 37%, white 15%

Language: Spanish 83%, Quechua 13%, Aymara 1.7% and other native languages

Religion: Christianity: Roman Catholic 81%, Evangelical 12.5%

Currency: Peruvian sol

Important Exports: Copper, gold, asparagus

Where in the World is Peru?

GEOGRAPHICAL NOTES

◉ Peru is divided into **three distinct regions**: the coast (*la costa*), the mountains (*la sierra*) and the rainforest (*la selva*). Each region has its own climate, wildlife, culture and history. The dry coast was where the Spanish mainly settled, and where the capital, Lima, is found. The Andes Mountains were the home of the Inca Empire and where Inca culture still resides. The Amazon Rainforest is on the other side of the Andes and is home to many other indigenous groups and tropical wildlife.

Chinchansuyu

Antisuyu

Cuntinsuyu

Collasuyu

Living largely up in the Andes Mountains, the Incas carved **terraces** into the hillsides in order to be able to grow crops and prevent erosion. →

Inca Terraces

The **potato** was first cultivated in the Andes about 8,000 years ago near Lake Titicaca. The Incas introduced Europeans to the potato and it's now eaten all over the world. There are thousands of varieties of potatoes grown in Peru, in many shapes, colors and sizes. →

Potatoes

The **Inca Empire** ↑ was named *Tawantinsuyu* or the "four regions," reflecting the four different regions or "suyus" that made up the empire. It stretched from what is today Ecuador down through Peru to northern Chile and Argentina. The Incas built a great **road system** connecting

Condor

their empire. The roads were used by Inca relay runners called *chasqui* who carried royal messages at a speed of up to 145 miles (240 km) per day, as well as by troops of soldiers and llama caravans. Some of the roads, which could be as wide as a five-lane highway or simply narrow pathways, still survive today. ↓

Inca Road

Condors are some of the world's largest birds → with wingspans of up to 10 ft (3 m). They rarely flap their wings once they have taken off, using warm air currents to keep them soaring. The condor is a national symbol of Peru.

← Inca architecture used stones cut so perfectly that **no mortar** was used between them. The buildings have proven to be remarkably earthquake proof and those that the Spanish did not tear down remain standing.

Inca Wall

MAP OF INCA EMPIRE ROAD SYSTEM

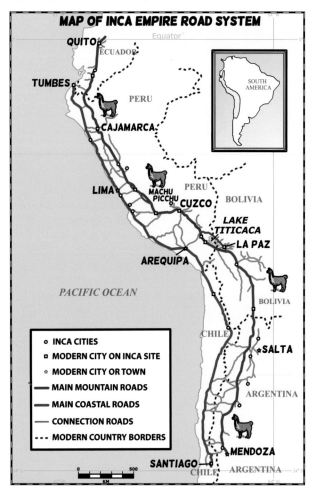

QUITO

Equator

ECUADOR

SOUTH AMERICA

TUMBES

PERU

CAJAMARCA

PERU

LIMA

MACHU PICCHU

CUZCO

BOLIVIA

LAKE TITICACA

LA PAZ

AREQUIPA

PACIFIC OCEAN

BOLIVIA

CHILE

SALTA

ARGENTINA

○ INCA CITIES
□ MODERN CITY ON INCA SITE
★ MODERN CITY OR TOWN
— MAIN MOUNTAIN ROADS
— MAIN COASTAL ROADS
— CONNECTION ROADS
--- MODERN COUNTRY BORDERS

MENDOZA

SANTIAGO

CHILE

ARGENTINA

0   500
KM

Inti

Inti was the Inca Sun god and the state god of the Inca Empire. The Incas believed that Inti was their divine ancestor. Inti is the inspiration for the suns on the flags of both Argentina and Uruguay. There were many gods in the Inca religion, but Inti was probably the most popular. →

Pizarro

Atahualpa

Francisco Pizarro was aided in his conquest of the Inca Empire by the spread of small pox and a resulting civil war. The Inca ruler, Huayna Capac, and his chosen successor were both killed by a disease brought in by the Europeans. Royal brothers, Huascar and Atahualpa, fought over the throne. **Atahualpa** won and was subsequently kidnapped by Pizarro. The chaos of both the epidemic and the civil war made the conquest of the large empire possible.

Horse Mounted Police in Lima

← The Spanish made Peru into a Christian → country, converting the natives and building **churches** all over. The Spanish were also the people to reintroduce **horses** to the Americas. Prior to their arrival, there had not been horses in the Americas for many thousands of years. Though Spanish culture spread throughout Peru, their population still has more Amerindians (45%) than those of European (15%) or mixed descent (37%). ↓

Cathedral in Lima

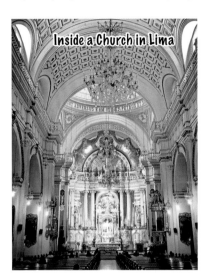

Inside a Church in Lima

Moorish Balcony

Marinera Dancing

↑ The **marinera** is a couple's dance that originated in the 19th century and is sometimes referred to as Peru's national dance. The woman dances barefoot in fancy embroidered dress with a wide skirt. The man wears a large straw hat and both the man and woman carry a handkerchief. The man and woman circle one another dancing, waving their handkerchiefs, her skirt and his hat to great effect, telling the story of a passionate courtship, coming very close together but generally not touching. Every year there is a national marinera competition in Trujillo.

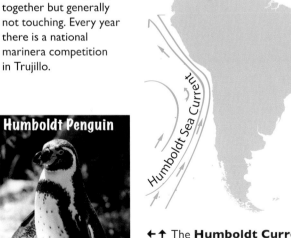

Going to School

↑ **Moorish balconies** in Lima were built during colonial times and reflect the influence of Moorish culture on Spain and its colonies. The Moors were Muslims from North Africa who invaded and ruled over large parts of Spain from the 8th century CE until they were eventually all driven out in 1492. (See S is for Spain.) It was only 40 years later that Pizarro defeated the Incas. These beautiful carved wooden balconies were originally designed to give women the ability to be outside and see the street without being seen.

← Most **school children** in Peru wear uniforms. The weather in the mountains and the coast can be quite cool, though rarely freezing.

Humboldt Penguin

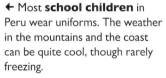

Humboldt Sea Current

←↑ The **Humboldt Current** is a sea current that sweeps up the western coast of South America from the South Polar Ocean. It brings cold water to the Peruvian coastline, allowing cold-water species like penguins to survive on the coast of Chile and Peru. It also cools the climate, giving Peru's coast very mild temperatures considering how close it is to the equator. The Andes Mountains keep rain clouds from moving past the Amazon Basin, leaving the coast very dry. But the cool air from the Humboldt current brings in a lot of fog and low-lying clouds to Lima, the capital. So while it rarely rains there, it is frequently humid, damp or cloudy.

Ceviche

← **Ceviche** is a raw fish dish that is very popular in Peru and much of coastal Latin America. Ceviche is marinated in a citrus pepper mixture that "cooks" the fish, making it opaque and firmer. It is served as a refreshing salad mixed with herbs and onion and with sides like avocado or sweet potato.

Lima's Coast

Papas Rellenas

← **Papas rellenas** or stuffed potatoes are a popular Peruvian dish. Meat, olives, herbs and eggs are surrounded by a mashed potato dough and then deep fried.

Government Palace

← The **Government Palace** is in the Central Plaza or Plaza Mayor of Lima, on a site originally chosen by Francisco Pizarro. As such, it is sometimes referred to as "La Casa de Pizarro" or "Pizarro House." Part of the palace is home to the president and his family.

The **rainbow flag** is a → symbol of the Inca or Quechua people of the Andes. It is the official flag of Cusco, which was once the capital of the Inca Empire. It can also be seen flying in other cities in Peru and Ecuador as a symbol of Tawantinsuyu (the Inca Empire).

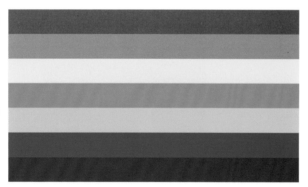

Weather in the Peruvian **Andes Mountains** is sunny, cool and dry. Most of the year, the high temperature in Cusco is in the upper 60s°F (19°–20°C). The high altitude is the reason for the low temperatures and also makes the air "thin," meaning it is less rich in oxygen than at lower altitudes. Humans adapt to the thinner air, but unaccustomed tourists may have to take it easy until they do. ↓

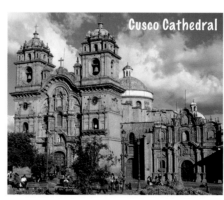
Andes Mountains

Traditional Clothing

← As the former capital of the Inca Empire, **Cusco** is still the center of Quechua culture today. There you can find people speaking Quechua and wearing Quecha traditional dress. (The most traditional styles are usually worn for festivals or for tourists.) Traditional **Quechua clothing** today is a mix of Inca and Spanish colonial styles. Brightly woven and embroidered garments date back to Inca times when men and women wore long woven tunics and headdresses. The men also wore ponchos and the women, a woven shawl. Today, these elements are still worn, but with traditional Spanish shirts, trousers and skirts.

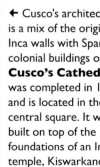
Cusco Cathedral

← Cusco's architecture is a mix of the original Inca walls with Spanish colonial buildings on top. **Cusco's Cathedral** was completed in 1654 and is located in their central square. It was built on top of the foundations of an Inca temple, Kiswarkancha.

Machu Picchu is an Inca ruin that was untouched by the Spanish. Located high in the Andes Mountains, not that far from Cusco, Machu Picchu was unknown to the Spanish and the outside world until American Hiram Bingham encountered it in 1911. It may have been a royal retreat for the Inca emperor Pachacuti that was later abandoned. The trail through the mountains from Cusco to Machu Picchu is often called the "Inca Trail" and it is very popular with backpackers. It was part of the original Inca road system, but the trail is narrow, reflecting the exclusivity of the city. Machu Picchu is the most popular tourist site in South America. ↓

Vicuña

Guanaco

← ↑ Llamas, alpacas, vicuñas and guanacos are all Andean **camelids**. Llamas and alpacas are domesticated while vicuñas and guanacos live solely in the wild. **Vicuñas** are the national animal of Peru and have the softest wool. ↓

↑ **Llamas** were bred for their meat and wool and to be beasts of burden, carrying loads through the mountains. **Alpacas** in contrast are smaller and are raised solely for their wool and meat. Alpaca wool is the softer and more prized wool. Vicuña wool is extremely expensive and rare as the animals are wild. ↓ →

Machu Picchu

Alpaca

Llamas

Ponchos

Coca tea is made from leaves of the coca plant, which is also an ingredient in Coca-Cola. Coca tea helps with altitude sickness and is known for decreasing fatigue and improving endurance. A stimulant as mild as black tea, coca tea has been used in the Andes since before the time of the Incas. Cocaine is also made from coca leaves, but it takes hundreds of leaves and a special chemical process to produce a tiny amount of cocaine. Unlike coca tea, cocaine is harmful to the health and causes brain damage. →

Coca Tea

Ponchos originated in ↑ the Andes and we get the word poncho from the Quechua word *punchu*. Ponchos are woven woolen blankets with slits for the head. They keep the body warm while allowing for a full range of movement, making them excellent wear for running and climbing in the mountains.

Cuy

← Guinea pigs originated in the Andes and **cuy**, or roasted guinea pig, has been a food there for thousands of years. Cuy is raised as food and tastes like rabbit. Cuy is a delicacy and not a part of the daily diet for most people.

If you're not feeling so adventurous, you might prefer **lomo saltado**, a popular dish of stir-fried steak, tomatoes and french fries served with rice. →

Lomo Saltado

Traffic in Iquitos

← Isolated within the Amazon Rainforest there are no roads from **Iquitos** to any other major city, hence there are very few cars in Iquitos. Goods are brought to the city by plane or by boat going up the **Amazon River**, and it is far easier to transport smaller vehicles like motorcycles. So, there are an abundance of motorcycles, bikes and motorickshaws in Iquitos. Iquitos is considered the capital of the Peruvian Amazon. It got its name from an ethnic group, the Iquitos, who lived in the region when the Spanish arrived. →

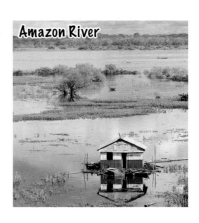

Amazon River

Making Juanes

↑ **Juanes** are a typical food in Amazonian Peru. Juanes are made from cooked rice and a filling that typically includes meat or fish, eggs, olives, herbs and spices. Somewhat like Mexican tamales, juanes are wrapped up in large leaf and then boiled in a clay pot. →

Floating House

On the Amazon River, there are many **floating homes** ↑ and houses built on stilts so that when the river floods, residents can stay in their homes and use boats to get around. Outside of Iquitos, there is a "floating neighborhood" called Belen that is made up of homes on stilts and houseboats.

Uakari Monkey

Macaw

The Amazon is a center for diverse **native peoples**. Neither the Incas nor the Spanish ever took complete control of the region, and so many distinct cultures have survived. This is a native Yahua man using a blowgun. ↓

Yahua Man

←↑There is an abundance of wildlife in the Peruvian **Amazon**, from dozens of types of monkeys and hundred of types of birds to the capybara, the largest rodent on earth. For more about the Amazon, see page 24. ↓

Baby Emperor Tamarin

Poison Dart Frog

Capybara

Lake Titicaca, which straddles the border → of Peru and Bolivia, is the largest lake by volume in South America. It is also often called the "highest navigable lake" in the world, located 12,500 ft (3,800 m) above sea level.

Lake Titicaca

Floating Island

↑ Living on Lake Titicaca, the Uros people are famous for using **tortora reeds** to build boats, **floating islands** and homes. They live on over 40 floating islands, originally constructed as a defensive measure so that they could move their homes when in danger. Today, tourists love to take a ride on a reed boat and visit a floating island. →

Reed Boat

↑ **Inca Kola** is a popular soft drink in Peru. Sweet and fluorescent yellow, Inca Kola is made with lemon verbena and tastes a bit like bubble gum.

Bowler Hat

Corn Varieties

↑ Thousands of different types of potatoes, sweet potatoes and corn are grown in Peru. ↓

Potatoes

← **Bowler hats** have been worn by ↑ Quechua and Aymara women since the 1920s. According to legend, a shipment of bowler hats was sent to sell to European railroad workers in the Andes. The hats were too small and so were distributed among the local women. Today they are considered symbols of native women's dress in the Andes.

Nazca Lines

Long before the Inca Empire (13th century–1532), great civilizations lived in Peru, and you can see many of their monuments today.

The **Nazca Lines** are huge drawings in the desert → of southern Peru that were made by the Nazca culture (200 BCE–600 CE). Undisturbed by the desert climate, the largest drawings are over 650 ft (200 m) wide and can be seen only from the air or surrounding hillsides.

← **Chan Chan** was a large city built by the Chimu people in 850 CE that held up to 30,000 people before being conquered by the Incas. The Chan Chan ruins, not far from the city of Trujillo, are filled with fascinating art and architecture.

Chan Chan

Listen to the SOUNDS of PERU

"El Condor Pasa" "El Condor Pasa" is the most famous Peruvian song. It was composed in 1913 by Daniel Alomía Robles, who based it on traditional Andean folk songs. "El Condor Pasa," meaning "The Condor Passes," became known worldwide when Simon and Garfunkel made a cover of the song in 1970, writing lyrics for it. It remains purely a song without words in Peru and has been declared part of Peru's national heritage.
YOUTUBE SEARCH: el condor pasa Peru

Zampoña Andean panpipes, known as *siku* in Aymara, zampoña in Spanish and *antara* in Quechua are probably the best known Andean instrument.
YOUTUBE SEARCH: zampona Peru

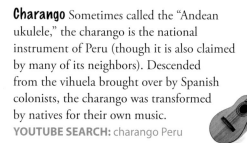

Charango Sometimes called the "Andean ukulele," the charango is the national instrument of Peru (though it is also claimed by many of its neighbors). Descended from the vihuela brought over by Spanish colonists, the charango was transformed by natives for their own music.
YOUTUBE SEARCH: charango Peru

Cajón A percussion instrument originally created by Afro-Peruvians but now popular all over Latin America, the cajón looks like a wooden box that players sit on. It is theorized that slaves originally made them from shipping crates on the coast. Chincha is the Peruvian province most associated with Afro-Peruvian culture.
YOUTUBE SEARCH: cajon Peru, cajon chincha, musica negra Peruana

Landó Landó is one of the styles of "música criolla" or "Creole music" made from a mix of African and Spanish rhythms. Landó is often compared to blues due to its slower tempo and minor key. **YOUTUBE SEARCH:** toro mata, lando peruano, maria lando susana baca

Huayno Huayno is the most famous type of Andean music and dance. Try the song "Virgenes del Sol."
YOUTUBE SEARCH: Virgenes del Sol, huayno peruano

Other Suggestions:
Uchpa's "Por las Puras" or "Chachaschay" (Quechua Rock)
Los Shapis' "El Aguajal" or "El Ambulante"
(Peruvian-style Cumbia, also known as *Chicha*. Cumbia music is originally from Colombia.)

READ:

Love and Roast Chicken: A Trickster Tale from the Andes Mountains by Barbara Knutson. Cuy the guinea pig must trick the fox to avoid becoming dinner. Ages 4 & up.

Martin De Porres: The Rose in the Desert by Gary D. Schmidt. The poor Peruvian son of a Spanish nobleman and an African slave becomes a saint. Ages 7 & up.

Lost City: The Discovery of Machu Picchu by Ted Lewin. A picture book detailing the story of how American professor Hiram Bingham encountered the lost city of Machu Picchu, guided by a Quechua boy. Ages 7 & up.

Up and Down the Andes: A Peruvian Festival Tale by Laurie Krebs. Set off from Lake Titicaca to journey to Cusco for the Inti Raymi Festival. Ages 6 & up.

Before Columbus: The Americas of 1491 by Charles Mann. Get the real story about life in the mighty Inca Empire and how it was defeated. Ages 11 & up.

Investigating Machu Picchu: An Isabel Soto Archaeology Adventure by Emily Sohn. A graphic novel. Ages 8 & up.

You Wouldn't Want to Be an Inca Mummy! by Colin Hynson. A humorously gruesome take on Inca history. Ages 8 & up.

Machu Picchu: The Story of the Amazing Inkas and their City in the Clouds by Elizabeth Mann. Ages 9 & up.

DON'T MISS WATCHING (online)

Marinera & Festejo Dancing The Marinera dance, originating in colonial Peru, shows the mix of Spanish, native and African music and dance. Festejo (*fays-TAY-ho*) is the Afro-Peruvian dance and musical style that has become popular all over Peru. **YOUTUBE SEARCH:** marinera peruana vigo, festejo peruano

Secrets of the Inca Empire There are great documentaries on the Inca by NOVA and the History Channel. National Geographic has one on the mysteries of Machu Picchu. **YOUTUBE SEARCH:** Secrets Inca Nova, Machu Picchu national geographic

Lake Titicaca See the floating islands on Lake Titicaca. **YOUTUBE SEARCH:** Titicaca floating islands

Nazca Lines Was the world's largest artwork, only visible from the sky, made by aliens? **YOUTUBE SEARCH:** Nazca Lines

MAKE PERUVIAN
Ceviche

Ceviche is raw fish "cooked" (though never heated) in lime juice. Served cold, it is the perfect summertime food. Unlike Japanese sushi, ceviche fish is actually "cooked" by the acids in the lime. After marinating for a couple of hours, the flesh of the fish becomes firmer and more opaque. Ceviche is popular throughout coastal Latin America, and there are numerous recipes and sides. In Peru, ceviche is usually served with sweet potato or avocado slices and sometimes popcorn. This recipe includes avocado in the ceviche and has sides of both sweet potato and popcorn. Try and see which side you prefer!

1. Keep all ingredients cold in the refrigerator in advance. Prepare garlic, cilantro, chili and onion first; put to the side in a small bowl.

2. Remove tilapia from the refrigerator and cube it, then place it in a glass or ceramic bowl. Cut limes in half, and squeeze lime juice on fish, using a sieve to catch any pulp. Make sure lime covers fish.

3. Add bowl of garlic, cilantro, chili, and onion. Stir, sprinkle with salt and pepper, and stir again. Cover and put back in the refrigerator to marinate for 2–3 hours or overnight.

4. Once "cooked" by the marinade, the fish should be more opaque and firm. Add avocado cubes, stir. Taste to see if it needs any additional salt. Serve cold with cool slices of cooked sweet potato and popcorn. Some people love to put a little sweet potato in each bite – scrumptious!

*Fresh or frozen fish? Traditionally, ceviche is made with fresh fish, but this recipe is made with frozen tilapia that has been given a full day to thaw in the refrigerator. (Do NOT speed the thawing process.) Unless you can get very fresh fish from a reputable vendor, frozen is both the safest and tastiest option, as it is flash frozen when it is very fresh.

½–1 lb frozen tilapia filets *
  thawed overnight in the refrigerator
2 garlic cloves, minced or crushed
1 tablespoon cilantro leaves, chopped
½ habanero chili, minced
  (to taste, optional)
½ cup red onion cut in slivers
5–8 fresh limes
¼ teaspoon black pepper
salt (to taste)
1 ripe avocado, cubed

Sides:
1–2 baked sweet potatoes,
  cooled in refrigerator
Popcorn (optional)

SPEAK QUECHUA! (Runasimi)

Allin P'unchay!	Good day!	al-yin **POON**-chigh (with explosive P sound)
Allin ch'isi!	Good afternoon!	al-yin **CHEE**-see
Allin tuta!	Good night	al-yin **TU**-tah
Allillanchu?	Are you well?	ah-yil-YAHN-choo
Allillanmi.	I'm fine.	ah-yil-YAHN-mee
Qamri?	And you?	kham-REE
Ima sutiyki?	What's your name?	EE-mah soo-TEE-ee-kee
Sutiyqa..	My name is...	soo-TEE-ee-kah
Maymanta kanki?	Where are you from?	my-MAHN-tah KAHN-kee
Cosqo manta.	I'm from Cusco.	... MAHN-tah
Allichu	Please	al-YEE-choo

Sulpayki	Thank you	sul-PIE-kee
Ari	Yes	ah-REE
Mana	No	MAH-nah
Mama	Mother	MAH-mah
Tayta	Father	TIE-tah
Kuchumasi	Friend	ku-chu-MAH-see
Munayki.	I love you. (platonic)	mu-NIGH-kee
Ripusaq	I have to go./ Goodbye	ree-PU-sahk
Q'ayakama	See you tomorrow.	ky-yah-KAH-mah
Tutakama	See you tonight.	tu-tah-KAH-mah

Imaynatan munanki chaynallatataq munasunki.
Just as you love others, so they will love you.

Q is for Qatar

Persian Gulf

North Natural
Gas Field

BAHRAIN

Gulf of
Bahrain

☆ DOHA

Persian Gulf

SAUDI
ARABIA

Khor Al Udaid
(Inland Sea)

Our **Q** is for **QATAR**

(which rhymes well with **"water,"**

the Q like a "K" or a "G").

It's a rather **small country**

that's rich in resources

with oil and now gas from the sea.

Pearl

Qatar is found

on the *PERSIAN GULF,*

just a dot on a smaller world map.

To find it you first locate Saudi Arabia,

it's an eastern appendage to that.

This **SANDY** peninsula's

not great for farming

due to its DRY, HOT terrain.

But they've always had riches

like *Pearls* and dried fishes

and access to great shipping lanes.

Oil Well

Museum of Islamic Art

Their **oil** made them wealthy

and **natural gasfields,**

the largest now known of by man,

Fund *museums,* **UNIVERSITIES,**

SKYSCRAPERS, **stadiums** –

the emir's grand development plan.

Their king or **EMIR,**

was *Sheikh Hamad Al-Thani,*

who came to considerable fame.

He gave women the vote

and began **AL JAZEERA,**

an Arab news network whose aim...

Is providing the region

with much more press freedom

to criticize leaders and laws.

Its reporting has helped

to topple regimes

and gave voice to democracy's cause.

Sheikh Tamim
bin Hamad

**qatar
2022**

Qatar's 2022 World
Cup Emblem

The emir today

is Sheik Tamim bin Hamad,

a leader who already boasts

That he'll bring the football

WORLD CUP here to Qatar.

In 2022, they'll be host!

Most people in Qatar

are from other countries,

guest workers from all 'round the globe.

Other Arabs, South Asians,

Iranians come here –

most are men who do not wear a **thobe.**

Men in Thobes

Local men wear white thobes

and a **ghutra** (a headdress),

in red and white checked or plain white.

Most women in contrast

wear long black **ABAYA**   [ah-BY-yah]

that hides most of them from plain sight.

Family in Qatar

Doha's Corniche

Most Qataris live

in the capital **DOHA**

and stroll on its bayside **corniche.** [cor-NEESH]

They watch whimsical **SKYSCRAPERS**

spring from the desert

and shop in both **souks*** and boutiques.

Doha's Skyscrapers

They listen and dance

to **KHALIJI** style music, [kah-LEE-jee]

which comes from the Bedouin tribes. [BEH-doo-in]

They may watch **CAMEL RACES**

or train **falcon hunters** —

both desert traditions survive.

Singing Sand Dunes

Falcon Hunting

Outside of the capital,

you can hear **sand dunes**

that sing when the weather is dry.

You can visit the **ORYX**,

their national animal,

on a farm that is also nearby.

Oryx

Farther afield

take a **DESERT SAFARI**

to the inland sea, Khor al-Udaid, [KOR al- oo-DAYD]

Where you'll swim in the waters,

go skiing down sand dunes

or rest under canopied shade.

Khor al-Udaid

*A **souk** [like soup with a k] is an open air market.

So come now to Qatar
and say your **"Salaam!"** [sah-LAHM]
to this desert peninsula land.
You'll find an **OASIS,**
a ***pearl*** of great wonder,
amidst sun, sparkling sea and soft sand.

Oryx

Salaam [sah-LAHM] means "Hello" or "Peace" in Arabic.

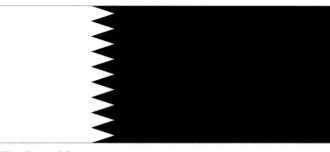

Qatar written in Arabic

Some believe **QATAR** got its name from Zubarah (called Qatara by the Greeks), an ancient Qatari port city that was a center for trade, particularly in pearls. Zubarah comes from the Persian word *gwadar*, which means port.

The **flag of Qatar** is very similar to the flag of nearby Bahrain. The white mast symbolizes peace and the maroon represents the blood lost by Qataris in battle. The serrated edge with nine points represents that Qatar was the 9th emirate to gain full independence (after Kuwait and the seven United Arab Emirates.) Qatar gained its independence in 1971.

Persian Gulf States

Official Name:
State of Qatar

Population: 2.1 million
Capital: Doha

Largest City: Doha

Comparative Size:
Slightly smaller than Connecticut, a bit larger than Lebanon

Ethnicity: Arab 40%, Indian 18%, Pakistani 19%, Iranian 10%, other 14%

Language: Arabic

Religion: Muslim 68%, Christian 14%, Hindu 14%, Buddhist 3%

Currency: Qatari rial

Important Exports:
Oil, gas

Where in the World is Qatar?

GEOGRAPHICAL NOTES

◉ Qatar is part of the **GCC** (Gulf Cooperation Council), a group of Arab states on the Persian Gulf. The GCC includes Bahrain, Kuwait, Oman, Qatar, Saudi Arabia and United Arab Emirates (UAE). Arab states do not call the Gulf "Persian" though, it is the **Arabian Gulf** on their maps.

Gas Flare at an Oil Well

← Qatar has huge amounts of **oil** and **gas** deposits → and a relatively small population. The combination has made them frequently ranked as the richest country in the world in terms of average income per person. Qatar has the 12th-largest oil reserves and the 3rd- or 4th-largest natural gas reserves of any country. The world's largest known natural gas field is off the coast of Qatar and it is divided between Qatar's "North Dome" and Iran's South Pars.

Map of Qatar's North Field

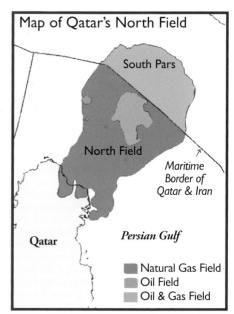

South Pars

North Field

Maritime Border of Qatar & Iran

Qatar

Persian Gulf

■ Natural Gas Field
■ Oil Field
■ Oil & Gas Field

Pearl

Sheikh Hamad Bin Khalifa al Thani, the emir of Qatar from 1995 to 2013, was known for modernizing his nation. He made the Qatari government more democratic, drafting a constitution that made Qatar a constitutional monarchy with a "Consultative Assembly" to advise the emir and approve budgets. The Emir also gave women the right to vote and hold office. He built the Education City, brought many international sporting events to Qatar and founded the news network Al Jazeera. The women in Sheikh Hamad's family were important to his rule. His second wife, Sheikha Mozah, has been a high profile advocate for Qatar's Education City and represents Qatar around the world. His daughter Sheikha Hind was his chief of staff; and his daughter Sheikha Al-Mayassa is the head of the Qatar Museums Authority and a leading figure in the international art world. ↓ →

Sheikh Hamad & Sheikha Mozah

← Qatar used to make money through harvesting **pearls** and fishing. From ancient times, pearl divers would harvest oysters found on the sea floor in the waters around Qatar. Thousands of pounds of oysters had to be brought up to find just a few pearls. Without modern diving equipment, it was very dangerous work – divers had to have huge lungs. When Japan developed the art of making cultured pearls more cheaply in the 1930s, Qatar's economy suffered. However, oil was discovered soon after and has been the main source of wealth ever since. ↓

↑ *A fountain in Doha representing Qatar's history and original source of wealth.*

Sheikha Mozah at the UN Alliance of Civilizations

Al Jazeera was the first international news network based in the Arab world. For the first time, international news was available in the region that was neither from the British (BBC) or American (CNN) perspective. This explosion of local information and analysis in the region has been instrumental in many of the democratizing campaigns taking place in the Arab world. Though Qatar itself is not yet a full democracy, and Al Jazeera rarely criticizes the Qatari government, Sheik Hamid Al-Thani's continual support for Al Jazeera has been a liberalizing force in Qatar and the region. →

شبكة الجزيرة
ALJAZEERANETWORK

Education City

The state religion of Qatar is **Islam**. While 99.9% of Qataris are Muslim, not all of their guest workers are. In total, about 68% of people in Qatar are Muslim, 14% Christian, 14% Hindu and about 3% Buddhist. ➜

Islamic Cultural Center in Doha

⬆ Qatar has used some of its wealth to create an "**Education City**" in Doha that hosts universities from around the world. Prestigious universities are able to have a second campus in Qatar so their students can study in Qatar on semesters abroad. And, Qataris can receive a world-class education without leaving their own country. The architecture of the Education City is as imaginative and modern as the city itself. ➜

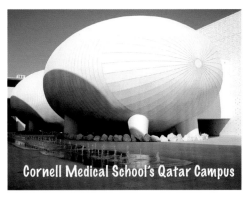

Cornell Medical School's Qatar Campus

Men Wearing Thobes and Gutras

Guest Workers

← **Guest workers** make up 80% of the population in Qatar. They work in the oil and gas industry, as well as hospitality, service and every other sector of the economy. Their restaurants bring food from around the world to Qatar. The largest groups of expatriates are from South Asia and Iran.

Men in Qatar wear long white robes called **thobes** ⬆ with loose white pants underneath. Thobes are very comfortable and shield them from the desert sun. On their heads, they wear a headdress called a **gutra** secured with a black coil called an *aghal*. The gutra protects them from sand and sun. Together, thobes and gutras are perfect desert wear.

Women in Qatar usually wear ➜ black **abaya** when out in public. Like the men, they cover their arms, legs and heads in loose flowing fabric. Black is not cooling like white is, but it is traditional and seen as being very elegant. Women in Qatar today are actually more educated than men, but traditionally they stay in the home. However, there are increasing government initiatives to make women a greater part of the workforce, including giving them senior-level positions in the government. Qatar was the first country in the Arab Persian Gulf to give all women the right to vote. They participated in Qatar's first elections in 1999 for municipal council seats.

Dr. Hessa Al Jaber is Qatar's Minister of Communication and Information Technology.

← **Emir Sheikh Tamim** bin Hamad Al-Thani became Qatar's new emir in June 2013. He had already helped Qatar win the right to host the World Cup in 2022.

qatar 2022

Walking on the Corniche

← **Doha** is Qatar's capital and largest city, → home to over 60% of the nation's population. It is known for its inventive modern architecture – from its skyscrapers, to its stadiums, to the Education City, to the new Museum of Islamic Art.

Doha has a **hot** desert climate, the average high each day from May–September is over 100°F (38°C). In "winter," January–February, the average high is about 72°F (22°C). Average rainfall is less than 3 inches (80 mm) per year.

Doha Skyscrapers

Doha's Corniche

←↑ Doha's **corniche**, or seaside walkway curves around Doha's bay. It is a popular place to stroll or jog and a great place to see the city's growing skyline and many monuments.

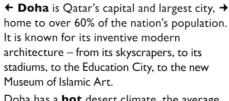
Machboos

↑ **Machboos** is a rice and meat dish that is popular all around the Persian Gulf. It includes spices like cardamom, cinnamon, cumin, ginger and rosewater.

Falconry is the art of training falcons → and other birds of prey to hunt for wild animals for humans. It has been a popular sport among nobility in the Arabian Desert for thousands of years and it is still widely practiced in the Gulf.

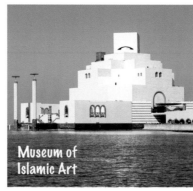
Falconry

Playing Khaliji Music

↑ **Khaliji** music and dance is popular in Persian Gulf States (Qatar, Bahrain, UAE, Kuwait and Saudi Arabia). Khaliji itself means "of the Gulf." The music largely comes from the Bedouin tribes that lived in the interior of the Arabian Peninsula. "Bedouin" comes from the Arabic word for "desert dweller." The music is known for the use of tabl drums and the oud, a stringed instrument.

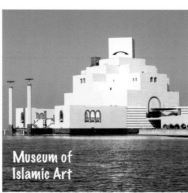
Museum of Islamic Art

← The **Museum of Islamic Art** sits on its own man-made island at the end of Doha's corniche. Designed by I. M. Pei, the building alone is a work of art, inspired by ancient ziggurats. Inside is art from all the Muslim empires. Islam frowns on the depiction of people and animals (to avoid creating idols) so Islamic arts tend to be decorative: carpets, tiles, geometric and floral pattens and calligraphy. ↓

Camel Race

← **Camel races** have been around since ancient times. Today camels are specially bred and trained to race, and winning camels can be worth quite a lot. Just like horse racing, there are bets on the races and big prizes. Camel races are also a tourist attraction. Camels can run at speeds up to 40 mph (65 km/h) in a sprint, and 25 mph (40 km/h) for longer distances.

↑ Islamic calligraphy (white on blue) rings this tile mosque dome with a center made of a geometric design.

Camel

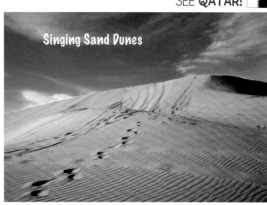

Singing Sand Dunes

Can sand really sing? Singing **sand dunes** → are a phenomenon that occurs on high dunes when sand is very dry. When winds cross the dunes, it may cause a mini avalanche of sand to fall down the dune. The sand vibrates together, making a droning sound, between the noise of swarming insects and the low note of a cello. The dunes continue to vibrate even after the sand stops, echoing off the high dunes as if the desert is humming or moaning.

↑ **Camels** were called the "ships of the desert" by Bedouins (traditional desert dwellers). Camels were once the only way to cross the desert and were essential to desert life. Their milk and meat were a food source, their dung was used for fire, even their hair was used to make fabric for tents. Camels eat desert shrubs but can go long periods without food or water as their humps store fat and water. When they go long without eating or drinking, their hump begins to sag. →

Camel

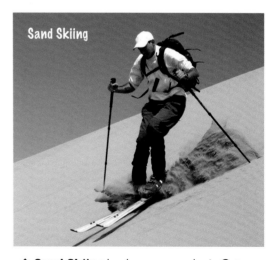

Oryx

↑ The **oryx** is the national animal of Qatar. In 1972, the Arabian oryx had become extinct in the wild. With the careful work of many Gulf countries, breeding oryx in captivity and then releasing them in the wild, the wild oryx population has resurged. Outside of Doha, there is an oryx sanctuary you can visit. Oryxes can go without drinking water – getting liquids instead from root and tubers they dig up to eat.

Inland Sea Beach

← The **Inland Sea** or *Khor Al Udaid* is a body of water created by a narrow inlet from the Persian Gulf. Huge sand dunes surround it and the water is crystal blue and calm. The Inland Sea is located on the border between Qatar and Saudi Arabia, and is shared by both nations. ↓

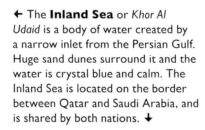

Sand Skiing

↑ There are many desert attractions offered near the Inland Sea: desert camping, camel safaris, sand skiing and dune "bashing." Dune bashing is racing up and down dunes in a four-wheel drive vehicle, something like a desert roller coaster. →

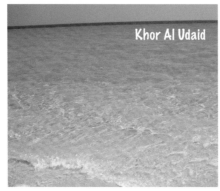

Khor Al Udaid

↑ **Sand Skiing** has become popular in Qatar as a tourist attraction. It is similar to snow skiing, but it's warmer and has softer landings. With no trees to run into, the only safety concern is keeping hydrated. The sand dunes surrounding the Khor Al Udaid are particularly powdery and perfect for sand skiing.

What would your name be in Qatar?

The former emir:

Sheikh	Hamad	bin	Khalifa	Al-Thani
Title	Personal Name	Son of	Father's Name	Family Name

His wife:

Sheikha	Mozah	bint	Nasser	Al-Misnad
Title	Personal Name	Daughter of	Father's Name	Family Name

His daughter (and chief of staff):

Sheikha	Hind	bint	Hamad	Al-Thani
Title	Personal Name	Daughter of	Father's Name	Family Name

His son, the current emir:

Sheikh	Tamim	bin	Hamad	bin
Title	Personal Name	Son of	Father's Name	Son of

Khalifa	Al-Thani
Grandather's Name	Family Name

What would your name be if you lived on the Arabian peninsula?

Your personal name or "first name," remains unchanged. Then comes your father's name, and in very formal situations, your grandfather's name as well. These names are preceded by a "bin" meaning "son of" or "bint" meaning "daughter of."

Finally, a family name may be used, but it isn't standard. The family name is frequently preceded by "Al" or "El," which mean "the." The family name might come from a hometown, profession or adjective like "the just." The Al-Thanis are named as descendents of their first leader to settle in Qatar, Sheik Thani bin Mohammed. When using a hometown, an "i" is traditionally added to the end. For instance, Al-New Yorqi would mean "the New Yorker."

While children take their father's name, parents take the name of their first child as an honorable title. Abu, "father of," or Umm, "mother of," would precede their child's name. These names are not used on official documents, but they are very respectful and used among communities. Palestinian President Mahmoud Abbas is frequently called "Abu Mazen" in the press.

What would your name be? What would your parents' names be (both officially and in the community)?

Listen to the SOUNDS of QATAR

Khaliji Music
Khaliji or Khaleeji is an adjective for Arab states on the Persian Gulf including Qatar, Bahrain, Saudi Arabia, UAE, Kuwait, Oman and Iraq. Khaliji music relies on the tabl drum and the oud. **YOUTUBE SEARCH:** khaliji music

DON'T MISS WATCHING (online)

Spotlight Qatar There are a few great news specials introducing Qatar including one by CBS News and one by CNN. **YOUTUBE SEARCH:** Qatar CBS, Qatar CNN

Sword Dance See a men's sword dance at a Qatari wedding.
YOUTUBE SEARCH: Qatar wedding dance

SPEAK Gulf Arabic!

As-Salaam Alaikum Greeting
(Peace be upon you) *ah-sah-LAHM ah-LIGH-koom*

Wa alaikum as-salaam Response
(And upon you be peace) *wah ah-LIGH-koom as-sah-LAHM*

Salaam	Hi! (peace	*sah-LAHM*
Shlonik *(to male)*	How are you?	*SHLOH-nik*
Shlonich *(to female)*		*SHLOH-nich*
ib khayr	I'm fine	*eeb KIGH-R*
Wa ant? *(to male)*	And you?	*wah ahnt*
Wa anti? *(to female)*		*wah ahn-tee*
Shukkran	Thank you	*shuh-KRAHN*
Afwan	You're welcome	*ah-FWAHN*
Na'am	Yes	*nah-AHM*
Laa	No	*lahh*
Inshallah	God willing/hopefully	*in-shah-LAH*
.... ismee	My name is	*iss-mee*
Ma-a salaama	Goodbye	*mah-ah sah-LAH-mah*

MAKE QATARI CHICKEN MACHBOOS

Machboos is a popular dish in many countries on the Persian Gulf including Bahrain, UAE and Qatar. Saudi Arabia has a similar dish called *kabsah*. In Qatar, it is the favorite lunch food, and many Qataris have machboos nearly everyday. Machboos is made with lamb, chicken or fish.

1. Measure all powdered spices (except turmeric) into a pan to toast. Toast spices on your stove top on medium-low heat, stir continually or shake the pan to keep them from burning. They will produce a strong perfume of spices when ready. Pour into a bowl and set aside.

2. Salt chicken pieces well and rub with some of toasted spices.

3. Put oil in large pan or soup pot (nonstick is ideal), bring up to medium heat. Fry chicken on all sides until skin is golden brown. This will take at least 10 minutes; give it time to brown the skin under the spices. Remove chicken from the pan and set aside.

4. Add onions to the remaining oil in the pan and sauté until they begin to brown. Add garlic and ginger; cook one minute longer.

5. Add the spices to pan including turmeric; stir well and cook for an additional minute.

6. Add chicken back to the pan, stir to coat with onion mixture. Then add tomato, black lime, water and bouillon cube. Bring to a boil, then turn heat to low. Cover and simmer for one hour.

7. Meanwhile, soak basmati rice in a bowl of water and chop cilantro. When simmering is complete, drain rice and add to pot. Stir, cover again and wait 15 minutes until rice is almost cooked.

8. Add chopped cilantro and raisins. Stir gently. (If rice is already drying out, add another ¼ cup water.) Cover and cook another 5 minutes until rice is cooked and liquid absorbed.

9. Add lemon juice and butter, stir gently, then move the dish to a platter, putting chicken pieces on top. Sprinkle rosewater on top.

10. Serve when warm (not hot) with a fresh green salad.

Spices to toast*:
¾ teaspoon ground black pepper
¾ teaspoon paprika
1 teaspoon ground cumin
1½ teaspoons cinnamon
¾ teaspoon ground cardamom
½ teaspoon ground cloves
½ teaspoon ground nutmeg

Other ingredients:
1½–2 lbs chicken pieces
  (dark meat, with skin and bones intact)
salt (to sprinkle on raw chicken)
3 tablespoons oil
1 onion, diced
3 cloves of garlic, crushed
1 tablespoon fresh ginger,
  peeled and minced
1 teaspoon turmeric
1 large tomato, diced or 1 can drained
1–2 black limes cut in half (optional)
1 cup water
1 large bouillon cube, or two small
1½ cup basmati rice
2 tablespoons chopped cilantro
½ cup raisins
Juice of 1 lemon
2 tablespoons butter
1–2 tablespoons rosewater (optional)

Modifications and Substitutions:

Black Limes: Also called dried limes, loomi or Omani limanu, black limes are a very popular ingredient in Gulf cooking. They have a smoky, sour flavor and are made by boiling limes in very salty water, then leaving them to dry out in the desert sun for a week. You could order them online, but the flavor is very subtle, so you can also omit them.

Rosewater: Rosewater can also be difficult to find, but it can be omitted or ordered online. Not everyone immediately likes the perfumed flavor.

***More authentic:** If you do have access to an international market with black limes and rosewater, you might also buy *baharat*, an Arabic spice blend that is traditionally used in machboos. This recipe makes a substitute for baharat when you toast the spices together.

R is for Russia

ARTIC OCEAN

ARTIC OCEAN

SIBERIA

FINLAND

ESTONIA
LATVIA

ST. PETERSBURG

☆ MOSCOW

URAL MOUNTAINS

⊙ YEKATERINBURG

Bering
Sea

Sea of
Okhotsk

LITHUANIA
BELARUS

UKRAINE

KAZAKHSTAN

CAUCUS

Black Sea

Caspian Sea

GEORGIA
AZERBAIJAN

⊙ NOVOSIBIRSK

MONGOLIA

CHINA

CHINA

CHINA

⊙ VLADIVOSTOK

Our **R** is for **RUSSIA,**

the Russian Federation,

Whose *nine time zones* make up

the **world's largest nation**!

Straddling **two continents,**

Russia's divided

By mountains named **URAL**

into parts quite lopsided.

Russia's Time Zones

Reindeer in tundra

Birch Forest

Part of  **EUROPE,** the west

is much smaller in size,

But many more Russians

have homes on this side.

To the east is **SIBERIA**

(the Asian side's name),

Where not half of the people

have twice the terrain.

Russian Orthodox
Church

Both have **TUNDRA** and **TAIGA,**

great forests of birches

And **onion-shaped domes**

of Orthodox churches.

Czar Nicholas II

In this vast Russian land

that was once ruled by CZARS, [ZARZ]

there are Black Sea coast beaches

and black *caviar.*

Black Caviar

For everyday though,

the people eat BREAD,

Potatoes and soup,

like borscht that's bright red.

Borscht

Blini

They drink **tea** all day long,

and love pancakes called **BLINI.**

They use **rubles** for buying

matroyshka so teeny. [mah-TROYSH-kah]

Ruble

Matryoshka

Their writing's 𝓒𝓨𝓡𝓘𝓛𝓛𝓘𝓒;

for transport there're trains;

And Grandfather Frost

is their Santa Claus's name.

In the center of **Moscow**

is its famous **RED SQUARE** —

Saint Basil's Cathedral

and the **KREMLIN** are there.

Grandfather Frost &
the Snow Maiden

The **KREMLIN** is huge,

it's a workout for legs.

The president lives there

with **Fabergé eggs.** [FAB-er-jay]

Saint Basil's Cathedral

From Vladivostok

to **Saint Petersburg,**

Russians aren't smiley,

and grinning's absurd.

Fabergé Egg

Though their teeth may be hidden,

their passions are not.

If you ask them **"Kak dela?"** * [KAHK dih-LAH]

they'll tell you a lot.

Swan Lake
Ballerina

The Russians are made

of **MELANCHOLIC JOY** –

From Tchaikovsky's **ballets**

to the books of Tolstoy –

Icon

From their **icons of gold**

to the works of **KANDINSKY** –

From the verses of **Pushkin**

to the sounds of **Stravinsky.**

Kandisnky's
"Moscow I"

Pensive and playful,

gloomy and proud,

Generous friends

whose parties are loud.

Stravinsky

Russians will charm you

although they are **BEARS.**

Their great **Slavic** land

is like no place elsewhere.

Privet!*

*__Kak dela?__ means "How are you?" *__Privet!__ [pree-VYET] means "Hi!"

← The **Russian flag** was originally adopted in 1896. It was used until the last tsar, Nicholas II, was overthrown in 1917, causing the Russian Empire to dissolve. In 1922, the empire was replaced by the Soviet Union. The flag was readopted in 1991 when the Soviet Union fell and the Russian Federation was established. *For more information about the Soviet Union, see page 244.*

Россия

Russia written in its native Cyrillic alphabet

The name **RUSSIA** came from the Rus people. Who were the Rus? One theory is that they were a group of Swedish Vikings who settled in Western Russia and Ukraine.

Kaliningrad

Time Zones in Russia

Official Name:
Russian Federation

Population: 142 million

Capital: Moscow

Largest Cities:
Moscow, Saint Petersburg, Novosibirsk, Yekaterinburg

Comparative Size:
The world's largest country, 1.8 times the size of the United States

Ethnicity: Russian 80%, Tatar 3.8%, Ukrainian 2%, Bashkir 1.2%, Chevash 1%

Language: Russian and many minority languages

Religion: Christian 73% (Eastern Orthodox), Muslim 10%

Currency: Russian ruble

Important Exports:
Oil, gas, metals

Where in the World is Russia?

GEOGRAPHICAL NOTES

⊙ Russia is the world's largest country and currently has nine time zones. (They used to have eleven!) Northern Russia spans almost halfway around the Arctic circle.

⊙ Russia straddles both Europe and Asia. The **Ural Mountains** divide Russia's European side from its Asian side, which is also known as **Siberia.**

⊙ Russia is a federation that is divided into 83 **federal subjects**. Each regional subject elects two representatives to the Russian Federation Council, which is similar to the US Senate.

Tundra

← **Tundra** is a biome around the Arctic Circle where the ground is permanently frozen and too hard for large-rooted plants like trees to grow. The top layer of soil is warmed by the sun and supports grasses. Caribou (reindeer), musk ox, arctic foxes and hares, polar bears and snowy owls are some animals that live in the tundra.

Taiga is the biome just south of the tundra. It is filled → with coniferous forests. Most of Russia is taiga. Temperatures are below freezing roughly half of the year but warm considerably in the summer.

Taiga

The **czar** *(ZAR)* or tsar of → Russia was the nation's supreme leader. Czar is derived from the Latin word *caesar,* meaning emperor. Ivan IV (the Terrible) was the first to declare himself czar of Russia in 1541. He was part of the **Romanov dynasty**, which continued to rule over Russia until the Russian Revolution in 1917. The great power of the czar was one reason that the **Russian Revolution** killed the last czar, Nicholas II, as well as his wife and children, ending the Romanov dynasty.

Czar Nicholas II

Birch Forest

← The white-trunk **birch** is the national tree of Russia. It is a beloved symbol of purity, spring and renewal, and the birch is one of the few deciduous trees in the taiga. Birch bark is used to make boxes, and birch juice is drunk as a tonic.

Onion-shaped domes are → hallmarks of Russian Orthodox churches. Some claim that they look like lit candles, but from a practical standpoint, they repel snow.

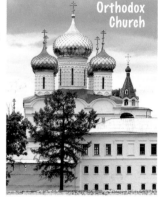
Orthodox Church

Black Sea

Sturgeon

← **Caviar** is the salted fish eggs of sturgeon. It is an expensive delicacy used as a spread on festive occasions. The most expensive variety of caviar, beluga, can be $5,000 a pound. It is harvested only from beluga sturgeon in the **Black Sea** or Caspian Sea. →

Caviar

Eating **soup** everyday is considered good for the health in Russia. **Borscht** is a bright red beet soup originally from the Ukraine. It is popular all over Russia, as is a cabbage soup called *schi*. Soup is traditionally eaten very hot with **wooden spoons** that will not heat up and burn the mouth. Each family member has their own wooden spoon that is not shared to avoid spreading germs. ↓ →

Wooden Soup Spoons

There is an expression in Russia, "**Bread** *is everything's head*," that expresses how central bread is to the Russian diet. It is traditional to welcome guests with a ← plate of bread and salt. Guests take a pinch of bread, dip it in salt and then eat it. →

Offering Bread & Salt

Borscht

A **samovar** is a tea → server and symbol of Russian hospitality. Tea is the most popular beverage in Russia and is drunk all day long. Samovar means "self-boiler" and uses a central metal column filled with coals to keep the tea hot. (Electric samovars are available today.) Samovars were traditionally kept ready to serve to guests all day long.

Samovar

Blini are thin pancakes, somewhat similar to French crepes. They are eaten with many different fillings and toppings like butter and sugar, caviar and sour cream, smoked salmon, jam, or berries and chocolate. ↓ →

Blini

Grandfather Frost & the Snow Maiden

Grandfather Frost or *Ded Moroz* → and his granddaughter, the Snow Maiden, bring New Year's gifts to all good Russian boys and girls. Unlike Santa Claus, Grandfather Frost typically arrives in person to give children their gifts at New Year's Eve parties.

Matryoshka

↑ **Matryoshka** are nesting dolls, carved from a single piece of wood. Typically there are five dolls nested together, but there can be over a dozen dolls, each progressively tinier.

← Russian money comes in **rubles**, which can each be divided into 100 *kopecks*.

АБВГДЕЖ ЗИЙКЛМН ОПРСТУФ ХЦЧШЩЪ ЫЬЭЮЯ

↑ The **Cyrillic alphabet** is used to write Russian as well as other slavic languages like Bulgarian, Serbian, Belorussian, Ukrainian, Macedonian and Montenegran. It was created by followers of Saint Cyril, a Christian missionary to the Slavs.

Fabergé eggs are bejeweled eggs created by jewelry designer Carl Fabergé to celebrate Easter. The eggs he designed for the czars of Russia were incredibly elaborate and contained further eggs and jewels within. →

Red Square

← Why is **Red Square** called "red?" The words 'red' and 'beautiful' used to be the same in Russian. Beautiful was how people described St. Basil's Cathedral, which sits on Red Square, and the name became a description of the square as well. The Kremlin also sits off of Red Square. All of Moscow's main roads originate in Red Square and so it is seen as the central square of Moscow (and all of Russia).

↓ **Saint Basil's Cathedral** was built in 1555 by Ivan IV (the Terrible) in celebration of his victory over the Mongols.

Moscow's Kremlin

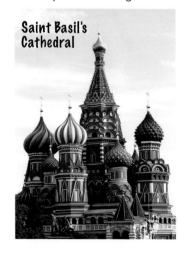

Saint Basil's Cathedral

The **Kremlin** is a walled enclosure built in central ↑ Moscow during Medieval times. *Kremlin* simply means "fortress," and many old Russian cities have kremlins that were used to protect a city and its citizens from attack. The Moscow Kremlin is famous because it is the home of the Russian president. In fact, the government of Russia is frequently called simply, "the Kremlin" in international news stories. Reporters frequently stand in front of Saint Basil's Cathedral to report on the Kremlin, even though it is unrelated to the Russian government and is simply located near the Kremlin in Red Square.

Russian Smile

← It's not that Russians never **smile**, they just don't smile without a reason. A neutral expression does not mean that Russians are feeling unhappy or unfriendly. Russians smile in amusement or joy, but it is not the typical expression for greeting others as it is in North America. Similarly, "How are you?" is not part of standard greetings. If you ask a Russian that, they will expect that you want a real answer, not just, "Fine, thanks. And you?"

Swan Lake

← **Tchaikovsky** (1840–1893) is one the world's most famous composers. He wrote the music to many famous ballets including *Swan Lake* and *The Nutcracker.*

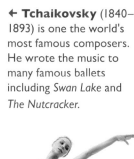
Ballerina

Wassily **Kandinsky** was a Russian painter who was a pioneer in creating *abstract art.* Abstract artists don't try to create pictures of people, things or nature. Instead they use color, line and shapes to express themselves. This painting entitled → *Moscow I* does not show a scene of exactly what Moscow looked like, instead it expresses the feel of a Moscow sunset. Kandinsky claimed that art could be like music – it does not need to represent something else in order to be beautiful or evocative. Paintings only about the interaction of color, line and form can be as beautiful as a symphony.

Kandinsky's Moscow I

Russia has helped to create **ballet** → as we know it in the 20th century. It is famous for the amazing dancers it has produced, like Anna Pavlova and Mikhail Baryshnikov, and its world-renowned dance companies: the Bolshoi Ballet and the Kirov Ballet.

Stravinsky

← **Stravinsky** was one of several famous Russian composers all living at about the same time including Rachmaninoff, Rimsky-Korsakov, Shostakovich and Prokofiev. Stravinsky, like Tchaikovsky, composed several famous ballets including *The Rites of Spring* and *The Firebird.*

Trinity is the most → famous **Russian icon** and is considered one of the greatest masterpieces in Russian art. Created by Andrei Rublev in the 15th century, it is a painting of the three angels who appeared to Abraham in the Bible. The Russian Orthodox religion has been making icons (religious paintings) ever since Russians first converted to Christianity in 988. In fact, they were frequently used as an aid in giving religious construction and in converting people who could not read. Icons are typically painted on small wooden boards and use gold leaf as an accent for halos and background areas. Icons are considered to be the gospel written in paint, and artists are very careful to represent Bible stories accurately. Most religious Russians have a corner of their home dedicated to icons and praying before them is a traditional part of Orthodox worship.

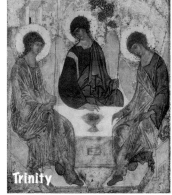

Trinity

Leo Tolstoy (1828–1910) → is the Russian writer who wrote the classic novels *Anna Karenina* and *War and Peace.* He is known as one of the world's greatest novelists. *War and Peace* is famous for being one of the longest novels ever written. It was said that Tolstoy's writing was so realistic that is was not art, but an actual slice of life.

Tolstoy

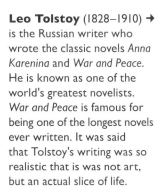

Russian Bear

← **Bears** have long been used as a symbol of Russia and are probably the most beloved animal within the country. Bears are plentiful in the forests of Siberia and friendly big bears are often characters in Russian fairy tales.

What was the Soviet Union?

Lithuania
Estonia
Latvia
Belarus
Ukraine
Moldova
RUSSIA
Georgia
Armenia
Kazakhstan
Azerbaijan
Turkmenistan
Uzbekistan
Kyrgyzstan
Tajikistan

The Soviet Union (1922-1991)

The **Soviet Union** or **USSR** (United Soviet Socialist Republics) was a union of 15 republics with a single federal government in Russia. (The republics had all previously been part of the Russian Empire before becoming part of the Soviet Union.) The word *soviet* means "governing council" and the first Soviet councils met during the Russian Revolution (1917) to plan the overthrow of the czar and a communist revolution. The motto of the Soviet Union was "Workers of the World, Unite!" They wanted to replace an incredibly unequal society ruled by a czar and aristocrats, with an equal society governed by workers and dedicated to improving life for Russian peasants. In order to do that, the state took over land and industry, ending private ownership and private enterprise in order to control the economy.

The influence of the Soviet Union extended far beyond its borders, creating a sort of "Soviet Empire." That empire included Soviet Satellite States, independent communist countries whose governments were heavily influenced by the USSR. Many of these countries were in Central and Eastern Europe and were occupied by the USSR after World War II. Soviet Satellite States included: Bulgaria, Cuba, Czechoslovakia, East Germany, Hungary, Mongolia, Poland, Romania and Yugoslavia.

The USSR and the United States were engaged in a "Cold War" from the end of World War II until the Soviet Union dissolved in 1991. For more about the Cold War, see page 293. For more about communism, see page 37.

The USSR was known as the **CCCP** in Russia, as those were its initials in Cyrillic, the Russian alphabet.

The Soviet flag featured the hammer and sickle, a symbol of the unity of farmers and workers. The red color symbolized revolution and the star, the rule of the communist party.

*A matryoshka of the most famous Soviet leaders from right to left: **Lenin** (1922–1924), **Stalin** (1924–1953), **Krushchev** (1955–1964), **Brezhnev** (1964–1982) and **Gorbachev** (1985–1991)*

Listen to the SOUNDS of RUSSIA

READ:

Balalaika

Balalaika A traditional instrument of Russian folk music, a balalaika can be a big as a bass or as small as a ukulele. **YOUTUBE SEARCH:** balalaika virtuoso

"Kalinka" & "Korobushka" Two of the most famous Russian folk songs.

Peter and the Wolf by Prokofiev. A charming children's story in which each character is represented by an instrument in the orchestra.

1812 Overture by Tchaikovsky. A work with cannon fire that celebrates Russia defending itself against the invading French army of Napoleon.

Other Classical Russian Works

Stravinsky's "Rite of Spring," which you can hear and watch as a dinosaur action movie on Disney's *Fantasia*

Rimsy-Korsakov's "Flight of the Bumblebee"

Rachmaninoff's "Rhapsody on a Theme by Paganini," which will make you wonder if the pianist has extra fingers

Shostakovich's "The Second Waltz"

DON'T MISS WATCHING (online)

Russian Dancing From Cossack men's dancing with high jumps and flips to Russian folk dancing in colorful dress, dancing is a joyful element of traditional Russian celebrations of all kinds. **YOUTUBE SEARCH:** Russian folk dance, Cossack dancing, Kalinka Russian dance

Cheburashka If Mickey Mouse had had a Russian soul, he might have been like Cheburashka, a character from classic stop-motion films first put out in 1969. Fun for all ages, Cheburashka reflects the positive values of Soviet society. **YOUTUBE SEARCH:** Cheburashka

Tale of Tsar Saltan There is an animated 1984 version of this Pushkin fairy tale where you can hear his wonderful Russian verse while seeing subtitles in English verse. A favorite Russian tale beautifully retold. **YOUTUBE SEARCH:** Tale of Tsar Saltan

Trans-Siberian Railway See Russia and understand the history and importance of the world's longest railroad. **YOUTUBE SEARCH:** Trans-Siberian railroad

The Magic Goldfish: A Russian Folktale by Demi. An adaptation of Pushkin's version of this famous fairy tale. Beautifully written and illustrated. Ages 5 & up.

The Gigantic Turnip by Aleksei Tolstoy and Niamh Sharkey. A funny tale about a harvesting a huge vegetable. Ages 3 & up.

The Magic Nesting Doll by Jacqueline Ogburn. A magic matryoshka, given to Katya by her grandmother, helps her save a prince from a wicked spell. Ages 5 & up.

The Sea King's Daughter: A Russian Legend by Aaron Shepard. A classic Russian fairy tale of a poor musician and his invitation from the Sea King. Ages 8 & up.

Tale of Tsar Saltan by Alexander Pushkin. Though sadly not in verse like the original Pushkin tale, this translation was beautifully illustrated by Russian Gennady Spirin. With evil sisters, a magic swan, an island exile and a royal love story, this Russian classic has many more plot twists than your average fairy tale. Ages 7 & up.

Three Questions by Jon Muth. This picture book is based on a charming tale of the same name by Tolstoy (which can be found online). This book changes the main character from a tsar into a boy, but the three questions remain the same. Try reading both versions. Ages 4 & up.

Tales about Baba Yaga by various authors. Baba Yaga is the quintessential Russian witch and she appears in many folktales. Sometimes villainous, sometimes helpful, she is always hideous and lives in a hut that stands on chicken legs. Find selections like the following at your local library: **Baba Yaga and Vasilisa the Brave** by Mariana Mayer. Ages 8 & up.

Angel on the Square by Gloria Whelan. Katya, whose mother is lady-in-waiting to the empress, lives at the palace at the eve the Russian Revolution and the fall of the Romanov Dynasty. Age 10 & up.

Grigory Rasputin: Holy Man or Mad Monk? by Enid Goldberg and Norman Itzkowitz.
Ivan the Terrible: Tsar of Death by Sean Price.
Catherine the Great: Empress of Russia by Zu Vincent. All from the "Wicked History" series, which present historical figures in an entertaining manner, with humor, true wickedness and grisly details. Ages 12 & up.

Anastasia: the Last Grand Duchess by Carolyn Meyer.
Catherine: the Great Journey by Kristiana Gregory. Both books are historical fiction from the "Royal Diaries" series, and they plunge the reader into key points in Russian history. Ages 9 & up.

MAKE RUSSIAN BLINI

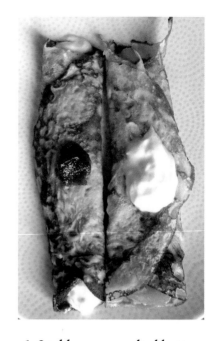

Blini are delicious and so easy to make. Super-thin pancakes you can fill with almost anything, they are popular year-round but particularly during the festival of ***Maslenitsa***, (mahs-len-NEET-sah) which roughly translates to "Butter Week." Similar to Mardi Gras or Brazilian Carnival, Maslenitsa is a celebration in early spring before the season of Lent, the forty days of Christian fasting that leads up to Easter. The festival is thought to date back to pagan times when the buttered blini represented the sun, which has begun to return for spring. What fillings do Russians use with blini? Well caviar is always popular, but for more everyday fare, jam and sour cream, smoked fish and sour cream, mushrooms and onions, condensed milk or just sugar and butter.

1. **Melt butter** and set to the side to cool.

2. **Beat together egg, one cup milk, salt and sugar.**

3. **Add flour and beat together until smooth.** It should be the consistency of American pancake batter.

4. **Add 1/2 cup milk, mix again.** It should now be the consistency of heavy cream. (Add more milk if needed to thin. The milk is added in two phases because it is easier to get all the lumps out with a thicker batter.)

5. **Add melted butter** (or vegetable oil) and stir well.

6. **Prepare pan.** Heat a small nonstick pan to medium heat. Add a small pat of butter and swirl around pan to coat.

7. **Pour batter in pan.** Using a ¼ cup as a ladle, fill it a little over half full. Pour batter into the pan while tilting the pan with your other hand to spread the batter. Keep tilting and swirling until all the batter is set. Sending extra batter to the outer edges of the blini makes it uniformly thin so that its is not thicker in the middle.

8. **Flip.** Using a spatula, flip pancake when it starts to look a little brown on the edges.

9. **Remove from pan to stack.** The second side takes less time to cook. Once it starts to brown, remove to a plate where you can stack all the blini.

10. **Repeat** until all batter is used. Serve immediately, putting out fillings on the table for people to top their own blini and then roll them up like cigars.

1–2 tablespoons melted butter
  or vegetable oil
2 eggs
1½ cup milk (1 cup + ½ cup)
½ teaspoon salt
1 tablespoon sugar
1 cup flour

butter for greasing pan

Popular Fillings
•jam •condensed milk
•berries •honey •sour cream
•smoked salmon •meat
•mushrooms •cheese
•onions and potatoes

SPEAK RUSSIAN!

Privet!	**Hi!** (Informal)	*pree-VYET*	**Привет!**
Zdrastvuite!	**Hello!** (Polite)	*ZDRAHST-vui-tyeh*	**Здравствуйте!**
Kak dela?	**How are you?**	*kahk deh-LAH*	**Как дела?**
Spasibo, Horosho. A u vas?		*spah-SEE-bah huh-rah-SHO ah oo vahs*	
	Thanks, good. And you?		**Спасибо, хорошо. А у вас?**
Spasibo:	**Thank you**	*spah-SEE-bah*	**Спасибо**
Horosho:	**Good**	*huh-rah-SHO*	**хорошо**
Da/Nyet:	**Yes/No**	*dah nyet*	**Да / Нет**
Do Svidaniya:	**Goodbye** (Polite)	*doh svee-DAHN-eeya*	**До свидания!**
Paka:	**Bye!** (Informal)	*PAH-kah*	**Пока!**

Cyrillic	letter sound	example of sound	cursive
А а	ah	**fa**ther	*Аа*
Б б	b	**b**oy	*Бб*
В в	v	**v**ote	*Вв*
Г г	g	**g**o	*Гг*
Д д	d	**d**og	*Дg*
Е е	eh, yeh	**e**gg, "**ye**" in yes	*Ее*
Ж ж	zh/j	like the "s" in measure	*Жж*
З з	z	**z**oo	*Зз*
И и	ee, ih	b**ee**, b**i**t	*Ии*
Й й	y/i	to**y**, "y" or "i" in a dipthong	*Йй*
К к	k	**k**ick	*Кк*
Л л	l	**l**uck, wi**ll**	*Лл*
М м	m	**m**o**m**	*Мм*
Н н	n	**n**o	*Нн*
О о	oh	s**o**ldier	*Оо*
П п	p	**p**ark	*Пп*
Р р	r	**r**un, tea**r**	*Рр*
С с	s	**s**i**s**ter	*Сс*
Т т	t	**t**ickle	*Тт*
У у	u, oo	tr**u**e, b**oo**t	*Уу*
Ф ф	f	**f**ork	*Фф*
Х х	kh	lo**ch,** ye**ch**! (yuck!)	*Хх*
Ц ц	ts	pi**zz**a, **ts**ar	*Цц*
Ч ч	ch	**ch**icken	*Чч*
Ш ш	sh	**sh**eep	*Шш*
Щ щ	shch	fre**sh ch**eese	*Щщ*
Ъ ъ	-	sound separator, so two letters aren't blended	*Ъъ*
Ы ы	ee	similar to и, used to signal that previous consonant is hard	*Ыы*
Ь ь	no sound	softens previous consonant	*Ьь*
Э э	eh, "a" in at	usually the "e" used to start words, used in foreign words	*Ээ*
Ю ю	yu, ew	**u**niversity	*Юю*
Я я	yah, a	**ya**cht, l**a**mb	*Яя*

Read and Write in Cyrillic!

The Cyrillic alphabet was created in the 9th century by followers of Saint Cyril. It shares letters with both the Greek and the Latin alphabet. In some ways, the Cyrillic alphabet is easier to learn than our Latin alphabet, as most of its upper and lower case letters are identical except in size. However, the cursive form of Cyrillic letters can change significantly, just look at the cursive versions of **Д** (d) and **Т** (t).

1. On a piece of paper, try to print all the letters of the Cyrillic alphabet, noting their equivalent letters in English.

2. After writing the alphabet, can you decipher and answer these questions with Russian words?

Do you like **рэп** music? What about **опера**?

Do you like to read **фэнтези**?

Would you rather go to a **кафе́** or to **Макдоналд'с**?

Could you live without the **интернет**?

Do you like to wear **джинсы**?

Do you love **шоколад**?

Is **водка** the most popular Russian drink, or **чай**?

Do we have an **экзамен** in **класс**?

3. What do these Russian words mean?

Президент Влади́мир Пу́тин

Чайко́вский **Толсто́й**

Анастаси́я **Аме́рика**

студе́нт **ро́бот**

футбо́л **чемпио́н**

телефо́н **ви́део**

фильм **Актер**

гита́ра **аэропо́рт**

рестора́н **меню́**

4. Can you write your own name, or the names of your friends and family in Cyrillic?

(You can check your answers online, internet search "write name in Cyrillic.")

S is for Spain

ATLANTIC OCEAN

Bay of Biscay

FRANCE

BILBAO

PYRENEES MOUNTAINS

BARCELONA

☆ MADRID

Menorca

Mallorca

PORTUGAL

VALENCIA

Ibiza

SEVILLA

Mediterranean Sea

Strait of Gibraltar

TUNISIA

MOROCCO

ALGERIA

España takes our **S** for **SPAIN**, [ays-PAH-nyah]

a **sunny** land up late.

And why should Spaniards sleep

when there're **fiestas*** every date?*

Gibraltar to the **PYRENEES,**

ATLANTIC to the **Med,**

The Spanish love to party

and with OLIVE OIL they're fed:

Olive Oil

*Literally, Spain claims to have more festivals (fiestas) than days of the year.

Tapas

Paella

Ham, paella, tapas, wine, [pah-AY-yah, TAH-pas]

soups and fresh gazpacho, [gahz-PAH-cho]

Queso, garlic, and egg tortillas – [KAY-soh, tor-TEE-yahs]

but never spicy tacos!

Spaniards talk and **talk** and **TALK** –

an all-at-once technique –

In which they hear their friends

all while continuing to speak:

Tortilla

Gazpacho

In Basque, Galician, Catalan

and Spanish (Castellano), [cah-stay-YAH-no]

a language that's called **Español**

by Latin Americanos.

Spain's regions are diverse in language –

climate and hist'ry too.

They really weren't one country

until **1492.**

King Ferdinand II
of Aragon

Spain before 1492

When Ferdinand and Isabella

united faith and land,

And sent **COLUMBUS** sailing

to extend the Spanish hand –

Queen Isabella I of
Castile

Spanish Empire in
the Americas

Flamenco

Saint James
(Santiago)

Picador

Fútbol

Across the ocean claiming

all the **NEW WORLD** for the old.

The Spanish spread their tongue and faith

for empire and for gold.

Spain's sunny south retains a flair

from Roma* and the **Moors**,*

From whom they got **FLAMENCO**

and bull-fighting picadors.

The green northwest with Celtic roots

is where **Saint James** now lies.

Spain's patron saint,

he rests below **Galicia's** cloudy skies.

Northeast some speak in Catalan [CAT-ah-lahn]

and **BARCELONA** sits,

A second capital of art,

competing with **MADRID**.

Spain's favorite sport is **football**,

their symbol is a **BULL**,

They're famed for their fun way of life

and artists' daring cool.

*Roma or Romani people were once called Gypsies in English and are typically called Gitanos (hee-TAH-nos) in Spain.
*Moors are Muslims from North Africa who once conquered and ruled over most of Spain.

Don Quixote

Cervantes' **Don Quixote** fought

against the windmills here,

Picasso's Guernica expressed

war's terror, waste and tears.

Dalí

MIRÓ, abstract and whimsical,

DALI's dreams made real –

and Gaudí, architect of wonder,

made Spanish art surreal.

Gaudí's Casa Batlló

So whether **TAPAS**, talk or **ART**

appeal to you the most –

FIESTAS, sunshine or the *beaches*

on its endless coast –

White Architecture
of Andalucía

WHITE VILLAGES, MEDIEVAL TOWNS

or castles from long ago,

FLAMENCO dance or RUNNING BULLS,

España's where to go!

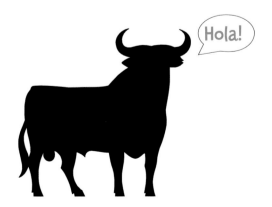

Hola!

← The red and yellow stripes of the **Spanish flag,** or Rojigualda, were first designed as a naval flag under King Charles III in 1785. The current design was approved in 1981 by a new Spanish constitution that established the country as a constitutional monarchy (an elected democratic government with a king or queen as ceremonial head of state). The former king of Spain, Juan Carlos, who ruled from 1975 to 2014, helped the country become a democracy after the reign of dictator Francisco Franco. Franco ruled Spain from 1939 until his death in 1975 and designated Juan Carlos as his heir. The king, however, was committed to handing over power to a democratic government. For that reason, the monarchy is seen today as a preserver of democracy in Spain.

Spain's local name is **ESPAÑA** [ays-PAH-nyah], which comes from its Roman name, "Hispania." The Romans may have gotten "Hispania" from a Phoenician term, "Ispanihad," meaning "land of rabbits."

Map of Spain's Autonomous Communities

(Off the coast of southern Morocco)

Official Name: Kingdom of Spain

Local Name: España,

Population: 47.7 million

Capital: Madrid

Largest Cities: Madrid, Barcelona, Valencia, Seville

Comparative Size: Slightly more than twice the size of Oregon, a bit larger than Sweden

Language: Spanish (Castilian) 74%, Catalan 17%, Galician 7%, Basque 2%

Religion: Christian 79% (Roman Catholic), Muslims 2%, none 19%

Currency: Euro

GEOGRAPHICAL NOTES

◉ Spain is made up of 17 **Autonomous Communities** (ACs). Many ACs were once independent historical kingdoms, and six have a second official language in addition to Castilian Spanish.

◉ Government in Spain is very decentralized. Similar to states in the United States, each AC enjoys a great deal of independence and governs its own health, education, courts and social services.

◉ Spain and Portugal make up the **Iberian Peninsula.**

Where in the World is Spain?

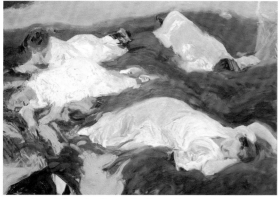

← The famous Spanish **siesta** is typically from 2:00 PM to 5:00 PM when businesses close and people go home to eat a large meal with their families and possibly take a nap. Work begins again at 5:00 PM and goes until 8:00 PM. Some kids go to school from 9:00 AM–2:00 PM, then go home for the day. Others are at school 9:00—12:30 and then come back 3:30–5:30. Many Spaniards eat a light supper around 9:00 PM. In big cities, some businesses do not follow the siesta schedule, but it is still in place for much of the Spanish population. →

Detail from La Siesta *by Spanish artist Joaquin Sorolla (1863–1923), made in 1911*

↑ *Tomatina Festival in Buñol, a city in Valencia*

↑ *Carnival in Verín, a city in Galicia*

↑ *Making a traditional* castell, *or human tower, in Barcelona, a city in Catalonia*

↑ *Women in flamenco dress at April Fair in Seville, a city in Andalucía*

← ↑ Spaniards claim to have more festivals, or *fiestas*, than days of the year. Most cities and regions have local festivals that honor their patron saint or their founder. Fiestas typically involve parades and parties in the street that are attended by all ages. Spaniards of all ages are also known for staying out late, sometimes all night, having fun and visiting with friends. In general, they sleep about an hour less than other Europeans and bedtime for children is later, usually between 9 and 11 PM. ↓ →

↑ *Fallas Festival in Valencia*

← *Running of the Bulls at the Festival of San Fermín (Saint Fermin) in Pamplona, a city in Navarre*

↑ *The "Semana Grande" Festival in Bilbao, a city in Basque Country*

Olive oil is one of Spain's → largest exports and an essential part of the Spanish diet. It is considered a key to good health and appears in the middle of the **Spanish food pyramid**, on the same level as fruits and vegetables. ↓

Olive oil

Ham or **jamón** → *(hah-MOHN)* has been a specialty of Spain since Roman times. It is dry-cured and aged for many months, but then may hang in a pantry indefinitely and not go bad. Super thin slices are eaten with bread.

Jamón

Spanish Food Pyramid

Paella

← **Paella** is a popular rice dish from Valencia made with saffron (which turns it yellow), olive oil, meat or seafood and vegetables.

Gazpacho

↑ Soups, or *sopas (SOH-pahs),* are a popular first course to daily dinner. **Gazpacho** is a cold soup made from tomatoes and cucumbers. One consistent feature of Spanish (and Mediterranean) food is a lack of hot peppers. Spanish food is typically seasoned with herbs and garlic. Mexican food is difficult to find in Spain and has little in common with Spanish cuisine.

A Spanish **tortilla de patatas** is a sort of potato omelette eaten as a main course or snack. It has nothing in common with the Mexican tortillas used in making tacos. Tortilla means "little cake" in Spanish. ↓

Tortilla

Tapas

↑ **Tapas** are snack foods like queso (cheese), bread, olives and ham that are typically served in the evening with drinks.

Pyrenees

↑ The **Pyrenees Mountains** separate Spain and France.

Vino

← Wine or **vino** is considered a healthy drink in Spain, and an essential part of many meals. *Do Spanish children drink wine?* Many may have a small glass with dinner, but it is mixed with sparkling water and has very little alcohol. There is also a popular drink in Spain called a calimocha, in which wine is mixed with cola.

Castilian Spanish, or → **Castellano** [cah-stay-YAH-no] is the main language of Spain. Spaniards prefer to call it Castilian (Castellano), rather than Spanish (Español), as there are many languages in Spain. Several regions have a second official language. Basque is spoken in Basque Country. Catalan is spoken in Catalonia and is similar to Valencian, which is spoken in Valencia. Galician is the second language in Galicia. Some other regions also have local languages that are not official.

Galician

Basque

Catalan/Valencian

Castilian Spanish

- Astur-Leonese
- Aragonese
- Aranese
- Extremaduran
- Fala

Languages of Spain

Bullfighting developed as a sport in Spain and Portugal in part because the Iberian bull was known as being particularly fierce, preferring to fight and die rather than run away. Over hundreds of years, many cultures added to the ceremony of modern bullfighting, including the Moors, who introduced *picadors* who fight the bull on horseback. (Moors were Muslims originally from North Africa who invaded and ruled over large parts of Spain from 711 to 1492.) Today, the final deathblow comes from *matadors* who fight the bulls on foot, with swords and a cape used to distract the bull. Matadors can be injured and even die from being gored by the bull. Bullfighting is considered an art in Spain, though some Spaniards feel that it is cruel to the bull. ↓

Flamenco

Bagpipers in Galicia

Bullfighting

↑ **Galicia** in northwest Spain is wet and green, and many people living there have ancient Celtic ancestry. The bagpipe is played and people speak Galician or *Gallego*, which has some Celtic words but is very similar to Portuguese.

← **Flamenco** is a type of music and dance that uses singing, Spanish guitars and clapped or stomped rhythm to create a dramatic outpouring of emotion. Flamenco fuses styles from Andalucía and Roma culture. **Roma**, who were once known as Gypsies and in Spain are known as *gitanos* (hee TAH nos), make up 2% of the Spanish population. Spain has the largest community of Roma in Western Europe.

Both men and women perform flamenco. Some moves are similar to a matador's flourishes when bullfighting.

Flamenco Shoes, Fan & Castanets

Saint James is called *Santiago* in Spain, an → abbreviation of Santo Iago. Saint James was one of Jesus's apostles who is believed to have traveled to Iberia (Spain and Potugal) to spread Christianity. After his death in the Holy Land, Spaniards believe his body was returned to Spain and rests now in the Cathedral in Santiago de Compostela, where pilgrims still flock from around the world. Santiago is the patron saint of Spain. ↓

Santiago

Santiago de Compostela Cathedral

In 711, the **Moors** (Muslims from North Africa) invaded Spain; and by 718, they had succeeded in gaining control of almost the entire peninsula. Moors called their kingdom Al Andalus. Jews and Christians were permitted to stay in Spain, but paid a special tax. Small Christian kingdoms in the northwest mountains survived the invasion and fought over the next eight centuries to retake the peninsula in a process known as the *reconquista*. Andalucía in the south was the last to pass into Christian hands and retains the most Moorish influence in its culture. This former mosque in Córdoba was transformed into a cathedral. ↑

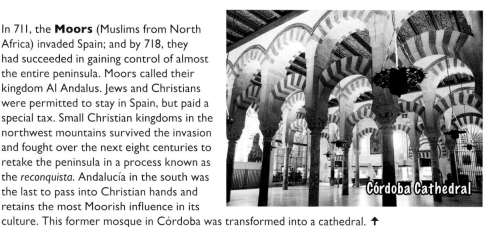
Córdoba Cathedral

King Ferdinand

Queen Isabella

← **King Ferdinand II of Aragon** and **Queen Isabella of Castile** → created Spain as the nation we know today. They unified Castile and Aragon through their marriage and took Granada from the Moors. They annexed Navarre in 1512, making the modern map of Spain. They created a national culture by declaring Spain a Catholic country, pushing out the Muslim Moors, expelling their Jewish population and starting the Spanish Inquisition to enforce religious conformity. They made Spain into an empire by supporting Christopher Columbus's voyage in which he encountered the Americas and claimed them for the Spanish crown. They are known as "Los Reyes Católicas" or "The Catholic Monarchs" in Spain.

1492

1492 is the most important year in Spanish history and one of the most decisive turning points in world history. 1492 made three major changes that created Spain as we know it. First, Ferdinand and Isabella pushed the last of the Muslim Moors out of Spain (and Western Europe) by defeating them at Granada. The Moors had originally taken over almost the entire Iberian peninsula (Spain and Portugal) in 711. It took close to eight centuries for the Christian kingdoms of the northwest to reconquer the peninsula in a process know as the *Reconquista (ray-con-KEE-stah)*. Second, Ferdinand and Isabella declared Spain to be a Catholic country. They expelled the Jews and used the Spanish Inquisition to enforce religions conformity. People were forced to convert to Christianity, leave the country or be tortured and possibly killed. Though such religious intolerance seems purely barbaric today, religion was the tool they used to unify a kingdom of many different languages and cultures. Lastly, they supported Christopher Columbus on the journey in which he encountered the Americas, claiming them for Spain and beginning the **Spanish Empire** in America. →

Spain Before 1492

Football (soccer) is incredibly popular in Spain and many cities have their own professional teams. There is a fierce rivalry between the two most famous teams, Real Madrid and Barcelona. The Spanish National Team won the 2010 FIFA World Cup, ranking it as the best team in the world. ↓

Barcelona Football Player

Viceroyalty of New Spain

Viceroyalty of New Grenada

Viceroyalty of Perú

Viceroyalty of Rio de la Plata

SPANISH EMPIRE IN THE AMERICAS IN 1800

The Osborne **bull** was created ↑ as an advertisement for the Osborne Sherry Company. In 1956, the company began placing the bulls off major roads in the Spanish countryside. Their large black outlines became part of the landscape and eventually symbols of Spain itself. Today in Spain, roadside advertising is illegal, but the bulls remain due to their popularity.

Don Quixote →
by Miguel Cervantes was the world's first modern novel. Originally published in two parts in 1605 and 1615, it is a comedy about an aging gentleman who becomes so obsessed with reading books about heroic knights that he goes crazy. Determined to be a knight, he sets off on his own quest to perform chivalrous deeds and rescue fair ladies from dragons. One of the most famous scenes is of Don Quixote fighting windmills that he mistakenly believes to be monsters.

Don Quixote

Guernica is a painting by Spanish artist Pablo Picasso commemorating the 1937 aerial bombing of the town of Guernica, Spain, during the Spanish Civil War. The attack was made by German and Italian planes at the request of Spanish Nationalist forces. The bombing of cities and unarmed civilians became a common tactic in World War II but was still new at Guernica. The painting is a testament to the horrors of war and the intense expressive capabilities of Picasso's *Cubist* style. ↓

↑ *Tiled mural that recreates Picassso's* Guernica *in Guernica, Spain*

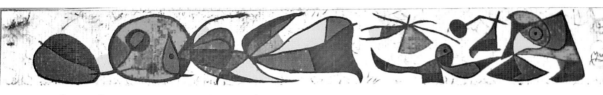

← *Miró mural on the front facade of Madrid's Convention Center.*

Joan Miró was a Spanish artist whose whimsical ↑ style experimented with both surrealism and abstraction. Surrealism attempts to visually represent dreams, thoughts and the ideas of the subconscious mind. Abstraction is painting forms and colors for their intrinsic beauty, not trying to use art to necessarily represent something else. Miró's style has been described as conveying childlike wonder.

Salvador Dalí →
is famous for his surrealist paintings of melting clocks and elephants on stilts. He attempted to capture the irrational visions of our subconscious minds and to express that our dreams are as important a view of the world as what we see with our eyes.

Dalí

Gaudí's Casa Batlló

← **Antoni Gaudí** is a famous Spanish architect with a completely unique style. He preferred the strength and beauty of curves and natural forms and used few straight lines or right angles. He wanted his structures to "stand like trees," with little internal or external support. He also loved the practical ornateness of nature – his creations could be as colorful and functional as the wings of a butterfly or the spirals of a seashell. This apartment building by Gaudí, *Casa Batlló*, has a roof that was designed to resemble a dragon's back.

Ávila's Medieval Walls

Spain could be described as the Florida of Western Europe. Many northern Europeans come to Spanish **beaches** on vacation to enjoy the sunny climate. →

← There are several **medieval towns** that remain largely intact in Spain, including Ávila.

Beach in Catalonia

Listen to the SOUNDS of SPAIN

Spanish Guitar A Spanish guitar, also known as a classical guitar, has six nylon strings and is typically played by plucking rather than strumming. Andres Segovia and Pepe Romero are two of the most famous Spanish masters of classical guitar. Listen to them playing "Asturias" (also called "Leyenda") by Isaac Albeniz or "Recuerdos de la Alhambra" ("Memories of the Alhambra") by Francisco Tárrega. **YOUTUBE SEARCH:** Segovia Asturias, Romero Recuerdos Alhambra

Flamenco Flamenco is a style of Spanish music and dance that has roots in the Roma culture of Andalucía. Its singing and dancing are usually accompanied by Spanish guitar and its rhythm is syncopated by stomping, clapping and the use of castanets.
YOUTUBE SEARCH: flamenco, flamenco Ramon Ruiz

Manuel de Falla's "Spanish Dance."
De Falla's playful, dramatic music seems to tell a story just in its notes. You might also enjoy his "Ritual Fire Dance" or music from the "Three Cornered Hat." Manuel de Falla (1876–1946) was one of Spain's great modern composers.
YOUTUBE SEARCH: De Falla Spanish Dance

READ:

And Picasso Painted Guernica by Alain Serres. A tribute to the power of art as protest, this book also covers Picasso's background and the history behind his art. It enables readers to see the artist's process of creating and to understand the symbols within this masterpiece. Ages 9 & up.

Don Quixote and the Windmills by Eric Kimmel. There are numerous condensed versions of Don Quixote, even a graphic novel of his adventures. This picture book tells Don Quixote's most famous adventure and is a great introduction to the main characters. You might also enjoy reading the first few chapters of the original Don Quixote, which introduce you to the hero and Cervantes' droll sense of humor. Ages 5 & up.

Salvador Dalí and the Surrealists: Their Lives and Ideas, 21 Activities by Michael Ross. A guide for young artists to explore the ideas of surrealism and make their own surrealist art. Ages 10 & up.

Building on Nature: The Life of Antoni Gaudi by Rachel Rodriguez. A wonderful introduction into the life of Antoni Gaudi and his unique architecture. Ages 5 & up.

SPEAK Like a Spaniard

¿Habla español?

The language we call Spanish is called "Castilian" or *Castellano* in Spain (cah-stay-YAH-no). Castellano has one main pronunciation difference from the Spanish spoken in the Americas that is sometimes called "**the Spanish lisp.**" The Spanish lisp is when the letter **Z**, and sometimes **C**, are pronounced as **TH**.

The letter **Z** in Spain is always pronounced like our **TH**. For instance *zapato,* or shoe, is pronounced *tha-PAH-toh.* **C** is also pronounced as a **TH** when it is before **I** or **E**. (In American Spanish, C before I or E is pronounced as an S, and Z is always pronounced like S.) So in Spain, *cinco,* or five, is pronounced *THEEN-koh,* but in the Americas it is *SEEN-koh.* If you think you've got it, try these Spanish words with and without a "Spanish lisp."

Gracias-thank you
GRAH-thee-ahs

Corazón-heart
co-rah-THOHN

Feliz-happy
fay-LEETH

Cena-supper
THAY-nah

Hace mucho sol.-It's very sunny.
HAH-thay MU-choh sol.

Cebra-zebra
THAY-brah

DON'T MISS WATCHING (online)

Flamenco Flamenco is almost always performed with dancing. See if you can mimic some of the stomping and clapping performed by men and women.
YOUTUBE SEARCH: flamenco, Daniel Navarro

Running of the Bulls Pamplona's annual festival is (usually) a non-gory celebration of the Spanish love of bulls.
YOUTUBE SEARCH: Pamplona running bulls

Tour the Alhambra & Cordoba's Mezquita Tour the greatest architectural jewels of Spain's Moorish rulers with Rick Steves. He gives the historical background behind two of world's most beautiful buildings and their mix of Muslim and Christian styles.
YOUTUBE SEARCH: Steves Alhambra, Steves Mezquita

God's Architect: Antoni Gaudi CBS's *60 Minutes* has a fascinating piece on Gaudi's masterpiece, the Basilica of the Sagrada Familia (Holy Family) in Barcelona, which is still being completed today after 130 years. **INTERNET SEARCH:** God's Architect Gaudi 60 Minutes

MAKE SPANISH
Gazpacho

Gazpacho is a cold soup that originated back in Roman times as a use for stale bread. Mixed with olive oil, garlic, salt, vinegar and water, yesterday's bread became a delicious summertime soup that helped to keep people hydrated in the heat. With the arrival of tomatoes and peppers from the Americas, the recipe changed to today's refreshing "liquid salad." With a blender, this recipe is incredibly easy and quick. Gazpacho is served cold, so it will need an hour to chill in the refrigerator to taste its best. Refrigerating the cucumbers and peppers in advance can speed cooling.

1. Grate your bread into fine crumbs, or crumble it with your fingers. (If you don't have stale bread, toast bread on low heat until it dries out.)

2. Quarter tomatoes and pepper, and chop peeled cucumber into large pieces. Put all ingredients in a blender. Add a sprinkling of salt.

3. Blend, then salt to taste.

4. For the most refreshing flavor, chill in the refrigerator for one hour.

5. Serve in a bowl, or as a beverage you can drink.

1 piece stale bread, ideally white bread, french bread or dinner rolls

1 ½ lbs very ripe tomatoes (two very large tomatoes or several smaller ones)

1 cucumber, peeled

1 bell pepper, green or red

2 cloves of garlic, crushed

2 tablespoons vinegar, red wine ideally

⅓ cup olive oil

salt (to taste)

Optional Modification: Omit the bread; it's still creamy and delicious without any.

MAKE (Nonalcoholic) SANGRIA

The word "sangria" comes from the Spanish word for blood, which refers to the drink's dark red color. Traditionally, sangria is a red wine punch made at home with lots of fruit. Other additions may include lime soda, ice, sugar and sometimes hard alcohol. Nonalcoholic sangria mimics wine sangria's color and flavor by using cranberry juice cocktail. There is no one traditional sangria recipe. Spanish families alter the drink according to taste and what's available, including almost any fruit: oranges, apples, peaches, pears, watermelon, kiwis, pineapple, berries, etc.

1. Wash all fruit well, including peel.

2. Cut up fruit and put in pitcher, punch bowl or soup pot.

3. Add frozen lemonade on top, then pour in juice and stir well.

4. Put in the refrigerator and allow to soak at least 30 minutes, ideally for a few hours.

5. Add soda, taste, add sugar if needed, stir well.

6. Using a ladle, or assisted by a wooden spoon, pour sangria into glasses, putting a spoonful of fruit in each glass.

fruit

1 orange, sliced into circles & quartered

1 apple, diced

1 peach, diced

1 lime, sliced into circles

or 3–4 cups of any type of fruit

liquids

1 small frozen lemonade concentrate

4 cups cranberry juice cocktail

3 cups club soda or seltzer water

sugar to taste

MAKE A SPANISH
Tortilla de Patatas

A tortilla de patatas is a sort of potato omelette that can be eaten at lunch or dinner and is a very popular snack or tapa. Making tortillas is a bit like making pancakes – they will always be delicious, but your first one might not look perfect. Don't worry; once you've made a few, it's easy. Just be very careful cooking with hot oil.

- **1 medium baking potato**
- **½ yellow onion,** medium
- **¾ cup virgin olive oil**
- **4 eggs**
- **salt** (to taste)

1. SLICE POTATO AND ONION: Put on some exciting flamenco music and an apron. Peel baking potato and quarter it lengthwise. Then slice it into ⅛ inch segments. If your slices are thicker, it will take a little longer to cook. Quarter onion, and cut into thin slices. Salt both onion and potatoes liberally, as you would french fries.

2. FRYING THE POTATOES: In a small, nonstick frying pan, pour oil and heat to medium heat. (Don't make it too hot, olive oil burns easily.) Gently place potato slices in the oil and place onions on top of potatoes. It should gently bubble. Fry for 15 minutes, stirring occasionally to make sure potatoes on the bottom don't burn.

3. DRAIN OIL: Place a nonplastic bowl in your kitchen sink; and put a metal sieve on top. With great care, pour potatoes, onion and oil into sieve. Allow to drip while you prepare the eggs. (If the oil doesn't burn, it can be used for making another tortilla. Once cooled, store it in a cool dark place and use within a month.)

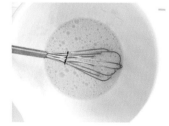 

4. MIX EGG & POTATO: Beat eggs until frothy. Add a small pinch of salt for each egg. Mix potatoes and onions into eggs once they are fully drained.

5. POUR IN PAN: Clean the bottom of the small frying pan, but not the inside, leaving a little oil in the pan. Reheat it to medium heat and add a couple of spoonfuls of reserved olive oil. Pour egg and potato mixture in.

6. STIR AND COOK: For the first 1–2 minutes, gently stir your tortilla as you would scrambled eggs, pulling the cooked egg from the bottom. Stop while it is still mainly liquid. Then spread it out flat and leave it alone to cook for a few more minutes, until it is lightly browning on the bottom. Use a spatula to gently loosen the sides.

7. FLIP & BROWN THE BOTTOM: When it is more solid than liquid, and the sides have been loosened, it is time to flip. Place a large plate over the top of your frying pan. Take the frying pan to your sink, holding the plate on top with one hand. Over the sink, quickly flip the plate and frying pan upside down. The tortilla will fall onto the plate. Return to the stove top and slide the tortilla back in the frying pan, runny side down. Continue to cook for another 3–5 minutes until bottom also browns.

8. SERVE: Use a spatula to slide the tortilla onto a plate. Allow it to cool, then serve it either warm or at room temperature, slicing it as you would a pie.

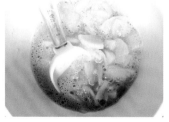

T is for Turkey

Our **T** is for **TURKEY,**

WHERE EAST AND WEST MEET,

A crossroads of cultures

where hist'ry runs deep –

Helen of Troy

Constantine I
Byzantine Emperor
(306–337 CE)

Way back to the HITTITES

and *Helen of Troy,*

Then to **Constantine,** *Suleiman –*

empires galore!

Here, in between

four sparkling sea coasts,

Is where **DERVISHES** whirl

and swirling meat roasts.

Suleiman I
Ottoman Sultan
(1520–1566)

Whirling Dervish

Here the **Byzantine** and *Ottoman*

Empires once reigned,

And their sultans and emperors

liked to rename.

The city, **Byzantium,**

two continents' jewel,

Became **Constantinople**

and then Istanbul.

Istanbul : A City
on Two Continents

The **Hagia Sophia,** (ah-YEE-ah soh-FEE-yah)

once the biggest of churches,

Changed into a mosque,

then a museum for searches –

Hagia Sophia

Turkish Tile

Kilim Rug

By tourists who wander

from sights to bazaars

Buying carpets and **kilims,**

blue tiles and **NAZARS,** [hah-ZARS]

Nazar

Then to a **HAMAM** (hah-MAHM)

where they bathe away cares,

Next out to eat *meze,* (MEH-zeh, *appetizers*)

which everyone shares.

Hamam

For dinner, **kebabs**

served with yogurt as well

and then sweet **baklava,**

oh it's all **çok güzel!**[*] (CHOKE goo-ZELL)

Baklava

Oh the food of the Turks

is such a *delight!*

And the natives are sure

to greet and invite –

Adana Kebab

Chai

You to *tulip-shaped glasses*

of sweet amber **chai,**

Or to **coffee** so thick

it will open your eyes,

Turkish Coffee

[*]**"Çok güzel"** means "so good." Güzel can mean good, delicious, or beautiful.

Minaret

And your ears, which will hear

from tall mosque **MINARETS**

An **EZAN** (call to prayer) (eh-ZAHN)

lest the faithful forget –

To *pray five times a day.*

Turks are Muslim but proud

Of their **SECULAR STATE**,

where all faiths are allowed.

Seal of Turkey's Parliament
(Grand National Assembly)

Here religion can't govern,

their republic is ruled

By a **PARLIAMENT** chosen

by voters and schooled

Fez Hat Banned in
1925 by Atatürk

In respect for reforms

that created their nation –

From headwear to letters,

vast **Westernization.**

This country remains

so *magically mixed,*

Between continents, cultures

so *perfectly fixed*

Atatürk Teaching the New
Alphabet ca. 1929

As a land that is **neither**

European or Asian –

But why should Turks wish

to be either persuasion?

For so true are the words

of KEMAL ATATÜRK,

"BLESSED IS THE MAN

WHO CAN CALL HIMSELF TURK!"

Atatürk
Turkey's Founding Father

Merhaba!*

Folktale Hero Nasreddin Hoca [hoh-JAH]

*"**Merhaba**" [MAIR-ha-bah] means "Hello!"

Turkey's local name, **TÜRKIYE** means "land of the Turks."

← Turkey was the heart of the Ottoman Empire and the **Turkish flag** is a modified version of the Ottoman flag. As the Ottoman sultan was the head of the Islamic Caliphate (the leader of Sunni Islam) from 1517 until its dissolution in 1923, the symbol of the Ottoman Empire (the crescent moon and star) came to be viewed as a symbol of Islam, though it has no religious meaning. Many Muslim countries now use the crescent and star on their flags. →

Algeria Mauritania

Tunisia Pakistan

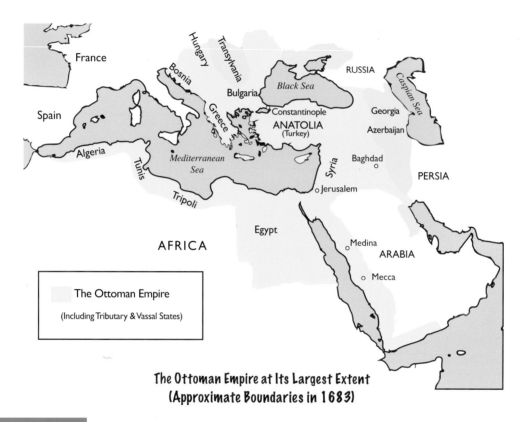

The Ottoman Empire at Its Largest Extent (Approximate Boundaries in 1683)

Official Name: Republic of Turkey

Local Name: Türkiye

Population: 81.6 million

Capital: Ankara

Largest Cities: Istanbul, Ankara, Izmir

Comparative Size: Slightly larger than Texas, slightly smaller than Pakistan

Ethnicity: Turkish 70–75%, Kurdish 18%, other minorities 7–12%

Language: Turkish, Kurdish

Religion: Muslim 98% (mostly Sunni)

Currency: Turkish lira

Important Industry: Clothing manufacturing

Where in the World is Turkey?

GEOGRAPHICAL NOTES

◉ The **Ottoman** (or Turkish) **Empire** ruled from 1300 until 1922 when the last sultan, Mehmed VI, was exiled. Constantinople (today Istanbul) became the capital of the empire when it was captured in 1453. Ottoman Turks held large parts of the Middle East, Eastern Europe and North Africa up until World War I.

◉ The northwest corner of Turkey, west of Istanbul, is part of Europe. The rest of Turkey is part of Asia and is called **Anatolia** or **Asia Minor**.

◉ Turkey's fertile land and its location between Europe, the Middle East and Asia made it an ideal place for trade and empire building for millennia.

Hittite Chariot

← The **Hittites** were an ancient civilization centered in Anatolia, which was at its height 1600–1200 BCE. The Hittites were excellent charioteers and some of the first people to smelt iron. Their empire grew in power and rivaled the Egyptian, Assyrian and Babylonian Empires.

Helen of Troy

← The ancient city-state of **Troy** was located on the western coast of Anatolia. The Trojan War (between Greeks and Trojans in the 12th century BCE) was a main theme in Greek literature and Homer's *Iliad* is an account of the war. The war started when **Helen**, the world's most beautiful woman and wife of a Greek king, was abducted by a Trojan named Paris. The war ended when the Greeks tricked the Trojans into accepting a giant wooden horse as a gift. Inside the horse were Greek soldiers who opened the gates of Troy, causing the city to be destroyed. ↓

Trojan Horse

Constantine

Suleiman I

← **Suleiman I** (the Magnificent) ruled 1520–1566 and was the sultan who expanded the **Ottoman Empire** the most, making it one of the world's great powers and supporting a golden age of arts and culture. ("Suleiman" is the Muslim version of the biblical name Solomon.)

Suleiman was known as "the Lawgiver" to his subjects. By studying Islamic law and the legal decisions of previous Ottoman sultans, he created a written legal code for his whole empire. His treatment of the Christians and Jews of his empire was so fair that groups of both moved there to escape persecution in other lands. Suleiman is one of 23 great lawmakers in world history whose images appear in the US House of Representatives. →

SULEIMAN

↑ Roman Emperor Constantine created the **Byzantine Empire** in 330 CE, when he moved his capital to Byzantium, which became known as Constantinople.

Constantine's Empire

337 AD

Constantine was the first emperor to convert to Christianity and as the empire became Christian, he became a saint in Byzantine churches. The Byzantine Empire ended when Ottoman Turks conquered Constantinople in 1453.

Doner Kebab

←There are many types of Turkish **kebab**, called *kebap* in Turkey. Kebab simply means roasted meat. Shish kebab is small pieces of meat on skewers (shish means skewer). Doner kebab has meat stacked on a vertical spit that is continually turned. (Doner means turning.) Shavings from doner kebab can be made into sandwiches or other famous Turkish dishes like *Iskender kebab*.

Istanbul

↑ **Istanbul** is the world's only major city that sits on two continents. Separated by the Bosphorus Strait, the western half is part of Europe and the eastern half is in Asia. Originally the city was called Byzantium until Constantine made it his capital and it became Constantinople. Even before the Turks, locals began referring to it as "Stambul," coming from Greek words meaning "in the city." The name stuck but did not become official until 1930. →

Istanbul

Europe   Asia

Whirling Dervishes

↑ **Whirling dervishes** perform a type of Sufi Muslim meditation. As they twirl, dervishes enter a trance of religious ecstasy, letting go of the self to be one with God. *Could you spin for several minutes?* The turning is gentle, dervishes don't focus their eyes and they keep their spines straight. When they stop, they focus on a spot on the ground until they are not dizzy.

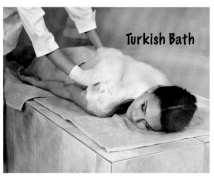

Hagia Sophia

↑ The **Hagia Sophia** was the largest church in the world for over a millennium. Dedicated in 360 CE, it is considered the greatest example of Byzantine architecture. It was turned into a mosque by the Ottoman Turks, and after the founding of the Turkish Republic in 1923, it became a museum. The Hagia Sophia is a popular tourist attraction, both for its architecture and the fact that it clearly shows Istanbul's many layers of history. The Hagia Sophia is spelled **Ayasofya** in Turkish; both mean "Holy Wisdom." →

The Sultan Ahmet Mosque, also → known as the **Blue Mosque**, was built next door to the Hagia Sophia. Though the Hagia Sophia had become a mosque under Ottoman rule, the Turks wanted to build something equally impressive. The Blue Mosque was completed in 1616 and its many domes are filled with gorgeous tilework. It got its name from the blue color in the tile design. →

Blue Mosque

Tile Ceiling of the Blue Mosque

↑ Turkey is famous for its beautiful **tile work**. Influenced by Persian and Chinese ceramics, the Ottoman Empire began making intricately painted tiles for walls, ceilings and floors of mosques and palaces. ↓

Inside the Hagia Sophia

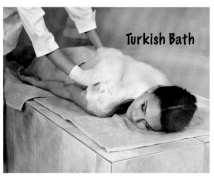

Turkish Bath

↑ **Turkish baths** leave bathers incredibly clean and relaxed. Separated into men's baths and women's baths, bathers pay an entrance fee, then strip down and wrap themselves in a cotton wrap. Bathers first lie on a very warm marble block in a steamy room. Their bodies sweat out impurities until their muscles seem to melt into the stone. Then a bath attendant comes and thoroughly massages and washes the bathers, stretching the muscles, removing large amounts of dead skin (loosened by the steaming), then washing the hair. After, bathers can stay at the bath and continue steaming and then cooling themselves with cool water from taps around the room. They can then relax in a "cool" room with tea until their body readjusts to regular temperatures. Baths are a social as well as a cleansing experience, a wonderful way to relax with friends.

Nazar

← **Nazars** are amulets used to protect people from the "evil eye." A traditional belief in Greece, Turkey and the region is that if someone is jealous of you, they can give you the "evil eye" and thus bring you bad luck. Hanging a nazar in your home or wearing one can protect you from this misfortune.

Turkish Tile

This tile features tulips, a flower that originated in Turkey.

← **Kilim** is a flat weave Turkish carpet. Kilim weaving dates back as far as 7000 BCE in Anatolia. Turks have also been famous for their knotted carpets since 1100 CE.

Flaky, sweet **baklava** originated in the kitchens of Ottoman sultans. Baklava is made of thin layers of pastry and nuts drenched in syrup or honey. ↓

Adana Kebab

← **Adana kebab** is made from minced meat. Like most kebabs, it can be served with a yummy yogurt sauce.

Baklava

Chai

Turkish coffee is so thick that a sludge of coffee grounds remain in the cup when you finish. The coffee is ground to a fine powder, then boiled twice to produce a foamy top. When you finish a cup, your fortune can be read in the shapes of the remaining grounds. This cup is served with Turkish delight or *lokum*, a sort of gummy candy. ➜

Turkish Coffee & Turkish Delight

↑ Turks drink **tea** or *çay* [chai] all day long. In the morning, in the afternoon, before a meal, after a meal, it is always tea time. Tea is an essential part of Turkish hospitality, both in homes and businesses. Tea is typically taken with sugar (but never milk) and served in tulip shaped glasses. To not burn their fingers, tea drinkers hold the glass at the rim, which never gets hot.

Ayran

↑ If you prefer something cool to drink, you might like **ayran**, (EYE-ran) a refreshing salty yogurt drink.

Minaret

← What makes a mosque a mosque?
One standard element of mosque architecture around the world is minarets. **Minarets** are towers that send out the call to prayer. One of the main requirements of Islam is that practitioners pray five times a day and the call to prayer, or *ezan,* helps Muslims to remember. The call to prayer is sung by a *muezzin* who used to walk up to the top of the minaret five times a day to make the call. Now, with recordings and sound systems, that is not the case. Some mosques still have muezzins who make live calls to prayer, but others use recordings. The call to prayer is sung in Arabic and starts "Allahu Akbar" or "God is the greatest." ⬇

Minaret with Speakers

What does **Turkey** *have to do with* **turkey?**
Turkey's local name is Turkiye, meaning "land of the Turks." The American bird, the turkey, got its name in a roundabout way from the Turks. When British colonists first saw the bird in America, they thought it was similar to a type of guinea fowl called a "Turkey fowl" in England, as it was imported to Europe by way of Turkey. (The birds were originally from Africa, but they were sold to Europeans by Turkish merchants.) Incidentally, the Turks also named turkeys after another country. They call turkeys **hindi,** which comes from their name for India, *Hindistan.* They associate turkeys with peacocks that come from India.

Turkey

Ataturk, meaning "father of the Turks," is the honorific last name given to Mustafa Kemal, the leader of Turkey from 1923 until his death in 1938. Ataturk was the Turkish Republic's first leader after the fall of the Ottoman Empire, and he instituted widespread reforms to modernize Turkish society. He felt that Ottoman rule had been holding Turkey back from progressing along with its neighbors in Europe. Here are a few of his reforms:

1. Changing the **alphabet** in which Turkish was written from the Arabic alphabet to the Roman alphabet (the same used for English).

2. Declaring the government of the Turkish Republic to be **secular**; that religion had no place in schools, government or law-making.

3. Banning the **fez**, and creating a law that women could not wear their headscarves in schools or public buildings.

4. Requiring people to select their own "last names" or **surnames**. Previously, people would state their father's and grandfather's name and their hometown as identifiers. Still today, adults may be called by their first names with the honorific *-bey* (for men) or *-hanim* (for women). For instance, Osmanbey is a respectful term for Mr. Osman Gül.

5. Making **women** equal before the law, including giving them the right to vote in 1934, before many European countries.

Ataturk before and after the fez was banned.

Ataturk teaching the new alphabet

All Turkish men used to ➔ wear **fezes** and they became a symbol of the Ottoman Empire among Europeans. Ataturk wished to reject Ottoman traditions and so he banned the fez. He wished to integrate Turkey with European society because he felt that Europe represented progress and modernity in the 20th century.

Fez

Turkish Alphabet

The Turkish alphabet is similar to our own, but it has some additional letters- can you find them?

A B C Ç D E F G Ğ H I İ J K L M
N O Ö P Q R S Ş T U Ü V Y Z

C - j as in joy, the name John is written Can
J - zh, like the s in pleasure
Ç - ch as in chair
Ş - sh as in shadow
Ğ - unpronounced, lengthens previous vowel
ı - uh as in but, written as an i with no dot.
İ - ee as in bee, written with a dot even uppercase
Ö - in between eh and uh
Ü - yu or u as in university

Some other vowel sounds:
ay - long i, as in high   **o** - oh, like "Oh no!"
ey - long a, as in "hey!"   **e** - eh, as in bed
oy - oy as in toy   **u** - oo, as in too
uy - we, French "oui!"   **a** - ah, as in father

All letters are the same as in English, but some sounds, like **W** and **Th**, do not occur in Turkish.
Could you spell your name in Turkish?

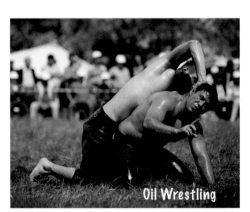

Oil Wrestling

← **Oil wrestling** is the national sport of Turkey. Wrestlers wear handmade leather pants called *kisbet* and cover themselves with olive oil to make it difficult to hold them. The match is won when a wrestler gets a good hold on an opponent's kisbet. Though football (soccer) is Turkey's most popular sport, wrestling is the most traditional.

Library at Ephesus

Cappadocia is an ancient city in central Turkey with a unique landscape. Its odd, moon-like surface is covered with endless fields of "fairy chimneys," whimsically-shaped cones and towers made from the uneven erosion of soft volcanic rock. People have made homes here inside rock towers, caves and underground tunnels since prehistoric times. ➔

Cappadocia

↑ **Ephesus** was a large, thriving city of the ancient world. A Greek city that became a Roman city, Ephesus is located on the Aegean Sea near modern-day Izmir. It was home to the Temple of Artemis, one of the Seven Wonders of the Ancient World. Saint Paul preached in Ephesus and his letter to the Ephesians is in the Bible. As one of the largest and best-preserved Roman sites, Ephesus is a tourist attraction for people who want to imagine life in an ancient city.

Listen to the SOUNDS of TURKEY

Kanun & Kemençe (traditional instruments)
Listen to the gorgeous sounds produced by two of Turkey's traditional instruments.
YOUTUBE SEARCH: kanun, kemence

Tarkan Turkey's biggest pop star. Listen to "Simarik," his first international hit, as well as "Kuzu Kuzu," "Dudu" and "Firuze."

Classical Turkish Music
Recommendations: **Sarband**'s "Nikriz Pesrev"
Muzeyyen Senar's "Benzeme Kimse Sana"
Munir Nurretin Selcuk's "Omrun Seni Sevmekle"

Turkish Pop
Song Recommendations: **Yalin**'s "Aski Sonunda," **Demet Akalin**'s "Turkan," **Sezen Aksu**'s "Sanima Inanma," **Murat Dakilic**'s "Bir Hayli," **Hande Yener**'s "Ya, Ya, Ya, Ya"

Call to Prayer from the Blue Mosque
Hear an ezan as it echoes out over the Bosporus in Istanbul, a sound that hasn't changed for centuries.
YOUTUBE SEARCH: Blue Mosque call to prayer

"Istanbul, Not Constantinople"
Though not Turkish in origin, Turks like this song. Try the original recording made by "The Four Lads" in 1953.
YOUTUBE SEARCH: Istanbul Four Lads

Kemençe

READ:

Hoja

Stories about Nasreddin Hoca Folk hero Nasreddin Hoca (HO-jah) is a wise fool from Turkey about whom there are innumerable humorous stories told through much of the Islamic world. The following are a selection of Hoca books; look at your library.

The Hungry Coat: A Tale from Turkey by Demi. Ages 5 & up.

The Wise Fool by Sharukh Husain. Ages 5 & up.

Goha the Wise Fool by Denys Johnson-Davies. Ages 6 & up.

Rumi: Whirling Dervish by Demi. Meet this mystical Turkish poet from the 13th century and his timeless words. Ages 10 & up.

Mosque by David Macaulay. Meet an aristocrat from the Ottoman Empire as he plans to build a mosque and its adjoining school and bath. Ages 10 & up.

SPEAK Turkish!

Merhaba	Hello	MAIR-hah-bah
Çok	Very	choke (like I choked on a fishbone)
Güzel	Good, beautiful, delicious	goo-ZELL
Hoş Geldiniz!	Welcome!	HOHSH GELL-dih-niz
Nasılsınız?	How are you?	nah-suhl-SUH-nuhz
Iyiyim sağol.	Fine, thanks.	eem sahll
Teşekkür ederim.	Thank you.	teh-SHEH-kur eh-DAIR-im
Çok teşekkür ederim.	Thank you very much.	
Adın ne?	What's your name?	AH-duhn neh?
Adım...	My name is...	AH-duhm....
Memnum Oldum.	Pleased to meet you.	MEM-noon OL-duhm
Seni Seviyorum.	I love you.	SEN-ee seh--vee-YOR-um
Türkiye Seviyorum.	I love Turkey.	TUR-kih-yeh seh-vee-YOR-um

Ne Mutlu Türküm diyene. (said by Ataturk)
Happy is the one who says "I am a Turk"

DON'T MISS WATCHING (online)

Visit: kids.mfa.gov.tr/kids for fun, cartoon-hosted introductions to Turkish culture made for kids and teens.

Whirling Dervishes A form of prayer and meditation created by the poet and mystic Rumi, dervishes whirl around in order to let go of the self and experience God.
YOUTUBE SEARCH: Whirling Dervish

Tour Istanbul & Turkey BBBTV (Biggest Baddest Bucketlist TV) takes you around Istanbul in under five minutes. Their special is called "Harems, Haggling and Hamams," Discovery Channel has a longer introduction called "Flavors of Turkey." **YOUTUBE SEARCH:** Istanbul harems hamams, Discover Channel Flavors of Turkey

Ottoman Empire History Find out why the Ottoman Empire was one of the most tolerant places on earth in its time. Learn how they trained young Christian boys to become much of their army and bureaucracy.
YOUTUBE SEARCH: Ottoman Empire PBS

Ataturk Biography To understand Turkey, you have to understand its founder and father, Mustafa Kemal Ataturk.
YOUTUBE SEARCH: Ataturk Biography

MAKE TURKISH
Köfte

Köfte (KUH-fteh) or Turkish meatballs are traditionally made with lamb or a mix of lamb and beef. Köfte is usually served with flat bread, salad and savory yogurt sauce. The shepherd's salad or *çoban salatası* (CHO-bahn sah-lah-TAH-suh) recipe below is probably the most popular salad in Turkey.

1. If using breadcrumbs, pour milk over them and set aside to soak. (Bread crumbs, egg and milk make the meatballs softer and less dense. Some Turkish cooks use them, some don't; both ways taste good.)

2. Assemble all other ingredients except egg in a large bowl. (Use a cheese grater or food processor to turn the onion into a pulpy slush. If using a grater, watch your fingers and don't try to grate the whole onion.)

3. Add the breadcrumbs and egg, kneading and mixing it all together with your hands. Be very thorough mixing the meat until it is uniformly smooth. (Make sure to wash your hands well immediately before and after handling raw meat.)

4. Form long ovals of meat and then flatten them slightly so they are not too thick to cook through.

5. Cook köfte on medium heat in a frying pan or put them under the broiler, four minutes on either side.

6. Serve with shepherd's salad, yogurt sauce and toasted flatbread. It is so, so good!

½ cup breadcrumbs (optional)
1 tablespoon milk (optional)
1 lb ground lamb or beef
1 teaspoon salt
1 teaspoon cumin
½ teaspoon cayenne pepper
½ teaspoon black pepper
½ onion, grated into a slush
2 garlic cloves, crushed
1 handful of fresh parsley leaves, chopped
1 handful of fresh mint, chopped (optional)
1 egg (optional)

Yogurt Sauce

Yogurt sauce really makes köfte amazing – make sure you don't skip it! Mix all ingredients.

1 cup plain yogurt, full fat
1 clove of garlic, crushed
1–2 pinches of salt
Small handful of parsley, chopped
½ teaspoon lemon juice (optional)

Flatbread

Though Turkish flatbread isn't easy to find in the US, any flat bread (including pita bread) will work. Just toast it with a little olive oil.

1. Brush olive oil on flatbread and sprinkle with salt and optionally a little garlic powder and fresh parsley. Bake or toast until warm and slightly crisp.

Köfte, Flatbread, Shepherd's Salad and Yogurt Sauce

Shepherd Salad

(Çoban Salatası)
Mix all ingredients and season to taste.

2 large ripe tomatoes, chopped
1 cucumber, peeled and chopped
1 green bell pepper, cored, seeded and chopped
½ onion, chopped
1 handful parsley leaves, chopped
3 tablespoons olive oil
1 tablespoon vinegar (balsamic or red wine)
or lemon juice
black pepper (to taste)
salt (to taste)

MAKE A TURKISH EVIL EYE (NAZAR)

A *nazar* is a Turkish talisman that is hung in homes and businesses and worn as jewelry to protect against the evil eye. The "evil eye" is a superstition that people can bring down misfortune on someone by simply looking at them with deep dislike or jealousy. Typically made of glass, a nazar is believed to break when the blue can absorb no more evil and should then be replaced. This wax paper version won't break and is an excellent suncatcher.

1. Cut out circles of tissue paper in descending sizes of dark blue, white, light blue and black. Use everyday household objects to trace your circles onto the paper first. (This evil eye was made tracing around a DVD, a canned good, a spice jar and the inside ring of the DVD.)

2. Cut a round hole in the dark blue circle, making it donut shaped. Make the hole slightly smaller than the white circle, so that the blue donut overlaps the white circle slightly when placed on top of it. The other circles can stack on top of the white circle.

3. Stack circles in eye design between two pieces of wax paper, with paper towels stacked above and below to protect your iron from wax.

4. Iron over the paper towels on the lowest heat setting, until wax paper melts onto the tissue.

5. Cut off the extra wax paper, leaving a thin border.

6. Use a needle and thread to put a string through the evil eye so that it can hang on a window.

Alternative Methods: If you don't have blue shades of tissue paper, trace your circles on thin white paper and color in the nazar with markers or paint.

⬆ *The four circles of tissue paper cut out to go between wax paper.*

THE HISTORY OF TURKEY THROUGH MEN'S HATS

What's in a hat? Why does Turkey have a history of banning headwear?

⬆ *Suleiman I in his turban and Mahmud II in his fez* ⬇

First of all, it's important to understand that headwear was once considered an essential part of men's dress. People were as likely to go out barefoot as bareheaded (meaning they simply didn't). Back in early Ottoman times, Turkish men wore **turbans** that were wrapped and decorated in such a way as to signal their occupation, rank and religion. The more important you were, the larger and fancier your headdress (hence the enormous turban of Suleiman the Magnificent). People's tombstones might even have their turban carved on top to symbolize their place in society.

Sultan Mahmud II banned the turban in 1829. He adopted the **fez**, a hat named for Fez, Morocco, where it was originally made. Turks began to wear the fez, which was seen at the time as being a very modern and equalizing reform – all men wore the same hat. You couldn't judge them on their appearance alone. The fez was sleek and didn't have a brim, which was useful because Muslims are expected to lower their forehead to the ground during prayers. The fez became so ubiquitous in the Ottoman Empire that it came to represent Turks to the West.

When **Ataturk** began his modernization campaigns, he banned the fez. He felt that it separated Turkey from the West and stood for old Ottoman ways. Once it was illegal to wear fezes, Turkish men struggled to find other headwear and most ended up abandoning hats altogether except during winter.

⬆ *A fez and Ataturk hatless* ⬇

U is for United Kingdom

HIGHLANDS

SCOTLAND

★ EDINBURGH

◉ GLASGOW

NORTHERN IRELAND

☆ BELFAST

Irish Sea

IRELAND

North Sea

◉ MANCHESTER

◉ BIRMINGHAM

ENGLAND

WALES

☆ LONDON

CARDIFF

ATLANTIC OCEAN

English Channel

FRANCE

Our **U** is **UK,**

four nations united

In a kingdom where authors

and rock stars are **knighted.**

Medieval Knight's Armor

Ball Sports from
Britain:

Football
(Soccer)

Cricket

Rugby

Golf

Northern Ireland and Scotland,

England and Wales –

Four nations of *teatime*,

FOOTBALL and **Rails.**

They make one sovereign state

with a **QUEEN** at its helm,

Though it's **parliament's** power

that rules all the realm.

The Brits had an empire

that spanned round the globe,

Spreading faith, British law,

ball sports and **railroads.**

Though no longer an empire

or ruler of seas,

Britain's language remains

in the lands that they seized.

And how lucky for us!

We can travel with ease,

With a language that's second

to only Chinese!

London Underground Train
or "The Tube"

Palace of Westminster
The UK's Parliament Building

19th Century Steam Train

Sherlock Holmes

Robin Hood

And the British have given

the world many stories:

From **Shakespeare's** great plays

to **King Arthur's** glories.

ROBIN HOOD, **Harry Potter**

and *Winnie the Pooh,*

Sherlock Holmes, PETER PAN

and greedy old **Scrooge,**

Alice in Wonderland,

Paddington Bear,

WillyWonka and FRODO

all came from there!

Hallelujah Chorus from
Handel's Messiah

The Beatles

They all came from these isles

where the Beatles first sang,

Where *Handel's Messiah*

first joyously rang.

Where they eat **fish and chips,**

snacktime **biscuits and tea,**

Chicken tikka masala

and *Sunday roast beef.*

Roast Beef Dinner

Fish & Chips

BBC'S on the telly.

Cars drive on the left;

And they still can use **stones**

to measure their heft.

Pounds

For shopping it's pounds

and pence that they'll use,

To buy **WIMBLEDON** tickets

or *WELLINGTON BOOTS.*

Wellington Boots
(Rain Boots)

So go get some pounds

and head off to see

This country of **bagpipes,**

biscuits and *tea,*

RUGBY and **RAIN,**

old stone **castles** and knights,

PUBS and museums

and so many sights!

Bagpiper

Rugby

Fancy a cuppa?

← The flag of the United Kingdom is called the **Union Jack**. The current version was created in 1801 to represent the United Kingdom of Great Britain and Ireland. The design combines three separate flags: the Saint George Cross representing England, the Saint Andrew's Cross representing Scotland and the Saint Patrick's Cross representing Ireland. The flag's design was maintained even after most of Ireland gained their independence in 1922. Scotland and England still use their own flags when they want to represent their nations specifically, but Northern Ireland officially uses only the Union Jack. Wales has its own flag, the "Red Dragon."

Saint George's Cross
Flag of England

Saint Andrew's Cross
Flag of Scotland

Saint Patrick's Cross
Former Flag of Ireland

The Red Dragon
Flag of Wales

Official Name:
United Kingdom of Great Britain and Northern Ireland

Population: 63.7 million

Capital: London

National Capitals: London, England; Belfast, Northern Ireland; Edinburgh, Scotland; Cardiff, Wales

Largest Cities: London, Birmingham, Glasgow

Comparative Size:
Slightly smaller than Oregon, a bit larger than Ghana

Ethnicity: White 87%, South Asian 4%, black 3%, mixed 2%, other 4%

Population by Nation:
England 84%, Scotland 8%, Wales 5%, Northern Ireland 3%

Main Language: English

Religion: Christian 64%, Muslim 5%, Hindu 1.4%, unaffiliated 28%

Currency: British pound

Shetland Islands

Orkney Islands

Outer Hebrides

SCOTLAND

North Sea

NORTHERN IRELAND

Isle of Man

Irish Sea

WALES

ENGLAND

Isle of Wight

Celtic Sea

English Channel

Where in the World is the United Kingdom?

GEOGRAPHICAL NOTES

⊙ The **UNITED KINGDOM** includes the nations of England, Northern Ireland, Scotland and Wales. The UK terms itself "four countries within a country."

⊙ **Great Britain** is an island containing England, Scotland and Wales.

⊙ The **British Isles** historically included Great Britain, Ireland and many smaller islands. Today, they are frequently called the "**British and Irish Isles**" or just Britain and Ireland.

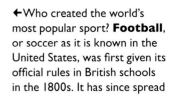

← Would you like to be a **knight** or **dame**? The queen (or king) of the UK still gives this high honor to people who have made a great contribution to national life. Scientists, authors, actors, musicians, educators, business and government leaders have all been "knighted." Even people from other countries can receive an honorary knighthood or damehood, but they cannot use the titles "Sir" or "Dame."

Sir Paul McCartney was part of the Beatles.

Dame Judi Dench is an actress.

Football

←Who created the world's most popular sport? **Football**, or soccer as it is known in the United States, was first given its official rules in British schools in the 1800s. It has since spread throughout the world.

The British **railway** is the → oldest in the world, dating back to the 1830s. The British Empire built railway networks that are still active today in India and Africa.

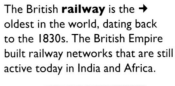

← London is also home to the oldest **underground train** system, nicknamed "the tube."

Sir Arthur Conan Doyle wrote the Sherlock Holmes mysteries.

Biscuits & Tea

← **Teatime** can be a snack taken in the afternoon (3:00–5:00 PM) or a meal taken in the evening (5:00–7:00 PM). Tea is generally served with milk.

Palace of Westminster

Queen Elizabeth II → is the head of state of the United Kingdom as well as 15 other Commonwealth realms including Canada, Australia, New Zealand and South Africa. As a figurehead, her role is largely ceremonial. She does not govern the country or make laws.

One day Prince William and his wife Catherine will be king and queen consort.

↑ The United Kingdom is governed by a **parliament** that meets in the Palace of Westminster. The palace is home to "Big Ben," a clock tower that was named for the huge bell that tolls within it. Scotland, Wales and Northern Ireland also have their own separate parliaments or national assemblies that are somewhat similar to state legislatures in the US or provincial and territorial legislatures in Canada.

← *Why is English so widely spoken around the world?* One reason is that the British Empire was so large. They left behind English language, soccer, cricket, British laws, and railways in many former colonies. This map shows all the places that were ever part of the British Empire in its 400-year history. In 1922, roughly 20% of the world's population was part of the Empire and it was said that, *"the sun never sets on the British Empire."* But by the 1970s, the British Empire had largely dissolved.

Anachronous Map of the British Empire
(All the lands that were ever part of the Empire)

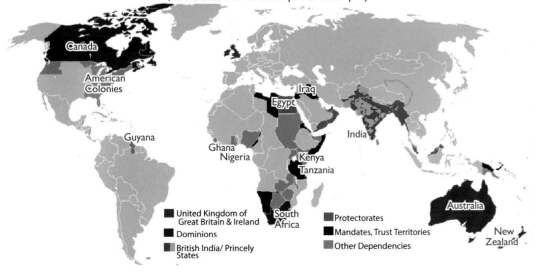

British stories have spread around the world. From Shakespeare's *Romeo and Juliet*, to Tolkien's *Lord of the Rings*, to Jane Austen's *Pride and Prejudice* and Charles Dickens' *A Christmas Carol*, British literature has more internationally known stories than any other country. It has produced numerous famous characters like Sherlock Holmes, James Bond, King Arthur and Robin Hood. In particular, British children's literature is vast and popular. Do you know stories about Winnie the Pooh, *Peter Rabbit, Alice in Wonderland, Peter Pan,* Paddington Bear, Harry Potter, *Charlie and the Chocolate Factory* or *The Lion the Witch and the Wardrobe*?

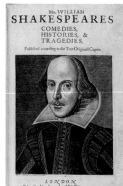

↑ King Arthur

← William Shakespeare's First Folio

↑ *The world's most famous detective: Sherlock Holmes*

J.K. Rowling reading from → *her first Harry Potter book*

Lewis Carroll's Alice in Wonderland ↓

↑ *Beatrix Potter's Peter Rabbit*

Robin Hood

Chicken Tikka Masala

Legends of Robin Hood, the heroic English outlaw, date back to the 14th century. →

What is the national dish of the UK? ↑ →
The most popular dishes served in restaurants now are spicy and usually Asian in origin, quite unlike traditional British foods, which are not spicy. The most famously popular dish is a curry called **Chicken Tikka Masala,** a dish of chicken marinated in a spicy tomato-yogurt sauce and baked in a tandoori oven. In terms of fast food or pub food, **fish and chips**, a fried fish filet and french fries, is the most popular. The most traditional meal for a Sunday dinner is **roast beef**, gravy, Yorkshire pudding and vegetables. Yorkshire pudding is a savory puffy bread originally made with drippings from the roast beef. (See recipe in UK activities.) ↓

Fish and Chips

The **Beatles** were a British rock band that ↑ became the most successful musical group in history. They recorded over 200 songs and had 20 number one hits. They were together from 1960 to 1970, and their songs are still popular around the world.

Roast Beef Dinner

Handel's "**Hallelujah Chorus**" was first sung in Dublin in 1742, when Ireland was still a part of the UK. "The Hallelujah Chorus" is part of a larger choral work in English called *Messiah.* Handel was born in Germany but moved to Britain and became a British citizen. His work helped to define the sound of British classical music. Some of Handel's pieces are used in royal ceremonies and have become the sound of British royalty to international audiences. →

The **BBC** or ➜
British Broadcasting
Company is the largest
public television network
in the world. The BBC
is funded by UK citizens
through an annual fee
for all households that
watch television. The
BBC has 10 television
channels in the UK, and it is the most-
watched television source. The BBC also has a large
worldwide radio presence. Many BBC programs are
exported to the US and around the world.

← Cars **drive on the left**
side of the street in the UK.
There are 50 other countries
that drive on the left, including
several in this book: Australia,
India, Japan and Zimbabwe.

↑**Wimbledon**
is the oldest tennis
tournament in the
world, held since
1877 at the All-
England Tennis Club
in Wimbledon, a
district of London.
Wimbledon is the
only major tennis
tournament still
played on grass
courts.

Annual Average	Rainfall (inches)	Sunshine (hours)	Humidity (high/low)
London	23	1481	92 / 70
Edinburgh	28	1421	89 / 69
Cardiff	45	1536	90 / 74
Belfast	34	1353	90 / 74
Plymouth	37	1677	89 / 76
New York	49	2535	71 / 54
Seattle	37	2170	83 / 62
Atlanta	50	2738	81 / 52
Chicago	37	2508	80 / 57
Toronto	33	2066	81 / 61

↑ *Why is the UK so
cloudy?* The Gulf Stream.
The Gulf Stream is a warm
ocean current that sweeps up
the east coast of Florida and
crosses the Atlantic Ocean
to run by Ireland and Britain.
The warm water in the Gulf
Stream creates fog as it meets
the colder northern air.
It also warms the climate of
the UK by several degrees,
making winters milder than
they would otherwise be at
that latitude. Though it is
often damp in much of the
UK, annual rainfall is not very
high as there are few heavy
showers. ➜

Wet Weather

The **pound** sterling is the currency in the UK ➜
Each pound can be divided into 100 **pence**,
the singular of which is a penny. The word *pound*
is also used as a unit of weight, though only
to measure human weight. Everything else is
weighed in kilograms. One weight measurement
used only in Britain and Ireland is a **stone**,
which is equivalent to 14 pounds. Human weight
is generally described in stones and pounds. A
100-pound person would be 7 stone 2 pounds.
↓ *How many stone do you weigh?*

Pound coins

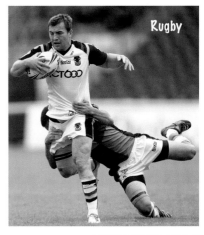

A scale measuring stone and kilos

Scotland has long been associated
with **tartan** (plaid) and **bagpipes**.
Both originated in other parts of
the world, but they are now part
of Scottish national identity. Each
Scottish clan (extended family) has
their own tartan pattern.
*What colors would you want in your
family's tartan?* ➜

Cardiff Castle

← Originally the site of a
Roman fort, **Cardiff Castle**
was built just after the reign
of William the Conqueror
(1066–1087), the first Norman
king of England. Many noble
families in England gained their
estates as conquerors from
Normandy, France. Most of
Britain's castles were built
during this period.

Rugby is a sport that ➜
got its name from Rugby
School, an English *public
school* (meaning an elite
private school). American
football is a relative of
rugby and the games are
similar. Rugby, however, is
played without protective
gear, and there are fewer
pauses in the game as
the same players stay on
the field for offense and
defense.

Rugby

Listen to the SOUNDS of the UNITED KINGDOM

Bagpipes Though bagpipes are traditional in many areas of the world, the bagpipes of Scotland and Ireland are the most popular today. Listen to the Royal Scots Dragoon. Guard. **YOUTUBE SEARCH:** Scottish Highlands bagpipe

Handel's Water Music The sound of British royalty to American ears. Listen to Handel's *Water Music* while having afternoon tea. Also try his "Music for the Royal Fireworks."
YOUTUBE SEARCH: Handel Water Music

The British Invasion The Beatles, the Rolling Stones, The Who, the Yardbirds and many more invaded the American music scene beginning in 1964, changing the face of rock music. For an overview of many Beatles songs, watch *The Yellow Submarine*, an animated movie.

God Save the Queen (or King) National anthem and tribute to the reigning monarch.
YOUTUBE SEARCH: God Save the Queen

SPEAK BRITISH English!

Biscuit cookie	**Pudding** dessert
Chips french fries	**Crisp** potato chip
Pants underpants	**Knickers** panties
Skivvies men's underclothes	**Flannel** washcloth
Trousers pants, slacks, trousers	**Jumper** sweater
Public school private school	**State school** public school
Holiday vacation	**Flat** apartment
Lorry delivery truck	**Dustman** garbage man
Lollipop man crossing guard	**Bobby** policeman
Rubbish garbage	**Telly** tv
Barmy, Potty crazy	**Nutter** crazy person
Old codger eccentric old man	**Bloke, Chap** guy
Cheesed off annoyed	**Chuffed** proud
Zed Zee (pronunciation of "Z")	**Loo** toilet
Lavatory restroom	**Bog roll** toilet paper
Fortnight two weeks	**Brolly** umbrella
Skive avoid work, shirk	**Whinge** whine
Nick steal	**Fancy** like
Cheers! Thanks! or Goodbye!	**Brilliant!** Great!
Blast! Oh no!	**Blimey!** My goodness!

It's monkeys outside. It's very cold.
And Bob's your uncle And there you go, it's that simple.
Donkey's years Ages. I haven't seen you in donkey's years!

READ:

This Is Britain and **This Is London** and **This Is Edinburgh** by Miroslav Sasek. Originally published in the 1960s and '70s, these books take readers on charmingly illustrated trips around some of the UK's top sites. Updates in the back reflect changes since first publication. Ages 5 & up.

Off With Their Heads!: All the Cool Bits of British History by Martin Oliver. A fun overview of British history from the prehistoric times to the present. Ages 9 & up.

George Vs. George: The American Revolution as Seen by Both Sides by Rosalyn Schanzer. See how American and British accounts of mutual history differ. Ages 9 & up.

Castle by David Macaulay. Discover all the inner workings of a typical medieval castle in Wales. Ages 10 & up.

Tales from England by James Reeves. **Tales from Wales** by Gwyn Jones. **Tales from Scotland** by Barbara Kerr Wilson. All part of the Oxford Children's Myths and Legends Series, enter worlds of witches, wizards, elves, fairies, knights and royalty with these famous tales. Ages 9 & up.

Not for Parents London: Everything You Ever Wanted to Know by Lonely Planet. A fun, irreverent (and violent) introduction to the city. Ages 9 & up.

DON'T MISS WATCHING (online)

Horrible Histories: The British Empire
The CBBC has a humorous kids' history show filled with gore, villains and all sorts of historical wickedness. They have a delightfully brief history of the British Empire.
INTERNET SEARCH: Horrible Histories British Empire

BBC Hands on History
The BBC has several other delightful kids' shows about both British and world history. One is entitled "Hands on History" and includes several animated videos of a ten-year-old boy experiencing life in a different era in Britain. Each episode is entitled "A Day in the Life of..." You can see all their kids' history resources at: www.bbc.co.uk/history/forkids/ **YOUTUBE SEARCH:** BBC Hands on History

The Secret City of London
C. G. P. Grey has a number of interesting, short YouTube videos explaining: the City of London, the true cost of the royal family, "How to Become the British Monarch" and "The Difference between the United Kingdom, Great Britain and England Explained."

MAKE BRITISH
Yorkshire Pudding

Yorkshire pudding is a puffy golden bread that Americans call "popovers." Yorkshire pudding was traditionally made as a side to roast beef and was cooked in beef drippings. The puddings are perfect for soaking up gravy, but they can be served as a side to anything, or as a scrumptious treat by themselves, still warm from the oven. "Pudding" is a British term for the dessert, which can also be called "sweets," "afters" or dessert. Calling this bread a pudding is in part a tribute to just how delicious it is!

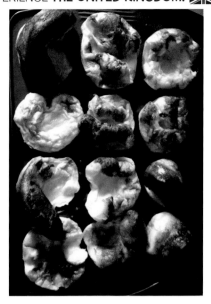

1. Beat together eggs, milk and salt.

2. Sift in one cup flour, then beat until smooth with electric beaters.

3. Allow mixture to sit for 10 minutes. Make sure there is an oven rack available in the middle to lower half of your oven. Preheat oven to 425˚.

4. Grease muffin tins generously, both sides and bottom of each tin, with slightly soft butter capable of making a thick coating.

5. Sprinkle a little flour into each tin. Shake pan to make sure it covers the bottom of each tin. Then turn pan over the sink and tap on the back to get out extra flour.*

6. Place muffin tin in the oven and heat until butter melts. Be careful not to burn the butter.

7. Carefully remove hot pan from oven, close the oven and immediately pour batter into each tin. You can use a ¼ cup as a ladle; fill it mostly (not fully) to evenly distribute the batter among the 12 cups.

8. Put muffin tin back in the oven as quickly and safely as you can.

9. Cook popovers for 20 minutes.

10. Remove from oven and allow to cool slightly. The golden puffs will sink a little, but they should not collapse entirely.

11. Serve warm, either plain or with butter.

3 eggs
1¼ cups milk
½ teaspoon salt
1 cup flour + 1 tablespoon
butter (or oil) to grease pans
12 muffin tin

* Most Yorkshire pudding recipes call for greasing the pans generously with either oil or butter without the addition of flour. But if your tins aren't perfectly "seasoned," the bread may stick on the bottom. Yorkshire pudding tins are typically cast iron and never washed with soap in order to stay perfectly seasoned. For regular muffin tins, adding a sprinkling of flour to the bottom of each tin prevents sticking (the sides don't need flour). Some British recipes call for a 1/2 inch of oil in each tin so that the popovers literally float and can "pop over" (turn over) while cooking. Experiment and see which method you like best!

Yorkshire puddings taste best when fresh and still warm from the oven.

MAP Your Favorite British Characters!

Do you have any British writers or characters on your bookshelves? Research where your favorite British authors and characters are from. Then, print out a large map of the UK as well as small pictures of character or authors (or just print their names or the names of the books). Attach your printed pictures and names to pins, and stick them into their location on the map like flags. You will have to be a literary detective in your research. For instance, Harry Potter grew up in Little Whinging, Surrey. While Little Whinging is fictional, Surrey is a real county in England. Robin Hood lived in Nottinghamshire, another county, or you could look for Sherwood Forrest, also a real place. Winnie the Pooh lived in a woods based on Ashdown Forest in Sussex. With books with unspecific or fantastical settings, use the author's hometown instead.

Alternative Map: Map famous Brits of all types, both fictional and real. Put the Beatles in Liverpool, Charles Darwin in Shrewsbury, Isaac Newton in Lincolnshire, etc.

V is for Vietnam

CHINA

CHINA

Red River

South China Sea

HANOI ☆

Ha Long Bay

LAOS

⊙ HAI PHONG

Gulf of Tonkin

Hainan (CHINA)

THAILAND

⊙ DA NANG

ANNAMITE MOUNTAINS

CAMBODIA

Gulf of Thailand

⊙ HO CHI MINH CITY (SAIGON)

Mekong Delta

VIETNAM is our country for **V**,

a long **S** on the *South China Sea,*

where the rivers and rain

and mountains sustain

farming **COFFEE**, **RICE** and **TEA**.

Growing Rice on Terraces

Vietnamese Dragon

The descendents of a **dragon** and **fairy**

who met and decided to marry.

Their children were divided

where their parents resided

To live by the sea or hills airy.

Mountains

So the myth-loving Vietnamese

are a people of **MOUNTAINS** and **seas**,

Rural towns and big cities

and house boats for fishing

And many exotic fruit trees.

Fishing Boats on the
South China Sea

River deltas: the southern **MEKONG**

and the northern **Red River** (Song Hong)

Are where most people dwell.

The economy's swell

For both making and spending their **DONG.**

Dong

Gong

In the middle ,the highlands are where

coffee grows in the cool mountain air

And they play on the *GONG*

near to houses called "long"

Up on stilts with movable stairs.

Long House

Water Puppets

Pagoda

In their capital city **HANOI**, [hah-NOY]

there is much to allure and enjoy:

Water puppeteer troops,

pagodas, *pho soup* [fuh]

And an old quarter street filled with toys.

And in **Ho Chi Minh City** (Saigon),

you will ride on a zooming *xe om*. [say ohm, *motorcycle taxi*]

Two wheels are preferred

in their traffic absurd,

In this city of grand goings-on.

Pho

Ho Chi Minh City Traffic

And if beauty you want to survey,

visit villages on **Halong Bay**

Floating by soaring stones

are the fishermen's homes

Where they'll greet you

"XIN CHOW!" or "Good day!" [seen chow]

Halong Bay

Woven conical hats will protect

them from sun and the rain they expect —

Everyday in **monsoon**

in the late afternoon —

A **NON LA'S** a most useful object.

Non La

Wearing an Ao Dai

And the school girls in long white **AO DAIS** [ow die-z]

are a pleasure for anyone's eyes.

For the tongue, there's filled crepes

called **banh xeo** that are dipped [bahn seoh]

In **nuoc cham,** a fish sauce that is prized. [nwohk chahm]

Banh Xeo &
Nuoc Cham

So come meet the **BLUE DRAGON'S** clan,

and enjoy all their beaches' white sand.

You'll find culinary bliss,

and rich history in this

Indochinese peninsula land.

Xin Chào!*

Water Puppets

*****Xin Chao** [seen chow] means "Good day!"

← Vietnam's flag was created in 1940 to use in a uprising against French colonial power in Cochinchina (southern Vietnam). In 1941, it was adopted by the Viet Minh, a communist group formed during World War II to fight Japanese occupation of French Indochina (today Vietnam, Laos and Cambodia). After World War II, Vietnam fought for independence from France in the First Indochina War (1946–1954). After the war, the country was divided into North Vietnam (led by Viet Minh) and South Vietnam. North Vietnam used the flag for their new communist republic, which fought to take over (and reunite with) South Vietnam through the Vietnam War (1955–1975). Red represents the blood spilled in revolution, and the star is for the five people of communist Vietnam: peasants, workers, intellectuals, traders and soldiers.

VIETNAM is a variation of "Nam Viet," meaning "Southern Viet," a name used for the region in ancient times. The "Viet" were originally a people who lived in southernmost China and northern Vietnam. Vietnam has used several other names in its history, including "Đai Nam," meaning "Great South."

Vietnam in Southeast Asia

Official Name:
Socialist Republic of Vietnam

Local Name: Viêt Nam

Population: 93.4 million

Capital: Hanoi

Largest Cities:
Ho Chi Minh City, Hanoi

Comparative Size:
Slightly larger than New Mexico, slightly smaller than Japan

Ethnicity: Viet 86%, Tay 1.9%, Thai 1.8%, Muong 1.5%, Khmer 1.5%, Mong 1.2%, Nung 1.1%, others 5.3%

Language: Vietnamese

Religions: Buddhism 16%, Christianity 8%, traditional 45%, unaffiliated 30%

Currency: Vietnamese dong

Export Crops: Rice, coffee, rubber, tea, fish

Top Exports: Clothing, shoes, electronics

GEOGRAPHICAL NOTES

◉ **Southeast Asia** consists of all the Asian countries south of eastern China.

◉ The Vietnamese sometimes describe their skinny country as "*two rice baskets hung on either end of a carrying pole.*" The two fertile river deltas in the north and south are separated by a long, high strip of mountains.

◉ Vietnam has the world's 13th-largest population.

Where in the World is Vietnam?

Fishing on the Mekong River

← **Fishing** and growing **rice** are → both important parts of Vietnam's economy and the Vietnamese diet. Rice is grown mainly in the river deltas (particularly the Mekong) and on terraces up in the northern highlands. Vietnam is the world's fifth-largest producer of rice and its second-largest exporter. Fishing boats fill up the harbors and rivers and many families live on houseboats. ↓

Rice Terraces

The creation myth of the Vietnamese is that a sea **dragon** fell in love with a mountain **fairy** and they had 100 children, who hatched from eggs. Eventually the dragon wished to return to the sea and the fairy to the mountains, so the two parted, each taking fifty children with them. Vietnam is a skinny country of mountains, river delta and seacoast. People either live by the water or in the mountains. ↓ →

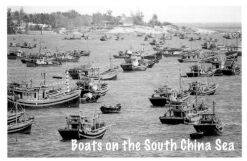

Boats on the South China Sea

Sapa is a town perched in the mountains in northwest Vietnam. ↓

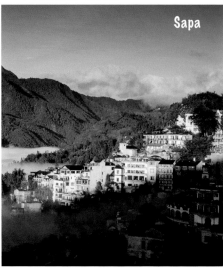

Sapa

Dragon

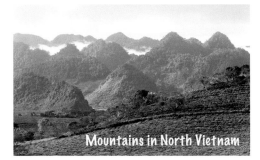

Mountains in North Vietnam

Durian

Many **fruits** grown in Vietnam are rare outside Southeast Asia.

← The most famous is probably the **durian**, which is as stinky as it is delicious. Some compare the durian's odor to strong cheeses, while others find it similar to dirty gym socks. Durians smell so strongly, there are laws against carrying them on public transportation in many cities.

The name of the **longan** fruit means "dragon eye" as people think the peeled fruit looks like an eyeball. The **Rambutan** also has a white orbed center, its name means "hairy." Both are sweet and taste a bit like grapes. →

Longans

Rambutans

"No Durians" Sign for Buses & Trains

Dragon Fruit

Mangosteen

↑ Creamy **dragon fruit** or *pitaya* are originally from the American tropics but are now very popular in Southeast Asia.

Only the white flesh of the **mangosteen** is ↑ edible; it tastes a bit like a cross between a peach and an orange.

← **Bananas** originated in Southeast Asia many thousands of years ago and grow abundantly in Vietnam. Many people have a banana tree in their garden, and there are many dishes steamed in banana leaves.

Banana Tree

← The **dong** is the currency in Vietnam. Pictured on the bills is Ho Chi Minh, the North Vietnamese leader who helped to make the country communist and united.

Gong

← The **gong** is a traditional East Asian instrument not unlike a bell. In the highlands, there are gong orchestras, and gongs are frequently played at community events and cultural ceremonies.

Long houses are built by many ethnic groups in → the highlands of Central Vietnam. Made to hold extended families, long houses have many rooms, one behind the other. Behind a large communal space, each room has its own small kitchen and can hold a nuclear family. This house, made by the E De people, reserves the back room for the family matriarch and her spouse. Beside her is the family of her youngest daughter, who will become the next matriarch.

Long House

Pho (pronounced *fuh*) is considered by many Vietnamese to be their national dish. Traditionally eaten for breakfast, it has become so popular that it can be eaten for any meal. Thin slivers of beef are in a broth with rice noodles, spices and fresh herbs. ↓

Hanoi

Hanoi sits on the Red River.

← **Hanoi** was the capital of North Vietnam (1954–1976) and is the capital of Vietnam today. It's been the capital of the region for most of its history, dating back to about 1010 CE. In the old quarter there are streets dedicated to selling just one thing. For instance, there is a street filled with vendors who only sell toys. Other streets sell items like candy, meats or silk. →

Pho

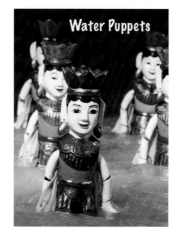

Water Puppets

Dolls on Toy Street

← **Water puppetry** is a popular art form from northern Vietnam. The stage is the surface of a 13 ft (4 m) square tank of water. Puppeteers hide behind a screen at the back of the stage and manipulate the lacquered wooden puppets to glide around the stage with long bamboo poles and strings hidden under the water. A traditional Vietnamese orchestra accompanies the performance, which typically tells folktales.

A **pagoda** is → a stacked tower with multiple eaves that is a common part of Buddhist temple complexes in East and Southeast Asia. This pagoda, named Tran Quoc, is the oldest in Hanoi. It was built in the 6th century CE by Emperor Ly Om De and has become a symbol of Hanoi.

Pagoda

Ho Chi Minh, Vietnam's first communist leader (1945–1965)

↓ A **xe om** is a motorbike taxi that you can pick up from almost any street corner in Vietnam. *Xe* means "motorbike" and *om* means "hug," meaning you should hold on tight when your driver is whipping through traffic. Two-wheeled vehicles (including bicycles) are the most practical way to get around Vietnamese cities. Getting through traffic and parking are quicker, and the natural air conditioning is generally quite effective.

Two-Wheeled Traffic

Ho Chi Minh City

← Saigon was renamed **Ho Chi Minh City** in 1975 after South Vietnam was reunited with North Vietnam. Saigon had been the capital of South Vietnam, which fought to remain independent from the communist North. Ho Chi Minh City is Vietnam's largest city.

Houseboats on Halong Bay

← **Halong Bay** is considered one of the most beautiful natural wonders in the world. There are over 1,600 little limestone islands in the bay, jutting out of the water like mini mountains covered in lush tropical vegetation. These little islands are too steep to live on and so remain perfectly wild and seem to almost float in the water. →

Halong Bay

A **non la** is the perfect hat for Vietnam's sunny, humid climate. Its width shades the entire face and neck and helps to keep you cool in the heat of the tropical sun. Its open shape allows for free circulation of air around the head so moisture and heat aren't trapped. Non las even help to keep you drier in the rain. They don't replace a rain coat, but they do keep water out of your face and from seeping into your collar. ↓

↑ **Carrying poles** are used widely in East Asia to enable people to carry heavy, unwieldy loads long distances.

Ban xeo means "sizzling pancake." Fried stuffed pancakes made from rice flour, ban xeos usually have savory fillings like pork, shrimp and bean sprouts. **Nuoc cham** is the most popular condiment in Vietnam. It is a slightly sweet, sour, spicy, salty fish sauce eaten with almost anything savory. ↓

Ban Xeo

Nuoc Cham

Non La

The **ao dai** is the national dress → for the women of Vietnam and high school girls wear white ao dais as school uniforms. Ao dais consist of matching loose-fitting trousers and long-sleeved tunics with side slits up to the waist. They are made from cool flowing fabrics and aim to be both elegant and practical in the tropical weather. Long pants and sleeves help to protect the skin from excessive sun exposure. Many women wear casual Western clothing and save ao dais for dressing up. ↓ →

Ao Dai

← You only see traditional men's dress in Vietnam on special occasions. Their **ao gam** is a long brocade tunic that is worn over pants. It is similar to the ao dai, but the tunic is looser. This man is wearing ao gam for the Vietnamese New Year, or **Tet**, and holding a string of firecrackers. →

Ao dais come in every color of the rainbow, not just white. →

Ao Dai

Schoolboy

← School children frequently wear a **red neckerchief** to show they are "young pioneers," a group similar to Scouts that is run by the communist party.

Blue Dragon in Vietnam

➜ The West first started calling Vietnam the "**Land of the Blue Dragon**" in the 1800s. Vietnamese do associate their nation with a dragon, but not specifically a blue one. Perhaps a blue dragon symbolizes a dragon from the sea, like the one in their creation myth. Or it could be that Western travelers misheard the original name for the capital Hanoi, *Thang Long,* which actually means "ascending dragon" and thought they heard *Thanh Long,* or "blue dragon."

Beach at Phan Thiet

⬆ Vietnam is known for its gorgeous sand **beaches** on the South China Sea.

Would you like to ride on a ➜ *water buffalo?* In rural Vietnam, children are usually responsible for caring for the family water buffalo. On farms, the water buffalo is used like a tractor to help till the land. They are also valued for the milk they produce. Water buffalo are not driven like cattle; they naturally follow their owners. They are treated like pets and members of the family. Children care for their water buffalo by leading them to good grazing areas to eat. ⬇

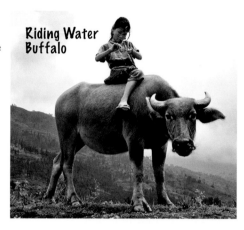

Riding Water Buffalo

Buddha Statue

Riding Water Buffalo

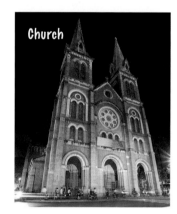

Church

⬅ Officially, Vietnam is a communist country with ⬆ an atheist state, but other religions are allowed by the government. About 16% of the country are practicing Buddhists and 8% are Christian. Though not widely practiced, Buddhism, Taoism and Confucianism influence the Vietnamese outlook on life – placing a large value on harmony, family, respect for elders, diligence and personal contentment. One widespread traditional belief is the importance of honoring ancestors and the dead. Every year on the anniversary of a family member's death, an offering will be made in their memory.

Cham women dance outside a temple; a Red Dao girl and a Hmong girl wear their traditional dress. All three groups are Vietnamese, though they are not ethnically Viet. There are many different cultural traditions alive in Vietnam. ⬇ ➜

Cham Dancer

Red Dao Girl

Hmong Girl

⬅ ⬆Though 85% of the Vietnamese population is Viet (also known as Kinh) there are 54 other ethnic communities in Vietnam, many up in the Central Highlands. The Cham, Red Dao and Hmong people are just three examples.

The Vietnam War Q & A

1. When was the Vietnam War and who fought in it?

The war was fought from 1955 until the fall of Saigon in 1975. The fighting was primarily between North Vietnam and South Vietnam. North Vietnam was supported by its communist allies in China and the Soviet Union and by a South Vietnamese rebel group called the *Viet Cong*. South Vietnam was supported by the United States and other anticommunist allies.

2. What do Vietnamese call the Vietnam War?

They call it "The American War" or *Chiến tranh Mỹ*. Its longest title amongst communist leaders is "The War Against the Americans to Save the Nation."

3. Why was the Vietnam War so painful for the United States and Vietnam?

The Vietnam War was America's longest war to date and cost the lives of over 58,200 American servicemen. A draft for the war sent many unwilling young American men, some only teenagers, to fight. Well over one million Vietnamese people lost their lives during the Vietnam War; some analysts place the figure closer to two million.

4. Why were they fighting?

The Vietnam War was part of the "Cold War" fought between communist countries (the Soviet Union and China) and the United States and its allies. While the US and the Soviet Union never fought directly, thus making the war "cold," they supported fights between communist and noncommunist forces around the world. The Korean War was also part of the Cold War.

5. Why was there a Cold War?

After World War II, Europe's global empires began to dissolve, and their colonies in Africa and Asia gained their independence – forming many new nations. As Europe's great powers had suffered through the war and were largely war-ravaged and bankrupt, two new superpowers emerged, the United States and the Soviet Union. The United States and the Soviet Union both attempted to exert their influence over the newly independent countries. The Soviet Union wanted to spread communism, and the United States wanted to spread capitalist democracies. The fight was ideological; what sort of society was best for the world's people? The fight between ideologies and forms of government even split three countries in two, creating North Vietnam and South Vietnam, North Korea and South Korea and East Germany and West Germany.

6. Why couldn't the capitalist democratic nations and the communist nations peacefully coexist?

Both believed that the two societies were a danger to one another and could not peacefully live as neighbors. Also, in Europe, nations were recovering from the war and reforming their societies and government. Those nations near the Soviet Union became communist giving support to the idea that the "Red Menace," communism, could spread like a disease and affect neighboring countries. People believed that communism would spread from the Soviet Union and China and take over the world. The Soviets themselves believed that eventually all peoples would demand communism as their form of government.

7. Why did the US lose the Vietnam War?

There are many factors, but the greatest one is that Vietnam had been fighting to be free from colonial rule for over a century and the communists claimed that this was yet another war of independence. Vietnam had been struggling to be free of French and Japanese (during World War II) foreign occupiers, and America was demonized as one more foreign force trying to govern their land. While the Chinese and Soviets supplied the North with weapons, they did not send in any troops, so they weren't seen as occupiers. Also, the South Vietnamese government wasn't a shining example of freedom and democracy; they could be corrupt and sometimes brutal. Another big issue was war tactics. The Viet Cong and North Vietnamese army used their knowledge of their own country to conduct successful guerilla warfare instead of large open attacks. The US had little way to distinguish Viet Cong enemies from South Vietnamese friends. The US used high-tech attack strategies that frequently killed innocent civilians, giving more South Vietnamese reason to support the Viet Cong. Finally, the Vietnamese had every reason to continue fighting to "protect their homeland" forever; they would never give up. The US was half-way around the world from home, and the high casualties on both sides, as well as war atrocities, made the war deeply unpopular in the United States.

A tour guide shows the entrance to an underground tunnel used by the VietCong.

8. When did the US and Vietnam resume normal diplomatic relations?

In 1995, the countries reopened their embassies and began to work toward agreements on trade and other bilateral issues. Today, the US and Vietnam have much more positive relations and views of one another, helped in part by the Vietnamese-American population in the US, and the embrace of market capitalism in Vietnam.

Listen to the SOUNDS of VIETNAM

Gong Music
Gongs are used as percussion throughout Vietnamese traditional music, but gong solo music is traditional in the highlands. Unesco has a great video explaining the "space of gong culture" in the central highlands. **Y**
OUTUBE SEARCH: Gong Vietnam UNESCO

Nha Nhac
Imperial court music, Nha Nhac means "elegant music" and it is played with many traditional Vietnamese instruments. UNESCO has a video explaining Nha Nhac, but for a good song, try the Hue Imperial Orchestra.
YOUTUBE SEARCH: Nha Nhac UNESCO, Nha Nhac Hue

Vpop
Vietnamese pop or Vpop seems to specialize in fun music videos, many of which tell whole stories, almost like mini-movies. There are several YouTube channels devoted to V-pop. Here are some suggestions to listen to and watch:
Nhat Kim Anh's "Yeu That Kho"
365daBand's "Saigon" or "No Love, No Life"
Khoi My's "Goc Nho Trong Tim"
Mister Band's "High"
YOUTUBE SEARCH: VPop, (band +song name)

DON'T MISS WATCHING (online)

Water Puppets See traditional water puppet theater, an Vietnamese entertainment that originated in flooded rice fields and is close to 1000 years old.
YOUTUBE SEARCH: Vietnamese water puppets

Street Food Tours Vietnamese street food has been called the best in the world, and there are innumerable YouTube videos taking you on tours around the best of it. You can watch ban xeo being made, as well as countless other yummy dishes. Prepare to salivate!
YOUTUBE SEARCH: Vietnam street food

See Vietnam's Top Tourist Destinations
For a nine-minute overview of Vietnam's tourist sites, try a video from Vietnam Airlines called, "Bringing Vietnamese Culture to the World." **YOUTUBE SEARCH:** title

See Vietnam's treasures with UNESCO
There are a few short UNESCO documentaries on World Heritage sites in Vietnam, like "Complex of Hué." Go to UNESCO's YouTube channel and search for Vietnam.

READ:

Children of the Dragon: Selected Tales from Vietnam by Sherry Garland. A charming picture book of Vietnamese tales, like "The Legend of the Monsoon Rains" and "The Bowmen and the Sisters," that includes the cultural, historical or geographical background for each story. Ages 8 & up.

Water Buffalo Days by Huynh Quang Nhuong. The memories of a young boy growing up in the mountains of central Vietnam before the Vietnam War. His best friend, Tank, is a water buffalo and their adventures make up this surprising page-turner. A wonderful look at daily life in the Vietnamese countryside, much of which has remained the same today. Ages 8 & up.

10,000 Days of Thunder: A History of the Vietnam War by Philip Caputo. Written by a journalist and veteran of the Vietnam War, this fascinating, photo-filled presentation includes both American and Vietnamese perspectives. It covers all aspects of the war, from the American draft to the Viet Cong, the history of Communism, Ho Chi Minh and the after-effects of the war on both Vietnam and the United States. Ages 10 & up.

SPEAK Vietnamese!

Vietnamese vowels have many tones and can be difficult for foreigners to pronounce correctly. Keep syllables short and crisp. Try VietnamesePod101's YouTube channel to hear the pronunciation of the simple words below.

Xin Chào	Hello	seen chow
Tôi tên là	My name is	toy ten la
Cảm Ơn	Thank you	gahm uhn
Tạm biệt	Goodbye	tahm byet

Gừng càng già càng cay.
The older the ginger, the hotter it is.
The older we get, the wiser and more experienced we become.

Thùng rỗng keu to.
The empty vessel makes the most noise.
Those with the least knowledge often have the most to say.

Gần mực thì đen, gần đèn thì sàng.
Black if near ink, bright by the lamp.
People are influenced by their upbringing and environment.

Visit www.australiatozimbabwe.com for links to online activities.

MAKE VIETNAMESE
Banh Xeo

A crispy crepe made with rice flour, coconut milk and shrimp, banh xeo can be tricky to make at first, but they are so divinely delicious that they are absolutely worth the effort. Typically, banh xeo has both shrimp and pork in it. This recipe uses only shrimp and it omits hot peppers, which are sometimes thrown in the pan as well. In the north of Vietnam, beer is typically used instead of coconut milk. Makes 6–7 crepes.

1. Make the batter: Mix rice flour, turmeric and salt. Add coconut milk, then enough water to make the mixture as thick as heavy cream, usually ¾–1 cup. Set batter aside to rest.

2. Prepare the filling: Cut up the onions and mushrooms into thin slices. Each shrimp is halved, cutting it lengthwise down its back.

3. Pre-cook the filling: Using a non-stick pan, sauté onion and mushrooms in a little oil until mushroom has shrunken and onions are translucent. Add shrimp to the pan, then sprinkle with salt to season all ingredients. Stir-fry shrimp for a minute or two, once it has begun to turn pink, remove everything from the pan and put on a plate to the side.

4. Prepare the pan: Clear pan, turn heat to medium high and brush frying oil around pan.

5. Pour the crepe: Whisk batter one last time. Then, using a ladle, pour some into the hot pan, tilting and swirling the pan as you pour to spread the batter *as thinly as possible*. Ban xeo won't get crispy if it's too thick. If gaps appear in the crepe while you are swirling, keep tilting the pan and most will close up. Add a small spoonful of batter to fill in any large holes. Don't make crepes too large in your pan; they are easier to remove when smaller.

6. Add the filling: Sprinkle some of the mushroom-onion-shrimp mixture over the crepe. Around six shrimp halves is plenty.

7. Cook the banh xeo and make nuoc cham: Put a lid on the pan and let it cook for 2 minutes. Remove lid, add small handful of beans sprouts and give the banh xeo several more minutes to cook uncovered. Banh xeo may need more than 5 minutes to cook uncovered. While waiting for it to cook, mix nuoc cham ingredients and set aside.

8. How to tell it's done and remove it from the pan: The edges of the crepe will become brown and crispy before it is ready. When they start to look done, turn your spatula over and gently start prying up the edges by sliding the back edge of the spatula underneath. By prying them off of the pan, the edges get further from the heat and give the thicker center longer to cook. The entire crepe will become easy to loosen as it becomes crisp. If one side is done before the other, fold it over, giving the bottom half more time to cook. Some cooks recommend drizzling oil around the edges to keep them from sticking. Usually, if it cooks for long enough, it will easily peel up. When it is ready and loosened from the pan, fold over and slide onto a plate. It's quite difficult to burn, so don't rush to get it out of the pan.

9. Serve banh xeo: Serve right away with lettuce, fresh herbs (mint, basil, parsley or cilantro) and nuoc cham. Cut banh xeo into about 6 pieces. To eat: wrap up each piece with fresh herbs in lettuce and dip into nuoc cham sauce. YUM!

Warning: It is difficult to serve banh xeo to an entire party, as they need to be eaten while still fresh. It's better to make a couple and share them among a group, then make more. You could also have two pans going at once.

Each bite of banh xeo is wrapped up with fresh herbs in lettuce and dipped in nuoc cham sauce. This nuoc cham was made with the substitutions listed below.

Batter
1 cup rice flour
⅛ teaspoon turmeric
¼ teaspoon salt
1 cup coconut milk
water

Filling
¾ cup sweet yellow onion, chopped small
1 cup mushrooms, sliced thin
15–21 raw shrimp, peeled and halved lengthwise
3–4 tablespoon oil for frying
salt to taste
2 cups bean sprouts

Fresh herbs
Bunches of mint, basil and parsley or cilantro

Nuoc Cham
2 tablespoons fish sauce*
2 tablespoons sugar
juice of one lime
¼ cup warm water
½ clove of garlic, minced
1 bird's eye chili,** chopped into thin rings

Substitutions
*if you can't find fish sauce, use a half-and-half mix of soy sauce and Worcester sauce
**or use any fresh hot chili

stands for the WORLD,

Our dear home,

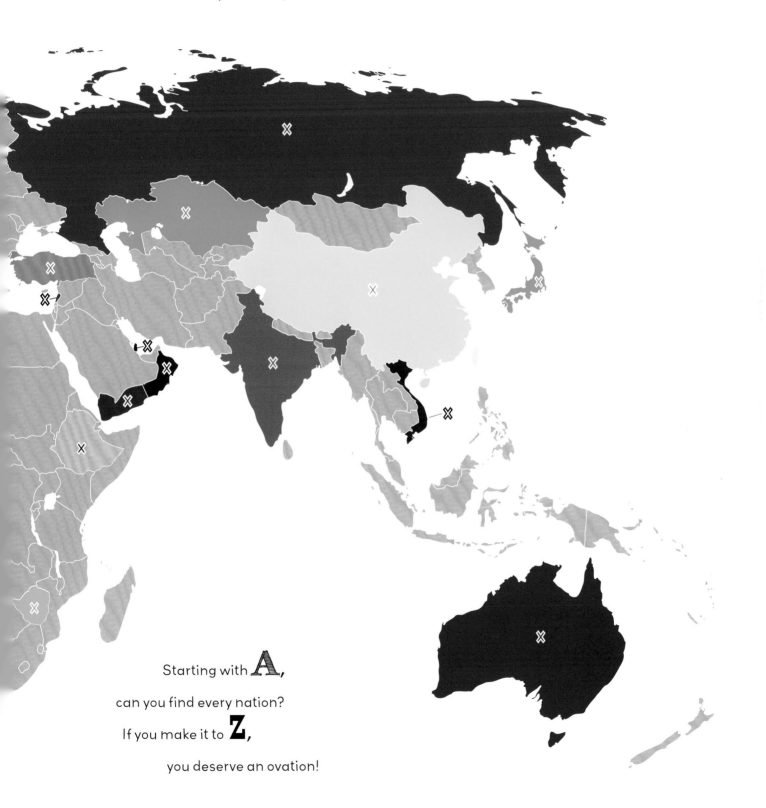

and  marks the spots

in which this book roams.

Starting with **A**,

can you find every nation?
If you make it to **Z**,

you deserve an ovation!

Y is for **Yemen**

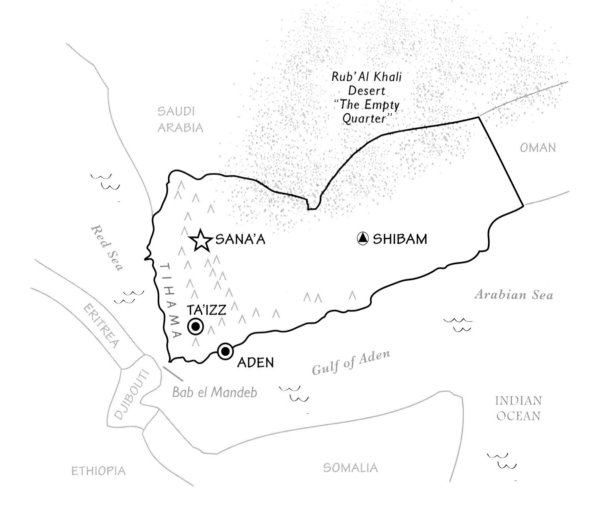

Rub' Al Khali Desert "The Empty Quarter"

SAUDI ARABIA

OMAN

☆ SANA'A

⛰ SHIBAM

Red Sea

TIHAMA

ERITREA

TA'IZZ ⊙

⊙ ADEN

DJIBOUTI

Bab el Mandeb

Gulf of Aden

Arabian Sea

INDIAN OCEAN

ETHIOPIA

SOMALIA

YEMEN is our land of **Y**,

Arabia's point with mountains high.

Though in its east are desert sands

And seaside, hot **TIHAMA** lands,

Its highlands are the greenest place

In all Arabia's arid space.

Yemeni Farmland

Man Chewing Qat

Honey

Here valleys grow plump **GRAPES** and **wheat,**

TOMATOES, **coffee,** HONEY sweet

And **QAT** that's used to stimulate

Their daily gossip and debate.

Jambiya

Each afternoon just after lunch

Good friends assemble in a bunch.

They've eaten well on **SALTAH** soup

With tasty flatbread used as scoop.

And now a **qishr** coffee drink [KISH-er]

Refreshes them to sit and sink —

Reclining into cushions placed

Around the room at each wall's base.

Qishr & Dates

Wearing Futa

The men wear daggers called **jambiya**.

Tied to belts, they still can be a

Weapon but are used much more

For wedding-dancing and decor.

With that, a long white robe with sleeves

And coat and turban if they please.

Or instead they'll wear a futa skirt

wrapped around a button down shirt.

Yemeni Men

Women's Fabric Store

Wearing Veil and Abaya

The women wear bright jewel-tone dress

But you'll not see their clothes unless

You visit a home where women have fun

at afternoon parties where men can't come.

Outdoors they mostly wear **abayas** [ah-BYE-yahs]

(Black robes), and veils that shield men's eyes

Here MEN AND WOMEN never mingle

Not when they're married, or when they're single.

Women find their son a bride.

The sexes never socialize.

In schools the girls and boys don't mix –

In seats or games or the friends they pick.

Yemeni Kids

Yemeni Kids

Called *"Arabia Felix,"* Yemen was known

In ancient times by those in Rome —

For riches brought by trade in scents:

Expensive MYRRH and ***Frankincense.***

And happy were the people here

The ***Queen of Sheba*** reigned and steered

Her people to a faith in one

Almighty god of Solomon.

Or so they say, 'twas not before

ISLAM arrived that shore to shore

The people prayed to one Allah

From Aden's port to old Sana'a.

Myrrh

Queen of Sheba

Sana'a

Sana'a is now the capital. [san-NAH]

It's an ancient city walled and full

Of towers iced like **gingerbread**

That hold one family who has tread

For centuries up stairs to floors

That stack at least to five or more.

Tower House

Another ancient city's *Aden*,

A port that welcomed ships all laden

Down with goods since times B.C.

(Not far from where the gulf meets sea).

At the **BAB EL-MANDEB,** Gate of Tears, [bob el MAN-deb]

Sailors pass in ships they steer.

Oil tankers, dhows and freighters squeeze

Between two **continents** and seas.

Aden

Bab el-Mandeb

Yemen hasn't as much **oil**

As other Arabian countries' soil —

So people mostly work in farming,

Industry and tourist-charming.

And charm they will, they're people who

Say **"Ya hala!"** and welcome you [YAH-hah-LAH]

Inside for coffee and to visit

Family, friends — you shouldn't miss it!

Ya Hala!
(Welcome!)

You might even have the chance

To learn a wild **YEMENI DANCE.**

Yemen is a destination

That's sure to flout your expectations.

Tribal and traditional,

Yet open and hospitable,

It is Arabia's unspoilt jewel

Where poetry thrives and parties rule,

The daily schedule making way

For **FRIENDS** to visit every day.

Come here to share their *love of leisure*

And see their land – an **ANCIENT TREASURE.**

Jambiya Dance

Old Friends

Ya Hala!*

Ya Hala [YAH hah-LAH] means "Welcome!" or "Hello" to a guest.

Yemen or "Al Yaman" in Arabic

← **Yemen's flag** was adopted in 1990 when North Yemen and South Yemen reunited as one country. It is essentially the Arab Liberation Flag, adopted first in Egypt in 1952 to celebrate Arab freedom from colonial power. It was also the basis for the flags of Egypt, Iraq, Sudan and Syria.

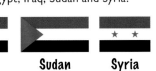

Egypt   Iraq   Sudan   Syria

The name **YEMEN** comes from the Arabic word *yaman*, meaning "on the right." The right simply means to the south, as when you face the sunrise, the south is on your right. Yemen is Arabia's southernmost nation. The right side is considered auspicious (lucky), so being "on the right" is also another way of saying "happy."

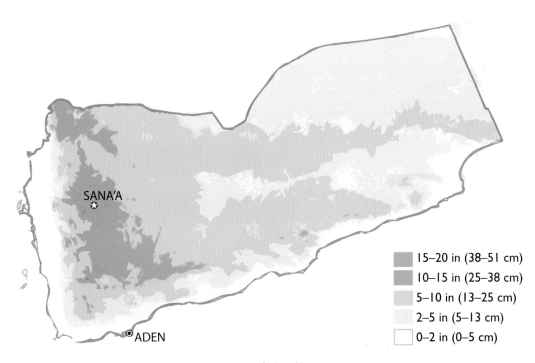

SANA'A

ADEN

15–20 in (38–51 cm)
10–15 in (25–38 cm)
5–10 in (13–25 cm)
2–5 in (5–13 cm)
0–2 in (0–5 cm)

Annual Rainfall in Yemen

Official Name: Republic of Yemen

Population: 26 million

Capital: Sana'a

Largest Cities: Sana'a, Ta'izz, Al-Hudaydah, Aden

Comparative Size: Larger than California, smaller than Texas and slightly larger than Spain

Ethnicity: Mostly Arab with some Afro-Arabs, South Asians and Europeans

Language: Arabic

Religion: Muslim 99% (including Sunni and Shi'a)

Currency: Yemeni rial

Important Exports: Crude oil, coffee

Where in the World is Yemen?

GEOGRAPHICAL NOTES

◉ Yemen has both the highest peaks in Arabia and the largest nondesert land area. In comparison to rainfall in the United States, Colorado and Montana both receive about 15 inches (38 cm) of rainfall annually, and Nevada receives about 9 inches (23 cm). The eastern United States receives more than 40 inches (102 cm) of rainfall annually.

◉ The southern tip of Yemen is only 20 miles (32 km) from the continent of Africa.

Tihama

Yemen has the largest **green region** in Arabia. While most of the Arabian Peninsula and Yemen are arid desert, Yemen's highlands get enough rain to farm grains, fruits, vegetables and qat. →

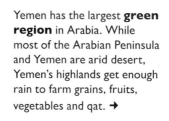

Farming

↑ The **Tihama** is a coastal fog desert. It rarely rains there, but due to moisture rising up from the Red Sea there is significant humidity. The Tihama is incredibly hot, with summertime temperatures regularly reaching up to 110°F (43°C), and humidity at 40–60%. Even Yemenis who are not from the Tihama find it very difficult to be there during the hot months.

Honey

← Yemen is known for producing sidr **honey**, the most expensive honey in the world. Made by bees who eat only from the sidr tree, it is harvested only twice a year in the Hadramut Mountains, where it has been gathered for about 7,000 years. It is believed to have medicinal value and can help heal wounds.

Chewing Qat

↑ **Qat** (KAHT) is a mild plant narcotic. People chew the leaves of the qat plant and leave the pulp in their cheek. Qat parties are held every afternoon and users say that chewing qat makes them more energetic and talkative. Qat is less addictive than either alcohol or tobacco, but the social habit of chewing qat each afternoon with friends is an ingrained part of the daily routine for many Yemenis. Qat is also popular in the Horn of Africa.

Saltah

↑ **Saltah** is the national dish of Yemen. → It is typically eaten for lunch with flat bread to scoop it up (a spoon is not needed). Saltah is made with meat, tomatoes, garlic and chilies and topped with a frothy sauce made from the herb fenugreek. Other vegetables, rice or potatoes may also be added.

Saltah may be eaten from a communal bowl. Everyone uses their right hand to tear off a bit of bread, then scoop up the saltah. ↓

Saltah

Qishr & Dates

Qishr is a drink made from the husks of coffee beans with the addition of ginger, sugar and sometimes cinnamon. Qishr is milder than coffee but has a spicier flavor. Drinks made from coffee husks are common in coffee-producing countries as the husks are widely and cheaply available. →

Mafraj

The living room, or **mafraj**, ↑ in Yemen is usually on the top floor of houses in the highlands. Seating is on the floor with long cushions to sit on and bolsters to lean against. A large group of men can comfortably sit around the room to visit or chew qat together. In fancy homes, there are frequently stained glass windows filtering in colored lights.

Men in Futa

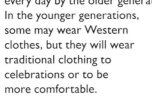

Traditional **men's clothing** in the highlands typically consists of a long white robe with a belt and **jambiya**, a curved dagger. A blazer is typically worn over the robe with a turban on their head. →

← On the coast, many men wear a type of woven wrap skirt, called a **futa**, with a shirt. Male sarongs actually originate in Yemen and are particularly popular on the coasts. Traditional dress is typically worn every day by the older generation. In the younger generations, some may wear Western clothes, but they will wear traditional clothing to celebrations or to be more comfortable.

Traditional Dress In the Highlands

↑ Dancing with jambiya at a wedding

Jambiya

← The **jambiya** is worn in its own fancy case. It is a status symbol and, like a men's watch, can be very expensive. It is virtually never used as a weapon, but it is taken out to perform the traditional dances that men do at weddings and other celebrations.

Musicians at a women's wedding party ↓

Women Musicians

Wearing a Niqab

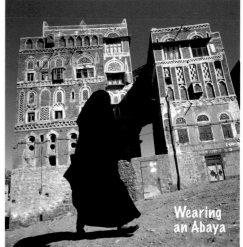
Wearing an Abaya

↑ Women and men outside the home are in separate communities and have their own separate cultures. They have their own parties, celebrations and dances. They typically attend separate schools, and even when they are in the same classroom, they sit on separate sides of the room. To celebrate a wedding, a men's party and a women's party are held at the same time. Some women have even developed their own language, a dialect of Arabic that men can't understand. In arranging marriages, fathers look for their sons-in-law and mothers for their daughters-in-law. Within immediate families, men and women are not separated.

A Yemeni fabric shop shows the normally colorful hues of women's clothing.

↑ Black **abayas** (large cloaks covering the head and body) as well as **niqabs** (face veils) are popular in many Yemeni cities as they allow women to be out in public without being seen by men. Outside of cities, many women do not veil their faces, and they may wear more brightly colored headscarves and coverings. Underneath the black abayas (also called *balto* in Yemen), women's clothing is much more colorful. At home with family and among female friends, women do not veil themselves.

↑ Play clothes

← Street clothes →

↑ In wedding clothes for separate women's and men's parties. ↓

School uniforms ↓ **What do Yemeni kids wear?**

Queen of Sheba

Mosque in Sana'a

Yemen was introduced to Islam in 630 CE, during the life of the prophet Muhammad. →

↑ The **Queen of Sheba** is mentioned in both the Bible and the Qu'ran. Historians believe she was the head of a kingdom known as *Saba* (or Sheba), which ruled over southwestern Arabia (present-day Yemen) from 1200 BCE to 275 CE. Called Bilqis by Muslims, both the Bible and Qu'ran tell how the queen visited King Solomon of Israel (ca 1000 BCE). In the Qu'ran, she was converted by Solomon to a belief in one god.

In ancient times, this region was known as "Happy Arabia" or *Arabia Felix* by the Romans, → due to their wealth from trade in expensive frankincense and myrrh. Yemen still harvests frankincense and myrrh, which are used as incense, in perfumes and medicinally. Both are resins gathered from special trees by cutting strips into the bark, allowing the resin to leak out and dry into "tears."

Myrrh Tears

Tower House

Sana'a, Yemen's capital, is located in the highlands. It is one of the oldest continually inhabited cities in the world. Legend has it that it was founded by Shem, one of Noah's sons from the Bible. It was a center for Christians and Jews before it was converted to Islam in 632 CE. →

Sana'a

↑ Sana'a is famous for its **tower houses**. The ground level is a storage area and may house livestock. The second floor has a common room for business transactions. The third floor has a divan used only for festivities and family gatherings. The fourth floor has private family rooms, the kitchen and usually an enclosed outdoor space where women can be outside without being seen. The fifth, or the top floor, is the *mafraj,* where men meet in the afternoons for qat parties. Many homes have separate staircases for men and women.

Decorative Plasterwork

←Sana'a's tower homes are known in part for the decorative white plasterwork on the outside, framing windows and wrapping the towers in latticework. It can give the old town the appearance of an incredible gingerbread city. They are also known for the use of colorful stained glass in the arches above windows

Shibam is a city in the desert of Yemen that is made up of tall tower houses that are 5–11 stories high. Most of the houses were built in the 16th century and they are made from mud baked in the desert sun. The homes were built so tall as a defense against Bedouin attacks. Shibam is one of the oldest examples of vertical urban planning and is sometimes referred to as the "Manhattan of the desert." ↓

Aden

Shibam

↑**Aden** is a port city and former capital of "South Yemen." Unlike Sana'a, which boasts spring temperatures though the year due to its high altitude, Aden is hotter and has a desert climate. It has been an important port since ancient times and the main stopping place for ships before entering the Bab el-Mandeb.

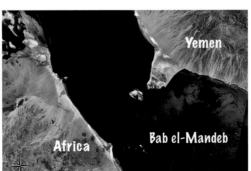

Yemen

Africa   Bab el-Mandeb

← The **Bab el-Mandeb**, or "Gate of Tears," is the narrow strait that separates Yemen from Africa and connects the Red Sea and the Gulf of Aden. Its name comes from the dangers ships used to face to navigate through these waters. Today, it is a major shipping lane and thoroughfare for oil tankers. It also helps to connect the Mediterranean to the Indian Ocean via the Suez Canal and the Red Sea.

Cairo Castle in Ta'izz

Fishing Boats at Al-Mukalla

Hilltop architecture is common in Yemen: Cairo Castle ↑ in Ta'izz and a village in the Harjaz Mountains ↓

Yemeni cities that are not perched in the mountains are typically coastal port cities like Al-Mukalla. ↑

Hilltop Village

The veiled chameleon is often called the **Yemen chameleon** and lives only in the mountains of Arabia in Yemen, Saudi Arabia and Oman. The chameleon changes its color based on its mood, age and temperature. ↓

Yemen Chameleon

Dancing with Jambiya

↑ Dancing with jambiya is done by men of all ages at celebrations. ↓

Old Friends

It is common in Yemen to have lifelong friends whom you see every day. Holding hands is common among friends of all ages.

Because Yemen doesn't have the large oil and gas deposits of some of its Arabian neighbors, it hasn't been developing at the same wild pace. You won't find big cities full of gleaming new high rises or foreign workers brought in to labor in the booming economy. Thus, Yemen has a very well-preserved culture. With the some of same buildings and clothing from a hundred years ago, and farmers and herders still using traditional methods, traveling to Yemen almost feels like visiting an earlier era. Here, daily routines give time for Yemenis to socialize with friends every afternoon. During these parties, epic poetry is still created and recited. Philosophers, wits and storytellers are still prized. And guests are warmly welcomed to take part. →

يا هلا

Ya Hala!
Hello! Welcome!

Dancing with Jambiya

Listen to the SOUNDS of YEMEN

Ayoob Tarish Absi
A popular musician and the composer of their national anthem, try his "Tair Ishbak."
YOUTUBE SEARCH: Tair Ishbak, Ayoob Tarish

Abu Bakr Salem Balfaqih
Another famous Yemeni musician, try his "yaMoraoweh." **YOUTUBE SEARCH:** yaMoraoweh, Abu Bakr Salem

Arwa
Arwa is one of the leading Arab pop singers. She's Yemeni, but her music is more international; she moved to Egypt when she was young. Try her "Marhaba."
YOUTUBE SEARCH: Arwa Marhaba

Other Singers:
Jameela Saad, singer & famous oud player
Ana Ma-Agdar
Hussin Moheb
YOUTUBE SEARCH:
Jameela Saad, Ana Ma-Agdar, Hussin Moheb

Oud

Yemeni Zaffa Music
Zaffa is the traditional wedding procession celebrating the bride and groom. Weddings are the biggest celebrations in Yemen, and there is always music for dancing.
YOUTUBE SEARCH: Yemen Zaffa

Yemeni Rap
Yemeni rap is still very new and gaining an audience. **Hagage "AJ" Masaed** is its pioneer in Yemen. Listen to his "Biladee Bilad Al-Yemen." Also try new voice Amani Yahya.
YOUTUBE SEARCH: Biladee Bilad Al-Yemen, Amani Yahya Yemen

READ:

From the Land of Sheba: Yemeni Folk Tales
by Carolyn Han. An anthropological collection of 27 short folktales. It is worth reading for the introduction alone, which begins:

We are all part of the same story. Stories allow dreaming and connect us to our intuition. They are vital to our well-being; as necessary as food and shelter. Without stories, how would we remember? Without stories, how would we nourish our souls?

In the collection, the most appealing and recognizable tales for Westerners may be the last two, "Henna Leaf," a Yemeni version of Cinderella, and "The Next Sultan." Ages 10 & up.

DON'T MISS WATCHING (online)

A New Day in Old Sana'a
A movie set in Sana'a's old town, it's a great view of Yemeni society and Sana'a's historic architecture. Romantic, humourous, tragic and only 86 minutes.
YOUTUBE SEARCH: New Day Old Sana'a

Tour the Old Town of Sana'a
Discover Sana'a's ancient tower houses. There are many great video tours, including one by UNESCO, which has named Sana'a's Old Town a world heritage site.
YOUTUBE SEARCH: Sana'a, Sana'a tower house

Tour Shibam
Visit Shibam, the medieval mud Manhattan, and learn its history and building techniques. Could you build a highrise from mud? **YOUTUBE SEARCH:** Shibam

Jambiya Dancing
Men's dancing at weddings includes waving around their jambiya while dancing in circles and lines, a beautiful tradition. **YOUTUBE SEARCH:** jambiya dancing

LEARN to Write Numbers in Arabic!

١٠	٩	٨	٧	٦	٥	٤	٣	٢	١	٠
10	9	8	7	6	5	4	3	2	1	0

Although Arabic letters are written right to left, Arabic numbers are written in left to right order, same as in English.
So, 10 is written ١٠ not ٠١.

0. Sifr ٠ (written as a dot)

1. Waheed ١

2. Ithnaan ٢

3. Thalaatha ٣

4. Arba'a ٤

5. Khamsa ٥

6. Sitta ٦

7. Sab'a ٧

8. Thamaaniyah ٨

9. Tis'a ٩

10. 'Ashara ١٠

1. Can you write your age?
2. What about the year that you were born?
3. What about your phone number?
4. Yemen has more than ٢٥٠٠٠٠٠٠ people.
5. How many people live in your country?

MAKE YEMENI FUL

Popular for breakfast or supper (the two smaller meals of the day), ful is a warm soup/dip that is usually eaten with flatbread to scoop it up – so scrumptious! Fava beans are the key ingredient in ful, but if you can find any, substitute black beans or kidney beans.

½ onion, chopped small

2 cloves of garlic, crushed

3–4 tablespoon oil

1–2 tomatoes, diced
   or ½ can of diced tomatoes drained

½ teaspoon salt

½ teaspoon cumin

black pepper (to taste)

⅓ green chili, minced (optional)

1 can fava beans*

fresh parsley or cilantro (optional)

*substitute kidney beans or black beans
if fava beans are not available

Fava Beans

> **Starting from dried beans?**
> 1. Soak overnight with 1 tablespoon baking soda, or boil for 5 minutes and then soak with soda for 1 hour.
> 2. Drain and rinse beans, then bring to a boil in a pot of salted water.
> 3. Turn down to a strong simmer and allow to cook for 3–4 hours.
> 1 cup of dried beans makes enough for this recipe. Once your beans are cooked, start the recipe below.

1. In a skillet, sauté diced onion and garlic in 3–4 tablespoons oil until onion starts to brown on the edges.

2. Dice tomato while you wait for onion to brown.

3. Sauté tomato with onion until oil turns red, about 10 minutes, mashing tomato as it cooks. Add cumin, pepper, salt and (optional) green chili. Sauté two more minutes.

4. Drain and rinse fava beans. Then, smash them with a fork.

5. Puree beans, tomato-onion mixture and about 1 cup water in a blender.

6. Pour back into the skillet and simmer with a lid for 20 minutes, stirring occasionally. Remove lid and stir until it is a thick soup. Taste and add salt until perfectly savory.

7. Sprinkle cilantro or parsley on top and serve with pita bread to scoop it up. Yum!

Z is for Zimbabwe

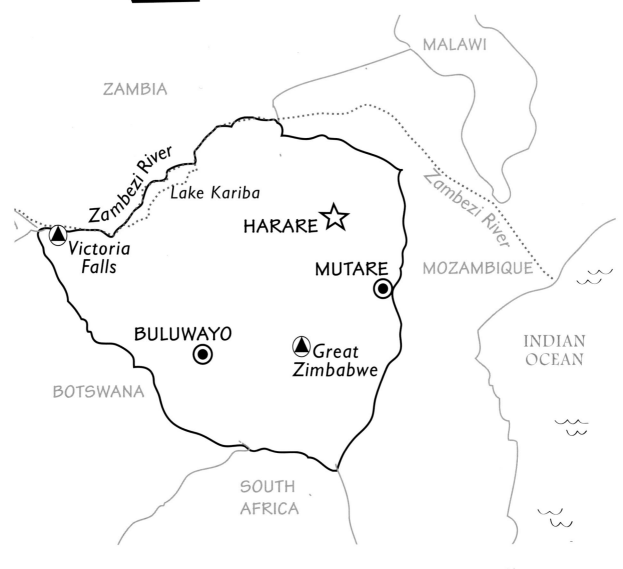

MALAWI

ZAMBIA

Zambezi River

Lake Kariba

HARARE ☆

Zambezi River

▲
Victoria Falls

MUTARE ◉

MOZAMBIQUE

BULUWAYO ◉

▲ *Great Zimbabwe*

INDIAN OCEAN

BOTSWANA

SOUTH AFRICA

Z is **ZIMBABWE**,

the great **"House of Stone,"**

Where ZEBRAS, giraffes

and elephants roam.

Mbira
(Thumb Piano)

Stone Sculpture

Sadza

Here you can hear

the **MBIRA's** soft sounds [em-BEER-rah]

Calling the ancestors

out of the ground.

Victoria Falls
"Mosi oa Tunya"

Here **VICTORIA FALLS**

from the river Zambezi, [zam-BEE-zee]

And across the plateau,

the weather is easy.

Here men find great **SCULPTURES**

hidden in stones,

Near fields where tobacco

and cotton are grown.

Cotton

But their food is from corn

served with sauce (just like pasta) —

For breakfast there's **bota**,

for dinner there's **SADZA.**

Once a colony British

called **Southern Rhodesia,**

This nation was founded

on historic AMNESIA

Bota

Cecil Rhodes
Rhodesia's Founder

Bird Sculpture from
Great Zimbabwe

Robert Mugabe,
Zimbabwe's First Prime
Minister

Brits believed civilization

arrived with the **WHITES**,

Who soon took the best land

and had all the rights.

Great Zimbabwe

They couldn't believe

GREAT ZIMBABWE had been

Constructed by locals —

by those with black skin.

This fortress in ruins

from medieval times

Had been city and home

to a culture refined.

Great Zimbabwe

White settlers built cities

and farms in this place,

And blacks became second class

due to their race.

But in **1980,**

democratic elections

allowed the majority

to make their selection.

Statue to
Unknown Soldiers

A new nation was born

and Zimbabwe was named

For a glorious past

when the ancestors reigned.

Now from bustling cities –

Bulawayo, **HARARE** – [bu-la-WAY-yo, ha-RAR-ree]

To villages tiny,

you'll meet dear **shamwari.** [sham-WAH-ree, *friends*]

Harare

They will say **"Makadee!"** [mah-kah-DEE]

while clapping their hands,

To mean "How are you?"

come enjoy our great land!

Clapping Hands in
Greeting

Makadee!
Salibonani!*

*__Makadee__ is a Shona greeting. __Salibonani!__ [sah-lee-boh-NAH-nee], means "Hello!" in Sindebele.

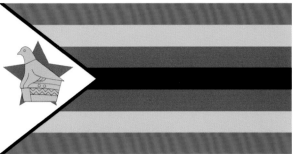

← **Zimbabwe's flag** was adopted in 1980 when the country gained internationally recognized independence and majority rule by black Zimbabweans. The bird pictured on the mast was part of the ruins found at Great Zimbabwe, an African kingdom that ruled here long before the arrival of Europeans in the 1880s. Beneath the bird is a star, which symbolizes the movement and struggle for independence. The white triangle represents peace. The green stripes represent Zimbabwe's abundant farm land, the yellow, its mineral wealth. The red stripes stand for the blood shed in their struggle for independence and the black stripe represents Zimbabwe's rule by its black majority.

ZIMBABWE got its name from **Great Zimbabwe**, the ruin of a medieval kingdom that was built with tall stone walls. Its discovery by archaeologists proved the existence of an advanced civilization here long before the arrival of white colonists. Zimbabwe means "house of stone" or "venerated houses" in Shona language.

Zimbabwe in Southern Africa

Official Name:
Republic of Zimbabwe

Population: 13.8 million

Capital: Harare

Largest Cities: Harare, Bulawayo, Chitungwiza (a suburb of Harare), Mutare

Comparative Size: Slightly larger than Montana, and a bit larger than Germany

Ethnicity: Shona 82%, Ndebele 14%, other African 2%, mixed and Asian 1%, white <1%

Language: English, Shona, Sindebele

Religion: Christian 87%, syncretic (Christian and traditional) 50%, traditional 4% none 8%,

Currency: Zimbabwean dollar

Important Industry: Mining

Top Export: Platinum

Where in the World is Zimbabwe?

GEOGRAPHICAL NOTES

◉ Though Zimbabwe is in the tropics, it sits on a high plateau, far above sea level. The high altitude makes the temperatures very moderate. In the capital, Harare, the temperature generally gets as low as the mid 40s°F (6°C) in June and as high as the mid 80s°F (29°C) in October. The rainy season is November –March, when there are heavy rain showers in the afternoons.

Zebra

← There are many national parks in Zimbabwe, and within the parks abundant wildlife roams, including zebras, giraffes, elephants, cheetahs, lions and hippos. Outside of parks, there are fewer wild animals, but elephants are known for sometimes getting into farms and eating the crops. →

Giraffe

Elephant

Hippopotamus

The **mbira** or thumb piano is a popular → instrument in Zimbabwean music, particularly that of the Shona people. The Shona use the mbira in ceremonies to call back the spirits of ancestors.

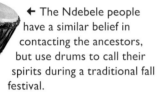

← The Ndebele people have a similar belief in contacting the ancestors, but use drums to call their spirits during a traditional fall festival.

Mbira

Cotton

← Zimbabwe has rich farmland and regularly exports tobacco, **cotton** and sugar. Commercial agriculture and mining are their two largest industries.

Sculptor with Her Work

← Zimbabwe is famous for its many **stone sculptors**, and their work is found in art museums around the world. Each sculptor has a unique style of carving, but a popular theme is semi-abstract depictions of human relationships. ↓

Sculpture

Victoria Falls

↑ **Victoria Falls** is locally known as *Mosi Oa Tunya,* or the "Smoke that Thunders," which describes the roaring sound and the cloud of mist it produces. It is the world's largest waterfall, as measured by the size of its curtain of water. The waterfall is over 5,000 ft (1524 m) across and 350 ft (107 m) tall. Victoria Falls is part of the Zambezi River and lies just on the border of Zimbabwe and Zambia.

Bota

Bota and Sadza are both made from *mealie meal,* the Zimbabwean term for corn meal.
← **Bota**, eaten for breakfast, is a type of corn porridge similar to American grits. It is usually seasoned with peanut butter, milk, butter or jam.

Sadza is thicker than bota, and it is eaten for → lunch and dinner along with sauces made from vegetables, meats or beans. It looks similar to mashed potatoes, but sadza is stiffer and can actually be picked up, rolled into a ball and then dipped into sauces. It is eaten using only the right hand.

Sadza

Southern Rhodesian stamps featuring Cecil Rhodes and the colonial ideal of "civilizing the natives" — see the figures under 1890 and 1940.

Great Zimbabwe Wall

↑ Prior to their independence, → Zimbabwe was known as **Southern Rhodesia**. Both it and Northern Rhodesia (present day Zambia) were named for the British empire-maker Cecil Rhodes. **Cecil Rhodes** was born in England but went on to make his fortune in the diamond business in South Africa. He founded De Beers, a company that still dominates the diamond mining industry. He helped to spread British mining rights north to present-day Zambia and Zimbabwe, eventually founding a colony there in 1890, which people called "Rhodesia" in his honor. Rhodes was a believer that British colonialism was a gift to the world. If the British Empire could spread round the world, it would bring "civilization" everywhere. This belief in the benevolence of British rule was widespread in Britain at that time.

Great Zimbabwe is a ruin of a city built from stone ↑ during the 11th to 14th centuries CE. It was the capital of the **Monomotapa Empire** and home to the king, his court and up to 18,000 others. Great Zimbabwe was a center for gold mining and international trade in its time. The walls surrounding it were as high as 36 ft (11 m) and were built using precisely cut granite blocks, stacked with no mortar. Covering over 7 sq km, it is the largest historical structure that has been found in Sub-Saharan Africa. When white colonists first saw the ruins of Great Zimbabwe, they developed many theories as to who could've built it: Arabs, Phoenicians, even the Queen of Sheba — anyone but the ancestors of the local population. The Rhodesian government even suppressed archaeological findings that suggest it was built by ancestors of the Shona. They wanted to maintain the myth that civilization only arrived with Europeans.
For the new nation, Great Zimbabwe became a symbol of black rule and indigenous civilization. ↓

Great Zimbabwe Bird

← Eight **bird** figurines were found on walls and atop totems at Great Zimbabwe. The bird, which is an African fishing eagle, may have been an emblem of the king and has now become another symbol of Zimbabwe, appearing on the flag and on coins.

Close-ups of the mortarless granite walls, which → still stand due to the precision of the stone cutting. ↓

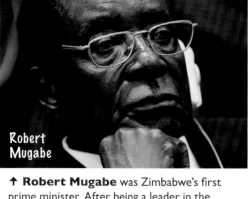

Robert Mugabe

↑ **Robert Mugabe** was Zimbabwe's first prime minister. After being a leader in the struggle for majority rule and becoming a national hero, he was elected in 1980. Ruling Zimbabwe for more that three decades, he has never been willing to leave office. Critics claim his unwillingness to let go of power has made the country a quasi-dictatorship. His reputed human rights abuses and oppression of opposition groups has damaged his reputation as a liberator of Zimbabwe. A new constitution has set term limits for all future presidents.

Harare is Zimbabwe's capital and largest city. It is home to the National Gallery of Zimbabwe, the University of Zimbabwe, the Zimbabwe Stock Exchange, the Harare International Airport and the National Sports Stadium. During the Rhodesian era, Harare was called Salisbury. ↓

Harare

Anglican Priest

← Eighty-seven percent of Zimbabweans are **Christian**, and the Anglican Church is the largest denomination in Zimbabwe. Though largely Christian, traditional healers called **N'angas** are still popular. N'angas use herbs, traditional medicines and spiritual advice to treat people. They also tell fortunes. N'angas may send people to regular doctors and hospitals for emergencies and complaints they can't cure. ↓

Clapping while greeting is a mark of respect among Shona people. They also clap before receiving a gift. Clapping is soft, slow and uses cupped hands. Men clap their palms parallel to one another, while women clap with palms crossed. Hand clapping is more frequently used in homes, rural areas and in traditional situations. Shaking hands is common everywhere and is the usual greeting among Ndebele people. →

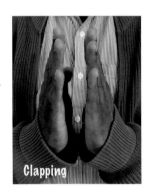
Clapping

N'angas have been important in Zimbabwe's history. N'angas were leaders in the first *Chimurenga* (independence movement) and advisors in beginning the second Chimurenga. N'angas communicate with the spirits of the ancestors and dispel bad spirits. Shona believe that the ancestors still reside at Great Zimbabwe and helped in the fight for independence. →

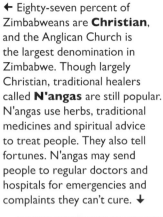
N'anga

Platinum

← Zimbabwe has the world's second-largest store of **platinum** (after South Africa). Mining is very important to the Zimbabwean economy, and the country is rich in mineral resources including platinum, gold, diamonds, copper, nickel, coal and tin.

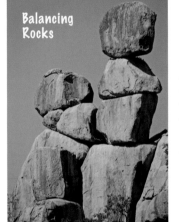
Balancing Rocks

← **Balancing rocks** can be seen in many areas of Zimbabwe. These stacks of enormous boulders appear as the softer rocks surrounding them erode over thousands of years – swept away by wind and water. This one, found in Matobo National Park, is called "Mother and Child." Balancing rocks have become a symbol of Zimbabwe and are even shown on their currency. ↓

The **Big Tree** → is a Baobab tree that is over 1,000 years old and is a tourist attraction located not too far from Victoria Falls. Baobab trees can live many thousands of years and grow in dry, tropical soils in Africa and Australia. They are exceptionally slow growing and drought resistant. *If this tree is over 1,000 year old, what year do you think it was planted?*

Big Tree

100 000 000 000 000 RESERVE BANK OF ZIMBABWE 100 000 000 000 000
I promise to pay the bearer on demand
ONE HUNDRED TRILLION DOLLARS
for the Reserve Bank of Zimbabwe
AA3905431
100 000 000 000 000 HARARE 2008
AA3905431

↑ Zimbabwe's currency, the Zim dollar, experienced skyrocketing **inflation** in the 2000s. It became worth so little that the government started to issue 100 trillion dollar bills. After their currency collapsed, they began using the US dollar, the Botswanan pula and South African rand instead.

Land Distribution Rhodesia 1965

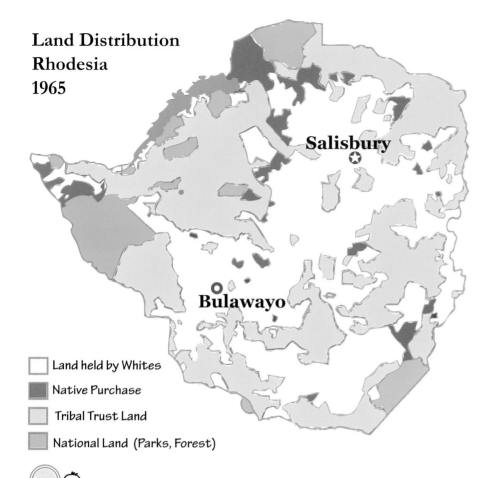

Salisbury

Bulawayo

- ☐ Land held by Whites
- ■ Native Purchase
- ☐ Tribal Trust Land
- ▨ National Land (Parks, Forest)

Who should own the land in Zimbabwe?

Reforming land distribution has been one of the most difficult issues facing Zimbabwe since its independence. Though whites never made up more than 5% of the population of Rhodesia, they held the majority of the most fertile farm lands in the central plateau. They were very successful at commercial farming techniques. Meanwhile, blacks farmed on small plots using traditional methods in the typically drier, less fertile soils available to them. While whites became wealthy through farming and mining in Southern Rhodesia, blacks were comparatively poor and reaped little benefit from the wealth of their nation's soil. Whites felt that as they brought the know-how to extract wealth from Rhodesia's soil and worked hard to do so, they had the full claim to that wealth. Blacks felt that whites had invaded their land and now exploited it to make themselves wealthy, while ruling over the much larger black population. Even independence and majority rule did not solve the land distribution problem. With whites still holding the most profitable parcels of land in Zimbabwe 20 years after independence, President Robert Mugabe started forcibly taking farms from white Zimbabweans in 2000 to give to blacks, particularly his supporters. This abrupt and sometimes violent "land reform" caused farm production to drop dramatically, which had a cataclysmic effect on Zimbabwe's economy – resulting in a severe food shortage and skyrocketing inflation. This created extreme hardship for the average Zimbabwean, causing many to flee the country to survive. In the long term, Zimbabwe hopes that most of its wealth will again be going to black Zimbabweans, who make up 98% of the population. Zimbabwe's economy, however, is still recovering from land reform.

Black Zimbabweans did not feel that they were fully free from Rhodesia's inequality when whites still owned much of Zimbabwe's wealth.

What is CHIMURENGA?

Chimurenga is a Shona word that means "struggle," and both of Zimbabwe's independence movements were called Chimurenga. The first unsuccessful Chimurenga was in 1896, soon after white settlers arrived in the region to found Rhodesia. The second Chimurenga was 1964–1979. Zimbabwe (then known as Southern Rhodesia) had a struggle for independence that was much more long, difficult and bloody than other African nations because white Rhodesians refused to give up their governing power. In 1960, the British Empire committed itself to a peaceful transition of power to local governance in all its colonies across the African continent. But they said that independence could only come after free and fair elections gave power to the black majority. The local white Rhodesians held political power and a disproportionate amount of the nation's land and did not want to give that up. Rather than give in to British demands for fair elections, Rhodesia declared its unilateral independence in 1965, claiming the British had no right to further meddle in Rhodesia's affairs. The Chimurenga armed struggle continued with two main rebel groups coming from the Shona and Ndebele engaging in guerilla warfare. Eventually white Rhodesians tried to give blacks a much greater role in government and to make the government more representative of them and responsive to their needs. But by this point, black Rhodesians wanted the full control of their government that majority rule would give. Eventually, violence and the armed struggle came to such a point that white Rhodesians effectively gave governing power back to Britain in 1979 for the British to hold elections and officially grant Rhodesia its independence. Robert Mugabe was the winner of those first elections, and the nation was then renamed Zimbabwe.

EXPERIENCE ZIMBABWE!

Listen to the SOUNDS of ZIMBABWE

Mbira Music

The mbira or thumb piano is played by plucking it with both thumbs. Frequently the mbira is played within a calabash half in order to amplify the sound.
YOUTUBE SEARCH: mbira

Thomas Mapfumo

Known as the "Lion of Zimbabwe," he and Oliver Mtukudzi are the most famous Zimbabwean musicians internationally. He is known in particular for his "Chimurenga" or "struggle" music, which conveys political protests. Prior to independence, he was one of the first popular musicians to write his lyrics in Shona, and his electric guitar playing mimicked the rhythms of the mbira. After becoming disappointed with Robert Mugabe's government, he put out an album called "Corruption." Try his songs, "Shumba," "Tombi Wachena," "Hanzvadi" and "Pidigori." **YOUTUBE SEARCH:** Mapfumo Shumba, Hanzdai, Tombi Wachena, Pidigori

Oliver Mtukudzi

A different sound from Mapfumo's, yet still distinctly Zimbabwean, his fans call it "tuku" music. Try "Neria," "Hear Me, Lord" and "Tozeza."
YOUTUBE SEARCH: Mtukudzi + song name

Other Song Recommendations:

"Chachimurenga" by **Stella Chiweshe**
"Hatisi Tose" by the **Bhundu Boys**
"Umoya Wami" by **Lovemore Majaivana**
"Banolila" by **Solomon Skuza**
"Train of Freedom" by **Ramadu**
"Chimoko" by **Alick Macheso**
"Handeyi Kumberi" by **Somandla Ndebele and Tongai Moyo** (two musical stars of Sungera, Zimbabwean pop)
"Idya Banana" by **Joseph Garakara**
"Chauta" by **Simon Chimbetu**
"Mawere Kongonya" by **Andy Brown**
"Urombo" by **Chiwoniso Maraire and Adam Chisvo**

Chiwoniso Maraire spent the first seven years of her life in the United States before her family moved back to Zimbabwe. She became a world-famous Zimbabwean musician and mbira player. ➜

READ:

Mufaro's Beautiful Daughters by John Steptoe. A beautiful imagining of Great Zimbabwe in this traditional folktale. Although the tale is actually from the Xhosa of South Africa, the setting and architecture are all from Great Zimbabwe. Ages 4 & up.

Where Are You Going Manyoni? by Catherine Stock. Follow Manyoni across gorgeous illustrations of the Zimbabwean countryside to her destination. Ages 5 & up.

Folk Tales from Zimbabwe: Short Stories by V. T. Kandimba. Four charmingly told stories, illustrated with photographs. Ages 6 & up.

Nelson Mandela's Favorite African Tales
Featuring two stories from Zimbabwe, the book also comes in an award-winning audiobook. Ages 6 & up.

The Girl Who Married a Lion And Other Folktales from Africa by Alexander McCall Smith. Filled with traditional tales collected from Botswana and Zimbabwe. Ages 12 & up.

Far from Home by Na'ima B. Roberts. Two girls, one white and one black, deal with their family's land being taken from them during two eras of Zimbabwean history. Their stories, woven together, give a striking portrait of Zimbabwe's complex history. Ages 13 & up.

DON'T MISS WATCHING (online)

Tour Great Zimbabwe Learn about the history of Great Zimbabwe, a medieval city that had the same population as medieval London. The BBC's "Lost Kingdoms of Africa" has an episode dedicated to Great Zimbabwe and there are other great documentaries about Great Zimbabwe. Check your local library and see clips online. **YOUTUBE SEARCH:** Great Zimbabwe, Great Zimbabwe Ancient City

See the Zambezi and the "Smoke that Thunders"
The BBC has another beautiful documentary on the Zambezi river and *Mosi oa Tunya* or the "Smoke that Thunders," also known as Victoria Falls.
YOUTUBE SEARCH: Victoria Falls smoke thunders

Matopo Hills Rock Art See paintings dating from the Stone Age in Zimbabwe's southern Matopo Hills.
YOUTUBE SEARCH: Matopo Hills Rock Art

Visit www.australiatozimbabwe.com for links to online activities.

MAKE ZIMBABWEAN
Muriwo Unedovi (Greens)

So very delicious, you will have a hard time believing it's leafy greens. Peanut butter, greens, tomatoes and onions make an unlikely but heavenly combination. In Zimbabwe, the greens they use for this recipe are similar to collard greens. This recipe uses spinach to make it a quicker and easier dish. If you'd like to use collard greens, see the substitution section below.

1. In a large skillet, sauté onion in oil until onion is translucent.
2. Add diced tomatoes, salt and chili and allow to simmer for about 5 minutes.
3. Add spinach to the pan, just enough to mostly fill the skillet. Stir, putting tomato-onion mixture on top of spinach to weigh it down. As the spinach wilts and shrinks, add more spinach to the pan, again pulling the tomatoes, onion and cooked spinach from the bottom and placing in on top. Continue until all the spinach is added but not fully cooked.
4. Add peanut butter to pan, and gently stir it in as it melts into the mixture.
5. Taste and add black pepper if you think it needs a bigger kick and more peanut butter if you would like for it to be creamier.
6. Serve as a side dish, or as a main dish with sadza or rice. It can also be an appetizer, served as a dip with crackers or pita chips.

1 medium yellow onion, chopped
1 tablespoon oil
4–6 tomatoes, diced and drained
   or 1 can of diced tomatoes drained
1 teaspoon salt
1 green chili, minced (optional)
1 bag washed spinach (12–14 oz.)
2 spoonfuls of peanut butter
¼ teaspoon black pepper (to taste)

Make with collard greens
Using well-washed collard greens, chop the greens, removing tough stems.
Put greens in a covered pot with one cup water and boil until they have softened but are not fully cooked.
Drain, reserving the remaining liquid, and then use greens in the above recipe. Cook with onions and tomatoes until done, using reserved liquid as needed for more moisture. Add peanut butter and taste test, just as in original recipe.

SPEAK SHONA!

Makadii	Hi! How are you?	mah-kah-DEE

(To be respectful, clap softly while saying this, hands in prayer position if you're male, palms crossed in an X for females.)

Ndiripo.	I'm fine.	ndee-REE-poh
Ndiripo, Makadiwo?	Fine, and you?	mah-kah-DEE-woh
Kanjan?	How's it going?	KAHN-jahn

(informal, to someone your age)

Mushe!	Fine.	MU-sheh
Masvita	Thank you	mas-VEE-tah

(formal, to an adult)

Ndatenda	Thanks	ndah-TAYN-dah

(informal)

Ehe	Yes	EH-heh
Aiw	No	EYE-W
Shamwari	Friend	sham-WAH-ree

LEARN SHONA PROVERBS!

Kupa Kuturika. To give is to save up.
Giving to others is an investment as they in turn will give to you.

Chinogova ruoko, muromo haugovi.
What gives is the hand, not the mouth.
Actions, not words, are what count.

Rambakuudzwa akaizoonekwa, nembonje pahuna.
Headstrong was found with a head wound.
Being too stubborn to listen to advice is likely to get you hurt.

Chada mwoyo hachikoni, mwoyo ndishe.
What the heart wants is not impossible, the heart is chief.

SPEAK NDEBELE!

Salibonani!	Hello!	sah-lee-boh-NAH-nee
Yebo.	(response to hello)	YEH-bo
Unjani?	How are you?	oon-JAH-nee
Ngiyaphila.	I'm fine.	nee-ya-PEE-lah
Yebo	Yes	YEH-bo
Hayi	No	HAH-yee
Ngiyabonga	Thank you	nee-ya-BON-gah

CARVE A SOAP SCULPTURE!

Carving in soap is a wonderful introduction to the type of sculpture made by Zimbabwean artists. There are even some Zimbabwean sculptures made from a very soft rock called "soapstone." This activity allows you to design a sculpture and make it take shape by removing the negative space around it. *Look at examples of Zimbabwean sculptures online before you start for inspiration.*

GATHERING TOOLS & MATERIALS:

SOAP: Ivory soap works well and can be bought in inexpensive multi packs. Almost any soap will work, but use a less scented one to avoid getting a headache – carving soap releases a lot of scent.

DULL KNIFE: A dull knife is the best tool, not just for safety reasons, but to avoid cutting too deeply into the soap. Ideally use a non-serrated knife that's sharp enough to cut cheese but not your fingers. A very dull paring knife works, or a butter knife or table knife. The knife isn't used to cut the soap, but shave off flakes of it.

TOOTHPICK: A toothpick can be used as a "detailer," to draw details on the sculpture. An unbent paper clip, nail, or any other small pointed instrument will also work.

MATERIALS: 1 bar soap
1 dull knife (butter/cheese knife)
1 toothpick

How to Carve a Soap Sculpture

1. Pick a shape.
Start with something basic for your first sculpture. Save difficult shapes and skinny legs for future designs.

2. Outline shape on your soap.
Use your knife or a toothpick to make a basic outline on one side of your soap. It doesn't have to be precise, but do make it as big as it can be, coming close to touching the soap edges. This fish is almost the length and width of a soap bar.

3. Gently shave off soap outside of your outlined shape.
Bit by bit, remove the soap outside of your shape in small shavings. As you get closer to the shape you outlined, your skill with your knife will improve.

4. Continue shaving to add contours and smooth.
After you get to a basic outline, continue to gently shave off edges to contour the shape to be as round or pointed, thick or thin as you like. Once you get your basic shape, continue very gently shaving off thin slivers to smooth the shape out.

5. Polish, then use your toothpick to add fine details.
Once you have a smoother surface, rub with your warm fingers to polish. Once smooth, draw in details with your finer point. You can also use other household tools to make shapes on the soap. A plastic pen top was used to make the round eye on this fish.

6. Make a stand for your sculpture. (Optional)
If your sculpture doesn't stand on its own, or if you simply want to add more details below, consider attaching it to a second bar of soap. This fish could have a half toothpick carefully inserted a few centimeters in its underside and then the other end gently eased into predrilled hole in a second bar below. The stand could be carved in advance to resemble a setting like water or waves.

Now look at that map

(the one in your brain)

and picture your world.

Does it look just the same?

I hope it is bigger,

more colorful too,

with new places to go

and things you must do!

For your journey's just started —

may the WORLD be your home,

and its people your family —

wherever you roam.

STATISTICAL SOURCES →

Country infobox information in this book comes from the CIA World Factbook. Religious statistics come from the Pew Research Center's "Global Religious Landscape." US infobox information comes from the US Census. Check **www.pewforum.org** and **www.cia.gov/library/publications/the_world_factbook** for the latest numbers.

RANKING COUNTRIES IN THIS BOOK

BY COUNTRY SIZE

1. Russia
2. China
3. Brazil
4. Australia
5. India
6. Kazakhstan
7. Mexico
8. Peru
9. Ethiopia
10. Nigeria
11. Turkey
12. France
13. Yemen
14. Spain
15. Zimbabwe
16. Japan
17. Vietnam
18. Oman
19. UK
20. Ghana
21. Denmark
22. Haiti
23. Qatar
24. Lebanon

BY POPULATION

1. China 1.35 billion
2. India 1.23 billion
3. Brazil 203
4. Nigeria 177 million
5. Russia 142 million
6. Japan 127 million
7. Mexico 120 million
8. Ethiopia 97 million
9. Vietnam 93 million
10. Turkey 82 million
11. France 66 million
12. UK 64 million
13. Spain 48 million
14. Peru 30 million
15. Yemen 26 million
16. Ghana 26 million
17. Australia 22.5 million
18. Kazakhstan 18 million
19. Zimbabwe 13.8 million
20. Haiti 10 million
21. Lebanon 5.8 million
22. Denmark 5.5 million
23. Oman 3.2 million
24. Qatar 2.1 million

COMPARATIVE DATA FOR THE UNITED STATES & CANADA

Official Name: United States of America

Population: 319 million, the world's 3rd largest country

Capital: Washington, DC

Largest Cities: New York, Los Angeles, Chicago

Comparative Size: About the same size as China, 3rd largest country in the world after Russia and Canada

Ethnicity: White 78%, black 13%, Asian 5%, Mixed 2.4% Amerindian 1% (Hispanic is not listed as an ethnic group in the US census. The US is 17% Hispanic.)

Language: English 79%, Spanish 13%

Religion: Christian 78.3%, Jewish 1.8%, Buddhist 1.2%, Muslim .9%, Hindu .6%, unaffiliated 16.4%

Currency: American Dollar

Official Name: Canada

Population: 35 million

Capital: Ottawa

Largest Cities: Toronto, Montreal, Vancouver

Comparative Size: Second largest country in the world after Russia

Ethnicity: Canadian 32%, English 20%, French 15.5%, Scottish 14.4 %, Irish 13.8%, German 10%, Chinese 4.5%, Italian 4.5%, Amerindian 4.2% (Canadians can select multiple ethnicities so the total is greater than 100%)

Language: English 59%, French 22%

Religion: Christian 69%, Muslim 2.1%, Hindu 1.4%, Jewish 1%, unaffiliated 23.7%

Currency: Canadian Dollar

LIST OF THEMATIC MAPS

Australia's Climates and States 10
Down Under Map of the World 17
Amazon Rainforest Map 22
China's Provinces & Regions 33
Nordic Countries (Denmark) 46
Greenland 49
Ethnic Regional States in Ethiopia 57
Ethiopia in Africa 59
French Empire in 1946 72
France, Administrative Regions 76
West Africa (Ghana) 84
Haiti & Its Caribbean Neighbors 99
Hispaniola 100
India, States of 112
India Language Map 113
Indus Valley Civilization 118
Japan's Four Main Islands 128
Ring of Fire 129
International Dateline 129
Central Asia (Kazakhstan) 144
Levant, The (Lebanon) 158
Phoenician Empire 159
Crusader Kingdoms 163
Mexico's States 172
Mexico's Climates 173
Mexico-Tenochtitlan 175
Mexican Cession of 1848 178

Nigerian States 188
Nigeria, Ethnolinguistic Regions 189
Niger River 189
Niger Delta 193
Omani Empire 201
Strait of Hormuz 205
Peru's Climates and Vegetation 215
Inca Empire (Tawantinsuyu) 216
Inca Empire Road Map 216
Humboldt Current 217
Persian Gulf States (Qatar) 229
Qatar's North Field 230
Russian Time Zones 240
Soviet Union Map 244
Spain's Autonomous Communities 252
Spain's Languages 255
Spanish Empire in the Americas 256
Spain Before 1492 256
Ottoman Empire 266
Nations of the United Kingdom 278
Southeast Asia (Vietnam) 288
Yemeni Rainfall Map 303
Bab el Mandeb 307
Southern Africa (Zimbabwe) 315
Land Distribution in Rhodesia 319

ACTIVITIES LISTED BY TYPE

RECIPES
Anzac Biscuits 14
Pineapple Mint Suco 26
Chinese Dumplings 41
Danish Apple Cake 51
Niter Kibbeh 66
Atakilt Wat 66
Quiche 78
Groundnut Soup 90
Pain Patate 105
Mango Lassi 122
Okonomiyaki 135
Baurasaki 151
Kazakh Chai 151
Tabouli 165
Hummus 165
Guacamole 180
Akara (Black-eyed Pea Fritters) 195
Swayweih 206
Ceviche 223
Chicken Machboos 235
Blini 246
Gazpacho 259
Nonalchoholic Sangria 259
Tortilla de Patatas 260
Kofte (Turkish Meatballs) 272
Shepherd Salad 272
Yorkshire Pudding 283
Banh Xeo 295
Ful 310
Muriwo Unedovi (Greens) 321

PLAY
Have Your Own Carnival Parade 27
Chopstick Challenge C11
Laenkfange (Capturing Chains) 50
Escargot 77
Ampe 89
Have a Haitian Storytelling Party 104
Kabaddi 122
Baiga (Horse Race) 150
Jebeshkek Bukender (Sticky Tree Stumps) 150
Eger (If) 150
Tasimaldu (Crossing Over) 150

SPEAK
Strine 14
Brazilian Portuguese 26
Mandarin Chinese 37
Danish 49
Amharic 63
French 76
Haitian Kreyól 104
Japanese 136
Kazakh 151
"Lebanese" 164
Spanish 180
Nigerian Pidgin English 194
Quechua 223
Gulf Arabic 234
Russian 246
Like a Spaniard 258
Turkish 271
British English 282
Vietnamese 294

Shona 321
Ndebele 321

INVESTIGATE
How to Avoid Being Eaten by a Saltwater Crocodile 16
Differences Between Australia and New Zealand 16
Down Under Map of the World 17
Animals of the Amazon 26
Life of Pelé 26
All About Chinese Writing 40
Vikings 50
Norse Gods & Goddesses 50
What Might Your Name be in Ghana? 92
Hinduism 123
Find A Favorite Lebanese Proverb 164
Aztec Food Safari 179
What Would Your Name be in Qatar? 234
What was the Soviet Union 244
History of Turkey Through Men's Hats 273
Map Your Favorite British Characters 283
Vietnam War 293
Who Should Own the Land in Zimbabwe? 319
What is Chimurenga? 319

CREATE
Boomerang 15
Dot Painting 16
Make a Ganza and Play Samba 27
Danish Paper Heart Baskets 51
Ethiopian Angel 64
Adinkra Stamps 91
Sequined Art Flag 105
Kolam and Rangoli 121
Art about the Four Seasons 136
Origami Waterbomb 137
Papel Picado 181
Turkish Evil Eye 273
British Literary Map 283
Soap Sculpture 322

LEARN HOW TO
Count to 10 on One Hand 39
Write 1-10 in Chinese 39
Write Love in Amharic 64
Write Salaam in Arabic 207
Read and Write in Cyrillic 247
Write Numbers in Arabic Y13

LISTEN TO
Didgeridoo 14
(& Sing) "Waltzing Matilda" 14
Samba & Bossa Nova 26
(& Sing) Girl from Ipanema 26
Gu Zheng, Pipa, Erhu or Dizi 38
"Mo Li Hua" 38
(& Sing) "I Love You, China" 38
"There Is a Lovely Land" 50
Krar Music 63
Teddy Afro 63
Edith Piaf 77
Ravel, Satie, Debussy 77
Le Marsellaise 77
Paris Combo & MC Solaar 77

Hiplife 89
Ghanaian Highlife 89
Talking Drums 89
Compas Music 104
"Jana Gana Mana" 115
"Mile Sur Mera Tumhara" 115
Saragi & Sitar 115
Tambur & Carnatic Music 115
Filmi (Bollywood Film Music) 115
Shamisen 134
"Kimigayo" 134
Jpop 134
Dombra 150
(& Sing) "Cielito Lindo" 179
Marcha de Zacatecas 179
Mariachi 179
Norteño Music 179
Banda Music 179
Nigerian Highlife 194
Juju 194
Afropop 194
Nigerian Hip Hop 194
Omani Khaliji Music 206
Al Bar'ah 206
"Mahbooba TV Oman" 206
"El Condor Pasa" 222
Zampoña 222
Charango 222
Cajón 222
Landó 222
Huayno 222
Khaliji Music 234
Balalaika 245
"Kalinka" & "Korobushka" 245
Peter and the Wolf 245
1812 Overture 245
Spanish Guitar 258
Flamenco 258
Manuel De Falla's "Spanish Dance" 258
Kanun & Kemençe 271
Tarkan 271
Call to Prayer from Blue Mosque 271
Classical Turkish Music & Pop 271
"Istanbul not Constantinople" 271
Bagpipes 282
Handel's "Water Music" 282
British Invasion 282
"God Save the Queen" 282
Gong Music 204
Nha Nhac 294
Vpop 294
Ayoob Tarish Absi 309
Abu Bakr Saem Balfaqih 309
Arwa 309
Yemeni Zaffa Music 309
Yemeni Rap 309
Mbira Music 320
Thomas Mapfumo 320
Oliver Mtukudzi 320

Due to their number, **READ** (148) and **WATCH** (103) activities are not listed.

COVER & INTRODUCTION

 ← All the "little man" drawings in this book (front & back cover, title page, introduction, activity pages & conclusion) are by **NLshop**/Shutterstock.com.
World with Headphones: 3DDock/SS; **Flag Globe with Chef's Hat**: Lightspring/SS; **Eye with Hands**: abdulsatarid/SS; **Colored Pencil Circle**: Ihnatovich Maryia/SS; **Globe on top of Books**: Dawn Hudson/SS;

BLACK AND WHITE COUNTRY MAPS

The simple country maps beginning each chapter were created from outline maps provided by **www.worldatlas.com**.

AUSTRALIA Dingo: Nicholas Lee/SS; **Kangaroo**: Smileus/SS; **Playing a Didgeridoo**: francosperoni/Fotolia; **Kookaburra Isolated**: joyfuldesigns/SS; **Saltwater Crocodile**: tratong/SS; **Great Barrier Reef**: Debra James/SS; **No Worries**: David Neubert of Berkshire County & NYC/Wiki, CC-BY-SA-2.0; **Captain James Cook**: Nathaniel Dance-Holland, UK National Maritime Museum, Wiki-PD; **Convict Chains**: Oleksii Iezhov/SS; **Gold**: Julia Reschke/SS; **Sheep**: Eric Isselee/SS; **Sydney Opera House**: Chester Tugwell/SS; **Outback**: Ralph Loesche/SS; **Surfing**: ohrim/SS; **Father Christmas on Manly Beach**: National Archives of Australia A1500, K26950; **Vegemite Toast**: Robyn Mackenzie/SS; **Emu**: pandapaw/SS; **Wombat**: Robyn Butler/SS; **Fly**: Le Do/SS; **Koala Isolated**: Eric Isselee/SS; **Australia Climate Map**: made from a map by Martyman/Wiki, CC BY-SA 3.0; **Aboriginal Dancer**: John Austin/SS; **Koala Climbing**: covenant/SS; **David Wirrpanda**: Jimmy Harris/Flickr & Wiki, CC-BY-2.0; **Didgeridoo Isolated**: ermess/SS; **Platypus**: worldswildlifewonders/SS; **Blue-Winged Kookaburra**: Michal Ninger/SS; **Boomerang**: gualtiero boffi/SS; **Clownfish & Surgeonfish**: Kletr/SS; **Australian with Asian Ancestry**: Barnaby Chambers/SS; **Uluru**: Stanislav Fosenbauer/SS; **Barron Falls**: Johan Larson/SS; **Great Dividing Range**: skyearth/SS; **Swimmers**: paintings/SS; **Snags on the Barbie**: val lawless/SS; **Shrimp on the Grill**: Stephen Coburn/SS; **Footy Kicking Ball**: Neale Cousland/SS; **Vegemite Jar**: CTR Photos/SS; **Cork Hat**: Leah-Anne Thompson/SS; **Flies on a Man's Hat**: Julian Loader/ www.bugbog.com; **Gold Coast**: Brisbane/SS; **Australian Flag Speech Bubble**: Andrei Marincas/SS; **Anzac Biscuits**: Shane White/SS; **Crocodile Warning**: Tourism NT, www.travelnt.com; **Footy Catching Ball**: Neale Cousland/SS; **Dot Painting**: Jkerrigan/DT; **Down Under Map of the World**: Made from "World Location Map (W3 Pacific)," by TUBS/Wiki, CC-BY-SA-3.0; **"Hereford Mappa Mundi" World Map from 1300**: PD-Wiki;

BRAZIL Isolated Samba Dancer: Guryanov Andrey/SS; **Toucan**: Fedor Selivanov/SS; **Sucos**: Leonid and Anna Dedukh/SS; **Isolated Sugarcane**: Swapan Photography/SS; **Guava**: irabel8/SS; **Papaya**: Viktar Malyshchyts/SS; **Brazilian Flag Soccerball**: ER_09/SS; **Amazon River**: Johnny Lye/SS; **Pink River Dolphin**: guentermanaus/SS; **Jaguar**: Ana Vasileva/SS; **Poison Dart Frog**: Eric Isselee/SS; **Mosquito**: Henrik Larsson/SS; **Anaconda**: cellistka/SS; **Feijoada Isolated**: diogoppr/SS; **Sao Paolo**: jbor/SS; **Capoeira Isolated**: ostill/SS; **Iguazu Falls**: DnDavis/SS; **Cafezinho Isolated**: Faraways/SS; **Amazon Rainforest Map**: NASA and Pfly/Wiki, PD; **Dilma Roussef**: Agencia Brasil/ Roberto Stuckert Filho, CC-BY-3.0-BR, Wiki; **Ronaldinho**: Reto Stauffer www.hopp-schwiiz.com/Wiki, CC-BY-SA-2.0; **Giselle**: Phil Stafford/SS; **Yellow Samba Dancer**: Val Thoermer/SS; **Xuxa**: Sergio (Savaman) Savarese/Wiki, CC-BY-2.0; **Pele Color**:

cinemafestival/SS; **Pele B&W**: Wiki-PD, AFP/SCANPIX; **Indigenous Brazilian**: "Amazonian Shaman" by Veton PICQ/Wiki, CC-BY-SA-3.0; **Blue Samba Dancer**: David Davis/SS; **Mango**: Viktar Malyshchyts/SS; **Sugarcane field**: margouillat photo/SS; **Futeboll Player Ricardo Oliveira**: Maxisport/SS; **Spider Monkey**: worldswildlifewonders/SS; **Vampire Bat**: kentoh/SS; **Piranha**: Razvani/DT; **Feijoada and Rice**: Alexander Bark/SS; **Rio de Janeiro**: Marc Turcan/SS; **Ipanema Beach**: Luiz Rocha/SS; **Capoeira Dancer on the Street**: Val Thoermer/SS; **Salvador da Bahia Street**: Jose Miguel Hernandez Leon/SS; **Cafezinho with Coffee Beans**: Zhukov Oleg/SS; **Bahian Woman**: Vinicius Tupinamba/SS; **Salvador da Bahia Coast**: ostill/SS; **Sucos**: Leonid and Anna Dedukh/SS; **Blue Morpho Butterfly**: ethylalkohol/SS; **Carnival Men**: David Davis/SS; **President Bush Playing a Ganza**: Agencia Brasil/Marcelo Casal Jr., CC-BY-3.0-BR, Wiki; **Hand Playing Ganza**: Skylines/SS;

CHINA Pipa: Denys Kurylow/SS; **Papercut Red Dragon**: polar/SS; **Peking Duck**: zcw/SS; **Duck Wrapped with Sides**: totophotos/SS; **Forbidden City**: Lukas Hlavac/SS; **Qing Emperor**: Emperor Xinfeng, Wiki-PD; **Dragon Kite**: Tjetjep Rustandi/Flickr; **Great Wall of China**: omers/SS; **Terracotta Warrior Isolated**: Tom Kuest - Fotograf/SS; **Panda Isolated**: Eric Isselee /SS; **Crowded Chinese City**: TonyV3112/SS; **Rice Farming**: pick/SS; **Himalayas**: Meiqianbao/SS; **Camel in the Gobi Desert**: 06photo/SS; **Yellow River Water**: "Hukou Waterfall," by Leruswing/Wiki, CC-BY-SA-3.0; **Fireworks**: adisornfoto/SS; **Rabbit in the Moon**: Wiki Users: Zemusu & Sailko, CC-BY-SA-3.0; **Chairman Mao**: Hung Chung Chih/SS; **Kung Fu Fighters**: testing/SS; **Kung Fu Stamp**: Oxlock/SS; **Shaolin Kung Fu**: by Kevin Poh/Wiki & Flickr, CC-BY-2.0; **Canton Rice**: Massimiliano Gallo/SS; **Pasta**: Jiri Hera/SS; **Dumplings**: ivylingpy/SS; **Peking Duck on a Pancake** & **In a Hand to Eat**: Joyosity/Wiki & Flickr, CC-BY-2.0; **Tiananmen Square**: gary718/SS; **Terracotta Warriors**: lapas77/SS; **Boy Walking on the Great Wall**: Hung Chung Chih/SS; **Qin Shi Huang**: PD-Wiki; **Hong Kong**: leungchopan/SS; **Bird's-eye View of Shanghai**: ssguy/SS; **Guangzhou**: ssguy/SS; **Yangtze River**: Stephen Rudolph/SS; **Yellow River Landscape**: Xidong Luo/SS; **Tibetan Plateau**: junjun/SS; **Porcelain Vase**: chungking/SS; **Chinese Tea**: Sandra Caldwell/SS; **Red Silk**: Erena.Wilson/SS; **Chinese Dragon on Porcelain**: Cyril Hou/SS; **Panda Eating Bamboo**: ex0rzist/SS; **Yuan**: bendao/SS; **Toilet Paper**: lukethelake/SS; **Guzheng**: Denys Kurylow/SS; **Pipa**: Denys Kurylow/SS; **Erhu**: Chinaview/SS; **Dizi**: Mau Horng/SS; **Hand with Chopsticks**: Volodymyr Krasyuk/SS; **Chinese Opera Singer**: DK.samco/SS;

DENMARK Viking Longship: photo25th/SS; **North Sea**: AR Pictures/SS; **Little Mermaid**: Andrei Nekrassov/SS; **Legos**: PerseoMedusa/SS; **Wind Turbine**: Jezper/ SS; **Bike Lane**: KN/SS; **Woodcut Thor Illustration**: Jef Thompson/SS; **Plate of Pickled Herring**: MaraZe/SS; **Egg Chair**: by Scott Anderson of Jakarta, Indonesia, CC-BY-SA-2.0, Wiki; **Viking Isolated**: Microprisma/SS; **Isolated Herring**: ra3rn/SS; **Map of Nordic Countries**: Modified from "Map of Scandinavia" by 000peter/Wiki, CC-BY-SA-3.0; **Oresund Bridge**: Bildagentur Zoonar GmbH/SS; **Climate Change Protesters**: Piotr Wawrzyniuk/SS; **Queen Margrethe**: Used by permission of the Danish Royal Family and photographer Steen Evald; **Hans Christian Andersen**: Christian Albrech Jensen, 1836, Wiki-PD; **Wind Turbine in Yellow Field**: Martin Bech/SS; **Copenhagen**: Yarygin/SS; **Woman Bicycling**: Jens Rost of Taastrup, Denmark CC-BY-2.0, Flickr "Comrade Foot"; **Windmills on the Sea**: TebNad/SS; **Danish Plains**: Dhoxax/SS; **Bike Green Light**: Claudio Divizia/SS; **Thor**: Marten Eskil Winge, 1872, Wiki-PD; **Hyggelig Brothers**: KellyBoreson/SS; **Boy Eating Herring**: Marcel Mooij/SS; **Hyggelig Christmas**: "Happy Christmas" by Viggo Johansen, 1891, Wiki-PD; **Danish Flatware** "Vintage George Jensen Stainless Flatware" used by permission of Kimberly Rhodes Roberts; **Ant Chair**: Iglazier618/ Wiki & Flickr, CC-BY-2.0; **Danish Chair Stamp**: IgorGolovniov/SS; **Danish Design Living Room**: Bertrand Benoit/SS; **Danish Architecture**: "Projecting Balconies" by Rob Deutscher/Flickr, CC-BY-2.0; **Smorrebrod**: Luigi Anzivino/Flickr; **Hamlet**: Gian Salero/SS; **Faroe Islands**: Spumador/SS; **Greenlandic Houses**: PavelSvoboda/SS; **Greenland Map**: AridOcean/SS; **Greenlandic Girls**: Visit Greenland/Flickr, CC-BY-2.0; **Man with Danish Flag Face Paint**: Monkey Business Images/SS; **Trees by the Sea**: KN/SS; **Viking**: Vasiliy Koval/SS; **Freya**: patrimonio designs ltd/SS; **Mute Swan**: pandapaw/SS; **Christmas Heart Ornament**: PD-Wiki, Jens Gydenkaerne Clausen;

ETHIOPIA Lucy's Bones: 120/French Wiki, CC-BY-2.5; **Axum's Stele**: trevor kittelty/SS; **Queen of Sheba**: Alan D. Coogan (A. Davey on

Flickr) CC-BY-2.0; **Orthodox Priest**: Clive Chilvers/SS; **Map of Ethiopia in Africa**: made from map by charobnica/SS; **Espresso**: Adrian Baras/SS; **Injera**: Sekitar, www.flickr.com/sekitar; **No Pork**: Lena Pan/SS; Blue Nile Falls: Pascal RATEAU/SS; CC-BY-SA-3.0; **Castle in Gonder**: JM Travel Photography/SS; **Gelada**: Rod Waddington from Kergunyah, Australia/Wiki, CC-BY-SA-2.0; **Carved Rock Chuch in Lalibela**: trevor kittelty/SS; **Lion of Judah**: Tribalium/SS; **Map of Ethiopia's Regions**: Made from a map by Golbez/Wiki, CC-BY-2.5; **Lucy's Face**: Cosmo Caixa in Barcelona, photo by 120/Frenech Wiki, CC-BY-SA-3.0; **Church**: Rod Waddington from Kergunyah, Australia/Flickr, CC-BY-SA-2.0; CC-BY-SA-2.0; **Mural of Mary and Jesus**: Miko Stavrev/Wiki, CC-BY-3.0; **Stele in Axum** (full View): Ondřej Žváček/Wiki, CC-BY-SA-3.0; **Crown**: trevor kittelty/SS; **Girls in front of a Mosque**: Jackmalipan/DT; **Mosque in Harar**: milosk50/SS; **Haile Selassie**:Wiki-PD; **Coffee Ceremony**: Elena Luria/DT; **Teff**: Rasbak/Wiki, CC-BY-SA-3.0; **Roasting Coffee**: Jenny Morgan; **Eating injera**: Richard from Kansas City/Wiki, CC-BY-2.0; **Girl in Dress with Blue Flowers**: Hector Conesa/SS; **Hamer Girl with Headband**: Hector Conesa/SS; **Girls in White Shawls**: Tomi Tenetz/DT; **Schoolgirls in Harar**: Vlad Karavaev/SS; **Ethiopian Man**: Hector Conesa/SS; **Highland Boy**: Jason Lewis/Expedition 360; **Priest Rowing**: Landroving Linguist/Wiki, CC-BY-SA-3.0; **Ethiopian Students Walking**: Adam Jones Ph.D./Global Photo Archive/Flickr, CC-BY-SA-2.0; **Boy in Papyrus Reed Boat**: Arthur Sacramento of Gibraltar/Flickr; **Blue Nile Falls**: Peter Jeschofnig/Wiki, **Semien Mountains**: Anton_Ivanov/SS; **Inside Lalibela Church**: trevor kittelty/SS; **St George Slaying the Dragon**: Alan D. Coogan (A. Davey)/Flickr, CC-BY-2.0; **Little Girl with Big Eyes**: naomii.tumblr.com/Flickr, CC-BY-ND-2.0; **Angels on the Ceiling of a Church in Bahir Dar**: JM Travel Photography/SS; **Church of St. George** (aerial view): Hector Conesa/SS; **St. George Church** (side view): Justin Clements (Giustino)/Flickr, CC-BY 2.0; **Lion**: Vishnevskiy Vasily/SS; **Ethiopian Coin with Lion**: Dereje/SS; **Addis Ababa**: PD-Wiki, Nani Senay; **Bekele**: Thomas Faivre Duboz of Paris, France/Wiki, CC-BY-SA-2.0; **Haile Gebreselassie**: Alexxx86/Wiki, CC-BY-SA-3.0; **Traditional Round Adobe House**: JM Travel Photography/SS; **Rural Village**: Galyna Andrushko/SS; **Highlands**: Alan D. Coogan (A. Davey)/Flickr, CC-BY-2.0; **Savannah**: Galyna Andrushko/SS; **Farmer Plowing**: milosk50/SS; **Lake Tana Pelicans**:Justin Clements(Giustino)/Flickr, CC-BY 2.0; **Afar Desert**: agrosse/SS; **Playing the Krar** Rod Waddington of Kergunyah, Australia/Wiki, CC-BY-SA-2.0; **Amharic Coca-Cola Bottle**: Justin Clements from Milan, Italy/Wiki, CC-BY-2.0; **Angels on the Ceiling of a Church in Bahir Dar**: JM Travel Photography/SS; **St. Michael Archangel**: Alan D. Coogan, "A. Davey"/Flickr, CC-BY-2.0;

FRANCE **The Alps**:Vaclav Volrab/SS; **French Riviera**: Vinicius Tupinamba/SS; **Louvre Museum Entrance**: Mihai-Bogdan Lazar/SS; **Monet's Waterlilies**: PD-Wiki, Neue Pinakothek, Munich, Germany; **Rodin's Thinker**: Rob Wilson/SS; **Notre Dame**: WDG Photo/SS; **Seine River**: alysta/SS; **Eiffel Tower Isolated**: viewgene/SS; **Eclaire**: Darryl Brooks/SS; **Louis XIV**:Wiki-PD, Charles Le Brun; **Guillotine**:James Steidl/SS; **Head**(tete): Viktoriya/SS; **Napoleon**: PD-Wiki, Jaque-Louis David; **Champagne**: nexus 7/SS; **Cheese Plate**: Yeko Photo Studio/SS; **Paris FashionWeek**: Simon Ackerman/Wiki, CC-BY-SA-3.0, **Renoir's Two Sisters On the Terrace**: Wiki-PD, Pierre-Auguste Renoir, 1881, Art Institute Chicago; **Mona Lisa**: Wiki-PD, Leonardo Da Vinci ca. 1519, Musee du Louvre; **Arc de Triomphe**: Ferenc Cegledi/SS; **Eiffel Tower**: Domen Colja/SS; **Boulangerie**:KN/SS; **Pain au Chocolat**: Madeleine Openshaw/SS; **Quiche**: noonday/SS; **Baguette**: bonchan/SS; **Gardens of Versaille**: Lyubov Timofeyeva/SS; **Versaille**: onairda/SS; **Hall of Mirrors**: Jose Ignacio Soto/SS; **Marie Antoinette**: PD-Wiki, Marten Van Meytens, ca. 1767; **Liberty Leading the People**: PD-Wiki, Eugene Delacroix; **French Cheeses**: Ev Thomas/SS; **French Strike**: Olga Besnard/SS ; **French Protester**: jbor/SS; **Wine and Cheese**: Alexander Chaikin/SS; **Map of French Regions**: Made from "French Location Map- Regions" by Eric Gaba (Sting)/Wiki, CC-BY-SA-3.0; **Lavender**: Andreas G. Karelias/SS; **Escargot**: marco mayer/SS; **Mont St. Michel**: Igor Plotnikov/SS; **Coast of Normandy**: Laurent Renault/SS

GHANA **Cocoa Beans**: tristan tan/SS; **Kente Cloth**: Dianearbis/SS; **Anansi Spider**: Dave from Guilford, England/Flickr, CC-BY-2.0; **Gold Coast Stamp**: IgorGolovniov/SS; **Independence Arch**: Felix Lipov/SS; **Martin Luther King**: Wiki-PD, Library of Congress, Dick DeMarisco for NY World Telegram, 1964; **Ghanaian Beach**: Sarah Shreeves/Flickr, CC-BY-2.0; **LionCoffin**: Emilio Labrador/Flickr, CC-BY-2.0; **Rolls of Kente**: Bottracker/Wiki, CC-BY-SA-3.0; **Jollof Rice**: Sharon McKellar/Flickr, CC-BY-ND; **Cedi Coin**: polosatik/SS; **Cocoa Farmer**: David Snyder/

DT; **Cocoa, Chocolate and Nibs**: Alena Brozova/SS; **Asantehene**: Walter Callens (Retlaw Snellac)/Wiki, CC-BY-2.0; **Royalty Wearing Kente**: David Snyder/DT; **Elmina Castle**: trevor kittelty/SS; **Weaving Kente**: Lisamildes/DT; **Door of No Return**: ZSM/Wiki, CC-BY-SA-3.0; **Soul Washer's Badge**: Claire H. from NYC/Flickr & Wiki, CC-BY-SA-2.0; **Schoolgirls in Yellow**: Sura Nualpradid/SS; **President Nkrumah with JFK**: Wiki-PD, by National Park employee Abbie Rowe, 1961, JFK Library; **Kwame Nkrumah**: USSR stamp, Wiki-PD; **Fantasy Coffins**: Askme9/DT; **Woman in Blue & White**: Lucian Coman/SS; **Woman in Green & Kente**: Lucian Coman/SS; **Stamping Adinkra**: Ronnie Pitman/Flickr, CC-BY-NC, (used with permission); **Tailor**: Shack Dwellers International [sdinet.org]/Flickr, CC-BY-2.0; **Adinkra Symbols**: John T Takai/SS; **Paying with Cedis**: trevor kittelty/SS; **Running to School**: Kate Fisher/Flickr, CC-BY-2.0; **Boy on Bike**: Jason Elliot Finch/Flickr, CC-BY-NC-ND-2.0; **Performer with Face Paint**: One Village Initiative/Flickr, CC-BY-SA-2.0; **Lake Volta Boat from Above**: Hugues (www.flickr.com/people/chugues) CC-BY-SA-2.0; **Lake Volta Fishing Boat**: Nora Morgan/Flickr, CC-BY-2.0; **Girls Carrying Loads of Firewood**: Stig Nygaard [www.rockland.dk]/ Flickr, CC-BY-2.0; **Boy Carrying Tray on his Head**: Anton Ivanov/SS; **Girl Holding Red Basket with Cushion on Head**: Anton Ivanov/SS; **Girl Carrying Mangoes**: Sura Nualpradid/SS; **Woman Carrying Baby in Profile**: David Bacon/Flickr, CC-BY-2.0; **Women Carrying Loads on Head and a Baby**: Anton Ivanov/SS;

HAITI **Columbus**: Unknown artist, Wiki-PD; **Taino Chief/Queen Anacaona**: Wik-PD; **Hammock**: Ersler Dmitry/SS; **Small Pox**: PD-Wiki, original by Edward Jenner (1749-1823); **Cotton**: natu/SS; **Sugarcane**: Swapan Photography/SS; **Coffee**: MIGUEL GARCIA SAAVEDRA/SS; **Slave Rebellion Icon**: SuslO/SS; **Cap Haitian Cathedral**: Rémi Kaupp/Wiki, CC-BY-SA-2.5; **Bassin Bleu**: Troy Livesay/ Flickr, CC-BY-SA-NC, **Citadelle La Ferriere**: PD-Wiki, US Army SBC, Gibran Torres; **Tap Tap Satisfaction**: Alex E. Proimos (flickr.com/proimos), CC-BY-NC; **Gourde**: Hayko/Wiki, CC-BY-SA-4.0; **Ti Maliss**: Jonathan & Amy Seponara-Sills (www.weareneverfull.com); **Pain Patat**: Teanna DiMicco, (www.sporkorfoon.com); **Black Pearl**: vector photo video/SS; **Sea Angel Sculpture**: SERVV, Comite Artisanal Haitien; **Haiti's Hills**: by Michelle Walz/ Flickr, CC-BY-2.0; **Canoe**: John Lindsay-Smith/SS; **Dominican Girls Dressed as Tainos**: hotelviewarea.com/Wiki, CC-BY-SA-2.0; **Girl Student**: Michael Swan/ Flickr, CC-BY-ND-2.0; **Caribbean Blue Water**: Kosarev Alexander/SS; **Indigo**: Ti Santi/SS; **Marron Inconnu**: Greg Moquin (Boston Gringo)/Flickr; **Palace San Souci**: Rémi Kaupp, CC-BY-SA-2.5; **Dessaline**: Wiki-PD; **Henri Christophe**: Wiki-PD, by Richard Evans, 1816; **President Pétion**: Wiki-PD, from Bibliothèque nationale de France; **Drapo Flag**: Sam Fentress/Wiki, CC-BY-SA-2.0, (Flag by Valris); **Tap Tap Back**: Cristian Borquez/Flickr, CC-BY-SA-2.0; **Pork Griyot**: Brian Kong; **Haitian Smile**: Alex E. Proimos (flickr.com/proimos), CC-BY-NC (used by permission); **After the Earthquake**: Michelle Walz/Flickr, CC-BY-2.0; **National Palace**: Michael Swan/Flickr, CC-BY-ND-2.0; **Cap-Haitian Students**: Alex E. Proimos (flickr.com/proimos), CC-BY-NC (used by permission); **Krik? Krak! Speech Bubbles**: madtom/SS;

INDIA **Bengal Tiger**: Eric Isselee/SS; **Asian Elephant**: shama65/SS; **Cricket Player**: EcoPrint/SS; **Namaste**: omkar.a.v/SS; **Chai**: Pete Niesen/SS; **Beach in Goa**: Val Shevchenko/SS; **Yoga**: Pikoso.kz/SS; **Lotus**: happystock/SS; **Peacock**: happystock/SS; **Chicken Curry**: bonchan/SS; **Autorickshaw**: paul prescott/SS; **Horn OK Please**: Bruno Fumari (Rigamarole)/Flickr, CC-BY-SA-NC-2.0, (used by permission); **Cow in the City**: Luciano Mortula/SS; **Crowded Train Platform**: Daniel Prudek/SS; **Ganesh**: Cindy Hughes/SS; **Dancing Shiva**: Miledy/SS; **Krishna Statue**: M. Trischler/Wiki, CC_BY-SA-3.0; **Sikh Man**: Ragne Kabanova/SS; **Church in Kerala**: Aleksandar Todorovic/SS; **Sign in Bangalore Museum**: Loodog/Wiki, CC-BY-SA-3.0; **Thali on tray**: Ashwin/SS; **Buddha**: Luciano Mortula/SS; **Ancient Indus Valley Statue**: Mamoon Mengal/Wiki, CC-BY-SA-1.0; **Chess**: SnowWhiteimages/SS; **Aishwarya Rai**: bollywoodhungama.com, CC-BY-3.0; **Taj Mahal**: Waj/SS; **Peacock Isolated**: cynoclub/SS; **Mango Tree**: DUSAN ZIDAR/SS; **Cricket Bat & Ball**: Sean Gladwell/SS; **Himalayas**: Roberto Caucino/SS; **Ganges River**: Mario Boutin/SS; **Varanasi**: Regien Paassen/SS; **Woman with Jasmine**: omkar.a.v/SS; **Jasmine**: Khomulo Anna/SS; **Curry Powder**: HLPhoto/SS; **Cycle Rickshaw**: Jorg Hackemann/SS; **Monkeys in Delhi**: John Haslam/Flickr, CC-BY-2.0; **Miss Pooja**: Atameetk/Wiki, CC-BY-SA-3.0; **Offering Prayers in the Ganges**: Neale Cousland/SS; **Hindu Temple**: VLADJ55/SS; **Krishna & Radhika**:PD-Wiki, National Museum Delhi; **Golden Temple**: Luciano Mortula/SS;

Flamenco Shoes and Fan: Penny Hillcrest/SS; **Cathedral in Santiago de Compostela**: Luis Miguel Bugallo Sánchez/Wiki, CC-BY-SA-3.0; **Great Mosque of Cordoba**: IMAG3S/SS; **Don Quixote Illustration**: Dn Br/SS; Picasso's **Guernica**: © 2015 Estate of Pablo Picasso / Artists Rights Society (ARS), New York, photo by Papamanila/Wiki, CC-BY-SA 3.0; Joan **Miró Mural on the Palacio de Congresos y Exposiciones in Madrid Spain**: © Successió Miró / Artists Rights Society (ARS), New York / ADAGP, Paris 2015, photo by Luis Garcia "Zaqarnal"/Wiki, CC-BY-SA-3.0; **Avila's Medieval Walls**: PHB.cz (Richard Semik)/SS; **Beach in Catalonia**: Kert/SS; **Spanish Guitar**: Melica/SS; **Mouth with Spanish Tongue**: Yuyula/SS; **Basilica of the Sagrada Familia**: Veniamin Kraskov/SS;

FONTS **Main text of the verse**: Grenadine 10 pt & many sizes of Billy. **Image captions**: Gills Sans 9.25 pt. **Image labels**: Marker Felt 9-10.5 pt. **Activity pages**: Adobe Garamond 10 pt. **Cover**: Billy & Stereofidelic. There are over 100 other wonderful fonts used in the verse. Email contact@australiatozimbabwe.com with any specific questions about the fonts used in this book.

AUTHOR ACKNOWLEDGEMENTS

Thanks to font makers, photo takers, illustrators and wiki creators, a vast creative community whose contributions to the world made this book possible.

Thanks to embassies, expats, experts and educators who saved me from errors and took time to suggest improvements for this book. In particular, I would like to thank the Embassy of Australia, the Embassy of Denmark, Embassy of Haiti and the Embassy of Oman for making recommendations that improved not only their own country's chapter, but the whole book. I would also like to thank my innumerable country content editors (whose names appear on the following page). Thanks especially to Patrick Ukata, who responded to years of questions about Nigeria and African politics. And thanks to Claire Sontag for offering many school years of support, and feedback from using chapters in her classroom.

Thanks to all my many editors and enablers. Beth Larson Richardson, my favorite co-conspirator, I hope you are as proud of this book as you are of our other international education projects—I couldn't have completed any of them without you. Thanks to Jenny and everyone at Love the World Books for helping to steer this book into print. Thanks to Jessica Glicoes for her endlessly helpful feedback and advice.

Thanks to the libraries and schools who educated me about children's books and gave me the skills to explore the world and write about it. Thanks to the Selma Public Library where I started writing this book and to both the Tuscaloosa Public Library and the DC Public Library, which gave me wonderful jobs so I could complete it. Thanks to New College at the University of Alabama for giving me experience working on long-term creative projects, and thanks to Indian Springs School for helping to raise me and send me out into the world.

Thank you to friends, family and colleagues who supported me and put up with me for this entire process. Thanks to my colleagues at the Georgetown Neighborhood Library for making my time there so pleasant that I've had plenty of energy to work on this. In particular, thanks to Liz, Stacy and Jess for helping me create the cover. Thanks to Paul Pickering, my earliest supporter and oldest friend, who told me when the book was in its awful infancy, "Just think how much easier the second book will be!" Seven years later, I still remember that, and can now see if it's true. Thank you to my brothers-in-law, Scott and Andres, for their innumerable marketing ideas and their completely biased enthusiasm for the book. Thanks to my parents, Alston and Anne Fitts, for all their prayers and edits and for the hereditary stubbornness, optimism and love of research that enabled me to see this through. And finally, thanks to my sisters, Lida and Mary Alston. Lida was my main traveling companion in exploring the world, so no one has done more to shape the way I see and understand it. Mary Alston was the diligent editor of many horrible first drafts of verse and always had specific suggestions for how to improve them. Thanks for letting me know how much the first ones stunk, and for sticking with me to the end!

AUSTRALIA:
The Embassy of Australia, Helen
Seidel, Rowena Bailey, National Archives of Australia
BRAZIL: The Embassy of Brazil, Fernanda Dias Afonso, Luciana
Brito CHINA: Theresa Wang, Tjetjep Rustandi; DENMARK: The Embassy of
Denmark, Jette Renneberg Elkjær, The Danish Royal Household, Steen Evald, Jens
Rost of Tastrup, Luigi Anzivino, Kimberley Rhodes Roberts ETHIOPIA: Worku Mulattu,
Arthur Sacramento, Rod Waddington, Justin Clements, Alan D. Coogan FRANCE: Alliance
Française of DC GHANA: Ama Asafu Adjaye, Ronnie Pitman, Jason Eliott Finch, Sharon McKellar
HAITI: The Embassy of Haiti, Stephane Rosenberg, Andre Guerrier, Michelle Walz, Alex Proimos,
Michael Swan, Greg Moquin, Troy Livesay, Brian Kong, SERVV INDIA: Anita Jayagopal Gouri, Shanthala
Raj Critz, Jayanthi Sambasivan, Bruno Fumari JAPAN: Lisa Kaufman, Mayumi Kiyokawa, Kayser Strauss
KAZAKHSTAN: The Embassy of Kazakhstan LEBANON: Abdallah Chahine, Voix de l'Orient MEXICO: Jenny
& Lupe Morgan, April Marquez Farrar NIGERIA: Patrick Ukata, Iheanyi Okpala, Chinwe Okeke, Yassin
Maisikeli, Jeremy Weate, Banning Eyre , Radio Nederland Wereldomroep, Christopher Peplin, Carmen
McCain OMAN: The Embassy of Oman, Hanan Al Kindi, Kathleen Ridolfo, Mohamed Elmenshawy, Hamed
Salam Al Suleimi, Charles Roffey, Dave Watts, D'Arcy Vallance PERU: Belisa de las Casas QATAR: The
Embassy of Qatar in DC, Samira Zaman RUSSIA: Oxana Holtman, Alla Anderson Patrick, Jack
Sontag SPAIN: Universidad de Alcalá de Henares TURKEY: Dilara Ekici, Terakki Vakfi Okullari
UNITED KINGDOM: Rebekah Smith, Chris Horton, Simon Bird VIETNAM: Laura Billings,
Jeremy Couture, Carolyn Vo ZIMBABWE: Zibusiso Ncube, BBC World Service
HELPFUL READERS: Sharon Fisher, Garret Watkins, Alina Stefanescu
Coryell, Anne Gibbons, Paul Pickering, Jessica Glicoes, Liane
Rosenblatt, Susan Harris, Claire Sontag, Dr. Jo
Sullivan, Africa Access

Thanks to a world of editors and contributors!

Many people from around the world helped assemble and edit this book.
From embassies which made sure that their country was represented accurately,
to photographers who contributed images, to natives who made musical
suggestions and cultural corrections, each chapter has been a collaborative
effort from a multitude of volunteers. This is truly a book about the world that
the world has helped create.

About the Author

Ruth Fitts worked with embassies, scholars and people around the world to create and edit this book. Before starting this project, she was the Director of Meridian International Center's International Classroom, a geography education program with the mission to "bring the world into Washington, DC Public Schools." In this role, she helped international diplomats and scholars create exciting classroom introductions to their home country, gave teachers' workshops on globalizing their curricula and created "culture boxes" about specific countries with hands-on materials for use in the classroom. With Beth Larson Richardson, the editor of this book, Ruth founded an International Children's Festival involving 16 embassies in hosting a funfair for kids to learn about their countries. She currently lives in Washington, DC and works in the children's room of a DC Public Library, giving story times and poring over children's nonfiction.

Ruth's first job out of college was selling carpets in Istanbul, Turkey; her boss said it was his worst month of business ever. Failing in the textile trade, she became an educator and avid traveler, visiting 35 countries as a tourist and living in two of them. Traveling to Yemen just days after 9/11, going overland down the coast of East Africa or discovering the big cities of South America, she encountered a world more wide and welcoming than she had ever imagined growing up in Alabama. To her surprise, she found that none of her classes in International Relations had given her an understanding of the countries she visited. Her studies had looked at the world as a group of problems to be solved, not as peoples and places to get to know and relate to. Ruth believes that geography education should inspire kids to feel both fascinated by the world and at home in it. It should make them eager to know our international neighbors and to experience and learn from their cultures. She wants to give kids a world that is no longer foreign, but filled with a wonderfully diverse human family. She wants to gift them the world that she loves.